002057 $24 95

SHEATHING THE SWORD

SHEATHING THE SWORD

The Demilitarisation of Japan

by

Meirion and Susie Harries

MACMILLAN PUBLISHING COMPANY
New York

To Harry M. Weinrebe,
founder of the
Hong Kong Conservatory of Music

Macmillan Publishing Company
866 Third Avenue, New York, N.Y. 10022
Collier Macmillan Canada, Inc.

Library of Congress Cataloging-in-Publication Data
Harries, Meirion, 1951–
Sheathing the sword.
Bibliography: p.
Includes index.
1. Japan—History—Allied occupation, 1945–1952.
2. Militarism—Japan—History. I. Harries, Susie. II. Title.
DS889.16.H35   1988   952.04′4   87-7859
ISBN 0-02-548340-4

Macmillan books are available at special discounts for bulk
purchases for sales promotions, premiums, fund-raising, or
educational use. For details contact:

Special Sales Director
Macmillan Publishing Company
866 Third Avenue
New York, N.Y. 10022

10 9 8 7 6 5 4 3 2 1

PRINTED IN THE UNITED STATES OF AMERICA

'Beginnings we say, Endings we say:
What began where; what ended?'

Patric Dickinson, 'To Go Hidden', 1985

Contents

ACKNOWLEDGEMENTS

In researching this book we were given a great deal of help by a great many people. In the Sources section we acknowledge the origins of copyright material, and specific ideas and information, but here we should like to thank:

Sally Abernethy; Dr. Gwyn Bayliss, Curator of Printed Books, Imperial War Museum, London; Duncan Bluck; Richard Boylan, Washington National Records Center, Suitland; Raymond Bushell; Julian Chancellor, Society of Authors, London; Professor Ernest Chew, National University of Singapore; Robert Donihi; Angela Earp; Haruhiko Fujite, National Diet Library, Tokyo; Dominic Lieven; Mikiko Fujiwara Lieven; Priscilla Goldstein; Hugh Hanning, International Peace Academy, London; His Excellency Tommy B. Koh, Ambassador of the Republic of Singapore to the United States; Basil Marriner; Lady Marriner; Charles Mason; Professor Marlene J. Mayo, University of Maryland; John Mendelsohn, Modern Military Branch, National Archives, Washington; Betsy Miller; Rick Morgan; Terri Naylor; Jiro Nozaka; General Indar Jit Rikhye, International Peace Academy, New York; Masaei Saito; John Taylor, Modern Military Branch, National Archives, Washington; Shigeru Wada, International Secretary, Japanese National Railway Workers' Union; Harry M. Weinrebe; Tom Weiss, International Peace Academy, New York; Dr. Justin Williams, Sr.

We should like also to thank the staff of:

the Japanese Embassies in Washington and London; the National Archives, Washington DC and the Washington National Records Center, Suitland; the Microform Room of the Library of Congress, Washington; the McKeldin and Hornbake Libraries, University of Maryland; the Wilson Library, University of Minnesota; the Oral History Research Office, Butler Library, Columbia University, New York; the New York Public Library; the Public Record Office, London, both Kew and Chancery Lane branches; the Lord Chancellor's Office, London; the Attorney General's Office, London; the National Register of Biography, London; the Imperial War Museum, London; the British Museum Newspaper Library, Colindale; the School of Oriental and African Studies, University of London; the British Library of Political and Economic Science, London School of Economics, University of London; the London Library; the Institute for the Study of Drug Dependency, London.

For permission to quote from original archive material, we are grateful to the following:

the East Asia Collection, McKeldin Library, University of Maryland, College Park, for the papers of Owen Cunningham, the Gordon W. Prange Collection, and the Justin Williams papers (and our thanks also to Dr. Justin Williams, Sr.); the Oral History Research Office, Butler Library, Columbia University, New York City; and the Asia Library, Harlan Hatcher Graduate Library, University of Michigan, Ann Arbor, for the papers of Alfred Rodman Hussey.

Lastly we should like to acknowledge the help and advice given to us by Hillel Black, Christopher Sinclair-Stevenson and Harriet Sumption. We are also particularly grateful to Professor Theodore McNelly, for the time and trouble he took discussing Article 9 with us, and reading the book in manuscript; to Joseph S. Sykes, former Executive Staff Secretary to General Paul J. Mueller, MacArthur's Chief of Staff, who brought the Occupation alive for us, and read the book in manuscript; to Frank Joseph Shulman, Curator of the East Asia Collection of the McKeldin Library, University of Maryland and, as expert bibliographer of the Occupation, our guide to much information we should otherwise have missed; to Patric Dickinson for permission to quote from one of his poems; and to Joe and Clarissa, in whose apartment this book began. Responsibility for the final product is, of course, ours.

GLOSSARY OF ABBREVIATIONS

ACJ — Allied Council for Japan

BCAS — *Bulletin of Concerned Asian Scholars*

BIPSD — Basic Initial Post-Surrender Directive

BRINDIV — British Indian Division

CIE — Civil Information and Education Section

CinCFE — Commander-in-Chief, Far East Command

COH — Oral History Research Office, Columbia University, New York

DoA — U.S. Department of the Army

ESS — Economic and Scientific Section

FEC — Far Eastern Commission

FEER — *Far Eastern Economic Review*

FO/F — Foreign Office Papers, Public Record Office, Kew

FRUS — *Foreign Relations of the United States*

G–2 — intelligence section

GS — Government Section

GWPC — Gordon W. Prange Collection, McKeldin Library, University of Maryland

HNMAOJ — *History of the Non-Military Activities of the Occupation of Japan* (Tokyo, 1951–2)

HP — Alfred Rodman Hussey Papers, University of Michigan, Ann Arbor

IMTFE — International Military Tribunal for the Far East

IPS — International Prosecution Section

J — Japan/Japanese

JCS — U.S. Joint Chiefs of Staff

JE — *Japan Echo*

JI — *Japan Interpreter*

JJS — *Journal of Japanese Studies*

JQ — *Japan Quarterly*

JWP — Justin Williams Papers, East Asia Collection, McKeldin Library, University of Maryland

LCO — Lord Chancellor's Office

MacA — MacArthur

MacArthur Reports — ed. Charles Willoughby, *Reports of General MacArthur, Vol. 1. suppl. MacArthur in Japan: The Occupation: Military Phase* (Washington, 1966)

NAS — National Archives, Suitland, Maryland

NAW — National Archives, Washington

NSC — National Security Council

NYT — *New York Times*

O/Occ — Occupation

OCP — Owen Cunningham Papers, East Asia Collection, McKeldin Library, University of Maryland

OSS — Office of Strategic Services

Patrick Memorandum — LCO2 2992. Memo by Lord Patrick, enclosed with letter

	Lord Normand/ Lord Jowitt, Feb. 5, 1947
PBAJS	*Proceedings of the British Association for Japanese Studies*
POLAD	Political Adviser to SCAP
Pritchard	eds. R. John Pritchard and Sonia Maybandun Zaidi, Project Director Donald Cameron Watt, *The Tokyo War Crimes Trial* (Garland Publishing, Inc.)
PRJ	*Political Reorientation of Japan, September 1945 – September 1948: Report of Government Section* (Washington, 1949)
PROC	Public Record Office, Chancery Lane
RG	Record Group
SCAP	Headquarters of the Supreme Commander of the Allied Powers
SDF	Japanese Self-Defense Forces
SNMAJK	*Summation of Non-Military Activities in Japan*

	and Korea (Tokyo, 1948)
SWNCC	State-War-Navy Coordinating Committee
T	Transcript of Proceedings of the IMTFE. (For almost four decades only the original hectographed transcripts were available, often incomplete, in a few British and American libraries. Now the edited transcript has been published – see *Pritchard*)
UKLIM	United Kingdom Liaison Mission to Japan
UNWCC	United Nations War Crimes Commission
UP	University Press
USIPSP	United States Initial Post-Surrender Policy
USSBS	United States Strategic Bombing Survey
WO	War Office Papers, Public Record Office, Kew

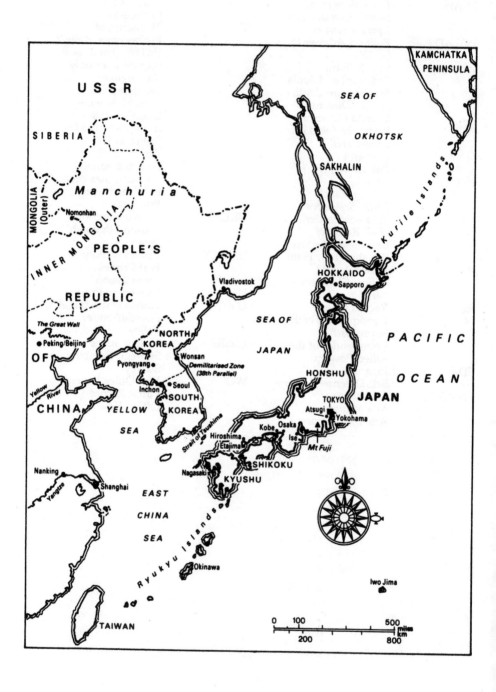

Prologue

Two days before Christmas 1948, at a few seconds before midnight, the door of the Tokyo death house opened. Four elderly Japanese men shuffled in from the dark prison yard, blinking at the brightness of the whitewashed chamber. They looked shabby and decrepit in their obligatory U.S. Army fatigues, dwarfed by the guards who flanked them, and for a fleeting moment the scene seemed a metaphor for the Occupation of Japan: the youth and strength of the American nation holding old Japan helpless in its grasp.

To one side of the prisoners were the official Allied witnesses detailed to observe the executions which were about to take place, and for their benefit the condemned were identified:

'DOIHARA, Kenji'. Army General. Aged 65. The newspapers dubbed him the 'Himmler of the East'; troops under his command tortured and murdered Allied prisoners.

'MATSUI, Iwane'. Army General. Aged 70. His troops had carried out the Rape of Nanking – the frenzied bloodbath eight Christmases before when thousands of Chinese civilians and prisoners-of-war trapped within the ancient walled city had been raped, tortured, murdered, mutilated.

'TOJO, Hideki'. Army General. Aged 63. Prime Minister of Japan from before Pearl Harbor to the fall of Saipan.

'MUTO, Akira'. Army General. Aged 56. His troops had committed widespread atrocities in Northern Sumatra and the Philippines, including thousands of murders during the infamous Bataan Death March.

Unaided, the four climbed the thirteen steps to the scaffold, took their positions and turned to face the witnesses. Black hoods were placed over their heads, and the nooses readied and tightened. From the platform, the chief executioner saluted the commander of the detail and reported that the condemned men were ready. There was no sound in the chamber besides the mutter of Buddhist prayers from the condemned. 'Proceed', came the command, and the four traps sprang open with a violent crack that echoed off the brick walls. By thirteen minutes past midnight all four had been certified dead. The corpses were fingerprinted and placed in plain coffins, and word was passed for the next batch to be brought in. At nineteen minutes past midnight the three remaining prisoners entered. Again official identification took place.

'ITAGAKI, Seishiro'. Army General. Aged 63. He withheld food and medicines from thousands of Allied prisoners-of-war.

'HIROTA, Koki'. The only civilian to be hanged. Aged 70. Former Prime Minister, and Foreign Minister during the Rape of Nanking. As he entered the death house his eyes met those of the American Official Witness: 'It was an exchange of glances in which he seemed to appeal to me for sympathy and understanding'.

'KIMURA, Heitaro'. Army General. Aged 60. Vice War Minister in Tojo's Cabinet. Negligent in his duty to restrain his troops from committing atrocities in Burma.

The ritual took its inevitable course, and by 12.35 a.m. the last of the major conspirators in Japan's 'aggressive war' had been certified dead.

*   *   *

But memories and hatreds are less easily eradicated than men. These seven hangings alone could hardly expiate the barbarities of the Pacific War. Neighbouring countries still monitor the pulse of nationalism in Japan, terrified that the dark spectre of militarism will once again rise to threaten them. In Asia, the post-war decades have been punctuated by mass demonstrations and protests at signs of revisionism within Japan. In the West, too, bitterness lives on, fed by an ever-swelling stream of literature, some of it unashamedly racist, which purports to expose fiendish Japanese strategies for renewed world domination.

Understandably, the most savage alarmists are men who themselves once experienced the horrors of which they warn. Where the war years are concerned, their polemics are solidly founded in fact. Throughout the Japanese Empire countless thousands were murdered, tortured and enslaved. Women were forced into prostitution and men into labour gangs. Vivisection and experiments in biological warfare were carried out on civilians and prisoners-of-war alike. Across Asia the Imperial Army conducted a massively profitable trade in narcotics. Conquered lands were ruthlessly exploited to fuel the Imperial war machine.

But the alarmists do not confine themselves to reviving memories of the past. Their fears also feed on the present. Japan has rearmed. Her 'Self-Defense Forces' are sustained by the eighth largest arms budget in the world. Imperial Army generals, including Tojo himself, are now honoured at Yasukuni, the principal shrine to the Japanese war dead. Prime Minister Yasuhiro Nakasone has made an official visit to the shrine to pay homage. Films are released which use Hiroshima and Nagasaki as an all-purpose excuse to cancel out the Bataan Death March and the Rape of Nanking. School textbooks are apparently rewritten to sanitise Japan's role in the Pacific War. The ritual suicide of Yukio Mishima, as a protest against the decay of *samurai* values, is held up by extremist groups as an example to the youth of Japan. Xenophobia manifests itself in many ways: all foreigners are finger-printed, and Vietnamese boat people are turned away. A right-wing political faction is inaugurated with a *yakuza*-style blood pact. A leader of industry celebrates Japan's racial purity and superiority. And so it goes on. Against the black background of the 1930s and 1940s, each new incident shines for some like a beacon warning that Japanese militarism is once again on the rise.

While we were living in the Far East, it was easy enough to comprehend, if not sympathise with, this renewed 'Yellow Peril' paranoia. It was harder to reconcile it with what we ourselves had seen of Japan and the Japanese. As Westerners, and Westerners too young to be carrying the wartime baggage of automatic mistrust, we instinctively recoiled from the alarmist thesis. We saw that this kind of propaganda, continually harking back to the past, still has a profound influence on the world's attitude to the Japanese. It has become almost a cliché now to describe Japan's economic progress, for instance, as a recreation of the reviled Greater East Asian Co-Prosperity Sphere of the 1930s. So we decided to try to confirm or deny the alarmists' prognosis by finding out for ourselves what has happened to Japanese militarism since the end of the Pacific War.

What struck us almost immediately was how little Japan's critics had to say about American involvement in the story. For the first seven post-war years, America actually occupied Japan. Over the last three decades, since Japan regained her political independence, America has been her principal sponsor and defender in the outside world. Nothing Japan has done since 1945 in the military sphere has been without American involvement.

The alarmists tend to gloss over America's responsibility for the present state of Japanese militarism. And there is another equally important omission – the fact that the bulk of the Japanese people were themselves victims in the 1930s and 1940s, and have as much to fear as anyone else from a resurgence of Japanese militarism.

They too suffered privations, and many of them degradation, imprisonment and torture no less severe than that inflicted on enemy prisoners-of-war. For the most part, they knew nothing of the crimes their troops were committing. The Japanese people were not conspirators, but tools in the hands of their military masters.

These two factors – American involvement and the past suffering of the Japanese themselves – shaped the book we have written. At the outset they helped define the questions we were intent on answering. We wanted to find out whether America truly demilitarised Japan during the Occupation. Did she try, and did she succeed in sheathing the Japanese sword? Is Japan now remilitarising, as the alarmists claim? And if so, are her people at fault? Or is America herself to blame?

*   *   *

On July 26, 1945, the Allies, speaking from the town of Potsdam in the heart of ruined and defeated Germany, offered Japan the alternatives of surrender or 'prompt and utter destruction'. Days passed without a choice being made, days in which Hiroshima and Nagasaki were obliterated and the Soviet Union, only now entering the war in the east, sent her Red Army smashing down from Siberia through the Imperial forces deployed on the plains of Manchuria, and on, it seemed, towards Tokyo. On August 15, Japan capitulated, the deciding vote for surrender cast by the Emperor. Eighteen days later, in a glittering ceremony held on board the United States battleship *Missouri*, anchored amidst the massed Allied fleets in Tokyo Bay, she formally agreed to the occupation of points in her home islands until such time as the Allies had fulfilled their declared objective of uprooting militarism and bringing to the Japanese people a 'peacefully inclined and responsible government'.

The Occupation of Japan, which lasted from 1945 to 1952, though Allied in name was almost exclusively American in substance. It was the first chapter in Japan's post-war relationship with the United States – a remarkable encounter, and the key to the story of post-war Japanese militarisation.

Looking back at the months following the surrender, it is tempting to see Japan as lying totally at America's mercy. The mere fact of defeat was traumatic for a nation which had never before been beaten in a foreign war. Losing her empire meant being starved of the raw materials so crucial for industrial survival. Months of saturation bombing of all the major towns and cities, culminating in the atomic holocausts at Hiroshima and Nagasaki, had left an urban wasteland which shocked even those who had created it. The Japanese people were stunned, exhausted, disoriented and despairing.

Nevertheless, America was to find that despite her overwhelming advantages, she could not do just as she pleased with Japan. By the time the fleet gathered in Tokyo Bay, visible proof of America's superior strength, the Occupation was already compromised.

At the very outset the Americans had pulled one important punch. They never took direct control of the Japanese people. Instead, after much heart-searching and calculation of the relative costs in terms of men and money, they chose to steer Japan's course at one remove, working through the Japanese government structure. Unlike Germany, Japan was not overrun by the Allies and the last wartime government was virtually intact and still functioning at the surrender, buttressed by an immensely influential bureaucracy.

America in effect set up a shadow government. Its head, to whom even the Emperor was subject, was General Douglas MacArthur. As the Commander-in-Chief of the American Forces in the Pacific, one of the most successful generals of the Second World War, MacArthur was a natural choice, in America's view, for the post of Supreme Commander for the Allied Powers. He already had a military hierarchy under him controlling the quarter of a million troops of the Sixth and Eighth Armies detailed to enforce the terms of surrender. But now beside this military structure, to deal with the Japanese government, MacArthur built a new semi-civilian bureaucracy.

The new organisation was known as SCAP, taking its title from MacArthur's own. (In this book, 'SCAP' always refers to the administration and not the man). MacArthur's bureaucracy was designed to mirror the Japanese structure through which it was to work, and had in consequence fourteen special staff sections, roughly corresponding with the major ministries of the Imperial Japanese Government. In the story of the demilitarisation of Japan, the special staff sections which will feature most often are the Government Section (GS), the Civil Information and Education Section (CIE), the Economic and Scientific Section (ESS) and, besides, the International Prosecution Section (IPS) in whose hands lay the responsibility for the trial of Japan's military overlords. Each SCAP section communicated with its Japanese counterpart through the Central Liaison Office. This was a purely Japanese invention set up without American prompting before the first troops arrived, and was staffed by experienced Foreign Office personnel.

SCAP sections evolved their policies within the framework of Washington's instructions and conveyed them in the form of directives, known as SCAPINs, to the Central Liaison Office. There they were translated into Japanese and passed to the appropriate ministry where they were expected to result in administrative instructions to local government or in legislation passed through the Diet, the Japanese parliament.

But involving the Japanese higher echelons in the task of setting Japan to rights had repercussions which the Americans had foreseen but could not avoid. By working through the Japanese system, the Americans were confirming in power men who were in many ways their natural enemies. The Japanese civil service, which bore most of the direct responsibility for implementing American policy, was hardly a promising agent of reform. Traditionally the bureaucrats identified themselves with, and were loyal to, the ruling élites – the landowners, industrial magnates and political bosses – and shared their vested interest in preserving the pre-war *status quo*. This essentially reactionary body was given, courtesy of America, a new lease of life which it employed, broadly speaking, in frustrating American intentions.

It would be going too far to suggest that there was a comprehensive government conspiracy. Between surrender and occupation individual departments certainly did what they could to cover their tracks and safeguard the future. The Foreign Office ordered the burning of selected records. The army frantically attempted to destroy all evidence of war crimes, and ordered military stockpiles to be distributed among the Japanese people or otherwise put beyond the reach of the invaders. On the day after Japan had formally surrendered aboard the *Missouri*, the Privy Council discussed methods of making American/Soviet tension work to Japan's advantage. But there had been no time to coordinate an official policy of non-cooperation.

Nevertheless, resistance to radical change is natural, especially when the change is imposed by a former enemy. With Japanese officials a vital link in every chain, progress from policy decision within SCAP to practical action in the field was never rapid and rarely smooth. Time was, of course, on Japan's side. The Occupation could not last for ever, and if action could be delayed long enough, it might never be necessary at all.

If procrastination was impossible, the Japanese could fall back on failures in communication. The Central Liaison Office might have been set up specifically to exploit the language barrier. (Few SCAP officials were fluent or even really coherent in Japanese when they arrived, and many left in the same condition.) SCAPINs and their implementing legislation were subtly but significantly altered in translation. And when Japanese officials were caught doing the opposite of what SCAP had intended, they could take refuge in a polite lack of comprehension. The unfortunate fact is that this was often quite genuine.

But in the end the most effective weapon was simple disobedience. To check that its 'suggestions' were in fact being followed, SCAP, itself centralised in Tokyo, relied on forty-six so-called 'military government' teams in the field to be its eyes and ears. But these teams were small and scattered, one in each of Japan's forty-six prefectures, and had not always had the training they needed to keep one jump ahead. Many of these young field officers knew little about Japan and had no practical experience of administration.

In any case, the teams had no authority to intervene directly. They could not 'govern', but merely observe and advise. MacArthur preferred to maintain the fiction that the Japanese government was acting on its own initiative: this way SCAP could not be accused of coercion, and there would be no automatic excuse for uprooting its reforms once the Occupation was over. So even if SCAP's directives reached the provinces intact, local Japanese officials could often afford to ignore them, secure in the knowledge that SCAP either could not or would not enforce obedience.

Viewed from the social scientist's perspective, too, the Occupation was flawed from the outset. On the face of it, post-war Japan was the perfect laboratory for controlled social experiment, because in the early years of the Occupation she was cut off from the outside world just as completely as she had ever been under the militarists. Many in SCAP regarded Japan, seemingly helpless, as an ideal patient for 'the world's most advanced techniques of socio-economico-political surgery'. But seeing the opportunity to reconstruct a defeated enemy on western democratic lines, and exploiting the opportunity effectively were two different things.

Part of the problem was the enormity of the change required. It was not simply a question of scraping off militarist barnacles. Beneath the repressive superstructure lay a culture which over the millennia had evolved, undisturbed by conquest or invasion, in its own unique way. Japan's development falls within the Chinese sphere of world history, being little affected by the Greek and Judaeo-Christian currents of western civilisation. In 1945, despite almost a century of western-style industrialisation, Japanese society remained fundamentally different from that of America.

The Americans were not attempting cosmetic surgery, but a massive transplant of alien values and social patterns. And they were proceeding without either the technique or the deep understanding of the patient which such a delicate operation demands. In the present decade, planning for change is an accepted mode of organising society. Forty years ago, however, the science was still in its infancy; only from the 1950s onwards was there routine collaboration between social scientists and policy makers. Certainly within the SCAP hierarchy, sociologists and cultural anthropologists held lowly and uninfluential positions.

But even had they been more closely involved, they would still have lacked the knowledge of Japanese society which would have enabled them to devise a coherent strategy. At that point, the West was profoundly ignorant of the sociology of Japan. Only one major field study had been carried out in the past, and there was no time now even to initiate, let alone complete the necessary research into existing Japanese customs before decisions had to be made on how to alter them. No one knew how long the Occupation would last, and this affected both the rate and the quality of change. Some observers suggested a minimum of a hundred years, others twenty-five. But when MacArthur let it be known that he favoured an occupation of no more than three or four years, 'the responsible officers in GHQ in 1945–6 hurried to get their primary missions accomplished so as to be ready whenever the termination date arrived'.

The deluge of reforms that swept Japan, unsupported by scientific research or any strategy of planned change, was in essence a simple act of faith in the American way of life. American values were held to be universally applicable; once the militarist blinkers were removed, the Japanese people were expected automatically to recognise the worth of the American way and embrace it lock, stock and barrel. But reforms which prosper in one culture mutate or die in another. The process of assimilation from one culture to another is complicated and slow. In this perspective it comes as no surprise that when the Occupation ended, many of the American reforms were sloughed off almost as if they had never been.

*   *   *

All these difficulties complicated America's task in Japan – the need to work through the Japanese, and the Japanese adroitness in exploiting this opportunity; the Americans' own inability to recognise the width of the chasm which yawned between the two societies and judge their cultural leap accordingly. But if in the event the Americans fell short of their objectives, it was principally because they could not agree on what these objectives were.

The Occupation spanned a period of far-reaching change in

world affairs. It coincided with the polarisation of the world into Soviet and American spheres of interest and, as the wartime alliance crumbled, the intensification of the Cold War between the superpowers. The Iron Curtain fell across Europe. Asia witnessed the struggles of countries like Vietnam and Indonesia against the reimposition of colonial rule; the independence of India; the progressive succumbing of China to Mao's Communists; and the Korean War.

During this time American foreign policy naturally underwent a complete metamorphosis. In its organisation, the State Department turned from a regional outlook – each foreign country the domain of a separate section of the bureaucracy – to a global approach in keeping with America's new perception of its focal position in the post-war world. The setting-up of the National Security Council as a coordinating agency with its pilot fish the CIA was the main outward sign of this revolution. Between 1945 and 1952, too, the Americans perceived increasingly clearly what their global role was to be. Eventually formalised in the Truman Doctrine, their mission was to 'contain' communism, by force if necessary, wherever it threatened the free world.

Both these innovations affected America's handling of Japan. Japan's problems – among which the threat of communism was one of the most pressing – could not be treated in isolation, but had to be seen as part of the overall world picture. How exactly Japan fitted into this picture, however, and into the strategies of containment, was something on which the American planners could not agree.

Planning for a defeated Japan began well before war had ended, and continued into the 1950s. During this period, the policy makers fell broadly into three warring camps. One wanted to see the old Japan obliterated entirely – its military machine, its reactionary social structure, and its onetime economic preeminence in the region. This group has been loosely labelled the 'China Crowd', because it wished Japan to be subordinated to the rising star of China.

The motives of this 'crowd' were afterwards to be called into question. Were they relics of the 'New Deal' mentality? typical of the post-war idealists who demanded a 'fresh start' worldwide? or were they simply heralds and supporters of communism? Joseph McCarthy thought the latter, and was able to point to similarities between their plans for Japan and the manifesto of the Japanese Communist Party, which had been framed in the mountains of Yenan under the guiding hand of Mao Tse-tung.

Against the China Crowd stood the old Japan hands within the Foreign Service and the State Department. This 'Japan Crowd' had perhaps a greater understanding of Japan as she had been before the war. They certainly had greater sympathy for her traditions and institutions, and in particular for the Imperial institution. To most of the China Crowd the Emperor was a war criminal, his political position an affront to liberal sensibilities, and they wanted both eradicated. The Japan Crowd saw the Emperor's prestige as the only means of preserving public order and some semblance of national cohesion in Japan. Nor did they wish to see Japan's economy ruined for the future.

On one point at least the Japan Crowd were in wholehearted agreement with their opponents – Japanese militarism must be smashed and the remnants of the Imperial Army destroyed. But their resistance to major elements in the China Crowd's programme left them open to manipulation by a third faction indifferent or opposed to reform.

The priorities of this third group were exclusively strategic. At its heart were the more hawkish figures in the U.S. Army and the War Department who, despite all the wartime rhetoric, were determined that Japan's strength, both military and economic, far from being reduced should be recruited on the American side in the battle against communism.

Other forces also made themselves felt in the mêlée that was policymaking for Japan. Congress, the Treasury, the White House, American big business, religious evangelists, educationalists, womens' rights activists, all brought their influence to bear in Washington. And in Tokyo, MacArthur plotted his own idiosyncratic course, with his SCAP organisation itself divided between radicals and conservatives, civilians and military. In the circumstances it is hardly surprising that over the period of the Occupation American policy in Japan displayed some remarkable inconsistencies, as first one group and then another gained dominance and imposed its will.

When the Occupation first began, it was the China Crowd which had the upper hand and, at its urging, an avalanche of social and political reform descended upon Japan. The planners' immediate aim was to disarm Japan and to destroy all trace of militarism wherever it might be found. At the same time, to ensure that the cancer would never regenerate itself, democracy was to be introduced into the body of the Japanese people as the antithesis of the regimentation and authoritarianism on which militarism feeds.

But by the time the new constitution drafted by SCAP as the centrepiece of reform was ratified in the middle of 1947, the liberal surge had already lost impetus. As the Occupation progressed, some of SCAP's early reforms were abandoned without being pushed to their logical conclusion, and others simply put into reverse. The attempt to smash Japan's big business monopolies, for instance, faltered and died. 'Reds' replaced ultra-nationalists as the targets of a nationwide purge. And first in secret, then at an official level, the Japanese were encouraged to rearm.

This did not reflect any change of heart on the part of the China Crowd, but rather the fact that their influence was on the wane. In the later years of the Occupation it was the Japan Crowd, helped by factors both outside and inside Japan, which saw its original policies prevail. Outside, the Cold War escalated; and this made it seem imprudent to go on tolerating internal developments which were weakening Japan as a potential ally. The success of Communist agitators in labour relations and politics, and the continuing failure of the economy to recover, cast doubts on the wisdom of the idealists' stance.

Most significantly, the interests of the Japan Crowd now converged with those of other factions in the policymaking struggle, and their combined weight carried the day. In broad outline, the Japan Crowd's aim was to reconstruct Japan as she had been before the militarists seized control and twisted and abused her institutions for their own ends. In the sense that this course offered a better chance of stability than the China Crowd's radical restructuring of the nation, it suited the American military. It also suited the leaders of American big business, anxious to resume lucrative trade links with their Japanese counterparts. The moguls found public support from *Newsweek*; and behind the scenes they exerted their influence through a singular and unofficial organisation called the American Council for Japan in which business stood shoulder to shoulder with the army to protect American vested interests in Japan.

In this perspective, it is the attempt at radical reform which was the aberration in American policy towards Japan. The reform programme seemed at first so typical of the time – a generous gesture of post-war idealism. But the late 1940s proved instead to be the era when in reality all hopes for internationalism and a universal morality finally died, and against this background America's original charter for Japan looks a little incongruous.

Nevertheless, though the wave of reform ebbed quickly, it left a permanent tidemark. What American hawks were able to achieve in Japan in the late 1940s, the 1950s and beyond, was influenced and in many respects limited by what the China Crowd had brought about in their brief period of power. One innovation in particular was crucial to the long-term demilitarisation of Japan – and this, though it was attacked as fiercely as the rest, could not be wholly undone.

Article 9 of the new Japanese Constitution reads:

Aspiring sincerely to international peace based on justice and order, the Japanese people forever renounce war as a sovereign right of the nation and the threat or use of force as a means of settling international disputes.

In order to accomplish the aim of the preceding paragraph, land, sea and air forces, as well as other war potential will never be maintained.

This was a remarkable gesture of idealism. As its architect, MacArthur, whatever his general political bias, must be counted amongst the radicals in Japan. And unlike many of the more drastic American reforms, Article 9 was in tune with the fundamental orientation of Japanese society, towards harmony and conciliation – so much so that it has survived over four decades.

In many respects, the history of the past forty years in Japanese-American relations is a catalogue of attempts by Americans in league with Japanese hawks to counteract the consequences of MacArthur's grand gesture. Even before Article 9 took shape, one of MacArthur's closest advisers was working hard to achieve the opposite effect – not to pacify Japan but to rearm her. The day after the surrender General Charles Willoughby, head of MacArthur's military intelligence organisation, renewed his acquaintance with his Japanese counterpart, General Seizo Arisue, in secret, and together they began to plan the rebuilding of Japan's army.

As the balance of power in Washington shifted, civilian policy-makers gradually moved closer into line with the military point of view. Behind the scenes America supplied money, expertise, arms and equipment, and applied mounting pressure until rearmament became an unspoken condition for granting Japan her political independence. When in 1952 America restored Japanese sovereignty, she also formally assumed responsibility for her external defence. But, discreetly, Japan continued her own rearmament programme. With the end of the Occupation American insistence came into the open. In 1953 Richard Nixon, on a vice-presidential visit to Japan, felt able to proclaim in public that Article 9 had been 'an honest mistake'.

By the following year Japan officially possessed 'Self-Defense Forces' on land, sea and air. Since then she has been groomed by the United States as an ally and potential junior partner in collective security arrangements for the Pacific region. Now in the 1980s Japan is the world's eighth largest spender on arms, and stands on the nuclear threshhold.

So which element in the American legacy is the more significant – the survival of Article 9, or the existence of the Self-Defense Forces? In the balance between reform and reaction, idealism and realism, lies the answer to our questions: did America demilitarise Japan? is Japan remilitarising? and if so, is America to blame?

*   *   *

In the 1980s a vast amount of material on the Occupation years has been de-classified. At Suitland, Maryland, the U.S. Government maintains an underground cavern the size of a football pitch, stacked eighteen feet high with boxes of SCAP files. (It was among these records that our research came a macabre full circle when we opened a file marked 'Tojo's Execution' to find ourselves looking at the fingerprint record taken from his still-warm corpse.)

Ploughing through the acres of paper, we were constantly reminded of the critical importance in the story of individual characters, occupiers and occupied, and their personal responses to the situation in Japan as they perceived it.

At SCAP, for example, within the broad boundaries of Washington's policy, senior and sometimes even junior officials were able to translate their own beliefs into actions which still affect the way 120,000,000 Japanese live their lives today. These beliefs were astonishingly diverse, for SCAP reflected 'the whole spectrum of post-war civilization . . . dumped by the shipload onto the docks in Yokohama lusting for a myriad of things'.

Recruiting was carried out in the States, and some of the civil servants in charge took the chance to reserve the choicer jobs for themselves, regardless of experience or qualifications. They were joined by hundreds of officers leaving the army, not yet ready to settle back into the civilian careers which the war had disrupted. There was, besides, the inevitable quota of 'would-be Marco Polos', opportunists and misfits. 'Civil service drunks who thought they could take advantage of a two-year dry cleaning (since who thought the military would allow booze? They got to Japan and found out that there was more booze available there at ten cents a drink than they had ever *dreamed* of). . . . Women of all shapes, sizes and ages, some hoping to get over a man, some hoping to get a man.'

Carpet-baggers got in, despite genuine efforts to stop them, but they were not the only ones to see the Occupation as the means of making a prosperous start to the post-war era. Hundreds of American bureaucrats worked more discreetly but no less avidly to build a nest-egg for their return. Present comforts beckoned too – all the advantages of a quasi-colonial life-style: status, space, servants. The SCAP empire was a little like the British Raj in its heyday. One American outsider, visiting Japan late in the Occupation, was disgusted by the oases of American luxury and comparative elegance in the midst of what was still a desert of Japanese suffering. He railed against MacArthur's minions and their 'shrill, cackling wives', relentlessly exporting American suburban values and behaving 'as if the war had been fought so that they could have six Japanese butlers with the divisional insignia on their jackets'.

But like the Raj, SCAP also included a large number of conscientious, hard-working men with no ulterior motive, merely a mission to relieve, repair and rebuild. MacArthur was to remark at one point that Washington had sent him 'a boatload of New Dealers' – a label which fitted quite neatly at least two individuals who were to be important in the story of demilitarisation. Charles Kades, a Harvard-trained New York lawyer, had worked from 1933 to 1937 for the Secretary of the Interior, his speciality the financing of public works: one of his staff described him as a 'dynamic libertarian', dedicated to freeing the Japanese people from the militarist stranglehold. Alfred Rodman Hussey, another Harvard man and more idealistic still, believed in a universal morality applicable to all men and all nations alike. He wanted this written into the new constitution of Japan, and felt it should be possible to legislate on ethical questions. He was later to court disaster by challenging his military superiors over their violation of the civil liberties not only of the Japanese but also of SCAP civilians who had become suspect for their leftist views.

Many in SCAP were indeed considerably more radical than either Kades or Hussey. Some, like Thomas Bisson, had profound emotional and intellectual sympathies with Mao's revolution in China, and were later to answer for them to McCarthy. MacArthur was aware that SCAP might even contain some Communist Party members, but was not inclined to take this very seriously. 'We have probably got some of them. The War Department has some. So does the State Department. It doesn't mean very much', a senior American official remembered him saying. But others within SCAP reacted far more fiercely.

The division between radicals and conservatives in SCAP coincided roughly, though not exactly, with the schism between civilians and the military. The SCAP structure coexisted alongside the military hierarchy of the Far East Command (FECOM), which MacArthur also headed as Commander in Chief, Far East. Problems arose because the two organisations had several departments in common – notably their military General Staff sections, and in particular G-2, the military intelligence section under Charles Willoughby. This gave the military some leverage within the quasi-civilian SCAP, and their position was strengthened by MacArthur's personal preference for army men as working colleagues. Even the special staff sections of SCAP, dealing with civilian affairs and staffed increasingly by civilians, found themselves with military chiefs who often had little experience or knowledge of their subjects. The Brigadier General originally deputed to reform the Japanese educational system did not even have a college degree. And the principal interest of the soldier heading the

Economic and Scientific Section, according to frustrated civilian subordinates, was to introduce professional baseball to Japan. The civilians felt their expertise being wasted and their progressive initiatives blocked by men more interested in making sure that the trains once more ran on time.

There were, of course, exceptions to the liberal civilian/ conservative military rule. Major General Courtney Whitney was the most glaring – one of MacArthur's most trusted military advisers, but at the same time as dogmatic a reformer in some respects as any of his juniors could desire. Whitney was in a key position to make his wishes felt, at the head of SCAP's Government Section, which supervised literally everything to do with the 'government' of Japan – Diet, Cabinet, ministries, political parties, local administration.

Whitney was not greatly beloved within SCAP. His enemies described him as pompous, rude, arrogant, and bullying, 'a stuffed pig with a mustache', and his juniors resented the exaggerated distance he put between himself and them. Much of the hostility of his peers, however, was due to jealousy. Whitney stood closer than anyone to MacArthur's elbow, and was the only SCAP official with direct access to him. A lawyer before the war, with a prosperous practice in Manila, when the Philippines fell to the Japanese and MacArthur was ordered to retreat to Australia, Whitney became one of his principal supports in what MacArthur regarded as a personal Golgotha. It was Whitney who masterminded the 'I shall return!' campaign.

Whitney and the members of the 'Bataan Gang', who had been through the war with MacArthur and shared his fluctuating fortunes, remained his inner circle throughout the Occupation – devoted and protective to the point of paranoia.* Quite often, however, the enemies against whom the gang members were defending him were each other, as they competed furiously for his attention. One of MacArthur's critics found the atmosphere of intrigue within the empire overpowering – strongly reminiscent of 'the latter days of the court of the Empress Catherine II', or the Kremlin under Stalin.

Whitney's bitterest rival, an enemy on ideological grounds too, was General Willoughby, a professional soldier and specialist in counter-intelligence. MacArthur referred to Willoughby unforgettably as 'my loveable fascist' – after he left the U.S. Army, he

---

* 'Some of them acted like men who had personally lifted him down from the cross after he had been crucified and they determined that nothing again should ever hurt him. . . . They formed an exclusive group that resented and suspected "outsiders".'

became one of General Franco's closest advisers – and he was the particular *bête noire* of SCAP's civilian reformers. To his mind nothing in Japan – the health or prosperity of the people, their human rights, civil liberties, intellectual freedom, political prerogatives, or any of the other benefits for which the reformers were fighting – was of the least importance as compared with the urgent necessity of securing the country against communism.

The Japanese were all too aware of the rifts within SCAP, and they exploited them to the full. Most adroit and most gleeful of the intriguers was Shigeru Yoshida, Prime Minister of Japan for five of the Occupation's seven years. Yoshida's nickname – 'One Man' – shows what his countrymen thought of him. Cantankerous, stubborn and outspoken – in his New Year's speech to the nation on January 1, 1947 he referred to Japan's trade union leaders as 'a bunch of bastards' – he was far more willing than most Japanese politicians to let his individual voice be heard. Indeed, he stamped his powerful personality so firmly on Japan in the post-war era that Richard Nixon included him in his list of seven twentieth-century leaders who changed the world. (The list also included MacArthur.)

To SCAP, and even among his own people, Yoshida epitomised the 'Old Guard' in Japan. A 'throwback' in his pince-nez and old-fashioned wing collar, his connections were with big business and the pre-war bureaucracy, and his greatest fear was the prospect of radical change to the traditional structure of Japan. He had every reason, therefore, to distrust Whitney and the Government Section reformers, whom he described variously as 'idealists', 'quite peculiar types', or Red subversives, depending on his audience. He infuriated Government Section by going straight over their heads to complain directly to MacArthur of the effects their reforms were having. The Supreme Commander became accustomed to finding little messages on his desk, unsigned but unmistakably from Yoshida.

Not surprisingly, Yoshida's natural affinities were with Willoughby and the other law-and-order men. He cultivated the right wing of the Occupation forces as assiduously as they appear to have supported him: when he was campaigning in the provinces for election as Prime Minister, they provided him with escorts and sent him sandwiches and other food to see him through long journeys 'because, they said, they knew it was in short supply'.

Yoshida was not, however, a militarist – it was a significant feature of Japanese politics that one did not have to be a liberal to oppose the militarists. He had consistently condemned the Pacific War as an 'unwinnable blunder' and the military leaders as dangerous socialist radicals, and he went to prison very briefly in

April 1945 for his views. As an opponent of rearming Japan, he was to be MacArthur's most unlikely ally in defence of Article 9, and the two leaders, despite their real differences, developed a healthy mutual respect and even affection. When MacArthur died in 1964, neither Truman nor Eisenhower came to his funeral, but Yoshida, then eighty-six, flew halfway round the world to be there.

In strong contrast stands one of the other key figures of the last four decades on the Japanese side – Yasuhiro Nakasone, Prime Minister since 1982. From the moment in January 1951 when, as a young conservative politician, he sent a personal appeal to MacArthur, complaining that 'servility caused by the defeat and occupation has much spoilt morals fostered in two thousand long years', Nakasone has been one of Japan's leading hawks. His personal campaign for rearmament, moral and physical, forms a counterpoint to the main story, and seems to give his continuing reign as Prime Minister a special significance.

Brooding over all the other Japanese characters in the story is the Emperor Hirohito. Trying to decide what to do with the Imperial institution, the Americans were face to face with an enigma. Was he the grinning gargoyle of wartime propaganda, stained with Japan's war crimes just as deeply as Hitler with Germany's? or the shy, gentle, myopic marine biologist, golfer and family man? Whichever myth came nearer to the truth – and the debate continues today, as Hirohito moves through his ninth decade – the Emperor had a crucial part to play in the drama of demilitarisation, both in political and religious reform, and, by his absence, at the trial of Japan's military leaders.

From prison, and then from the dock, Hideki Tojo emerges as old Japan's most dazzling defender during the early years of the Occupation. Resigned to death, unrepentant and unafraid, like a *samurai* at bay, he defied the serried ranks of Allied prosecutors, and offered his countrymen a rationale for their past conduct and some present pride in themselves. We gradually became fascinated by the proceedings against Tojo, a two-and-a-half-year marathon involving twenty-seven other defendants, which had been closely modelled on the Nuremberg Trial. A quarter of the book is devoted to the International Military Tribunal for the Far East, which, in our story, features as an integral part of the campaign for psychological demilitarisation.

In many respects the IMTFE was a microcosm of the Occupation, displaying a few of its strengths and almost all its weaknesses. Chief among these was the internecine warfare between so-called allies. The dignity of the Tribunal was hardly enhanced by the open dislike of its Australian President for the American Chief Prosecutor. The President, Sir William Webb, had just finished a lengthy report on Japanese atrocities for the Australian government, and his principal ambition was to see Hirohito in the dock. The Chief Prosecutor, on the other hand, Joseph Berry Keenan, had strict instructions that the Emperor was not to be implicated in any way. To the best of his abilities, he obeyed – but these abilities were by now severely limited. In the 1930s Keenan had been a formidable trial lawyer, scourge of America's mobsters. Ten years later he was a confirmed alcoholic, and as the trial progressed, he became an increasing liability. This emerges clearly from the papers of the chief British prosecutor, Sir Arthur Comyns Carr, a far more reticent and punctilious man, who was deeply uncomfortable under Keenan's erratic leadership.

All other personalities to some extent pale, however, in the presence of MacArthur. Any thumbnail sketch is bound to be misleading, so complicated and contradictory was his character. After eighteen years of research his most recent and most authoritative biographer was forced to conclude 'how little I know about MacArthur's inner self . . . My nearly two decades of tracking him have led me only to a few fascinating shells along the edges of a long beach and a wide ocean'.

One cannot read MacArthur's official writings, his letters, and records of his interviews and speeches without getting bogged down in a morass of inconsistencies. He talked almost unstoppably – his appointments had to be strictly limited because he discoursed at such length – and he had a tendency to tailor what he said to his audience. It is possible by selecting from the evidence to make anything one wants of him.

This seems always to have been the case. In otherwise hardboiled men, he inspired an uncritical devotion that was to last all their lives: both Willoughby and Whitney wrote biographies of him that verge on the fawning. Equally, he was the object of some near-pathological hatreds. Harry S. Truman had no particular liking for military men, especially those with presidential ambitions and pretensions to breeding. Before he ever met MacArthur he had consigned him to the same category as General Custer – 'Mr. Prima Donna, Brass Hat, 5-Star MacArthur . . . play actor and bunco man'. (To MacArthur, of course, Truman was simply 'a vulgar little clown'.)

MacArthur's detractors saw first his vanity. An exceptionally handsome man, in his sixties he was said to have begun dyeing his hair, and he used a lot of gestures in conversation, and fiddled endlessly with his pipe, to conceal the fact that his hands had developed the tremble of Parkinson's Disease. Whitney often gave him memos in large type because he hated wearing his glasses.

He had a bad habit of claiming credit for other people's successes (which accounted for many of his enemies in the services), and went to great lengths to shift the blame for mistakes. This was the product of an obsessive concern for his public image, which he was able to indulge to the full in Japan. He enjoyed seeing himself as an American proconsul or a colonial governor like his father (military governor of the Philippines from 1900 to 1901) and did not discourage people from referring to him as a blue-eyed *shogun*, or even likening him to the Emperor. The State Department was greatly irritated when he refused to help them by briefing foreign ambassadors, on the grounds that 'other heads of state' were not required to do it. Dean Acheson snapped that MacArthur 'had many attributes of a foreign sovereign . . . and was quite as difficult as any'.

MacArthur acknowledged only George Washington and Abraham Lincoln as his advisers – on the human plane, that is: Truman sneered at his apparent perception of himself as the 'Right Hand Man of God'. And his preoccupation with status lasted until his death and beyond. When he was eighty-three and in 'horrible' physical condition, the Pentagon consulted him about his funeral, offering him four days lying-in-state and burial at Arlington National Cemetery. MacArthur, ill or not, stipulated more than a week of lying-in-state at various different venues, and entombment in his own private memorial in Norfolk, Virginia. At Arlington, he said, he would be surrounded by his enemies.

Public image was a means to an end, however, not an end in itself. His fiercest critics claim that between 1944 and 1952 his aim was the Presidency, and this ambition alone guided his actions. They allege that he saw Japan simply as a springboard, and was more interested in the Occupation for its political convertibility than for itself – hence his efforts to keep absolute control of Japan and claim total credit, and also his agility in disassociating himself from projects he thought likely to fail. He kept well clear of the IMTFE, for example.

MacArthur's defenders admit some of these flaws. But to them, the vices are heavily outweighed by equally indisputable virtues. He was physically very brave, one of the most decorated American officers of World War 1. He had a quick and analytical brain and a phenomenal memory. And he had, it would seem, great personal magnetism. The people who detested him most tended to be those who had least direct contact with him. (Between 1945 and 1951, when he fired MacArthur, Truman, for example, only met him once.) Even when what he said was banal – and one critic wrote of him, 'The General's words steam along like warships with no great cargo of meaning' – the way he said it could be mesmerising.

More important, perhaps, MacArthur's admirers insist on his

greatness of heart. Sir Alvary Gascoigne, Britain's representative in Japan, was perhaps not intending a compliment when he wrote home, 'MacArthur really believes that he is the one man who could save the world'. But he had clearly felt the force of the Supreme Commander's crusading spirit, a readiness to champion causes much wider than mere personal interests.

MacArthur also saw the Occupation as a chance to bring a whole nation into the Light, and genuinely relished the idea of bestowing on the Japanese the benefits of the American way of life, in which he wholeheartedly believed. If he had a tendency to identify America's interests with his own, this was done sincerely and not cynically.

It is hard to see his behaviour as wholly calculating, because from time to time he would be visibly carried away on waves of enthusiasm, which as often as not landed him in trouble. He much preferred the broad sweep and the general principle to niggling little details of fact which confused the picture. Issues, to his mind, presented themselves in black and white, and he had a great fondness for Western movies, where the moral is never in doubt.

Both to the American public, fed on official press releases, and to the average Japanese citizen, knowing nothing of power struggles in Washington or within SCAP, MacArthur *was* the Occupation. In physical terms he held himself aloof. He lived in the old United States ambassador's residence, enclosed by high masonry walls and iron grilles, and very rarely socialised outside his own home. All traffic lights along the way were held on green as he swept through the centre of Tokyo on his way to the office; this route was all he saw of Tokyo, and in six years he never left the capital except to go to the airport.

But in every other sense, in the early years of the Occupation at least, he was at its heart. He was responsible both for its most disreputable cover-up (see Chapter 19) and for what was arguably its greatest and most enduring achievement – Article 9. And in Article 9 lies the most baffling paradox of all. The general who suggested spreading radioactive cobalt waste along the Korean frontier as a defence against the Red Chinese was also the man who said, 'Could I have but a line a century hence crediting a contribution to the advance of peace, I would gladly yield every honor which has been accorded by war'.

The staunch Republican, holding various beliefs which attracted the support of the most reactionary men in America, was in other ways a radical ahead of his time. Whatever his motives, he persistently sided with the reformers within SCAP to a degree that frustrated Willoughby and infuriated Washington. He may have demanded unfailing loyalty from his juniors, but long before the calamity of Korea he was openly insubordinate to his masters – the wild card in the Occupation of Japan.

* * *

It is not hard to understand why MacArthur felt any contribution to peace would be worthwhile. He had fought in three wars, and in the last fifty years of his life, he saw forty-five of the world's seventy-nine politically significant states suffer military coups. Since then, the potential for military interference in civilian affairs has ballooned, with some 400 billion American dollars spent annually to equip and maintain the 21 million men and women under arms worldwide.

Peace researchers have made strenuous efforts in recent years to explore and publicise the implications of militarisation for world affairs – political, social and economic. But it is not necessary to be a pacifist to fear and oppose militarisation. The objection is not merely that these huge arms budgets could be better spent, or even that the proliferation of weapons increases the risk of war. Even those who believe that war can be justified accept that militarisation is fundamentally antagonistic to the democratic way of life.

Broadly the symptoms of militarisation are an authoritarian political system within which the military holds significant power; a regimented, hierarchical society; and a spirit of aggressive nationalism.

These characteristics have been extrapolated from Bismarck's Prussia, Hitler's Germany, the dictatorships of Latin America and Africa, the Soviet Union, and many other militarised states. Needless to say, each militarised society differs from the theoretical model both in the degree of its militarisation and the form the process may take. Some states fall prey to a *coup d'état* and are ruled directly by a military junta. In others power-sharing, overt or covert, is possible. In his Farewell Address President Eisenhower warned his countrymen of the dangers of what he called the 'military-industrial complex', the alliance between soldier, bureaucrat, scientist and businessman which, however well-intentioned and patriotic its activities, may nevertheless possess what Eisenhower felt to be 'unwarranted' influence in a civilian democracy.

It is even possible for an unarmed society to display many of the symptoms of militarisation – the prime example being Germany in the post-First World War period. The Weimar Republic was democratic and largely disarmed, and yet the Germans clung to mass movements, organised privately, which were regimented, disciplined and hierarchical. In doing so, they voluntarily sacrificed their civilianism, making Hitler's task immeasurably easier.

The theoretical models of militarisation we now possess were not, of course, available to SCAP. We are applying modern terminology and modern insights to the problems of the past. In this book, 'demilitarisation' is a portmanteau word encompassing both the eradication of the symptoms of militarisation, and the creation of a democratic state. 'Militarism' we use in a narrower sense mainly to signify the spirit that pervades militarised states – ultra-nationalism, xenophobia, expansionism, and the glorification of war and the profession of arms.

PART ONE

SYMPTOMS AND STRATEGIES

1

Militarised Japan: The Nature of the Problem

There is no one word in western vocabularies which can adequately convey the precise nature of Japan's militarisation. 'Militarist', 'Fascist', 'Nazi' and so on show only parts of the picture; and when describing the state of affairs prevailing in Japan in the late 1930s and early 1940s, commentators often fall back on calling it simply 'Japanism', a law unto itself.

On the surface the regime was an authoritarian military-civilian coalition which kept itself in power by means of a powerful state apparatus for repression and control. But beneath the militarist superstructure lay a society which already contained within itself the seeds of militarisation: hierarchy and obedience, an obsessional stress on loyalty and self-sacrifice, and a group ethic. Arguably SCAP never fully appreciated that the menace had two levels, and this immeasurably complicated its task of demilitarisation.

The militarised Japan of the late 1930s was founded on a constitution dating back to the nineteenth century and modelled on the constitution of Prussia. Sovereignty was vested in the Emperor, and ranking equally below him were two groups of national servants and counsellors – the Imperial armed forces and the civilian government. As Japan progressed through the dark valley of the 1930s the military gradually achieved dominance over the civilians, in a period characterised as 'government by assassination'.

The extent of Emperor Hirohito's involvement in the military's rise to power, whether as a conspirator or an opponent, is still not entirely clear. It is important, however, in examining his role to distinguish between the man and the Imperial institution. (Roughly the same distinction can be drawn in the United States between the President and the Office of the Presidency.) The institution was unquestionably in the hands of the militarists, and they used it to legitimise their rule. Hirohito's personal involvement was undoubtedly less than the sum total of what was done in his name, but how *much* less, or conversely, how much he did actively to restrain the militarists is still obscure.

What is sure is that, though the military gained the upper hand within the home islands, they never took full control. The complexities of mobilising an industrialised nation for total war required them to take Japan's other vested interests into partnership. They enlisted the aid of the leaders of big business, whose expertise was crucial in exploiting the resources of the Japanese Empire and in designing and building new weaponry. They needed the good will of the large landowners, the sons of whose tenant farmers provided the cannon fodder. They recruited certain members of Hirohito's court, and even his family; politicians and ultra-nationalist leaders; and the prime movers in the highly centralised and immensely powerful bureaucratic machine, to guarantee the nation's day-to-day co-operation.

The broad mass of the Japanese people were simply pawns in the game. Their lives from cradle to grave were regimented and circumscribed, physically and psychologically. In 1940, for example, the Home Ministry established the *tonari-gumi*, or neighbourhood association, system. Throughout Japan every household was grouped with nine others, to form the basic unit of the wartime administrative system: through the *tonari-gumi*, rations of food and fuel were distributed and regular compulsory meetings were held at which official notices were read. Each *tonari-gumi* had its headman, the equivalent of the Nazi block leader, who used his local influence to ensure compliance with regulations and proper patriotic feeling amongst his charges. The *tonari-gumi* network proved so effective in mobilising local resources and solving local problems that it was retained by MacArthur for some time into the Occupation despite its distinctly totalitarian overtones.

The Way of the Subject, published in 1941 by the Ministry of Education, sums up the spirit in which the system was founded: 'It is unforgivable to consider private life as the realm of individual freedom where we can do as we like, outside the purview of the State. A meal at table or a suit of clothes, none is ours alone, nor are we purely in a personal capacity when at play or asleep. All is related to the concerns of the state. Even in our private lives we should be devoted to the Emperor and never lose our attitude of service to him.'

At work as at home, the individual was controlled. The National Mobilisation Law of 1938 gave the bureaucracy wide powers to oversee industrial production, wages and prices, and to draft labour from far and wide to meet national needs. The daily life of the farmer, too, was closely regulated. Rarely did he own his land, and he was entirely subject to the whims of the landowner. Under

[4]

wartime conditions he was told what to plant and when; seeds and fertiliser were issued by central authority and quotas set.

By the late 1930s, industry, commerce and finance in Japan were dominated by an interlocking series of monopolistic combines known as *zaibatsu*, the four biggest of which were Mitsui, Mitsubishi, Yasuda and Sumitomo. The *zaibatsu* were to be an issue of major concern throughout the Occupation. They were privately-owned corporations, and by the 1930s the controlling families were among the richest men in the world. They formed a dynamic working partnership with the government which over the first decades of the twentieth century had achieved an industrial miracle – and was to do so again, by much the same methods, in the post-war period.

Contributing significantly to *zaibatsu* efficiency was the government's tendency invariably to support the employer at the expense of the employee, in terms both of weighting the tax burden towards the peasant and worker, and in restricting organised labour. In school children had the virtues of industry and austerity incessantly dinned into them, emerging as a willing workforce with low expectations in terms of standard of living – a rare asset for an employer. And through a semi-official organisation called the *Kyochokai*, the government propagated 'an ideology of industrial harmony based on Confucian moral and ethical precepts'.

At the height of unionisation in 1936 only six per cent of the total workforce of around fifteen million was unionised, and most of these men were in 'enterprise unions', working largely for the benefit of their employers. In the cities, there existed huge discrepancies of wealth and political influence. Missing entirely from the socio-economic scene was any substantial middle class, and this gap obviously exaggerated the polarisation in Japanese society with which the Americans would have to cope.

There were strict controls too over news, public comment and even private opinion. Japan's geographical character as a nation of islands helped the militarists isolate the people from world events. Until the fall of Saipan, only short-wave radio signals could reach Japan from the West – and the possession of suitable receivers was prohibited. Consequently the Japanese had no scope for 'black listening', the tuning-in to Allied broadcasts that had proved so valuable in Europe as a counterweight to Nazi distortions.

Control of the airwaves and a strict censorship of the home media ensured that for a decade the Japanese heard, read and saw only that which the authorities wanted them to know. The Home Ministry used 'thought police' to monitor the pulse of public opinion for any unexpected quickenings; and they could take direct action against any dissenters or anti-government activists, thanks to draconian legislation dating from the nineteenth century. The civilian police were on hand to break up 'undesirable' public meetings, and at their shoulder stood the most brutal of all the forces of repression – the *Kempei Tai*. These were a military police force whose jurisdiction had come to extend to soldier and civilian alike. They rivalled the Gestapo in the interrogation techniques they employed on fellow-Japanese, and to support their reign of terror they had the sanction of an indescribably callous prison system. MacArthur viewed the *Kempei Tai* as 'the strongest weapon of the military clique', enabling them 'to spread a network of political espionage, suppress freedom of speech, of assembly, even of thought, and by means of tyrannical oppression to degrade the dignity of the individual'.

Indoctrination filled the vacuum left by censorship and repression. In schools, through compulsory military service, and throughout adulthood, the Japanese were force-fed a diet of militarism. From 1940 onwards some twelve and a half million elementary school children were subjected daily to drill, marching, singing army songs and bowing in squads towards the Emperor's Palace repeating the oath of loyalty: 'We are the children of the divine country Japan. We are the children of fighting Japan. We are the children of Japan which is building Greater East Asia.'

In part, the militarists were simply purveying through all the resources of the mass media the simplistic messages of conventional wartime propaganda. Japan, they said, was fighting for the freedom of the world. Her incursions into South East Asia were part of a crusade against colonial oppression by America, Britain, Holland and France, and her war in China a valiant attempt to stop the spread of communism in Asia. The Allies, on the other hand, were aggressors. Their imperialist ambitions had isolated Japan, forcing her to strike against Pearl Harbor and elsewhere in self-defence. As in the West, much energy was devoted to fanning the embers of patriotism – as far as the home front was concerned, to boost war production and sell war bonds – but the Japanese militarists took this to extremes almost beyond the comprehension of the Occidental mind.

They created a rigid and racist cult of fanatical nationalism centred on the Emperor. Through a perversion of the ancient mythology of Shinto, a religion central to Japanese culture, they portrayed Japan as a divine country created by gods – unlike other countries, which in the beginning had merely coalesced from mud and slime. Ruling over this divine land since time immemorial had been an unbroken series of Emperors, direct lineal descendants of the Sun Goddess – Amaterasu, the principal Shinto deity and *kami* (spirit) of the most powerful force in the universe. The Japanese people were themselves descended from lesser gods in the Shinto pantheon. Consequently the Imperial line was the trunk of the Japanese family tree, of which all other Japanese families were the branches.

In this way Hirohito added to his constitutional position as head of state the attributes of god, religious leader, and *paterfamilias* to the Japanese tribe. At its height, the cult portrayed the islands of Japan, the Japanese race, and the Emperor as one mystic and indivisible whole. 'The Emperor', as Hozumi expressed it, '*is* the state.'

It is hard to tell how deeply the Japanese people actually believed in this militarist ideology. Lip service to the cult was compulsory, and if ever doubts were raised – in academic circles, for example – they were swiftly and brutally suppressed. In all probability, the degree of indoctrination varied according to the sophistication of the background and education of the young peasant-soldier who was the backbone of the Japanese military monster. What is not in question is the benefit the militarists gained from the cult.

The political power of the Emperor had been for decades a tool to be used by others. By enhancing the prestige of the Imperial institution the militarists increased their own practical power. And the Emperor was an effective focus for intense religious and tribal feeling that readily crossed over into the kind of racism which is so strong and sustaining a motive force in time of war. The emphasis on Japan's divinity and, drawing further on Shinto mythology, her destiny to bring all the corners of the world under the Emperor's banner, bore all the hallmarks of master-race propaganda. Lastly, and perhaps most importantly, the Imperial institution was a channel through which the militarists could exploit certain characteristics inherent in Japanese society.

In the West the basic unit of society is the individual. Each person is regarded as autonomous and equal, and under the banner of liberty he is entitled to pursue his own self-interest, subject only to the laws governing society as a whole. 'Rugged individualism' (Herbert Hoover's phrase) is a most cherished quality, and it lies at the base of the democratic system in the West. In Japan, on the other hand, individualism is anathema. The basic unit of society is the group, and the Japanese can only exist happily and find self-realisation within the collectivity. In Freudian terms his super-ego function is diminished – though as if to underline the difference between Japanese and Westerners, some commentators deny that Freudian theories are even applicable to the Japanese mind, which is better understood, they suggest, in terms of interactionist rather than individualist theories.

The Japanese will invariably sacrifice his own interests,

ambitions and welfare to the good of the group. To prevent the group from fragmenting he will go out of his way to avoid confrontation – hence the Japanese passion for consensus: if no one feels excluded, no one can be antagonistic.

The organisation of each group – be it family, village, workforce, criminal gang or political clique – is hierarchical. Hierarchy is taken for granted as part of the essential nature of the universe. Even the Japanese language is status-referential, with many different forms of the same word enabling the user to reflect to a nicety the precise degree of superiority or inferiority of the listener. The bonding within each group is along these hierarchical, vertical lines. In the West, for example, the principal axis of the family is husband/wife. But in Japan, it is parent/child. The nature of this bonding is not so much love as mutual obligation. And looking at it from the perspective of the 'lower' of the pair, obligation is expressed as intense loyalty. In the 1930s and 1940s this loyalty – of child/subject to father/Emperor – operating within the national group was turned into the principal, almost the *only* ethical imperative governing Japanese behaviour.

For the soldier, the loyalty he owed directly to the Emperor who was father, god and Supreme Commander was loyalty unto death. This had been the supreme virtue of the *samurai* – constant preparedness for death in the cause of his master and consequent indifference to his own fate in the face of danger. The militarists were quick to exploit Japan's historic code of chivalry, just as they had twisted traditional religion. Ignoring the spiritual side of the *samurai* creed (the *bushido* or 'way of the warrior'), they emphasised the one feature which served a practical purpose – the extraordinary and terrifying strength of the fighting man in whom the instinct for self-preservation has been destroyed.

These twin dynamics in Japanese society – group orientation and unquestioning loyalty to one's superior – were harnessed by the militarists through the Emperor system. And it was the combination of, above, a totalitarian organisational structure and, below, an inherent predisposition to be organised which made the Japan of the 1940s so formidable an enemy.

*   *   *

There is no doubting the aggregate effect of 'Japanism'. The statistics of death are sufficient proof of its power over the people of Japan. Among Allied troops in the Pacific War the ratio of captured to dead was 120:1; among Japanese soldiers bound by the creed of loyalty unto death it was 4:1. And to this day many are convinced

[8]

that if the call had come, the entire home population too would have sacrificed itself on the guns of the invading American armies.

This then was the enemy the Americans faced, the problem they had to solve. 'Japanism' was a unique phenomenon – complicated, multi-faceted, its roots deeply embedded in the fundamental nature of Japanese society. How good were the prospects of reshaping a nation which had had both the spirit to fight to the last man at Iwo Jima and the discipline to lay down its arms without demur at a word from its Emperor? And how was change to be achieved? Hardly surprising that long before the war was over, the debate had already begun in Washington over the best means of winning the peace.

2

The Peculiar Chosen People: Planning the Occupation

Some ninety-five years before the Occupation began, Herman Melville claimed of himself and his fellow-countrymen, 'We Americans are the peculiar chosen people – the Israel of our time: we bear the ark of the liberties of the world. God has predestined, mankind expects, great things from our race; and great things we feel in our souls.' Ever since the Declaration of Independence, America's sense of her own unique status and divine mission has inspired and irritated, reassured and revolted the rest of the world.

Abraham Lincoln once referred to the Declaration of Independence as 'a standard maxim for a free society . . . augmenting the happiness and value of life to all people of all colors everywhere'. The American way, it would seem, was universally applicable; and many Americans still believe it to be so. Underlying the surface workings of the world are certain fundamental moral laws and spiritual values. Americans espouse these laws and values as by instinct, and have, they feel, a duty to open the eyes of others to them.

Even after the experience of the Vietnam War, Americans tend to assume, as Henry Kissinger recently observed, 'that the normal political evolution is towards the American pattern of government. That nations are shaped by their culture, their history, even their folk tales, that therefore their margin of change is finite, is not a view readily accepted by most Americans, even their leaders'.

That the margin of change was finite was certainly not a view accepted by the architects of the Occupation – a project which has been described by one (American) participant as a watershed in the American tendency to assume responsibility for 'the reshaping of not only Asia but some two-thirds of the world in our own image or as nearly like our own image as the world's less fortunate citizens can manage'.

Japan was not merely to be crushed but completely remodelled – that was taken for granted by American policymakers, who started planning the future of a defeated Japan only months after war against her had been declared. It is one of the saddest ironies of the Pacific War that, given the material and logistical potential of America, once she was roused to fight, the outcome was never in doubt. So while American troops were struggling bloodily from Guadalcanal to Saipan and on to Iwo Jima and Okinawa, back in Washington, in rather more civilised surroundings, American civil servants were deciding the ultimate fate of their enemy.

What is remarkable is not that they began to plan, but the dispassionate benevolence of their blueprints. For even away from the battlefront, the atmosphere in which the planners were working was ferocious, heavy with aggressive ranting in the press and acute public racial hatred. In the House of Representatives, Congressman John E. Rankin of Mississippi spoke of 'savage apes', while in the Upper House, Senator Richard B. Russell, displaying a fine command of the multi-purpose ethnic slur, declared the American Indian 'with his scalping knife and fiery stake' to be 'a chivalrous cavalier' in comparison with the 'bestial Japs'.

Nor would Russell and Rankin have appeared to be extremists in the eyes of many of their voters. In December 1944, thirteen per cent of Americans favoured killing everyone in Japan, and in April 1945 *The New York Times* was still devoting columns to a debate on the actual feasibility of exterminating the race. And all the while the planners were minuting proposals which appeared to extend to the 'savage apes' everything considered most precious in the American way of life. Japan was to be rid of the spectre of militarism – and the exorcist was to be democracy.

Early plans were centred on three – misplaced – assumptions. Firstly, the Allies must have a free hand to do with Japan as they pleased – in other words, Japan's surrender was to be unconditional. Secondly, capitulation was probably to be achieved by a military invasion. And lastly, invasion would be followed by a full-scale occupation, with direct military government established piecemeal in the wake of the troops as the advance was pushed gradually through the home islands.

Consequently, the Departments of the Army and Navy faced the need to brief and train thousands of officers for military government. Civil Affairs Training Schools and other study centres were set up to teach the rudiments of the Japanese language and culture, and the various techniques needed for administering war-wasted enemy territory – how to distribute and ration scarce food and fuel, how to restore transport and communications, control disease, prevent looting and banditry, and ensure the security of the occupying forces.

The military were happy to work out how the occupation should be run. But it was not yet considered to be their job to determine the governing policy. Once Japan was under control, where was she to be steered? – in the early 1940s at least, this question was for the civilian makers of foreign policy to decide. In the State Department, long-range planning for the post-war world had begun in 1939, with Europe's war barely three months old. Once America was directly involved in the struggle, activity naturally accelerated, and by 1943 the outlines of a policy specifically for a conquered Japan were emerging from a welter of research groups and advisory bodies. The most influential of these was the Interdivisional Area Committee for the Far East, an interesting mixture of academic theorists and hard-boiled Foreign Service officials.

For their practical planning to have point and focus, the military needed to know the lines along which the State Department's collective mind was working. In November 1943 the Office of Strategic Services (fore-runner of the CIA) framed some of the questions which required answering, and these were passed on to the State Department. 'What place do we want Japan to occupy in our post-war world political system?', they asked. 'How weak do we wish Japan to be? . . . What is to be Japan's industrial position?'

At this stage, there seemed to be three main alternatives. Should Japan effectively be removed from the picture of world affairs – 'pastoralised', in Henry Morgenthau's phrase, reduced to her pre-industrial status as a politically isolated and insignificant nation? Or should she simply be neutralised – left in her present state, but with her military power obliterated and her economy regulated through international trade controls? Alternatively, should Japan be enlisted as a future ally, and to that end reconstructed as quickly and efficiently as possible?

On the answers to these questions depended another: 'Do we wish to preserve or to undermine the position of the Emperor?' How much of the old Japanese governmental system was to be left intact depended rather on the role that the new Japan was to be allotted in the post-war world. But within the State Department, as officials attempted to answer the questions the military had put to them, opinion was sharply divided.

*　　　*　　　*

At one pole was the so-called 'China Crowd', a collection of policy-makers who, as they looked ahead to the post-war world, put their faith in China as America's most promising ally in the Far East. For some of these men, 'China' meant a China united under Chiang Kai-shek's Nationalists. But the 'Crowd' was largely composed of planners strongly influenced by contact with and hopes for the China of Mao Tse-tung and the Chinese Communists.

They included such figures as John K. Emmerson, John Stewart Service, John Paton Davies, and George Atcheson, all Foreign Service officials serving in China during the heady days when Mao was in Yenan planning revolution. Indeed, all except Atcheson spent time as official observers in Yenan. Sympathetic to many of the views of the proposed Chinese republic, Emmerson and the others were correspondingly critical of the old militaristic, imperialist, hierarchical Japan. Their views were most clearly reflected in the writings of leading left-wing scholars like Owen Lattimore, Thomas Bisson and Andrew Roth, whose books (particularly Lattimore's *Solution in Asia* and Roth's *Dilemma in Japan*) enjoyed a vogue in liberal circles.

Neither the pro-Nationalists nor the pro-Communists within the China Crowd wished to place Japan in a position to threaten China's rise. Both favoured a 'hard' and punitive peace, laying emphasis on the reform of Japan, not its recovery. They proposed that most of the existing political and economic structure should be dismantled, which would both slow up Japan's post-war progress to China's advantage and prepare the nation for recasting in a more acceptable mould. In particular, the Emperor system, the principal symbol of feudal prestige and unrepresentative power, should be abolished and the stranglehold of the *zaibatsu* on industry broken, as necessary preliminaries to the foundation of a peaceful democracy.

At the other pole within the State Department was the 'Japan Crowd'. This too had its hard core of Foreign Service officials, mostly rather older than the China hands. Joseph C. Grew was the leading light – a diplomat of the old school, and the last pre-war Ambassador in Tokyo. Round Grew clustered several of the staff who had been interned with him in the Embassy after Pearl Harbor. Eugene Dooman, a 'swarthy, pudgy' man, with pretensions as a gourmet, had been born and largely educated in Japan: Grew's second-in-command, he was also known as his *alter ego*. Robert Fearey, the ambassador's private secretary, had been appointed to this post because he was a pupil of Grew's own *alma mater*, Groton School. Joseph Ballantine, a key member of the group, had seen long service in Japan in an earlier period.

The rest of the Japan Crowd were academics who had specialised before the war in Japanese studies – men like George Blakeslee, a veteran of the brief American Occupation of the Rhineland, with a long career dedicated to the cause of peaceful international relations and the League of Nations; and Hugh Borton, Quaker, moderate New Dealer, and teacher of Japanese history.

Most members of the Japan Crowd were by absolute standards

unquestionably liberals too. Blakeslee, Borton and others like them had been appointed to the State Department by the Roosevelt administration precisely because they were obviously in sympathy with the ideals and principles of universal morality and internationalism so ringingly enunciated by F.D.R. and Churchill in the Atlantic Charter of 1941.

Despite the deep differences between the China and Japan Crowds, all – even Grew, Dooman and Ballantine, the especial bugbears of the China Crowd, attacked by name by Andrew Roth in *Dilemma in Japan* – freely acknowledged the need to rid Japan of militarism. The difference was that the Japan Crowd had more faith in Japan's capacity to reform herself. Where the China Crowd denounced the imperialist and militaristic Japan of the 1930s, the Japan Crowd chose to focus on the previous decade of fledgling democracy, seeing in it foundations on which, with the militarist shackles removed, Japan's liberal élite could and would build, leading the people towards a new society.

'Our idea', Ballantine explained later, 'was . . . to encourage those Japanese who in the past had shown progressive pro-western tendencies. . . . We wanted to encourage them to come forth and assume leadership. We felt that the strong forces of example, tutelage, and suggestion would be far more effectual in making the Japanese see the inconsistencies and inadequacies of their traditional order of life, and they would themselves then be willing to make choices in favour of democracy and liberalism.'

As students of Japan's history, with long experience of life there, the Japan Crowd wanted to preserve her cultural heritage. In particular, they were determined to maintain the Imperial institution: the Emperor alone, they felt, could hold the nation together in defeat, bolstering it against the threat of Russian intervention which, to Grew at least, was very real.

Many of these men had a genuine and idealistic affection for Japan as she had been before the militarists warped and twisted her out of shape – Blakeslee was unkindly known as '"poor dear Japan" Blakeslee'. But in the eyes of their critics this affection was vitiated by the less abstract and more personal interests in Japan's survival which several of them also had. For Grew, diplomacy was 'essentially a matter of personal relationships, the intercourse of nations being governed best by the code of gentlemanly conduct', and he had good friends among the more liberal of Japan's political leaders. Inevitably, given the intimate connections between Japan's various ruling élites, this meant some association, however distant, with the leaders of big business; and Grew's bitterest enemies took pleasure in pointing out that he was, after all, a cousin of J. Pierpont Morgan.

Other voices too besides the warring factions of the State Department made themselves heard in Washington. 'New Deal' economists, who had helped to carry out the 'trust-busting' campaign at home, tended to support the China Crowd in their hostility to the *zaibatsu*. U.S. military leaders, mortally afraid of a power vacuum in Japan which the Russians could all too easily fill, inclined towards the Japan Crowd's stress on the importance of stability. The Treasury was preoccupied first and foremost with the relative costs of the different proposals. And outside government circles, various pressure groups rode their own hobby horses. The argument seems simply to have been opened still wider by the foundation of the State-War-Navy Coordinating Committee (SWNCC) at the end of 1944, to align policies for the occupation.

In some areas planning had certainly reached a level of fine detail in the spring of 1945. But on key issues no final decision had been taken by the time America was called upon to turn plans into reality. This moment, of course, was reached sooner and more precipitately than any of the planners had expected. The atomic bomb, one of the reasons for Japan's capitulation, was also one of the best-kept secrets of the war. Not even MacArthur, it seems, was told of its projected use, and he continued to plan for the full-scale invasion of the Japanese homeland.

The suddenness with which surrender came, a full three months earlier than the date projected by MacArthur's headquarters, must explain much of the confusion and contradiction in America's immediate post-war policy for Japan. In the middle of July 1945, when America, Great Britain and China met at Potsdam and announced to Japan the terms on which the Pacific War might be ended, there was no clear statement as to whether government in Japan would be direct or indirect, whether her economic development was in the short term to be curbed or accelerated, and perhaps most urgent, whether or not the Imperial institution was to survive.

The balance certainly appeared to be tipping in the Emperor's favour. To depose him was to run the risk of appalling violence and anarchy in Japan. The occupying power would require thousands, maybe hundreds of thousands of extra troops to restore order, and this would make nonsense of all the Allies' promises – so crucial in political terms – to 'send the boys home'. A growing majority of policymakers firmly believed that the Emperor should be retained at least long enough to ensure the orderly and complete surrender of his armies, and probably well into the foreseeable future. He was, after all, a convenient figurehead who might be used, as Emperors had been used for centuries in Japan, to legitimise the actions of the governing power.

This was also the view of the British Foreign Office; but they were unwilling publicly to endorse the Imperial power, which was viewed by the British public, educated by Allied propagandists, in much the same light as the Third Reich. The Foreign Secretary commented acidly, 'I do not want us to recommend to the Americans that the Emperor should be preserved. They would no doubt like to get such advice, then say they had reluctantly concurred with us.'

President Truman, who had been in office, unelected, for only three months, therefore faced the problem of how to preserve the Imperial institution without immediately being seen to do so. With patriots at home calling for Hirohito's blood, Truman could hardly declare his intention of keeping the Emperor on the throne, without committing political suicide. In June 1945, thirty-three per cent of Americans wanted the Emperor executed. (But only half of those questioned actually knew his name. Five per cent thought it might be Tojo, and other shots in the dark included Hara-Kiri, Tito, Chiang Kai-shek and Yoko Hama.)

Truman's dilemma partly explains the evasiveness of the document which finally emerged at Potsdam. The Potsdam Declaration of July 26, 1945 made no explicit promise to spare the Emperor. But to all except the most idealistic interpreters, its reference to a government that would be 'established in accordance with the freely expressed will of the people' was a tacit pledge that the Japanese people might keep the familiar Imperial order. There was certainly no doubt in the minds of the Japanese government when they accepted these terms that the people's will would be to retain the Emperor.

The Potsdam Declaration represented, therefore, a victory for conservatism and the Japan Crowd. Their philosophy was represented particularly clearly in the provision that 'the Japanese government shall *remove all obstacles to the revival* and strengthening *of democratic tendencies* among the Japanese people'. Japan's democracy was to be homegrown, not an American transplant.

Throughout the early months of 1945 leading up to the Declaration the Japan Crowd had undoubtedly had the edge in the struggle for control of policy. Grew had risen almost to the top of the State Department – first as Director of the Office of Far Eastern Affairs (replacing Stanley Hornbeck, who was strongly pro-Chinese), and then as Under Secretary of State. And as he rose, the influence of his supporters increased. Ballantine succeeded him as Director of the Office of Far Eastern Affairs: and it was Dooman who was largely responsible for the wording of the Potsdam Declaration.

But then in August 1945, in the weeks after the Declaration when

MacArthur's instructions for the Occupation were finally drafted, the pendulum swung dramatically. Secretary of State Edward Stettinius had given Grew virtually a free hand where Japan was concerned. He now retired, and was replaced by James Byrnes whom Grew found far less accommodating. (Byrnes despised the career foreign service, and was on record as referring to 'those little bastards at the State Department'.) Grew himself resigned, and to the dismay of his supporters, his place as Under Secretary of State was taken by Dean Acheson – whose alignment was very definitely with the China Crowd.

From then on, there was a steep decline in the fortunes of the Japan Crowd, and a corresponding rise to power of new men whom a disgruntled Joseph Ballantine described as 'New Deal economists, political scientists, and law graduates with little experience in the world of practical affairs and none in Japan'. Ballantine himself was replaced at the Office of Far Eastern Affairs by John Carter Vincent, another China hand. And the post of Political Adviser to SCAP went neither to Ballantine nor Dooman, Grew's nominees for the job, but to a man formerly based in Chungking, George Atcheson. The first recruit to join Atcheson's office in Tokyo was China Crowd stalwart John K. Emmerson. It was hardly surprising, then, that the instructions which MacArthur carried with him to Japan had moved well beyond the moderate and generalised aims of the Potsdam Declaration.

General Whitney was to recall MacArthur outlining the plans for Japan as he paced the aisle of the plane taking him to Tokyo. 'First destroy the military power. Punish war criminals. Then build the structure of representative government. Modernize the constitution. Hold free elections. Enfranchise the women. Free the political prisoners. Liberate the farmers. Establish a free labor movement. Encourage a free economy. Abolish police oppression. Develop a free and responsible press. Liberalize education. Decentralize political power. Separate Church from State.'

The loyal Whitney portrays MacArthur behaving as though this neat script had come to him more or less by divine revelation. 'I still recall vividly the sight of that striding figure as he puffed on his corncob pipe, stopping intermittently to dictate to me the random thoughts that crowded his mind.' In fact, it had come by radio-telegram from the Joint Chiefs of Staff, in the form of the U.S. Initial Post-Surrender Policy of August 29, 1945.

In broad outline the USIPSP echoed the Potsdam Declaration: the occupying powers were to 'insure that Japan will not again become a menace to the United States or to the peace and security of the world'. This they would achieve by limiting Japanese sovereignty to the four home islands; by eliminating the influence of the militarists wherever it might be detected; and by bringing about the eventual establishment of a peaceful and responsible government conforming 'as closely as may be to the principles of democratic self-government'.

In some of its detail, however, the August policy directive had 'China Crowd' written all over it. The Japan Crowd, more pragmatic and less doctrinaire, had concluded that political ideals must be subordinated to hard economic facts. The advantages to be gained by attacking the *zaibatsu* – social justice and the wider distribution of wealth – were outweighed by the damage it would do to any chance of economic recovery, to which they gave top priority. But here was the USIPSP ordering 'the dissolution of the large industrial and banking combinations which have exercised control of a great part of Japan's trade and industry'. 'The plight of Japan is the direct outcome of its own behaviour', the August directive stated sternly, 'and the Allies will not undertake the burden of repairing the damage.' And when the USIPSP was confirmed and elaborated in the Basic Initial Post-Surrender Directive (BIPSD) of November 3, 1945, the instructions were even clearer. MacArthur was to assume *no* responsibility 'for the economic rehabilitation of Japan or the strengthening of the Japanese economy'.

As conservatives in Japan and America were quick to point out, Truman's directives to MacArthur corresponded at many points with the draft manifesto of the Japanese Communist Party, which had been shown to various members of the China Crowd visiting Yenan the previous year. Both, for instance, recommended the release of all political prisoners, the purge of militarists, and the establishment of unions in labour, industry and agriculture, where the Potsdam Declaration made no specific promises. And in other provisions – its advocacy of land reform, for instance – the Communist manifesto anticipated measures later adopted by the Occupation, though only hinted at in the initial directives.

In February 1950, in a speech to the women's Republican Club in Wheeling, West Virginia, Joseph McCarthy claimed that he 'held in his hand' a list of Communists in the State Department. A large subversive clique, he said, had sold China to the Reds. Eugene Dooman, for one, felt that this clique – which he identified with his old enemies in the China Crowd – had tried to do the same with Japan. At the heart of American policymaking for Japan had been men who were no better than tools of the Communists: how else had the American press and public and 'persons in all quarters of the Government' been persuaded 'to embrace theses espoused for years by the Japanese Communist Party. . . . I am not arguing that for one to advocate something also advocated by Communists makes one a Communist, but the advocacy by presumably loyal

Americans of so many Communist [proposals] seems to take on the color more of design than accident'.

'DOOMAN SAYS LEFT-WINGERS RAN JAP POLICY', blazed the headlines in September 1951 the day after Dooman had testified before the McCarran Committee, one of the many watchdogs of 'un-American activities' spawned by McCarthyism. Dooman's principal targets were Dean Acheson, Owen Lattimore, John Carter Vincent, and John Emmerson. Emmerson, one of the official observers reporting on the development of Mao's revolution, later recorded his experiences in Yenan, and their aftermath, in his autobiography *The Japanese Thread: A Life in the U.S. Foreign Service*. It does much to explain how the directives to MacArthur came to take the form they did.

The Chinese Communist Party of 1944 was, Emmerson argued, very different from what it had become in 1950, when the witchhunt began in earnest. It was not until the escalation of the Cold War that Mao Tse-tung's victory was set in a new and sinister context, and any American who had ever contemplated an alliance with Mao became no less suspect than he would have been had he suggested friendship with Stalin. In 1944 the link between Russian and Chinese communism was not taken for granted: several of the China Crowd believed, in fact, that alliance with Mao's China spelt America's best hope of resisting the Russian advance in Asia.

Japanese communism, as the China Crowd encountered it in Yenan, had Chinese and not Russian affinities. In their opinion the Japanese Communist Party was in any case unlikely, for practical reasons, to prevail in Japan in the foreseeable future. And its manifesto had, besides, much in common with liberal thought everywhere. Universal suffrage, freedom of speech and thought, freedom for trade unions, legislative power in the hands of an elected body – the programme, as described to Emmerson and others in 1944, 'sounded like a paraphrase of the American Bill of Rights'.

The atmosphere in Yenan was like that at 'revival meetings . . . where the converts suddenly got religion'. Emmerson dashed off enthusiastic and hopeful reports. 'No doubt influenced by the crisp air and the contagious zeal of Yenan, I used language that might not have found its way into a dispatch composed in the more disciplined atmosphere of a State Department or embassy office.' And back at home, 'Yenan was a glamorous word in the Washington of 1945'. Those who had actually been there were in great demand for lectures and briefings. The war was nearly over, and everywhere it was felt to be time for a fresh start. Here perhaps is the source of the high idealism and political radicalism of MacArthur's instructions – radicalism which surprised many in the United States, appalled Japan's surviving leaders, and disconcerted even the Allies who were supposed to be cooperating with America in determining Japan's future.

* * *

As planner and executant-in-chief, America's dominant role in the Occupation was never seriously challenged. America, and only America, had the men in place, the transportation available, the money to pay for the Occupation. The Allies were perhaps to be permitted, even encouraged, to contribute men to the occupying force, enabling American troops to be released in response to public pressure for speedy demobilisation, and impressing Japan with the number of nations involved in her defeat. Chinese troops would be especially welcome, as General Marshall put it, 'to obviate any feeling that the war was between orientals and occidentals'.

But in the end Allied military involvement was small. None of Chiang Kai-shek's forces could be spared from the battle against the Communists. Great Britain, Australia, New Zealand and India supplied a British Commonwealth Occupation Force of 40,000 men (as compared with the U.S. force of 250,000). But British troops were in Japan only a year before they were recalled in the face of acute manpower shortages in the British Army. The Indian troops left after India gained its independence in August 1947. And the New Zealanders were gone by 1948.

The Soviet Union markedly lost interest in sharing the administrative burden of the Occupation once it became clear that there was no prospect of dividing Japan into zones, one for each of the major powers, as had been done with Germany, and declined absolutely to send troops to serve under an American commander. The British saw in the withholding of Russian forces a darker purpose – 'The acquiescence of the Chinese and Russians in the American proposals . . . leads one to suspect some larger agreement between them and the United States'; and it was mooted in the Foreign Office that the price of Russia keeping its troops out of Japan was American acceptance of the communisation of North Korea.

But the modesty of their practical contribution did not, in the Allies' view, detract from their right to influence policy and monitor the progress of the Occupation. Each of the Allies had its own interests to promote or protect in Japan. Britain, anxious to preserve the vestiges of its prestige in the Far East, was even more concerned to safeguard the economic strength on which its moral authority had been founded. Initial suspicions that the Americans would simply squeeze out British trading interests in Japan – hence an unsuccessful bid by the British to have the Commonwealth Occupation Force based in the Osaka–Kobe area, with its major ports and long-established British merchant houses – were soon replaced by the fear that they would overstimulate the Japanese economy to the point where Japanese exports themselves became dangerously competitive again, especially in the crucial fields of textiles, ceramics and shipbuilding.

Australia's motives were more visceral – revenge, and the fear of renascent Japanese militarism again threatening the homeland. Her demands reflected 'Australians' concept of themselves as an underpopulated and isolated bastion of European civilisation among potentially hostile aliens', and the Australians pushed hard and persistently for punishment for Japan's past and crippling restraints for her future.

Russia's attitude might crudely be summarised as the desire to wean Japan away from America's orbit, or at least prevent her from settling too securely there.

However, despite America's preeminence, Allied aspirations in Japan could not simply be ignored, if only because it was essential to integrate policies in Asia with those in Europe, where America's hand was weaker. If the Soviet Union were to retire from what appeared to be a purely American sphere of interest in the East, it would be hard to resist demands for reciprocal recognition of Russian hegemony in Eastern Europe. Letting Russia in on the management of Japan was seen by the State Department at least as the price for retaining a foothold in Romania and Bulgaria.

In any case, the price was not exorbitant, as 'power-sharing' in Japan, as in the Balkans, was more apparent than real. It took the form of two Allied bodies, one in Washington and one in Tokyo. The senior body was the Far Eastern Commission (FEC) which sat in Washington. It consisted of representatives of eleven of the Allied nations involved in the Pacific War, and had nominal responsibility for formulating the policies which MacArthur would implement. The Allied Council for Japan (representing only the four major allies, the U.S.S.R., China, Britain and the Commonwealth, and the U.S.) sat in Tokyo as the FEC's 'eyes and ears' to advise MacArthur on the best methods of implementing these policies and to monitor his adherence to them.

In fact, MacArthur, who had done his best to resist the setting-up of these bodies, dismissed them both as 'useless' – an accusation which became self-fulfilling, since the United States had effectively reserved the right to take unilateral action should it happen to disagree with its Allied advisers. The FEC soon found itself doing little besides confirming, at best 'reviewing' American policies long after action had been taken on them. As for the Allied Council, since each representative had the right of veto, unanimous 'advice' was very rarely forthcoming. More usual was an atmosphere of stalemate and acrimony in which the United States and the Soviet Union could rehearse the aggressive gestures and attitudes of the Cold War.

3

First Encounters

Traditionally the Japanese host will not ask a guest what he would like to drink. He will already have considered what, in the particular circumstances of their meeting, his guest is most likely to want, and will simply offer him this. In the eyes of General Seizo Arisue, the Director-General of Japanese Military Intelligence, orange juice was the most appropriate refreshment for the first American advance party to reach Japan, and accordingly his staff set up a small buffet tent at the side of the runway at Atsugi airfield where it was to land on August 28, 1945.

However, the first contingent of Occupationaires was hardly in the mood for ceremony. Possibly suspecting treachery, they put down on the far side of the airfield from General Arisue's marquee, and Major Faubion Bowers, personal aide to MacArthur, later recalled his first glimpse of the ferocious Imperial Japanese Army: Arisue with all his aides-de-camp, running across the airport with their swords clanking, 'much flustered and much upset'.

Eventually hosts and guests congregated in Arisue's tent. Their conversation, necessarily stilted, dried up altogether when the American officer in charge was offered the orange juice. Instead of taking it, he turned and asked Bowers in a loud voice whether or not he should drink it, whereupon Arisue, rightly construing this as a suggestion that it might be poisoned, seized the glass back and drank it himself. It was all, in Bowers's phrase, a bit like a cocktail party that was not going very well.

This comic, even surreal first meeting of victors and vanquished was in strange contrast to the days of tension preceding it. Unlike the situation in Europe, where Allied troops had been obliged to fight across every inch of German soil, Japan had surrendered before her principal home islands were invaded. This meant she still possessed not only a government holding the reins of power, but also an undefeated army of some three million men. The Emperor announced the fact of surrender to his people shortly

[23]

after noon on August 14, 1945, and over the following ten days Japan walked a knife-edge between disciplined peace and armed insurrection.

The surrender precipitated a wave of ritual suicides, some in the Imperial Plaza in front of the Palace, of distraught civilians and soldiers alike, among them the Army Minister, General Anami. On the eve of the Emperor's broadcast, fanatical officers broke into the Imperial Palace and ransacked it in search of the recording of the Surrender Rescript that Hirohito had made for transmission the following day. Failing to retrieve it, they too committed suicide. Several of the navy *kamikaze* based at Atsugi flew over Tokyo dropping leaflets denouncing the Emperor's defeatist advisers, before fleeing with their planes to a remote base to make a last stand. Some *kamikaze* did fly out after the American fleet in the days following the surrender, never to be seen again. In the provinces, ultra-nationalists took over key municipal buildings and there was talk of a military *coup d'état*.

But all these sparks failed to find tinder. In the majority of Japanese, war-weariness had crushed every other emotion; and even the weather seemed to be working against the diehards. Once before, in the thirteenth century, Japan had been threatened with invasion: the hordes of Genghis Khan had attempted a landing which, had it succeeded, would have added Japan to the Mongol empire. Instead, a typhoon – known thereafter as the Divine Wind (*kamikaze*) – had battered the Mongol fleet and driven the invaders away. Now once again the Divine Wind struck, on the day originally projected for the arrival of the Allies' advance guard, delaying the landings and giving the Japanese authorities a breathing space of two extra days in which to secure calm.

Nevertheless, though Allied aircraft-carriers may have been in Tokyo Bay on alert only a few minutes flying time away, the first contingent of Occupationaires was exposed and entering the unknown. An OSS memo of August 1945 outlined the imponderables: 'In an unexpected or new situation, many Japanese exhibit uncertainty to a degree abnormal for most Occidentals. Under these conditions their behaviour may be characterised by anything from extreme emotional apathy and physical immobility to uncontrolled violence directed against their persons or almost any object in their environment. The fact of surrender presents such a new situation, and one which for years the Japanese have been taught to avoid beyond all others.'

MacArthur's own arrival at Atsugi after the advance party was itself an act of considerable courage. It was also impeccably stage-managed. 'The Second Coming couldn't have caused more commotion', recalled Ben Z. Kaplan, in an article entitled 'Tojo Doesn't

[24]

Live Here Anymore'. The cameo was flawless – a lone figure at the top of the aeroplane steps, corncob pipe in mouth (though in private MacArthur preferred a meerschaum), battledress shirt open at the neck and a war-torn but heavily gold-braided hat smartly tilted, casual yet masterful, and supremely confident. The Occupation had begun.

The same sense of style distinguished the formal rituals of surrender held on board the U.S.S. *Missouri* on September 2. The signing ceremony was accompanied by a massed formation of B-29 bombers flying low over Tokyo, presumably to hammer home to the natives the fact of their defeat. But the fly-past, if it achieved anything at all, served mainly to show the aircrews exactly what they had done to Japan during the last six months.

The extent of the destruction was greater than any of them had expected. Apart from the atomic bombs at Hiroshima and Nagasaki, the B-29s had dropped approximately one bomb for every fifteen people in Japan. Over 668,000 civilians had been killed or wounded, 125,000 in a single appalling incendiary and napalm raid on Tokyo on March 9, 1945, when timber-framed houses turned the city into a vast *hibachi*. An estimated 2,259,879 houses had been burned or blasted to ruins, and another 600,000 deliberately destroyed by the government in frantic efforts to build firebreaks and free-fire zones for coastal defence. At the heart of most industrial towns and cities the Occupationaires found total devastation: metal safes and filing cabinets standing solitary amidst acres of ash, brick dust and twisted iron girders; and everywhere a deep silence and a dreadful stench of excrement, rubbish, and smouldering embers.

Makeshift shacks, shanties and tents made of planks and boxes, scrap metal and rush matting, housed those survivors of the bombing who had not fled into the countryside. Many of these people were near to starvation: in November 1945 they were dying in Tokyo at the rate of two hundred a month. The Allied assault on Japan's merchant marine and the effectual blockade of her ports had both denied raw materials to her war industry and cut off the food supplies from overseas on which Japan had been dependent to a dangerous degree. Farmers for once were to be envied for the food they could provide for themselves, and such trains and buses as were still running out into the countryside were always crammed with city-dwellers and the possessions they hoped to barter for food: family heirlooms, scrolls, *netsuke*, jewellery, as well as humbler and less dispensable objects – clocks, china, cooking utensils. As the first winter of the peace approached, the 'onion skin economy' bit deeper, and people were compelled to peel off more and more layers of belongings simply to survive.

For those who had nothing to trade, and no money with which to take advantage of the thriving black market, distress was real and some of the remedies desperate. They made ersatz clothes from wood pulp, which came to pieces in the rain, clogs carved from bomb débris, pots and pans converted from steel helmets. Japanese housewives scanned charts of edible weeds printed in the newspapers, and the *Nippon Times*, with hollow comfort, extolled the nutritional virtues of mulberry leaves, normally the staple diet of silkworms but now hailed as rich in proteins and vitamins when dried as tea or ground to make flour. Where the average American could expect a basic intake of 3400 calories daily, most Japanese existed on less than 1500. The gifts of chocolate and chewing gum from G.I.s were welcome less as a friendly gesture than as the only sugar some of the recipients had had for months.

The plight of Allied prisoners-of-war at this time was equally desperate, and to liberate them was the Occupation forces' first priority. There were an estimated 36,000 prisoners-of-war in Japan – though only 32,624 were actually recovered. One or two days delay could have meant death to hundreds of them, so a system of food drops was instituted by the 20th Air Force. But this brought its own tragedies when parachutes failed to open, or drums and crates detached themselves from the consignments in mid-air, killing the recipients they were intended to save.

At the start, there was obviously mutual suspicion, some of it thoroughly justified. There were knife attacks on soldiers after dark, telephone wires were cut, dynamite was tossed into a passing jeep, and small-arms fire left bullet holes in the fuselages of Allied planes. An American sentry was murdered in Sapporo in December 1945 by a veteran of the Japanese navy, whom he had caught trying to steal U.S. Army goods for sale on the black market. In May 1946 a Japanese youth was sentenced to life imprisonment at hard labour for an assault on U.S. servicemen. At regular intervals rocks were thrown through the dining-car window of the *Dixie Limited* – though as one intelligence officer commented, 'When a comparison is drawn between the travelling conditions in military trains and in the normal trains used by Japanese, it is not in the least surprising that the occasional Japanese finds himself unable to restrain the urge to display his jealousy'. As trains reserved for Occupation personnel swept past half empty, the Japanese were squeezed out of packed carriages to ride on locomotives, couplings and running-boards. Between May and September 1946 303 were killed and 953 injured falling off or 'striking objects while clinging to the sides of trains'.

But on the whole the soldiers prepared for ambushes and sabotage that never came. The Japanese were compliant and orderly, and the Occupation progressed smoothly. Co-operation was, in fact, often taken to ludicrous extremes. In one rural area, as Mark Gayn reported, a sudden rash of traffic accidents followed the posting of signs indicating 35-miles-per-hour zones. 'The unhappy but obedient Japanese drivers were doing their best. The incident was cleared up after a local Japanese daily came out with an editorial conceding that democracy was fine, but was it necessary to drive that fast?' And as tensions eased, the Japanese who had sent wives and daughters into the countryside to escape the rape and licentiousness of which their military masters had forewarned them gradually called them back.

It does, however, take an uncomfortable stretch of the imagination to accept MacArthur's rosy view of his troops' rapport with the Japanese, whose hearts and minds he sensed being altered 'by the ennobling influence of the American way of life. . . . They saw and felt [the American combat soldier's] spiritual quality which truly reflected the highest training of the American home'. Throughout the Occupation there was a small but constant stream of the kind of offences, some of them gross, which are conventionally attributed to armies of occupation. Faubion Bowers, for instance, described rape, drunkenness and looting in Hokkaido when the first of General Swing's veteran paratroopers arrived, battle-happy and vengeful. And the Chief of Counter-Intelligence registered that the early respect for the Americans was 'being modified by the reported incidents of robberies, attacks, and rowdyism' committed by G.I.s. SCAP's official bulletin on the progress of the Occupation reported equivocally in November 1945, 'Contacts between Allied troops and Japanese civilians continue to be satisfactory. There have been six cases of rape involving Allied personnel.' And in January 1946 a G.I. was sentenced to death for killing two Japanese 'without provocation'.

But by the end of 1945, the process of American demobilisation was in full swing. Most of the long-serving soldiers were soon released, and a large proportion of the troops arriving in Japan were new draftees, with none of the bitterness and aggression bred by combat. They had more curiosity, more tolerance, wished for closer acquaintance with the Japanese. And for this there was a good deal of opportunity. After the first uneasy months of the Occupation, the American rules on fraternisation for the military were realistic and liberal to a degree which scandalised the officers of the British Commonwealth Occupation Force, whose relations with the natives were deliberately more distant. In MacArthur's inimitable phraseology, any order barring social contact would be 'violative of the inherent self-respect of the American soldier', and soon public transport, shops, restaurants and theatres were 'on limits'. Better this, it was felt, than that the G.I.s should look for illicit entertainment. By January 1946, twenty had already died from drinking black-market whisky heavily adulterated with methyl alcohol or gasoline.

In any event, such minor frictions and isolated abuses as did occur could in no way be compared with the hostility that existed between Japanese and their Russian conquerors in Manchuria and Korea, where the State Department logged 'constant reports of indiscriminate rape, pillage, looting . . . received from all areas occupied by Soviet forces', beside whom, according to *The New York Times*, 'the Americans have a half-apologetic attitude towards civil populations'.

Socially speaking, the most serious problems stemmed from an excess of friendliness – the less acceptable face of fraternisation. Wherever troops were concentrated, the garrisons soon developed a 'strip' of bars, brothels, bath-houses, black-market restaurants and gambling houses. Local residents objected both to the ambience and to the sight of Japanese girls with American soldiers, particularly blacks. A Japanese war criminal, returning to Japan after serving his prison sentence in Singapore, wrote to a fellow-prisoner: 'One of the first sights that struck our eyes on our return to Kobe was that of one of our own Japanese girls walking hand in hand with a coal-black American negro (sic) soldier. I cannot tell you how cut to the quick we were at such a sad state of affairs.' And as in Vietnam, the children, some 3–4,000 of them, born of liaisons or marriages between blacks and Japanese were outcasts from birth.

In the upper echelons of the army, contact with the Japanese was usually at a more luxurious level – and sometimes well over the border line separating 'fraternisation' from bribery and corruption. Mark Gayn, a left-wing journalist and scathing critic of the wealthy and entrenched élite both in Japan and in the United States, devoted much of his time as the *Chicago Sun*'s Occupation correspondent to unearthing what he saw as the Japanese reactionaries' efforts to undermine America's reforms.

An important element in this campaign was, he felt, the systematic attempt to subvert the morals, and thus the determination, of the American forces. In search of evidence, he set up an interview with Akira Ando, ultra-nationalist racketeer and owner of eighteen of the largest brothels in Tokyo. Ando wined and dined him lavishly, and orchestrated a meeting with a member of the Imperial Family whose connections with the ultra-right were allegedly intimate. As he was leaving the palace, Gayn glanced at the visitors' book and saw among those who had preceded him most of the highest-ranking officers in the occupying army.

This story cannot simply be dismissed as a leftist slur. Harry Emerson Wildes, one of the Occupationaires who was by no means a radical, alleged in his book *Typhoon in Tokyo* that another leading ultra-rightist had planted his son in the home of a commanding general as a spy, 'but this was unusual since women were preferred'. On March 27, 1946, the Office of the Chief of Counter-Intelligence, GHQ, reported: 'A frequent comment made among Japanese is that all American officers are drunkards. Some members of the *zaibatsu* boast that they are able to influence American officers in any way they want by giving them the right entertainment.'

This was, in fact, Ando's downfall. For boasting that a leading general was his chief protector, he was arrested for possessing black market goods. The visitors' book was confiscated and never seen again.

enemy were normally declared widows. An influx of former prisoners was not, therefore, something the Japanese authorities were expecting. But the Americans were aware that towards the end of the war the rate of surrenders had sharply increased: at Okinawa 7,400 Japanese were taken prisoner. They saw in the social rehabilitation of these renegades a valuable opportunity to debunk the militarists' creed of death or dishonour.

One group of prisoners-of-war were a problem from a distance – those seized by the Russians in Manchuria and Korea in the last week of the war, and now used, in defiance of the Geneva Convention, as slave labour. A Japanese warrant officer, one of the few to escape across the Amur, told of lumber camps in Siberia where the prisoners, dressed only in their thin summer uniforms, worked nineteen-hour days on subsistence rations. MacArthur's righteous anger – and he used the repatriation issue as a stick with which to beat the Russians throughout the Occupation – was slightly compromised by the fact that the British had also kept back 100,000 of the soldiers who had surrendered to them in the South East Asia Command, to help in the work of reconstruction.

The principal difference was that Russia saw its captives as potential cadres and subjected them to intensive indoctrination. The prisoners in the lumber camps of Siberia, for instance, ate their meagre meals to the accompaniment of diatribes against the *zaibatsu* and were taught to see their ordeal as preparation for 'the struggle upon returning home'. The most promising were sent to four indoctrination schools in or around Moscow for special training as intelligence agents; and in 1949 Russia seemingly unbent to MacArthur's pleas and poured no less than 95,000 Communist 'converts' back into Japan.

'What a terrifying lot our returned countrymen are!', wrote one wife to her war criminal husband imprisoned in Singapore. 'Grim and unsmiling, their hearts are as frozen as the country they left, and bellowing to everyone that the only true freedom is to be found in the teachings of Marx and Lenin. . . . The Soviet has taught them to think of themselves as being "iron men", superior to all others, and scorning such weaker feelings as love for their families, etc. . . . They are strong-willed and determined and as their homes are spread all over the country, their influence will be felt in even the tiniest hamlets.'

This naturally alarmed and incensed General Willoughby, who, as head of G-2, with oversight also of SCAP's Civil Intelligence Section, had responsibility for the surveillance and suppression of subversive activities. But it would seem that the Russians' campaign largely rebounded on them. The majority of repatriates sloughed off the thin skin of Marxist ideology within months of returning home. And the fact of their mistreatment provided excellent propaganda for the Americans (and continues to do so, since as late as 1970, it was plain that 300,000 prisoners were still unaccounted for).

Disarming Japan was a multi-layered operation, of which demobilisation was only one aspect. The Allies (for this was one of the British forces' main functions) had to locate and eliminate all arsenals, ammunition dumps and ordnance depots. In the process they unexpectedly found 100,000 tons of chemical warfare supplies which had been awaiting the invader. The Americans also had to devote a good deal of their time to neutralising their own weapons – unexploded bombs, and thousands of mines which were disrupting sea traffic round the coast and periodically washing ashore to kill Americans and Japanese alike.

All Japan's anti-aircraft equipment and coastal defences were to be destroyed, and the plans and drawings of fortifications and installations confiscated. What little military shipping she had left was to be appropriated. Particular attention was paid to the suicide craft which had been the most vivid symbol of Japanese fanaticism, and altogether 393 midget submarines, 177 human torpedoes and 2,412 suicide surface craft were discovered. (Three midget submarines were destroyed in action on September 12, 1945, in Picnic Bay, Hong Kong as they made their final futile gesture of loyalty to the Emperor.)

All aviation was prohibited. No Japanese was to learn to fly, since a body of trained pilots would be a military asset, and airfields were to be turned over, where practicable, to agriculture.

Civilians too had accumulated an appalling armoury during the months when a desperate government rallied them to resist invasion; in January 1945 the recorded sounds of B-29 bombers had been broadcast in the streets of Tokyo to prepare the inhabitants for what was to come. In April the Civilian Suicide Corps was warned to expect the call to arms, and in June hand grenades were issued to the general public. On July 12, most terrible and pathetic of all, a Blind Veterans Volunteer Corps was formed. The Americans' own estimate was that some 3,200,000 civilians were ready to fight them in August 1945 – and this figure was probably far too small. The weapons they confiscated included crossbows, armour, baseball bats, plumbing-pipe guns, bamboo bazookas, and explosive arrows. They left the small-arms used by the police, hunting guns (with licences), explosives for quarrying and chemicals for fertilising, but took dummy weapons used for drill in schools, and even the fencing sticks wielded by actors in the *kabuki* theatre.

As the Sixth Army had discovered, disposing of Japan's fire power once it had been marshalled was extraordinarily hazardous.

Dumps and caches of ammunition and explosives were heavensent for saboteurs, but even without booby traps they were highly volatile. Sometimes safety devices had deteriorated after months hidden in heat and damp; sometimes there were no safety devices in the first place. Prudently, the Allies relied a good deal on a Japanese workforce to collect and destroy Japanese munitions; but since most skilled technicians had already been demobilised, they were forced to use 'slow and unskilled labourers', and one officer commented, through gritted teeth, 'Their apparent disregard for personal safety, combined with the language barrier, made the job dangerous'. Ammunition exploded as it was being towed out to sea on barges to be sunk; dumps of parachute flares ignited, and in the 32nd Infantry Division Zone a cave full of propellant charges detonated, killing dozens of Japanese workmen. One American soldier and 'an undetermined number' of Japanese died when the American dropped a quantity of TNT at an ammunition dump at Tateyama airfield. Field guns, tanks, anti-aircraft equipment and aeroplanes were cut up with oxyacetylene torches or sprayed with liquid gas and set on fire by 'Destruction Incorporated' crews. Those ships which were not reserved for distribution among the Allies were scuttled or scrapped – though a few, including Japan's only surviving battleship, the *Nagato*, met a more dramatic end, requisitioned for use as 'guided missile targets and *other experimentation*' – the 'other experimentation' being the American atomic tests at Bikini Atoll in July 1946.

Not all that was collected was destroyed. Supplies that had peacetime uses were handed over to the government for civilian relief: rations (beans, beer, cereal, tea), fuel, vehicles, and twenty-one million pairs of army socks. Then as now, Japanese technology in some areas was ahead of the field, and much equipment was kept back for study and experiment. A USA Navy technical mission arrived in September to examine advanced naval technology: and in the first year over 180 tons of materials interesting from an intelligence standpoint were shipped to the States for scrutiny. (The Allies, too, benefited from what they could confiscate: a 'Self-Contained Mobile Command Post for four AA Gun Positions', for example, was sent by the British to India, where, with Partition approaching, it was obviously expected to be useful.) This was in addition to the 'Trophies Issued to Troops' scheme whereby each officer and man who had served in the region where arms were collected was entitled to claim either a rifle, a pair of binoculars, a pistol, a bayonet, a carbine or a sabre. (The latter was most highly prized and usually shown off as 'a samurai sword'.)

Other weapons were simply described as being 'in US army

custody for possible future use' – including 120,000 bayonets, 81,000 rifles and carbines, and 2,240 automatic weapons. As the Occupation wore on, the Russian member of the Far Eastern Commission, who missed very few chances to embarrass SCAP, began to complain of 'laxness' in American accounting procedures, with the hint that the Americans were earmarking more than their fair share of the weaponry. Certainly the excuses offered by MacArthur for American hoarding were a little lame. He ascribed one discrepancy between 'arms received' and 'arms destroyed' to 'typographical error': the figure of 369,017 20mm automatic AA cannon received was 'incredible', and should read 5,422. And a large number of 'tanks, assorted' in US possession were 'containers not combat vehicles'.

Physical disarmament was, in theory, a finite task, and one which should not have taken long. But there had been a crucial interval of two weeks between capitulation and occupation – time for the Japanese High Command and Imperial Japanese Government to plan for the future and cover up the past. On August 17, shortly after accepting the Potsdam Declaration, the government sent out urgent memoranda ordering the burning of all confidential and possibly incriminating documents. Two months later Allied investigators commented, 'Vital information concerning certain parties of prisoners-of-war who have not been accounted for as yet is singularly lacking'. Among them were sixty-three Americans who had died in a fire after an air-raid on their prison; it was only revealed later that Japanese prisoners had been removed as the sirens were going while the Americans had been bayonetted in their cells and left to their own bombers. On August 17, 1945 the War Ministry issued Order Number 363 instructing local commanders to distribute to the public as quickly and completely as possible their stores of fuel, oil, war materials, vehicles, gun-powder, even ships and land, for the purposes of 'reconstruction'. But that this was not purely humanitarian is suggested by the final paragraph – 'This order must by all means be burnt before the landing of the enemy. Every effort shall be made not to have it fall into the enemy's hands'. Supplies that *could* have alleviated civilian distress, estimated to be worth ten billion yen, were hoarded instead, and were later to find their way on to the black market.

Weapons were, strictly speaking, to be kept 'in custody', but many commanders preferred to 'distribute' these as well. In September 1945 a *New York Times* correspondent reported armed but unmarked trucks entering and leaving tunnels into a mountainside in the Tokyo/Yokohama area by night. In remote rural areas, Allied troops found tanks being used as tractors, and pillboxes housing tons of field artillery and ammunition disguised as traditional

Japanese houses, complete with sliding screens. Civilians loyally followed their government's lead, and few were prepared to part with heirloom swords. And almost to the end of the Occupation, surprise raids on shrines, police stations and schools were still turning up caches of grenades, mortars and bayonets.

In any event, it was not enough merely to confiscate weapons which the Japanese themselves would have discarded with the advance of military technology. SCAP had also to prevent their replacement with newer and more deadly equivalents, and so set out to implement a comprehensive programme of industrial disarmament in perpetuity: no research, no importing, and no production of arms.

Where research was concerned, it was the American intention to benefit fully from what the Japanese had already learned, and to share as little of this knowledge as possible with the Allies. They wished, in short, to 'enjoy such intelligence advantages as may properly be derived from the major role played by US forces' in Japan's defeat. When Allied pressure for information became irresistible, the Americans would make sure firstly that its disclosure would not be positively harmful. The JCS considered that 'sharing with other nations intelligence which the Japanese had collected against the United States', for example, would be 'contrary to United States interests'. Then 'they would ensure that they had themselves taken full advantage of a source before making it available. So when the Russians forced SCAP to allow them to question Japanese officers suspected of carrying out experiments in biological warfare on prisoners in Manchuria, SCAP arranged a prior appointment for Colonels Kukuchi and Ota with 'specially trained' War Department representatives. 'If any information brought out by preliminary interrogation [is] considered of sufficient importance that divulgence to Soviets should not be permitted, Kikuchi and Ota are to be instructed not to reveal such information to the Soviets . . . Prior to interviewing by the Soviets the Japanese Biological Warfare experts should be instructed to make no mention of US interviews on this subject.' The Japanese silence, as it turned out, had a price – amnesty from prosecution for the architects of the biological warfare programme. The evidence is overwhelming that the American government cooperated in concealing Japanese atrocities, whose victims included American servicemen, in order to secure information which would enable them to commit similar crimes. 'The value to the United States of Japanese biological warfare data', commented two of the American medical experts involved, 'is of such importance to national security as to far outweigh the value accruing from war crimes prosecution.'

Once America had taken what it wanted, however, research in

Japan was to develop no further. Institutes, laboratories and testing stations were to be closed, and until projects had been cleared of any possible military application, scientists were not to resume their activities. In particular, there was to be no further enquiry into the uses of atomic energy. During the war the Japanese had, like the Americans and the Germans, worked to develop atomic weapons; and though they had neither the materials nor the advanced scientific technique to make the final breakthrough, their research programme was sophisticated enough to attract the attention of SCAP. All atomic scientists were taken into custody, and all nuclear-related materials and facilities which had survived the bombing were seized (including supplies of radium and thorium compounds). Japan's five cyclotrons were destroyed as war materiel, apparently with the sanction of General Leslie Groves (head of the Manhattan Project) – to the chagrin of MacArthur who had approved their peacetime use in medicine, metallurgy and agriculture. In fact SCAP's attitude to atomic energy in Japan was to become increasingly more liberal, but at the outset the hard line favoured by the other Allies in the Far Eastern Commission prevailed, and further research of any kind was prohibited.

The ban on the importation of arms was in 1945 slightly academic, since Japan had neither the finance to pay for even the most essential of imports – food and raw materials – nor the merchant marine to carry them. But enough of the enormously expanded industrial infrastructure remained despite the bombing to make renewed arms manufacture at home a possibility. This threat was countered by a ban on all industrial activity geared specifically to war, and by proposals to limit industries indirectly fuelling the war machine. Japan was to be allowed to produce only so much steel, only so much rubber, oil, radio equipment, ball bearings and machine tools as were needed for peacetime domestic consumption and a very modest level of consumption at that. Japan's 'peacetime needs' in 1945 were interpreted by hard-liners as being approximately equivalent to her needs in 1930. Her requirements in heavy industry were set at approximately one-tenth those of the mid-thirties when the campaign of external aggression was well under way.

In the long term, the simplest method of confining Japanese industry within these bounds would have been to regulate the inflow of the necessary raw materials. The British had such faith in this method that many believed the physical presence of the Allies in Japan actually to be superfluous. Why tie up money and manpower when Japan could be manipulated at a distance by economic sanctions? But, in the short term, her industrial infrastructure was to be pared to acceptable proportions by simple subtraction – by scrapping of munitions equipment, and by enforcing the payment of reparations.

The Japanese were made liable to restore to the Allies anything they had taken from them. Burma lodged a claim for one of Buddha's teeth, and Holland a request for the skull of Java Man, looted from Batavia. Where the originals were not available, Japan was to find materials of comparable value – a system which worked well enough for, say, radio-active isotopes and railway equipment, but broke down over 'cultural objects'. The FEC puzzled long over whether Japan could make amends for a Thai statue or a Chinese vase with Japanese artefacts of 'roughly equivalent character'.

Reparations were to be made over and above these transactions – less paying back a debt than paying for a misdeed. Japan was to forfeit all property and equipment still in place in her lost colonies; and at home, all goods, facilities and machinery above the 'peaceful requirement' cut-off level were to be available for distribution among the Allies. This would both give them the satisfaction of revenge, and, more significantly, further their various economic objectives. It would curb Japan's economic strength in relation to China, pleasing the China Crowd. It would reduce the Japanese threat to the more vulnerable of the Allies' own industries. And the industrial equipment handed over would be of immediate practical use in repairing their own or their colonies' wrecked economies. By the time the Occupation began, Russia had already undertaken a certain amount of unilateral distribution of Japan's wealth, in order to compensate for the damage inflicted by Germany on the rest of the Soviet Union. During their week in Manchuria the Russians 'liberated' approximately two billion dollars worth of military and industrial equipment.

The reparations programme, which began in January 1946 when the first group of 394 plants was 'taken into custody', was in fact fraught with difficulties. The Allies could not agree whose wounds were the most severe and whose need of economic balm the greatest; smaller nations, like the Philippines, who saw themselves as Japan's principal victims, nevertheless anticipated the larger Allies hogging the lion's share of the compensation. Nor could they agree on the means of monitoring Japan's industrial output, or even on the level at which it should be pegged and 'the surplus removed'.

Hardliners, like Russia, would have been happy to have seen Japan virtually de-industrialised, certainly no more prosperous than the countries she had formerly colonised. But Americans faced the prospect of paying Japan's bills until she could support herself; and the reparations programme was to be fatally undermined by the failure of Japan's economy to recover from the war even to the level of self-sufficiency. With inflation rising grotesquely – average retail prices in July 1948 were forty times those of July 1945 – and over ten million unemployed, to give away the means of economic reconstruction seemed at best impractical.

5

Rooting Out Evil: The Purge

By May 1948, 210,288 of Japan's leading citizens had been removed from public life. They had committed no crime under pre-Occupation law, and they had received no trial. They were a motley and dynamic group – Cabinet ministers, newspaper publishers, generals, Diet members, village headmen, theatre producers, police chiefs, industrialists, editors, film makers and university professors. What they had in common, in SCAP's view, was abuse of power – the power they possessed, because of their public positions, to influence the opinions and behaviour of others.

This wide-ranging purge, pushed methodically through succeeding strata of Japanese society, illuminates America's conception of how responsibility for the war should be allocated – a conception elaborated in detail at Tojo's trial. According to this view, blame lay less with social forces, economic trends or political ideologies than with human greed, ambition and aggression. This assumption was implicit in the words of the Potsdam Declaration: 'There must be eliminated for all time the authority and influence of *those who have deceived and misled the people of Japan into embarking on world conquest,* for we insist that a new order of peace, security and justice will be impossible until irresponsible militarism is driven from the world.' To MacArthur, Japan's leaders were 'war potential' that he must neutralise – human equivalents of the spiked guns and exploded arsenals.

The object of the purge was to push 'undesirable elements' to the sidelines of power where they could do no more harm. Ultranationalist and militarist societies, the most obvious focuses of unacceptable ideas, were to be dissolved and prevented from reforming. And individual exponents of militarism and aggression were to be removed from, or denied access to, positions in public life from which they could again warp Japan's course in the direction of disaster.

The men whom America wanted to purge were those in whose past record could be detected any or all of the marks of militarism, as defined by SCAP. These were: participation in, or support of, military aggression and overseas imperialism; dissemination of ultra-nationalist propaganda; claims of ethnic superiority and attempts to act on them – assuming leadership of other Asiatic races, for example, or excluding foreigners from trade and commerce; advocacy of totalitarianism; the use of terror and violence to achieve political ends and crush opposition to the regime; an insistence on the special status and prerogatives of the soldier. And it was not only the Pacific war years which were under scrutiny, but also the subjects' public posture during the era of Japanese expansion in the late 1930s – and dating sometimes as far back as 1931 and the Manchurian Incident.

For a minority of extremists, Japan's surrender was the end; on August 30, 1945, the day of MacArthur's arrival, thirty-two members of secret societies committed *hara-kiri* publicly in Tokyo in 'a true patriotic spirit, eager to apologise to the Throne for their inability to win the war'. Far more, however, saw the Occupation as a passing phase and pursued their causes with increased fanaticism. In the first weeks of the Occupation, taking advantage of MacArthur's championship of freedom of opinion, thirty-eight new political parties sprang into existence. Most of these were exceedingly right-wing, some overtly fascistic, like the *Tenguto* or 'League of the Longnosed Goblins'. This took its name from characters traditionally believed to have taught swordsmanship to *samurai*. It was less cute than its title suggests, since the manifesto called for 'absolute support of the Emperor system' through 'justice enforced by strong-arm men'.

Many post-war ultra-nationalist societies were, in fact, little more than gangs of racketeers dressing straightforward thuggery in the trappings of patriotism and respect for ancient values. One such was *Shin-ei Taishuto* or the New Elite Masses Party (motto: 'Strong body produces strong thoughts'), which was financed at least to some extent by government money siphoned off from a subsidy for the relief of war sufferers. (In January 1947 two of its members, self-styled vigilantes, were to attack Katsumi Kinanumi, the leader of the more radical of the two major labour federations, with a knife bought for skinning rabbits. One was a recently repatriated veteran and typical of a class of men who, as the *New York Times* pointed out, 'have contrasted their meagre finances with the sometimes exorbitant union demands'. His professed aim was to convince Kinanumi of the treachery and unwisdom of strikes.)

Less selfishly motivated, more idealistic, and therefore perhaps more dangerous were the older ultra-nationalist organisations such as the *Dai Nippon Butoku Kai* or 'Great Japan Military Virtue Association', and the Black Dragon Society, also called the Amur River Society for its ambition to extend Japan's boundaries across Manchuria to that natural line of defence against Russia. The *Butoku Kai* had originally been formed in 1895 as a medium for keeping alive the *samurai* virtues in the face of corrupting Western influences. The arts of judo, *kendo* (fencing) and *kyudo* (archery) were practised, both as athletic training and for the improving effects they were believed to have on the character, but any military connotations were largely historical. In wartime, however, the militarists found the organisation a useful framework within which to whip up the martial spirit and, more practically, to offer civilians military training. In 1942 Tojo became the *Butoku Kai*'s president, army and navy instructors replaced amateur enthusiasts, and bayonet practice and rifle marksmanship were added to the list of 'martial arts'. By 1943 the U.S. Attorney General's Office had put the *Butoku Kai*'s Stateside branches on its growing list of organisations subversive of the American way.

On January 4, 1946 MacArthur ordered all suspect societies to be dissolved, and all new organisations of an even vaguely political cast to be registered with the government, listing their purposes, sources of funding, and members. Any society found to have more than a quarter of its members drawn from previously banned organisations was itself to be abolished. Under the provisions of SCAPIN 548, 'Abolition of Certain Political Parties, Associations, Societies, and Other Organisations', 'suspect' societies were those whose aims were interpreted as including support of Japan's military action abroad; the use of terrorism to influence policy (the New Elite Masses Party was the first to be dissolved on this count); or the provision of quasi-military training. Lest there should be any confusion, SCAPIN 548 named the societies that were to be disbanded (a list which totalled over 200 by 1951), among them groups with such evocative titles as The House of the Cry of the Crane, Imperial National Blood War Body, Society for the Ultimate Solution of the Manchurian Question, Anti-Foreign Similar Spirits Society, White Blood Corpuscle League, and Bayonet Practice Promotion Society.

Once dispersed, the key officials of these societies were then purged under a companion directive, SCAPIN 550, 'Removal and Exclusion of Undesirable Personnel from Public Office'. The logical corollary of SCAPIN 548, SCAPIN 550 was nevertheless far more dubious, both practically and morally. Part of the problem was that virtually from the outset Government Section decided to designate 'undesirables' by category. Even the JCS during the war had opposed the notion of purge by category on the grounds that it was too sweeping. The Occupation was after all trying to implement in the Japanese mind the concept of due process of law – whereas purge by category entailed the presumption that a man was guilty unless proved innocent. The Japanese suggested judging each individual case on its merits – not in the courtroom, but by means of a reviewing committee. But Whitney, aware that in occupied Germany proceedings of this type were slowing the purge to a crawl, curtly dismissed the proposal. As he explained, with characteristic directness, 'Until after the directive has been complied with, individual "guilt" (which requires inquiry into *intent* as distinguished from *act*) is irrelevant'.

Some purge categories were obvious. Given SCAP's aim of 'blasting from the command posts of the government all those who planned, started and directed the war', immediately designated were all those arrested as war criminals, plus the entire General Staffs of both Army and Navy, the members of Imperial General Headquarters, the Supreme Military Council, the Board of Field Marshals and Fleet Admirals, and all civil servants at policy-making level in the war ministries. With them went the Thought Police, the military gendarmerie (*Kempei Tai*), and all other special intelligence officers – not the makers of policies but inextricably implicated as their enforcers.

Then came those presumed to be the most stalwart supporters of the military regime – all career officers of the Army and Navy; all politicians 'recommended' by Tojo to the voters at the 1942 election; all branch chiefs of the Imperial Ex-Servicemen's Association: influential members of all banned ultra-nationalist organisations; senior members of financial and development organisations involved in Japanese expansion between July 1937 and September 1945, plus governors and chief administrators of occupied territories; and the most influential members of the principal 'rule-aid' organisations – the Imperial Rule Assistance Association, the Imperial Rule Assistance Political Society, and their affiliates. (The IRAA was a national front organisation used by the army to mobilise patriotic feeling at grass roots level, the IRAPS its political wing – a permanent power bloc ensuring Diet support for the war.)

Finally, to allow a little room for manoeuvre, SCAP provided a catch-all category with scope for interpretation, covering 'any person who has played an active and predominant governmental part in the Japanese programme of aggression *or who by speech, writing, or action has shown himself to be an active exponent of militant nationalism and aggression*'. And taking no chances, the purge directives reserved to SCAP the right to add further categories.

A particularly unpalatable aspect of the purge in Japanese eyes (introduced with the *zaibatsu* especially in mind) was the provision that for ten years after a man had been purged, no relative by blood, marriage or adoption (and this was taken to the third degree) could succeed to his post. The intention was obvious – to prevent purgees from perpetuating their influence by setting their families up as dummies; but Prime Minister Yoshida argued vigorously that visiting the sins of the fathers upon not merely their children but their nephews, cousins, stepmothers, brothers-in-law and great-grandchildren was less than democratic and progressive. In ancient China, when a man was found to have committed a grave offence, all his relatives used to be sentenced accordingly; but since then, he felt, notions of justice had surely developed a little.

Also expandable at will were the areas of public life from which undesirables were to be excluded. SCAPIN 550, issued three months before the first general election under Occupation auspices, was primarily intended to purify politics at the national level – the Diet, Cabinet, and central government ministries. Consequently, all incumbent government servants at or above a certain rank (that of *Chokunin*, or, broadly speaking, department head) were to be screened to discover whether they fell into any of the purge categories. The same scrutiny was made of those aspiring to public office in the future, including candidates for election to the Diet, except that *all* government posts, above or below *Chokunin* rank, were closed to those who failed to pass their screening. This tighter criterion was designed to prevent high-ranking 'undesirables' removed from their posts from re-entering the public service at a lower level where they could nevertheless continue to exert a malign influence.

SCAPIN 550 had drastic immediate effects in some national political circles. The Home Ministry, for example, (which had administered the thought control programme), lost 340 of its officials, the Imperial Household 118. Over 170 peers were removed from the upper house; and no more than ten per cent of Diet members were pronounced eligible for re-election in April 1946. Among those disqualified was the man on the verge of becoming the new Prime Minister – Ichiro Hatoyama, purged by special SCAP directive on the eve of the election.

But this, MacArthur considered, was not enough to remove the stain of militarism, and in 1947 the purge was officially extended into new fields – to the press and other media, to local government, and to big business.

In January 1947 SCAP rather belatedly acknowledged the role of newspaper proprietors and editors, writers, artists, scholars, publicists, film makers, broadcasters and theatre producers in the fomenting of war. The output of suspects was carefully scanned for signs of rabble-rousing propaganda, and the wider the circulation of the paper, book, film or speech, the greater the offence if it was found unacceptable. But the period under scrutiny was more limited than in other fields – from July 1937 only until December 1941 – because after the outbreak of war, government controls over the media were so tight that anything written or said could hardly be held to reflect the author's true opinion.

In extending the purge to local government officials, SCAP was casting the net very much wider than before. Hundreds of thousands more people were brought within the scope of the purge, and the Japanese government under Yoshida balked. Anarchy, chaos and communism, Yoshida predicted, would result if MacArthur filleted the Japanese nation of its backbone by removing the 'small men' from their niches in society – men who in any case had been pawns, not policy-shapers. Nevertheless, elections were approaching again, at which for the first time the Japanese would have the opportunity to vote for local as well as national executives. MacArthur saw a chance of encouraging the new democratic leadership he had promised, and so he allowed only minor modifications.

Altogether over 200,000 people were eventually purged by SCAP. The programme started slowly. In the first year everyone in Japan who held or was applying to hold important public office was required to fill out a questionnaire. In it each was asked to describe, among other things, his past military service, membership of political and patriotic organisations, his writings or speeches and his corporate positions. The penalty for omission, half-truth or outright lie was a moderate fine or a prison sentence of less than a year – not prohibitive if one had something serious to hide. These documents then went before a single central screening committee which either passed, removed or barred their authors. During 1946, 8,920 were screened on the basis of this documentation, and 1,076 removed or barred from office.

When the purge was extended in 1947/8 and the number of targets increased dramatically, a three-tiered structure of screening committees at national, prefectural and municipal levels was set up. In addition, it was decided to designate provisionally as a purgee *anyone* who could be counted as 'undesirable', whether or not he actually held or aspired to important public office. No questionnaire was required as proof of undesirability, merely 'reasonable evidence' that the subject fell into one of the proscribed categories. 'Provisional designation' meant that the person was to all intents and purposes purged, though he retained the right of appeal to a specially-constituted Appeals Board; and it accounted for an overwhelming majority of all those removed from the scene – some 193,000.

The final stage in the purge procedure was SCAP's surveillance of purgees to ensure that they did not return to political activity, make propaganda use of the media, nor attempt to perpetuate their influence with advice, instructions or financial help. They were neither to visit their former workplace 'except in a purely private capacity', nor confer privately with their erstwhile colleagues on a regular basis. In 1947 a Special Investigation Bureau was set up within the Attorney General's Office. The reintroduction of surveillance into Japanese life was the price to be paid, at the expense of civil liberties, for the defeat of militarism.

When the purge was well under way, SCAP's attention was drawn to the fact that dotted around Japan's cities in prominent positions were statues and monuments whose sole purpose was to glorify the very values which human purgees were being penalised for holding. The statue of General Omura, proponent of universal conscription, at the Yasukuni Shrine, for instance; the *Hakko Ichiu*/'Eight Corners of the Universe Under One Roof' Monument at the back gate to the Imperial Palace, with its inscription by General Araki, a 'Class A' war crimes suspect; and the Atago Shrine's monument to 'Twelve Loyal Men and Women who Died for Japan' – died, in fact, by their own hands, after attempting to murder the Marquis Kido for recommending Japan's surrender. Many such monuments, previously exempted from salvage drives as 'objects of worship', were now unceremoniously torn down and scrapped. Doubtless MacArthur would have been delighted had the purge of their flesh and blood equivalents proved half as easy or effective.

Needless to say, the purge was bitterly resented by those subject to it. It was no Stalinist pogrom, nor even as severe as the denazification campaign in occupied Germany. But for many of the principal victims it spelled catastrophe. They were generally middle-aged or elderly, and at one stroke they lost their livelihoods, pensions and social standing.* But dislike of the purge was not confined to those it affected at first hand.

The purge encouraged a return to the social behaviour of the era of thought control – mistrust, watchfulness and a readiness to turn informer in order to deflect suspicion from oneself. The citizens of Nara Prefecture, for instance, were invited by a military government team to tell their local screening committee about any school teacher 'who you know either had or has militaristic, ultra-nationalistic or feudalistic thoughts. . . . If you do not do so, you are not fulfilling your responsibility as a democratic citizen. Of course, if you can obtain newspaper items, speeches, books or

---

* Though in one sense, *not* to be purged carried more of a stigma. 'If you were purged, that meant you were a first-rank citizen of Japan.'

students' classroom notes and other such written evidence against bad teachers that is very fine, but if not, your statement will be sufficient'.

The definition of 'war guilt' was so imprecise that inevitably many were purged who had done nothing wrong. It would not always have been easy to demonstrate, for example, how a local village headman had helped in 'deceiving and misleading the Japanese people to embark on world conquest'. Many found it difficult to reconcile the purge with Article 39 of the new Constitution: 'No person shall be held criminally liable for an act which was lawful at the time when it was committed.' Others considered it unjust that men should be punished for belonging to the Imperial Rule Assistance Political Society or holding important office in the *Butoku Kai* when the former was compulsory and the latter frequently *ex officio*. The purge was abused by the Japanese authorities as a tool for incapacitating political opponents. While the Chairmanship of the Central Screening Committee was held by prominent Liberal Shikao Matsushima, the Democratic Party saw four members of its executive committee purged. When the Democrats came to power in 1948, practically the first person to have his appeal against purge upheld was Wataru Narahashi, one of the four.

There was equal discredit, on the other hand, when obvious candidates for purging slipped through the meshes. In the eyes of many, the entire programme was compromised by SCAP's failure to remove Japan's most exalted citizen – the Emperor – from *his* office.

Injustices and uncertainties such as these, in the view of the OSS, threatened to undermine the credibility of the Occupation as a whole. 'Ultimate and genuine democratisation in Japan rests much less on the somewhat haphazard exclusion of undesirable individuals than it does on the will and ability of the Japanese to utilise an existing institutional framework for the protection and expansion of democratic principles, principles *with which the purge is in direct conflict*.'

On a less theoretical level, the purge was simply too easy to evade. In line with general Occupation policy, SCAP regarded it as important that the Japanese government should appear to be purging itself. The Americans issued their SCAPINs and the Japanese were then expected to respond with legislation and bureaucratic action. But often the purge was in the hands of precisely those officials with the most to lose from it. Somehow the criteria for designation were subtly altered in the process of translation, and normal administrative inertia was greatly exaggerated. The bureaucracy was only too happy to sacrifice the military. It had always operated independently and could now be surgically removed without damage to the main body of the government machine. However, when the orders came to turn the purge directives against themselves, the bureaucrats demurred – and only two per cent of those screened were ever purged.

Evasion took many forms. There was the anticipatory move – the early retirement enabling the potential purgee to retain pension rights, or the hasty transfer from a purgeable position to a non-purgeable one. (The U.S. Army found itself unwittingly employing considerable numbers of the Home Ministry's former thought police who had had the foresight to quit their employment immediately after the surrender.) There was the simple failure to screen – thirty-six new members, some of them highly dubious, entered the House of Peers in March 1946 without any examination of their eligibility. And there was the failure to screen diligently: in December 1946 the Ministry of Education called upon the Tottori Prefecture Screening Committee for Teachers to resign. Out of 4,700 candidates screened, the Screening Committee had seen fit to reject only six, and the Ministry, as it put it, doubted 'the wholeheartedness with which the Committee was pursuing its task'.

6

Military and Magnates

In 1945 ten major families controlled seventy-five per cent of industry, finance and commerce in Japan. They bound the industrial sector with a spider's web of banks, holding companies, subsidiaries and affiliates intricately inter-connected by overlapping directorships, a centralised system of financing, contractual obligations, family ties and quasi-feudal loyalties. 'The world', in MacArthur's view, 'has probably never seen a counterpart to so abnormal an economic system. It permitted exploitation of the many for the sole benefit of the few. The integration of these few with government was complete and their influence upon governmental policies inordinate, and set the course which ultimately led to war and destruction.'

Given this attitude, MacArthur naturally relished the instructions he had received in the Basic Initial Post-Surrender Directive, to encourage 'wide distribution of income and of the ownership of the means of production and trade'. In these words he heard the death knell of the vast business empires which monopolised Japan's industrial wealth and had used it to finance military expansion.

However, MacArthur's motives for attacking the *zaibatsu* were rather different from those of the men who had actually issued the instructions. To the China Crowd planners who had framed these economic policies, the toppling of Japan's financial élite was merely one element in an overall assault on international monopoly capitalism. Before the war, international trading blocs and cartels had controlled almost half of world trade. They had fixed prices, artificially restrained output, eliminated smaller rivals – and in the process (according to the economic theories to which the China Crowd largely subscribed) created unemployment, depressed domestic markets and the other conditions favourable to the rise of totalitarianism. The dissolution of national monopolies, like those which flourished in Japan, was the first step towards the destruction of the international cartels.

MacArthur took only a passing interest in these theories, which were expressed persuasively in the writings of Bisson, Roth, Lattimore and other gurus of the China Crowd. In his eyes, the crime of the *zaibatsu* leaders was less abstract – that they had fuelled the Japanese war machine in the years leading up to Pearl Harbor.

In fact, the relationship between big business, the army and the bureaucracy was not as clear-cut as MacArthur alleged. To a considerable extent, during the 1920s and 1930s magnates and military were rivals for political power, and had sharply contrasting views on the rate and method, if not the principle, of imperialist expansion. But inevitably in the construction of the Greater East Asia Co-Prosperity Sphere, military and business interests coincided to an increasing degree. The *zaibatsu* factories were called upon to provide equipment, their shops to provide transport, their banks for finance, and their overseas branches were useful bases for intelligence-gathering.

Hardly less damaging, the four greatest combines – Mitsui, Mitsubishi, Sumitomo and Yasuda – served the militarists indirectly by perpetuating an almost feudal relationship between employer and employee throughout Japanese industry. They discouraged any sense of independence or solidarity among the workers which might have become politically troublesome. And by concentrating economic power in their own hands, the *zaibatsu* inhibited the growth of the kind of healthy and critical middle class which might have impeded the rise of militarism.

The objective, as set out in the 1945 directives, was simple – the deconcentration of Japan's economy; the problem was how to achieve it. In line with the Occupation policy of indirect control, the campaign had to be put into effect through the Japanese themselves. But with rare misjudgement, MacArthur pushed this principle to extremes and attempted to present the programme of monopoly dissolution as having originated with its victims.

In October 1945 he invited each of the four major houses to submit a plan for its own undoing. The Yasuda family responded quickly – and with the Economic and Scientific Section barely in existence, the General, no expert in company law, could not be restrained from hastily approving the proposals they put forward. That these were hardly likely to do more than temporarily inconvenience the *zaibatsu* was all too clear from the alacrity with which the other major families agreed to them.

Their compliance aroused SCAP's suspicions, and MacArthur asked Washington to send an advisory group of anti-trust experts to assess the Yasuda Plan. No more than a cursory glance was needed before the joint mission sent by the State and War Departments, under Professor Corwin D. Edwards, condemned it roundly. The Plan, as they declared in March 1946, was merely a cosmetic gesture – setting on one side the capstone of the power pyramid without so much as dislodging its next layer, let alone achieving the thorough fragmentation which might enable a 'system of competitive capitalism' to emerge.

In place of the Yasuda Plan, the Edwards Mission offered far more sweeping proposals, which were later adopted by the Far Eastern Commission as Directive FEC 230. The target was the 'excessive concentration of economic power', which Edwards defined as any company (in industry, finance, insurance or distribution) with a disproportionately large asset value, workforce, or share of the market. And the attack was three-pronged; the family companies and their major holding companies were to be dissolved and prevented from reforming, the network of subsidiaries and affiliates beneath them was to be broken up, and the leading *zaibatsu* figures removed from the financial scene.

For the dissolution of the holding companies, the Japanese government was instructed to set up a Holding Companies Liquidation Commission. This was empowered to define, designate and dissolve *any* over-large enterprises, and its initial list of some 325 companies reads like a *Who's Who* of Japanese business. In July 1947 MacArthur ordered the dissolution of the Mitsui and Mitsubishi trading companies – so gigantic that each gave birth to over 200 splinter companies.

To break the web of corporate ties below the holding company level – interlocking directorates, inter-corporate security ownership, family links, and other devices enabling large central combines to stifle competition – SCAP engineered the enactment of an anti-monopoly law defining and outlawing 'unreasonable restraints of trade' and unfair methods of competition. This was followed by the creation of a Fair Trade Commission to enforce the law.

As for action against individuals, SCAP intended to incapacitate all those who seemed unlikely to 'direct future Japanese economic effort solely toward peaceful ends' – in other words, all those who had in the past exercised controlling power in the combines which had helped to propagate war. The attack had two stages: first the culprits were to be deprived of their interests in monopolistic companies, and then they were to be debarred from the business scene.

All creditors, managers and stockholders of any company designated as an 'excessive concentration' were to be divested of their holdings in the company. These were then to be transferred to the Holding Companies Liquidation Commission and sold on the open market. The ultimate aim was to 'lay the foundations for a Japanese middle class and a system of competitive capitalism', so wherever possible small or medium entrepreneurs, trade unions and agricultural co-operatives were to be encouraged to buy up the securities – if necessary, by being offered them at a fraction of their real value. As an additional blow, MacArthur pressed the Japanese government to impose a heavy capital levy on war profits (up to 100% where purely war-related industries were concerned), to introduce more steeply graduated income and inheritance taxes, and to cancel war indemnities owing to the *zaibatsu*. Most swinge-ing, the entire assets of 14 *zaibatsu* families (including Mitsui and Mitsubishi) were frozen pending sequestration – though ulti-mately only 56 individuals were so penalised.

The second stage in SCAP's vendetta was the application of the purge to industry and commerce – its first major encroachment into the private sector. The instructions given to MacArthur on the economic purge had been unambiguous. 'In the absence of evi-dence . . . to the contrary, you will assume that *any persons who have held key positions of high responsibility since 1937, in industry, finance, commerce or agriculture* [our italics) have been active exponents of militant nationalism.'

On paper, SCAP looked like making a clean sweep. All the members of the major *zaibatsu* families and their appointees and all key officials of other designated companies (plus their relatives to the third degree) were to be prohibited from working in any com-pany within their own combines or for that matter in any other capacity in the business world. But in practice less than two thousand business figures were ever designated as purgees, and not all of these were actually removed from their jobs.

Moral issues aside – and there were many who saw the destruc-tion of hugely successful business concerns as criminally wasteful, smacking of anarchy or, worse, communism – did the proposals of the Edwards Mission ever have a chance of working? It seems that in fact the men in SCAP's Economic and Scientific Section had taken upon themselves a virtually impossible burden. To disman-tle permanently even one of the *zaibatsu* business empires would have required more time, more staff and above all far more experi-ence of Japanese business law and methods than they possessed. They might identify and dissolve the principal holding companies at the top of the pyramid readily enough, but when they moved against the myriad subsidiaries, the complexity of the task defeated them. The first line of *zaibatsu* defence was the claim, which could never be disproved, that all the documentation neces-sary for the efficient reorganisation of the companies had been destroyed in the bombing. If ESS surmounted this hurdle, they were soon hopelessly tangled in a web of contracts, loans and accounts, joint and nominee shareholdings, common directorships, family ties and *oyabun-kobun* patterns which held the business world together; as fast as they severed connections, the strands rejoined silently behind them.

'In dominating men or being dominated by them', wrote Shungaku Matsudaira in 1850, 'the issue turns simply on the question of who has the initiative.' Anticipating dissolution, large companies fragmented stockholdings secretly among dummies from whom they could later reclaim them. The delay in implementing the economic purge gave its targets time not only to nominate and groom successors but to fortify the corporations' defences and put snares in the path of the attackers. The initiative was something the *zaibatsu* never lost, from the Yasuda Plan onwards.

The Japanese bureaucracy undoubtedly understood the workings of the business world, having interacted closely with it throughout Japan's modernisation. But by virtue of this very intimacy and the benefits it had brought, they could hardly be expected to co-operate in guiding SCAP's men through the maze. Yoshida himself was a doughty defender of traditional business methods: 'It is a great mistake to judge the *zaibatsu* as having done only bad things. Japan's economic structure today was built by such old *zaibatsu* as Mitsui and Mitsubishi. It can be said that the prosperity of the Japanese people has depended in great part upon the effort of these *zaibatsu*. Thus, it is doubtful that the dissolution of these old *zaibatsu* will really benefit the people.'

Nor indeed was there support for SCAP from the sector these reforms were intended to benefit. MacArthur's ambition was to develop a *laissez-faire* economy in the American tradition, in which small and medium-sized enterprises would compete freely in an open market. But the notion of individualistic internal competition, foreign in any case to the Japanese group orientation, was virtually incomprehensible to a nation preparing to force its way back into international markets against stiff external resistance. Besides, such independent entrepreneurial talent, little enough, as had existed before the war, had been obliterated by bombing, blockade or by the post-war economic collapse. When the Holding Companies Liquidation Commission put the dissolved corporations' assets on the market, there were no other businesses, nor a large enough middle-class, with the money to buy them even at reduced prices. It is believed that almost all the 'redistributed' stocks were repossessed either by the original *zaibatsu* under false names, or by black marketeers 'laundering' their profits.

There was actually more potential for damaging the *zaibatsu* and fostering a democratic economy in encouraging the development of an independent trade union movement. This kicked away a vital prop in the edifice of monopoly capitalism: a pliant workforce, barely capable of organising itself to make demands, is obviously an enormous advantage to an employer.

The way in which labour was organised before the war had made concerted action next to impossible. Many workers, perhaps a majority, were isolated in tiny home industries which employed them on a part-time basis. Factory owners held thousands more, men as well as women and children, in a form of indentured servitude, housing them in dormitories (even sometimes in labour camps) and sending their pay directly to their families with whom terms (minimal) had previously been agreed. Labour 'bosses' built up their own individual workforces of casual labourers paid on a daily rate.

Labour surpluses made it unwise to resist any of these forms of exploitation – and in fact the national ethos largely undermined the will to do so. The individual in Japan expected, and was expected, to subordinate his will to the general good; more specifically, the individual worker in the first decades of the twentieth century was not accustomed to thinking in terms of his own material gain. In the drive for rapid industrialisation of the nation, all personal ills, social and economic, were to be endured. Workers were often bound to management less by contract than by something resembling filial piety – an attitude which gave to organised opposition, however justifiable in material terms, an air of treachery. To the dismay of SCAP officials preaching the doctrines of the dignity of labour and the wage offensive, the distinction between the interests of management and those of the workers had been blurred; and where unions had been formed, they were often seen by employer and employees alike as a useful device for increasing productivity and promoting company harmony.

SCAP's motives in encouraging the Japanese worker to fight for his rights were mixed. The large employer would no longer be able to pursue selfish interests completely unopposed: and since in the past these interests had often included overseas expansion, this could be considered a blow struck against aggressive militarism. To give the working man greater economic power would be to expand the domestic market for Japanese products, lessening the threat these products might otherwise pose in international markets. But besides the self-interest which inevitably underlies one country's occupation of another, there was also the sincere desire to promote democracy for its own sake, and the belief that a society cannot survive as a democracy without a liberated working class and thus by implication a healthy labour movement.

Unionism benefited indirectly at the outset from MacArthur's very first move to install democracy in Japan – the Civil Liberties Directive of October 4, 1945, which ordered the Japanese government to cancel all laws restricting freedom of thought, speech, press, religion or assembly, and to dissolve the secret police organisations which had enforced the laws. MacArthur also commanded the release of all political prisoners, among whom were many prewar union activists and even more Communists and left-wingers who would soon become leaders in the union movement.

Then in December 1945 labour was given its official freedom by the basic Trade Union Law which for the first time guaranteed the right of Japanese workers to organise trade unions, bargain collectively, and strike. Over the next two years fourteen different labour bills, passed at SCAP's insistence, set up local labour relations committees and the machinery for conciliation and arbitration; a separate Labour Ministry; vocational training schemes; and a network of labour exchanges which struck a shrewd blow at the labour 'bosses' by offering an alternative to a semi-feudal dependence on a single master. The Labour Standards Law of April 1947, more progressive than anything enacted in America, laid down minimum standards for safety, hygiene, wage scales, overtime pay, working hours, holidays, sick leave and accident compensation; it regulated the employment of women and children, and prohibited forced labour altogether. A formal programme of labour education was introduced, to teach Japanese workers how employees in a democracy regarded their employers.

In October 1945, before the wartime restraints had been effectively demolished, there were 707 registered trade union members in Japan. By June 1949 there were 6,655,483, accounting for almost half of Japan's non-agricultural workforce (a much higher membership proportionately than America). Unions mushroomed first at the local level, springing up in their thousands in the first flush of enthusiasm; but in August 1946 many of these small, disorganised and under-funded unions were welded into two national federations, infinitely more powerful – *Sodomei*, the General Federation of Trade Unions (Socialist in its political orientation), and *Sanbetsu*, the National Congress of Industrial Unions, Communist-influenced. Techniques of collective bargaining became more forceful, if no more sophisticated, and unions developed the new weapon of production control. SCAP had indeed made Japanese labour a force to be reckoned with – and not merely by the *zaibatsu*.

At the same time SCAP was making comparable changes in the other half of society, greatly improving both the status and prospects of the farmer. 'No democracy can be built on a foundation of agricultural serfdom', as W. Macmahon Ball, the Australian representative on the Allied Council for Japan, pointed out; and even in 1945 the analogy with the feudal system was fully justified. Almost half of Japan's arable land was cultivated by men who did not own it. Seven out of ten farmers were tenants of some or all of the land they worked, handing over between a third and half of their rice crop in rent to landlords, and receiving for the rest such low prices that few if any were able to buy their way out of what was indeed effectual serfdom.

SCAP's objective in agricultural reform was not to bring down a dominant élite. In a mountainous and grossly over-crowded archipelago, none of Japan's farmers owned estates large enough to be described as 'excessive concentrations' of wealth; only about two thousand owned as much as 100 acres, and most commanded no more than ten. It was not in this case the overlords who were accused of fostering militarism, but the underdogs – the tenant farmers and agricultural labourers struggling for a wretched livelihood with nothing better in view. Their frustration and resentment, which might easily have been directed against their masters in an agrarian revolution, had instead been skilfully channelled into aggressive overseas expansion. The militarists found bedrock support and willing recruits in a repressed, conservative and potentially violent peasantry with little or nothing to lose. Echoing official Occupation thinking, Edwin Martin wrote succinctly: 'So long as the 47% of the Japanese people living on farms are barely able to survive, they will continue to be a source of cheap labor and cannon fodder. They will be an uneducated and dissatisfied group, seeking a way to better their lot without too much regard for the morality of the means, or understanding of the probable consequences of their acts.'

SCAP's solution was to give Japanese peasants a stake in a peaceful future by the wholesale re-distribution of agricultural land. This was devised primarily by Macmahon Ball and other members of the Allied Council, one of its very few positive contributions to reform in Japan. Absentee landlords were outlawed: all land not cultivated by its owner was compulsorily purchased by the Japanese government and sold to its tenants at pre-war prices, payable over thirty years at 3.2% interest. (By the time the last sales were made, an acre of land in some areas cost little more than a carton of black market cigarettes.) Owner-cultivators were allowed a maximum of 7.5 acres for their own use plus 2.5 acres which they might rent out for additional income. Rent was to be paid in money, not in produce – MacArthur himself firmly believed in the inalienable right of a farmer to his crops – and maximum levels were set.

To oversee and enforce the massive and infinitely complex programme of land transfers, a network of eleven thousand land commissions was set up on each of which tenants, owner-cultivators and landlords from the localities were all represented. By December 1949, small land-owners farmed 89% of Japan's arable land, and a major source of social injustice and military aggression had been destroyed. That the land reforms at the same time had the effect of undermining the appeal of Communist doctrines, by entrenching a class of 'petty capitalists' with everything to lose from collectivism, was officially declared to be no more than a happy side benefit.

7

Changing Minds: The Re-Education of Japan

In the last week of December 1946, a military government officer chairing a meeting in Hiroshima prefecture was asked earnestly by a local farmer whether, in his opinion, the Allies' intention was that Japan 'should adopt Democracy along Ancient Greek, Marxist or Capitalist lines?' The question bears distinct traces of the Japanese Communist Party speakers who had toured the provinces recently, taking advantage of the new freedom of speech, and it was hardly typical of the issues taxing the average farmer in 1946. But it does suggest some of the bewilderment felt by those at the receiving end of Occupation reform. The gift of democracy could not be bestowed on the Japanese without explanation. Simply to install the machinery of democratic government was not enough: most machines will break down when operated without understanding, interest or care. Introducing democracy to Japan was not unlike faith healing; the patient had to believe in the cure, and want it, for it to work.

Teaching people to want and understand democracy was the necessary counterpart of teaching them to unmask and reject military totalitarianism. The purge was designed to deprive the Japanese militarist of his political power, and the dissolution of the *zaibatsu* his economic power, just as surely as the disarmament programme took his physical weapons away; his influence over the minds of the Japanese people was, however, harder to counter. 'Psychological disarmament' – correcting the education of youth and reorienting the ideas of adults – was to cost SCAP dear in terms of effort, expense and exposure to criticism.

The educational system of any country is undoubtedly the most effective tool it possesses, should it choose to use it, for indoctrinating its citizens*. In a sense, the Civil Information and Edu-

---

* 'A general state education is a mere contrivance for moulding people to be exactly like one another: and as the mould in which it casts them is that which pleases the predominant power in the government . . . in proportion as it is efficient and successful it establishes a despotism over the mind, leading by natural tendency to one over the body.' John Stuart Mill, *On Liberty*.

[61]

cation section of SCAP was no less intent on 'thought control' than the previous rulers of Japan, and it was of the utmost importance that Japan's schooling be refashioned to serve American ideals.

The first target was the teachers, cast in the 1930s and the 1940s as 'the drill sergeants of nationalistic orthodoxy'; to refuse the role was a sure symptom of 'dangerous thought', and many had been summarily removed under the Peace Preservation Law. Now it was the turn of those who had submitted. Anticipating Allied retribution, the Ministry of Education either sacked or accepted the resignations of 116,000 teachers even before the first purge directive was issued, and a further 6000 fell under its provisions in 1946 alone.

SCAP never claimed, however, to have detected every teacher capable of transmitting unhelpful ideas. In January 1948, an assistant principal of the Hongo Middle School in Tokyo was found to be teaching from a book he had written himself in 1943 on the virtues of ritual suicide as a means of atoning for the dishonour of defeat. Entitled *Seppuku* or 'Disembowelment', as a reminder of the yawning gulf between cultures which CIE had somehow to bridge, the book could hardly have been bettered. Particularly revealing was the tone of incredulity in which the author described the reactions of the Americans, British and Dutch to the necessity for surrender. 'With no sense of shame . . . they ask immediately that their families be notified of their capture. After that, they set about making their quarters as comfortable as possible awaiting the day of the return home. Their families, in addition, instead of disowning them for their cowardice, welcome them home with open arms.'

To take the place of the purged teachers, SCAP encouraged both new recruits and the reinstatement of liberals – many of whom had in fact been strongly influenced by the ideas of American educator John Dewey, fashionable in Japan in the internationalist years after World War 1. A formal programme of 'teacher reorientation' was devised by the Ministry of Education, at SCAP's dictation. This incorporated a five-week course of lectures on the part played by the militarists in leading Japan to disaster, the central concepts of democracy, and the aims of the Occupation. In addition, a Teachers' Manual issued in April 1946 laid great stress on the importance of assuming individual responsibility for the content of courses, of using one's initiative, experimenting with different teaching techniques and encouraging pupil participation – ideas potentially more disturbing to the 'drill-sergeant' mentality than any revelation of Japanese war guilt. Whether it was because the reorientation campaign was particularly compelling, or because the majority of teachers were in fact already chafing at the restraints placed on them by the militarists, the teaching world was transformed in the course of five years from the loud-hailer of hyperpatriotism to a principal focus of radical sentiment – or, as the Yoshida government would have it, a hotbed of subversion.

The institutional framework within which the teachers were to work was also dramatically rearranged. Education was henceforth to be for the benefit of the individual: never again should the government abuse a highly centralised educational system as a machine for manufacturing regimented servants of the state. The iron grip of the Ministry of Education on teachers, textbooks and curricula was to be relaxed, with primary responsibility for schools devolved to local education boards elected by the residents of their catchment areas. And the individual student was to have not only more education, but more options within it. Compulsory education was lengthened from six years of elementary school to six of elementary plus three of middle school with a further three years of senior high school available, on the standard plan of American schools; and the child need not choose so soon between purely academic studies and commercial or technical training.

Instituting the American 6:3:3 system meant finding more teachers at a time when hundreds of thousands, voluntarily or involuntarily, were leaving the profession. It also meant providing more school buildings, offering a wider range of facilities, at a time when there was little money even for the bare necessities of survival. One member of CIE recalls, 'I often felt as though we were dangling a beautiful, delicious steak before a very hungry lion' – or perhaps more appositely, cramming the steak down the throat of an animal too weak to chew and choking it half to death. Moreover, SCAP, because of its own centralised structure, had to work to a large extent through the all-powerful Ministry of Education to achieve its ends, dangerously delaying the growth of local autonomy, and weakening its eventual credibility.

These flaws, not fatal in themselves, would nevertheless later undermine genuine achievements. One such achievement was the cleaning-up of the content of lessons; there was little point, after all, in improving teaching methods, or lengthening the period of instruction, if what was instilled remained essentially undemocratic. In December 1945 two courses – history and geography – were temporarily suspended for re-thinking, and one – *shushin*, or the teaching of morals – was abolished altogether.

The Japanese history taught in schools was, in CIE's view, inextricably and invidiously entangled both with the Imperial mythology and with the cult of *bushido* – baleful influences centuries old, unlike National Socialism in Germany whose roots were far shallower. Geography teaching too had been tailored to reflect notions of Japanese racial superiority and divine mission. A typical wartime text-book called attention to the shape and position of the Japanese archipelago, curved and on the rim of the continent, as suggesting a natural leadership role: 'We appear to be standing in the vanguard of Asia, advancing bravely into the Pacific. At the same time we appear ready to defend the Asian continent from outside attack.' More obnoxious still was instruction in *shushin*, with its near-obsessive stress on loyalty, filial piety, obedience and the subordination of the individual will.

In place of *shushin*, Japanese children were now taught civics and social studies, with stress on 'reflective not customary morality', the ethical rather than the obedient citizen. In place of learning by rote, they were offered an 'experience curriculum' based on the 'problem approach' (in Dewey terminology), which required them to use initiative in finding answers for themselves. Schools radio broadcasts, which had featured nationwide co-ordinated calisthenics and such items as 'Juvenile Stories from the Co-Prosperity Sphere', now included a series called 'What Am I?' on the psychology of the adolescent, emphasising the naturalness of curiosity, rebelliousness, and other intense emotions.

Spontaneity and individuality were invoked even more vigorously in the sphere of physical education – where admittedly an antidote to discipline and regimentation was badly needed. Since 1936 military training in schools had been compulsory for children of all ages. Its harshness is graphically suggested by the stream of rescinding orders which poured out of the Ministry of Education as it tried to cover its tracks. 'Military science halls' were to be converted into gymnasia. Any suggestion of military drill was to be eradicated from the bearing of students – the manner of their 'gathering, marching, saluting and attending school'. Teachers too should 'be careful not to fall into vain, formalistic regulation discipline or uniform instruction . . . Stress must be laid on the sportslike or play-like treatment of subjects of study'.

Generally, competitive sports were greatly to be preferred to co-ordinated exercise. In devising sports programmes for their pupils, teachers should now give some consideration to the weather conditions, the age of the children and their stamina. 'Especially the harmony between exercises and rest must be balanced'. Most revealing were the lists of courses ordered deleted from the curriculum. For teachers, 'Short Training Course on Glider Repairs'. For elementary school pupils, between the ages of five and eleven, judo, *kendo*, *kyudo*, 'Walk With Measured Tread', 'Warships', 'Play at Soldiers', 'Fish Torpedos'. For secondary school pupils: aviation, halberd practice, Navy March, 'Strength of Iron (*Kurogane No Chikara*) shout of triumph', bayonet exercise, throwing of hand grenades.

In order to control the content of lessons, CIE, like the militarists, had to control the textbooks. Since the turn of the century all books used by secondary students had had previously to be authorised by the Ministry of Education, and all those used in compulsory elementary schooling were actually written and published by the Ministry. In the 1930s and during the war they had inevitably become heavily tainted with ultra-nationalist propaganda. SCAP's short-term emergency solution was to require schools to ink out all offending words and passages. But most headmasters found that the easiest method of carrying out this laborious task was to get the children to doctor their own books – the surest possible way of riveting their attention on the noxious material. And in some texts the harmless was so closely intertwined with the damaging throughout that the 'cleaning-up' process left them an indecipherable mess.

The urgent need for completely new books to be issued meant continuing, at least for a time, the system whereby the Ministry of Education compiled and published school texts. These were, of course, now subject to SCAP's approval as being in line with the new ideology. In October 1946 history teaching was resumed with the first 'clean' post-war textbook. Specially commissioned from teachers at Tokyo Imperial University, it was entitled *Kuni No Ayumi* ('The Footsteps of a Nation'), and placed the beginning of Japan's history in the Stone Age, discounting as myth the creation stories so closely associated with the Emperor's divine descent.

The eventual aim, however, was to break the Ministry's monopoly, and in 1948 a new procedure was instituted. Writers submitted manuscripts to a Textbook Authorisation Committee within the Ministry of Education; the Committee then produced lists of books approved for use, from which schools made their selection on the recommendation of teachers and administrators. This was very similar to the authorisation system employed in Japan in the 1880s and the 1890s, and could not be described as offering teachers a free choice, since a considerable number of the textbooks on the market were still proscribed either by the Ministry or by SCAP, which retained the ultimate power of review. But it did at least let into schools textbooks which had been written by independent authors outside the Ministry of Education.

For the re-education of Japan's adults, a more positive and slightly – but only slightly – more sophisticated approach was adopted. The 'Civil Information' function of CIE was seen by many as a gigantic public relations exercise – not least by those who appointed as CIE's first chief Brigadier General Kenneth Dyke, in civilian life an experienced and successful advertising executive. In the words of CIE's Chief of Policy and Programmes, John W. Gaddis, 'The product being advertised was democracy'.

Because of their personal idealism, few in CIE were inhibited by the fact that in some respects their approach resembled that of the pre-war Japanese Social Education Bureau which a SCAP consultant had recommended should be abolished as a 'propaganda ministry'. Some of their outlets too were the same. The radio network had been an indispensable propaganda tool during the war, centrally controlled with access to a huge audience, since Japan boasted the highest proportion of radio sets to households of any nation except America. SCAP was to find it equally valuable. In schools, until new textbooks were available, radio was a principal means of introducing children to the fundamentals of democracy, interspersed with useful items of public information and exhortation. (Features included 'The Policeman with the Mustache – *Theme*: Masakazu finds that the fierce looking policeman is really kind and helpful. The policeman is a public servant now whose purpose is to help and protect. In the old society they were to be feared.' 'Sweet and Astringent Persimmons – *Theme*: the uses of persimmons and the need for the city and rural people to co-operate.' 'Boast of Potato – *Theme*: a sweet potato tells the story of its life and all the uses of sweet potatoes.')

For adults the presentation was more subtle. To make it more readily assimilable, material recommended and sometimes drafted by SCAP was incorporated within already existing radio programmes – *The Farmers' Hour, The Woman's Hour, The Industrial Hour*, quiz programmes like *Fountain of Knowledge* and *Twenty Gates* (a version of *Twenty Questions* – 'Collective bargaining: animal, vegetable or mineral?'), and drama serials like *Good Neighbours*. In this way the Japanese people had explained to them the intricacies of SCAP's land reform, the legal rights of divorced wives, the benefits of widespread ownership of industry, and so on. More directly, freedom of speech and opinion was encouraged by example. 'Man on the Street' was the equivalent of today's radio phone-in; and in 'National Radio Forum' topical issues were debated by a panel composed equally of conservatives, liberals and radicals – a well-worn format in America, but little short of sensational to Japanese listeners remembering a time when broadcasters could be arrested for their private thoughts, let alone their public utterances. When a message was considered particularly urgent, it could be repeated, undisguised, several times a day in spot announcements – 'Don't forget to vote in today's national elections. This is your democratic privilege and duty.'

Films were also obvious vehicles for benevolent lecturing as they had been for the more pernicious propaganda of the militarists. SCAP relied principally on imported feature films illustrating the American way of life, foreign newsreels, army education 'shorts', and documentaries with sound tracks rewritten and translated to suit the Japanese audience. Japanese film companies were also encouraged to work along these lines, but domestic newsreels met consumer resistance. Audiences living with bomb damage, industrial depression and food rationing seemed to resent the publicising of their predicament, and film maker Akira Iwasaki claims that in some areas they threw stones at the screen.

A network of reading rooms was opened throughout Japan, making books and magazines available on open shelves to everyone for the first time. Most pre-war libraries had been open to men only, and the books were kept behind bars and handed over only on specific request. During the war information on the outside world had been rigorously suppressed; now a rich tapestry of American life was unrolled before Japanese readers. The picture was still a little selective. Books on medicine, business methods and public welfare were offered, but nothing on atomic energy, military hardware, or jet propulsion. Fiction 'with democratization value' was provided (under which heading came the works of Thomas Mann, *Random Harvest* and *Gone With The Wind*), but Westerns and murder thrillers were not, lest the Japanese derive a false impression of American culture.

The reading rooms also provided facilities for recorded concerts of Western music (including the music of the saxophone and the Hawaiian guitar, banned during the war as 'decadent'), 'Meet America' lectures, and square dancing, as a thriving community life was considered one of democracy's distinguishing features. CIE put a good deal of energy into promoting Citizens' Public Halls, run by locally-elected committees and used for art exhibitions and amateur theatricals as well as by parish-pump politicians practising 'local leadership', and debating societies whose aim was to develop the art of 'public speaking for democratic citizenship'. (This involved much *extempore* round-table discussion, rather than the 'traditional memorized-speech type of Japanese oratorical contest'.) Parent-Teacher Associations, another novelty, were set up in the hope that parents would be convinced never again to relinquish responsibility for their children's education to the state; women were expected to benefit especially from this kind of involvement in life outside the home. In the cause of increased opportunities for all, CIE pushed the Japanese government into an extensive programme of adult education – special courses for repatriated soldiers (in the spirit of America's own G.I. Bill of Rights), evening classes for miners and day labourers, correspondence courses for farmers, sex education classes, education for the handicapped and for those in prison.

One further aspect of public information the Americans considered distasteful but necessary. CIE was under instructions 'to make clear to all levels of the Japanese public the true facts of their defeat, their war guilt, the responsibility of the militarists for present and future suffering and privation'. First efforts to do this were neither subtle nor successful. In the first week of the Occupation, it was suggested that the national press should feel free to discuss its country's war guilt; and when the invitation was not taken up with any enthusiasm at all, the Press and Publications Division of CIE prepared a report on 'Typical Japanese Atrocities during the Liberation of the Philippines', complete with photographs and diary extracts which it required published over three pages of all the major dailies. This prompted one of the dailies, the *Asahi Shimbun*, to retort that the release of the report was intended to distract attention from comparable G.I. abuse of Japanese nationals. (The editor added that in his opinion the use of the atomic bomb had been a breach of international law, and *Asahi* was immediately suspended from publication for forty-eight hours).

Equally unimpressive was 'Now It Can Be Told', a serialised radio account of the slide to war, in the style of America's popular 'March of Time'. Even partisan observers felt it to be a little lacking in 'the nuances of Japanese thought patterns': Japanese critics dismissed it as noisy, vulgar and simplistic. The Japanese people might be supposed to be abashed by defeat – but not abashed enough to respond gratefully to advice administered at the nursery level. Mark Gayn attended a rehearsal of 'Now It Can Be Told' and recalled: 'The broadcast was opened by a Japanese narrator. "We, the people of Japan", he said in the best dramatic voice of the American radio, "know now who was responsible for the crimes committed against us". "Who? Who are they?", other voices asked. "Give me time", said the narrator. "I'll tell you. I'll give you some of their names. Above all, I'll give you the facts so you can draw your own conclusions".'

More effective was the matter-of-fact reporting, in the press and on the radio, of the proceedings of the International Military Tribunal for the Far East, and the trials of lesser war criminals at Yokohama. Regular coverage of the IMTFE, including a 10-minute radio bulletin on each day's proceedings, continued until the bitter end, providing, with little need for comment, a mass of incriminating data on the activities of the militarists. Meanwhile MacArthur, always sensitive to public opinion, called a halt to the worst of the finger-pointing and moralising early in 1946.

Almost as important to SCAP as the information they were implanting in the Japanese adult consciousness were the ideas they were attempting to keep out – though they did their best to keep secret from the public this aspect of their 'reorientation'.

Censorship of the Japanese media was no spur-of-the-moment decision, taken under the influence of urgent military necessities. It had been on the planners' agenda at least since 1943, and was referred to obliquely in the Potsdam Declaration under the heading of the 'suppression of ultra-nationalist ideology'. MacArthur promised 'an absolute minimum of restrictions upon freedom of speech', but the Basic Initial Post-Surrender Directive had already given him the power to impose censorship not only in the interests of military security but also 'as may be necessary [for] . . . the accomplishment of the purposes set forth in this directive'. These provisions were open to almost limitless interpretation, offering MacArthur a weapon not merely against the ultra-Right but also against enemies on the Left, or anywhere else that he chose to see them.

His principal target was the press, immensely influential in a country with a high literacy level, where most families took more than one paper, and most major papers published more than one edition per day. Under wartime controls newspapers did little more than parrot official army handouts and propaganda from the Board of Information. With the prospect of these restrictions being lifted, the press looked forward eagerly to flexing its muscles and expressing itself. There was in fact a brief burst of tabloid journalism of the most lurid kind. But MacArthur's ideas on the categories of information prejudicial to the objectives of the Occupation soon took depressing shape. 'News must adhere strictly to the truth . . . There shall be no destructive criticism of the Allied Forces of Occupation' – orders which were held to be not only consistent but virtually synonymous: it seemed that in MacArthur's view criticism of the Occupation would by definition be untruthful.

And his censors proved abnormally sensitive to slights. It was forbidden to incite mistrust or resentment of Occupation personnel, and understandably references to G.I. blackmarketeering, rape, theft, and drunkenness were suppressed (though some papers got round the problem by constant reference to delinquent 'blue-eyed nationals' and 'men with nine-inch footprints'). It was also forbidden to disparage or even imply disparagement of America's conduct of the Occupation or of world affairs. In some cases the unfriendly intent would have been hard to miss – as in the entry under 'denounce' in the *Dictionary of English Literature* of 1946 – 'No imperialism is more denounced today than the imperialism of the United States'. In other cases it required skilled detective work. A poem in the magazine *Kikuhata* (the organ of the 'patriotic' Chrysanthemum Flag Friends Society) was identified by an alert censor as a *waka* of nineteenth-century nationalist xenophobe Tomoo Otaguro. 'As the night becomes colder, I feel myself rest-

[69]

less to clean my foreign clothes for the winter' would readily be translated by *cognoscenti* into 'As the national situation becomes aggravated day by day, I feel myself restless to prepare to attack the foreigners'.

Even Americans were not allowed to express doubts. Walter Lippmann's column, syndicated all over America, was one of the most regularly censored features in the Japanese press. And only after MacArthur's personal intervention were Japanese editors allowed to reproduce a speech made by Henry Wallace in Madison Square Garden, in which he had remarked that the United States had no more right to be in Eastern Europe than Russia to be in Latin America.

In the early years of the Occupation, American censors found themselves in the improbable position of shielding Russia, still nominally an ally, against attack by Japanese conservatives, while at the same time discouraging radicals from castigating Britain and Holland as decaying colonial powers. (It was perhaps over-protective to suppress a letter reprinted in *Asahi* from the London *Times* on the decline of British forces in the Far East, given that it was written by Sir Robert Clive, former British Ambassador to Japan.) Most taboo of all were suggestions of any difference of opinion between the Allies – glancing references to tension in Korea, for instance, the reparations issue, or the Truman Doctrine. On this ground it was felt advisable to expurgate the minutes of the Allied Council for Japan, which on occasion consisted of little but the derogatory remarks of the Allies about each other.

Mention of Hiroshima and Nagasaki and the Tokyo fire-raid of March 10, 1945 (which killed outright more people than either atomic bomb) ranked high among subjects likely to 'disturb public tranquility'. Nothing more emotive than scientific reports of the after-effects (carefully screened) was allowed: a poem in *Kikuhata* centred round the figure of a man on a bridge, a charcoal statue still holding a bicycle, was roundly condemned as calculated to alarm. No pictures were permitted other than those of the mushroom clouds, which many have described as 'beautiful' and 'awe-inspiring'. (A Japanese film which had been shot in Hiroshima two hours after the explosion was suppressed until after the Occupation, as was John Hersey's best-selling account *Hiroshima*.)

Books were subject to the same restrictions, and literary censorship produced some even more striking results. *War and Peace*, which had been much admired in Japan for twenty-five years, was now cut, *The Grapes of Wrath* banned altogether (presumably for its unflattering picture of American weather and social welfare), and the *Kama Sutra* was kept even from some of the censors: '[The] entire text is of such a nature as to be unsuited for translation and typing by office staff'. Bank notes were withdrawn if they bore undesirable images – Shinto symbols, scenes from countries no longer under Japanese rule, photographs of military leaders, pictures of nationalist heroes, or militarist monuments (like the one on the ten-yen note, the Foundation Tower of the Universe/All The World Under One Roof Monument). Likewise stamps with such designs as 'shields and cherry blossoms', 'Rising Sun and airplane', 'map and coconut palm', 'juvenile flyer', 'surrender of enemy', all in use in 1947.

All letters and telegrams entering or leaving Japan, plus a certain proportion of internal mail, were checked against a 'flash list' of some 2,700 suspected names (a list that was also the basis of a selective phone-tapping campaign). The censors were primarily interested in evidence of subversive activity (ultra-nationalist or, increasingly, Communist), slanders against the Allies, threats of vengeance, along the lines of 'I shall get revenge by a great and superior bomb', and complaints of G.I. misbehaviour. Touchingly, they also gathered crumbs of praise of the occupying forces: 'Their efficiency in putting traffic in order is something for the Japanese to learn. As they are seeing moving pictures they are quiet and *take off their hats*. As people of the first country in the world, this might be expected.'

One of the principal casualties in the world of films was *Citizen Kane*, banned for its unmistakable and uncomplimentary allusions to one of MacArthur's principal supporters, William Randolph Hearst. But in general SCAP's policies towards the cinema, under the Motion Picture Unit of CIE, were progressive at least in intent. The weapon of censorship was employed almost exclusively against militarists and ultranationalists: the index of films ordered to be burnt consisted largely of such titles as *Swords Flash in the Cherry Blossom Time, General Attack at Singapore, The Day England Falls*, and *Human Bullet Volunteer Corps*. Even Kurosawa's *The Men Who Tread on the Tiger's Tail* was suppressed for exalting feudal values – which may well have amused Kurosawa, since the same film had previously been suppressed by the militarists as overly liberal.

Film makers were encouraged to work with such reformist themes as the significance of labour unions, the evils of the black market and the rehabilitation of prisoners-of-war as respected members of the community. The results were predictably turgid; and politically, in the view of SCAP conservatives, the Motion Picture Unit was opening the door to leftist propaganda in the shape of such films as *Children of the Atom Bomb*, which ends with the heroine leaving Hiroshima, her relatives all dead or dying in agony, while overhead American planes roar towards Korea.

The CIE officials responsible for sanitising the Japanese theatre were warier in what they positively recommended – a production of

The Mikado, which it was felt would encourage a healthier attitude towards the Emperor; Lilian Hellmann's *Watch on the Rhine*; John Drinkwater's *Abraham Lincoln*; and Arthur Miller's *All My Sons*. They went to even greater lengths than the Motion Picture Unit, however, to combat reactionary drama. The principal offender was the centuries-old *kabuki* theatre, one of Japan's great glories but viewed by SCAP as a vehicle for the glorification of feudalism and *samurai* virtues. The two youthful officials in charge of refurbishing the Japanese theatre found *kabuki* obnoxious for its cheap valuation of human life, relegation of women to inferior status, obsession with loyalty and revenge, and all-pervasive blood-thirstiness. They worried that the audience was more susceptible to corruption now that, theatre prices being what they were, it was composed no longer of intellectuals but of 'newly affluent factory workers and war profiteers'; and after reviewing 518 of the classic plots, they ordered 322 to be removed forthwith from the repertoire. This move was presented as originating with the Japanese – which was rather as if 'the Germans conquered England and suddenly the English announced that they had banned Shakespeare in perpetuity because he was feudal'. The reformers also encouraged the remaining plays to be performed with 'revolutionary' changes: the female role played by a woman instead of the traditional male impersonator: the heroine not killed but forgiven for her transgressions (shades here of Nahum Tate's *King Lear*): kissing on stage: a Buddhist monk permitting himself to fall in love. In the plaintive words of the official report, 'this innovation appeared to weaken interest in democratization of the *kabuki* art form'.

SCAP was not particularly proud of its censorship. MacArthur, like his Washington advisors, was aware of the incongruity of a crusader for democracy working with the tools of the dictator. Near the start of the Occupation he had invited Roger N. Baldwin, head of the American Civil Liberties Union, to come to Japan as an observer and consultant in the campaign for Japanese civil rights. Censorship was one of the surprisingly few Occupation activities which Baldwin criticised unreservedly: wrong in principle, often crass in practice, and an extraordinarily bad example to the people MacArthur was attempting to impress with the moral superiority of the democratic ideal. One solution – obviously the one Baldwin had in mind – would have been to suspend or at least modify the censorship. MacArthur received similar advice from the OSS at the end of 1947: censorship was a continuation of the 'authoritarian tradition' in Japan, which could only augur badly for the future. But he preferred simply to keep it underground, and the order went out, 'The public is not to be informed that the Civil Censorship Detachment is pursuing censorship activities'.

8

Making Shinto Safe

In the United Nations Church in New York, on the eve of Apollo Seven's flight to the moon, a Shinto priest performed a ceremony of purification to pacify restless spirits that might trouble the lunar module's mission. This service symbolised the complete rehabilitation in American eyes of a religion which in the early 1940s many American Christians seriously believed to be satanism by another name. The futurologist Dan Gilbert fulminated against Shintoism as 'the only [religion] in the world which constrains its followers to practise every vice recommended by Satan. No other religion, no matter how barbarous may be its adherents, glorifies lying, cheating, stealing, rape, plunder and pillage on the wholesale scale of Shintoism. . . . No other barbarous religion outlines a religious and racial destiny which contemplates the extermination of the entire remainder of the human race'.

With public opinion at home howling for the obliteration both of the religion and its high priest, it is to the credit of the SCAP officials in CIE that they saw their duty as being only to purge Shinto of the militarist trappings it undoubtedly then possessed – and in the American tradition of freedom of religion, to sever its connections with the state.

Japanese children experienced at first hand the demise of state-supported Shinto with the removal of the 'god-shelves' (*kamidana*) from their schools and the destruction or conversion into ordinary cupboards of the depositories where the Emperor's portrait and the Imperial Rescript on Education were kept. No longer would these be reverently unveiled at school ceremonies – the portrait to be honoured with deep obeisance, the Rescript on Education to be read aloud by the school principal with the utmost care. (Everyone present would have had in mind the example of Lieutenant Ishi-roku who, on stumbling over a syllable, had felt it necessary to commit *hara-kiri*.) Co-ordinated bowing in the direction of the Imperial Palace was no longer compulsory. Shinto doctrines were

[73]

to be expurgated from textbooks and teaching manuals. Nor were school teachers to escort their pupils on enforced trips to Shinto shrines; they were not even to suggest such visits or set homework which made them necessary*.

These reforms were the consequence of American efforts, through the Shinto Directive of December 15, 1945, to 'separate religion from the state, to prevent misuse of religion for political ends, and to put all religions, faiths, and creeds upon exactly the same basis' in fulfilment of the promise of religious freedom made in the earlier Civil Liberties Directive. Shinto was not the only target. The compilers of a schools radio programme on 'Great Educators' found themselves in trouble when it came to discussing the work of Jesus, Buddha and Confucius, since 'religious doctrine as such must be avoided'. The history of religion was permissible in schools, and the biographies of 'religious personalities'; but the discussion or propagation of teachings peculiar to *any* religion was forbidden. But since in the Japan of 1945 one religion alone was inextricably associated with the state, the campaign inevitably took on the complexion of an anti-Shinto crusade.

The Shinto Directive made itself felt most damagingly by cutting off all government funding of Shinto and Shinto shrines, and by making illegal the private 'contributions' extorted through neighbourhood associations, on which many smaller shrines depended. It also prohibited public officials from controlling Shinto observances or even attending them in an official capacity; no longer were new appointees to visit shrines to report on their assumption of office, or participate in purification ceremonies on completion of public buildings, roads or irrigation ditches.

The principal intention was to deprive state activities of their supernatural sanction. According to one authority on Shinto and Japanese nationalism, 'For two thousand years the ultimate authority by which government had imposed its will on the nation had rested on sanctions that transcended the right of subjects to criticise or to resist'†. If SCAP could help it, never again would defiance of a possibly misguided government be considered not merely subversion but sacrilege.

At the same time – and SCAP is usually given less credit for this than it deserves – the Shinto faith was to be rehabilitated as a reli-

* The effort to keep religion out of schools was occasionally taken to ludicrous lengths – as when one school refused a local priest permission to make a telephone call on the grounds that government property might not be used for religious purposes.

† And cf. Herbert Paul, *The New Alliance*: 'Patriotism and religion have been so often at variance that a country whose religion is patriotism has an obvious advantage.'

gion. Shintoism was not in itself obnoxious, at least to the better informed within SCAP. In its essence it consisted simply of 'a cluster of the beliefs and customs of the Japanese people centering in the *kami*, a term which designates spiritual entities, forces or qualities that are believed to exist everywhere, in man and in nature'. Life was to be lived in harmony with these forces, and in gratitude to them, but there were various ways of obeying these imperatives. Many believers joined sects centred around individual founders and studied their teachings on the *kami*. Others found the most natural expression of their faith in regular visits to shrines, symbolic *kami*-dwellings.

Neither 'Sect Shinto' nor 'Shrine Shinto' in its original form would have posed any threat to SCAP – both would indeed have been entitled to protection like any other faith under the Civil Liberties Directive. But Shrine Shinto in 1945 no longer took its original form. For almost a century it had been systematically exploited by Japan's ruling cliques and its rites turned into a powerful instrument for fostering military aggression. The Imperial institution, as a means of unifying and inspiring the Japanese people, generated much of the power behind the drive for modernisation and international recognition. Beliefs about the Emperor's divine descent, without constituting by any means the whole of the Shinto faith, were inextricably bound into it. Thus to promote Shintoism, or at least those elements which exalted the Emperor, was to accelerate Japan's rise to power*.

Accordingly, all Shinto shrines were taken over by the government; their priests became government employees, their funds were drawn from public money, their rites prescribed by law and supervised by government officials, and attendance was increasingly made compulsory. The Japanese people's emotional attachment to the Emperor was institutionalised into a state-run cult in which religious beliefs were deliberately and confusingly intermingled with nationalist propaganda and military ambitions. The cult required the Japanese to accept that the Emperor, his land and his people formed an indivisible entity which by association with him was divine. Divinity implied both racial superiority and the right and duty to extend the Emperor's rule over 'the eight corners of the world'.

It was as a result of these distortions that Japanese religion had become a prime target in the campaign for 'psychological disarmament'. In two areas in particular – the celebration of national

---

* When Hirobumi Ito, one of the founders of modern Japan, visited Europe in 1882 to study methods of modernisation, he was specifically advised by Bismarck to revive those elements of Shinto which could exalt the Emperor.

holidays, and the veneration of war dead – qualities which the Americans themselves prized highly had become suspect. Love of country and respect for its defenders had been perverted and diminished into a crude glorification of military values.

Festivals which had grown out of the old 'natural' Shinto – celebrations of the seasons, the harvest, the creation myths – had been twisted to reflect its new and more sinister character as a servant of the state. Often they were simply excuses for displays of patriotic fervour, small-scale imitations of the Nuremberg rallies, clothed in a thin veil of Shinto ritual. Much against its will the Japanese Cabinet was persuaded to review the roster of national holidays, discarding those with 'too much of a Shinto odor', and replacing them with celebrations more in keeping with the new enlightenment. November 3, for example, the Emperor Meiji's birthday, was traditionally an occasion for rejoicing in the expansion of Japan's empire under his aegis. Now it was renamed 'Culture Day'. 'National Foundation Day' (February 11), the commemoration of the enthronement of Jimmu, the first god-emperor of Japan, was dropped altogether. But enlightenment did not stretch as far as accepting the *Asahi Shimbun*'s suggestion that August 6 be named Atomic Bomb Day, as a permanent incentive to peace.

As for the war-dead shrines which so worried SCAP, the first had been built, ironically, to honour those who fell in battle after the arrival of Commodore Perry's 'black ships' and the first American 'liberation' of Japan. They contained no bones or ashes, only tablets on which were recorded each soldier's name, rank, unit and last action. But unlike the tomb of the Unknown Soldier and other western war memorials, Japanese war-dead shrines were no mere symbols of patriotic duty, but houses for the spirits, sacred places where relatives could console them for their untimely death, show gratitude for their sacrifice, and so appease their anger at the living. When the military clique seized upon the shrines – and in particular Tokyo's Yasukuni Shrine, the principal shrine to Japan's war dead – as an obvious focus of patriotism, this direct, natural and human relationship with the *kami* was overlaid with a thick and polluting layer of state propaganda. War dead, having gloriously fulfilled the duty that was expected of all the Emperor's subjects, and laid down their lives in his service, were now not merely to be consoled but worshipped and their exploits 'adored'. Shrine compounds were large enough for a whole regiment to pay its respects at once.

SCAP's problem was to eradicate such militaristic practices without denying the Japanese people the right to honour their dead fittingly and assuage their grief. Passing on to the head of CIE a request for permission to recover the bones of the dead from Iwo

Jima, William Bunce, head of the Religions and Cultural Resources Division, pointed out that Congress had recently guaranteed the right of every American mother to have her son's remains shipped home. This had been granted even though 'There is in our society no concept linking the happiness of a disembodied spirit with the way the spiritless body is disposed of or which concedes to that spirit any power to aid or harass the living'. In both Buddhist and Shinto faiths such powers are taken extremely seriously; and the prostitution of the war dead shrines for political ends did not affect the fact that they also performed a genuine religious function.

The CIE solution to the problem of war shrines and memorials shows considerable understanding, sensitivity and respect for Japanese beliefs. Shrines were prohibited from employing ex-soldiers as their priests, government officials were forbidden to participate in military funerals, or to make 'expressions of exaggerated respect' towards the military monuments – but the shrines and monuments themselves survived. It cannot be said that MacArthur was as restrained or as scrupulous.

Perhaps surprisingly, given the American missionary spirit and the pressure exerted by Christian lobbyists in Washington, MacArthur had no orders to propagate Christianity in Japan. On the contrary, in succeeding directives he had been clearly instructed to establish freedom of religion, and had himself issued a directive forbidding the ruling power to favour any one faith above others. However, for much of the period in which he was himself the ruling power in Japan, he deeply embarrassed many of his staff by championing Christianity quite openly, at the same time dismissing or disparaging indigenous faiths as morally inferior. (He liked to speak of Christianity's 'profound and beneficial influence upon the moral viewpoint and ethical standards of the [Japanese] race'. Remarkably naive in some respects, he then complained of his lack of appreciation among Buddhist and Shinto leaders.)

MacArthur's motives were mixed. Most important were his own religious beliefs. He did not go to church, but he had evolved his own secure faith apparently centred on the moral principles of the Sermon on the Mount, and he was in the habit of enlisting God as an ally and thanking Him in public pronouncements for His guidance. 'On one occasion after drafting a statement . . . following a noteworthy victory he is reported to have stepped out of his office and called his aide back with the shout, "We forgot God!".' In his *Reminiscences*, published in 1964, MacArthur referred to himself modestly as 'a theologian of sorts'. In the late 1940s he appeared to see himself more as a Protestant equivalent of the Pope, a spiritual leader ready to take advantage of 'the greatest challenge and opportunity Christianity has had throughout the Christian era'. He unquestionably believed that in absolute moral terms Japan would be a better place for being Christian. He also saw the strategic advantages, and to the horror of CIE, struggling to persuade the Japanese government to relinquish religion as a political tool, he touted Christianity as the best defence against communism. Nor can he have been quite unmindful of the electoral appeal in the Bible Belt of America of a conspicuously devout Presidential candidate.

MacArthur saw nothing odd in the fact that on the day the Shinto Directive was issued, ordering the separation of church and state, two large Christmas trees adorned SCAP headquarters. He called for missionaries in their thousands, and gave those who came special privileges – accommodation, food, transport and the right to associate freely with the Japanese – which infuriated Occupation personnel, let alone other religious leaders. He egged bible societies on to import ten million bibles: annual distribution of bibles before the war had been about 145,000, and many of the ten million were accepted purely as cigarette paper. He would seem to have protected from the purge Toyohiko Kagawa, Japan's best-known Christian preacher. Kagawa's leadership was essential to the Protestant evangelist campaign which MacArthur, christened an Episcopalian, keenly supported. But he had nonetheless made regular wartime radio broadcasts on behalf of the militarists, and MacArthur should perhaps have thought twice about sheltering a man who had attacked American Jews as the instigators of war, and proclaimed that 'President Roosevelt takes pride in owning a book-knife made from the bones of a dead Japanese soldier'.

MacArthur was also probably the source of the suggestion that the Emperor and members of his family were considering conversion. According to Billy Graham, MacArthur once told him the Emperor had offered to make the whole Japanese nation Christian – presumably Protestant, given the General's choice of confidant. On the other hand in 1948 rumours were rife that Hirohito was about to become a *Catholic*. SCAP official Justin Williams wrote flippantly to a colleague in June, 'Some think that [Bishop] Sheen and [Cardinal] Spellman are here trying to make a Catholic out of "Charlie"'. But in July a member of the British Legation to the Holy See informed the Foreign Office, 'The Vatican are not disposed to take seriously the tales which the Catholic press of Rome rather frequently prints, that the Emperor is about to become a Christian'.

Since Shinto rites continue to this day to play an important part in Palace life, it would seem that the Vatican was right. Despite the best that MacArthur could do, Christianity made little progress during the Occupation; the number of Catholics, for instance, increased only from some 120,000 in 1941 to about 157,000 in 1951. (The figures had, of course, been affected by the fact that the centre of Roman Catholicism in Japan was Nagasaki.) He was nevertheless guilty of abusing his authority for his own emotional and spiritual satisfaction; and it took an effort of will for those in the Religions and Cultural Resources Division to refuse to follow his lead. 'Standard Operating Procedure Governing Contacts and Relationships with Japanese' at the end of 1948 (when admittedly the General's ardour had cooled and he had acknowledged that 45 million Japanese were Buddhists and likely to stay that way) explicitly forbade CIE personnel to attempt to 'transfer the prestige of the Occupation forces' to a single faith by involving themselves in it as anything other than individual worshippers. But there was little that CIE staff in Tokyo could do to communicate their own scruples to the Occupation's army. G.I.s stole supplies to give to charities of their own religious persuasion, Army Chaplains bitterly attacked CIE for its lack of support; and in September 1946 military government officials in Kyoto prefecture requisitioned seventy acres of land belonging to the Kami Kamo Shrine, containing many sacred places and sanctuaries, to provide (for the entertainment of Occupation personnel alone) the largest golf course in the Orient.

9

'Ah-So San:' The Humanising of the Emperor

The edifice of the Japanese military state was built on the Imperial institution. As SCAP soon discovered, wherever they began to dismantle the superstructure, they always came down to the same foundation – the authority of the Emperor. Within weeks it was clear that this too must be refashioned; for the new Japan to rest on precisely the same basis as the old would, it seemed, be both futile and dangerous.

The Americans' problem was that they had no alternative but to work through the Emperor system. At the same time, they had somehow to alter it until it was fit to exist within the new and democratic Japan of which they were the architects. This meant redefining both the spiritual and political role of the Emperor – an intellectual challenge of great complexity which they were only part successful in meeting.

A major cultural difference handicapped them at the outset. Where the American approach tends to be legalistic, the Japanese, in the interests of group harmony, prefer a blurring of the edges. Both Shintoism and the Emperor's role within it to a large extent defied the type of rational analysis the Americans tried to impose. In effect, they were trying to change by written directive something which had its life primarily in instinct and emotion.

The Imperial institution was all-powerful because it combined spiritual and temporal authority, the one used by the militarists to buttress the other. The Emperor was the *locus* of all the powers of the state; any rights the people possessed were his 'gift'. He was also the spiritual leader of Japan by virtue of his lineage. As the senior member of a family tracing direct descent from the sun goddess Amaterasu, Hirohito had (and has) responsibility for presenting the wishes of the nation to the *kami* – in a sense, as the high priest of his tribe. Because of this special status, he joined the ranks of the very few Japanese – among them certain priests, national heroes, and other outstanding servants of the nation –

who might be worshipped as deities in their lifetime. (All men become *kami* after death.)

The dangers of Shinto-inspired Emperor-worship, as the main motivating force of the Imperial Army, had been made abundantly clear to the Americans. Their declared concern for religious freedom made it impossible to attempt to discredit Shinto itself; what they could do was to minimise the special status which the militarist perversion of Shinto had conferred upon the Emperor.

On January 1, 1946, the Emperor issued a rescript to his subjects. In the course of it he declared, according to the official translation, 'The ties between us and our people have always stood upon mutual trust and affection. They do not depend upon mere legends and myths. *They are not predicated on the false conception that the Emperor is divine*' [our italics]. MacArthur lost no time in publicly congratulating the Emperor on what is always described as his 'renunciation of divinity'. But there is much about this episode which is mysterious.

No one seems certain where the rescript originated. With the Emperor? The Imperial Household? MacArthur? CIE? All of them had apparently been weighing the advantages of cleansing the Imperial institution of its more obviously 'irrational' elements. But the drama was brought to the boil by an outsider called Reginald Blyth. Having been given access to the Palace as tutor in English to Crown Prince Akihito, he had then been invited to act as 'go-between' for SCAP, and played the part with panache, gyrating between the Imperial Household and CIE, reporting what each was thinking about the Emperor's future, and, it seems, egging both sides on to commit themselves more positively than either would necessarily have done if left to their own devices. The significant portion of the Imperial Rescript was actually drafted, as a result of Blyth's intercession, by Harold Henderson, head of the Education, Religions and Fine Arts Division of CIE, in his lunch hour. But as for authorship of the *idea*, an 'insider' from the Imperial Household, asked where the rescript originated, clapped his hands in front of him and asked, 'Which hand made the sound?'

More important, it is not at all clear what the rescript really signified. Hirohito did not explicitly deny the Imperial Family's connection with Amaterasu and its special position in the religious life of the nation. What he did deny was that he personally was to be worshipped as a living *kami* (or *Akitsu-kami*, loosely rendered in the rescript as 'divine') – the concept which the militarists had grossly exaggerated in order to fuel ultra-nationalism. In religious terms, the 'renunciation' actually achieved very little. In 1958 the Shinto Publication Committee for the Ninth International Congress for the History of Religions described it as 'merely a change in outward treatment'; the rituals continue, and the Imperial Family continues to play a central role in them on the nation's behalf.

But the political consequences were little short of revolutionary. The Emperor's obvious readiness to bridge the gulf between himself and his people paved the way for some rather more practical levelling by SCAP. From now on roles were to be reversed: the people were to be sovereign and the Emperor was to derive his position from *their* will. Government in the new Japan was to be 'a sacred trust of the people, the authority for which is derived from the people, the powers of which are exercised by representatives of the people and the benefits of which are enjoyed by the people'. And the Emperor was to be no more than a symbol for the people – 'a symbol of the State and of the unity of the people'. Such authority as remained to him depended on their affection, not their obedience.

In political terms he was more cipher than symbol since all his practical power was gone. He no longer commanded the military forces, issued laws or concluded treaties. In December 1948 he did no more than remark privately to Joseph Keenan, America's chief prosecutor at the International Military Tribunal for the Far East, that he would like to foster in Japan a counterpart of the American form of government. When Keenan passed this innocuous observation on to President Truman, Hirohito found himself accused of 'private dealing with foreign powers without reference to the elected representatives of his country', and he was publicly censured in the Diet – an event so far outside his pre-war experience as to be almost laughable. Nine months earlier, a Japanese audience had criticised the first performance of *The Mikado* ever seen in Japan as 'fantastic and unreal': but as a *New York Times* editorial asked, 'Can anything in Gilbert and Sullivan be more remote from reality as they used to know it than the Japan into which Hirohito and his family have been violently projected?'

Before the war the Imperial Family might well have been described as the largest *zaibatsu* of them all, owning more than three million acres and holding major interests in banks, shipping lines, trading companies and many of the financial concerns most deeply implicated in Japan's overseas expansion. Now, suddenly, the Emperor was liable to tax for the first time. The family was stripped of all real estate and property other than 'immediate personal belongings' (Hirohito's glasses were considered to be his own, but his desk was labelled 'property of the State'). Henceforth they were in effect to be on a salary, their expenses and allowances voted by the Diet. The Palace at Akasaka was turned over 'to the Japanese people' for use as a public building – though at first superstitious awe seemed to prevent government departments from pressing their claims. The staff of the Imperial Household was slashed from over 8000 to little more than 1000, the aim being to turn it from a hot-bed of reactionary intrigue at the Emperor's elbow into a small liaison office under the watchful eye of the Prime Minister. The family itself was pruned. Fourteen former members lost their Imperial status; and it was felt that the new compact family of seven no longer needed thirty doctors of their own, thirty cooks, and a stock farm devoted exclusively to supplying the Imperial table.

The Emperor also lost his privileged legal status with abolition of the crime of *lèse majesté*. He had at first a good deal to endure, as his subjects experimented with their new-found freedom to criticise him. One candidate for the Diet (Communist) opened his campaign speech with the question 'MacArthur is the navel. Why? Because it is situated above the *chin'*. *Chin* is a common Japanese word for the penis; it was also the word traditionally used by the Emperor, with a slightly different inflection, in referring to himself – a version of the royal 'we'. So the question, roughly translated, read 'MacArthur tells the Emperor what to do. The Emperor is a prick'.

More important, however, was what the mass of the people, with no political axe to grind, thought of the new Emperor; and since it seemed that in future the Emperor (and, of course, the Imperial Household) was to exist at the people's pleasure, the Household was not prepared to leave their reaction to chance. Instead it embarked on an ambitious long-term exercise in public relations to induce the people to take the Emperor to their collective bosom and guarantee the survival of the institution as part of the fabric of daily life. A stream of endearing facts issued from the Palace: the Emperor limits himself to four cigarettes a day, the same ration as his people; the Emperor only eats rice once a day because of the national shortages; the Emperor refused to give up his golf in the teeth of the militarists' ban on all alien sports. 'His collection of sea shells is . . . one of the most complete in existence. For another thing, it isn't everyone who can take a fan between his toes and fan himself. Not only can the Emperor Hirohito perform this stunt, but he is able to do so whilst swimming. He can also swim in the rain holding an open umbrella in one hand.'

The Princesses Atsuko, Kazuko and Takako were pictured washing dishes in their summer villa; the Emperor's youngest brother Mikasa was revealed as an addict of square dancing; the Empress was caught straightening her husband's tie in the street. But the Emperor was brought most directly face to face with his people in the tours arranged for him by the Household – to schools, farms, hospitals, factories and offices, or simply areas of war damage where he mildly deprecated the destruction and praised the efforts at reconstruction. Once when the Emperor had ventured abroad, whole countrysides were washed and disinfected for him, buildings mended and new roads built. Now 'the ruler of 80 million Japanese walked all through the plant [a fertilizer factory belonging to the Showa Electric Company] which is 80% destroyed by the air raids, following white chalked arrows, climbing up recently repaired stairs, followed by at least 50 company officials and continuously subjected to photographers' flash bulbs exploding within a few feet of his face'.

At first the Emperor's new 'homely' image was a strain for all concerned. His appearance had come as a disappointment to many of his people. When he first went to visit MacArthur at the American Embassy (a startling event in itself – the mountain going to Mahomet), a picture was taken of the two 'rulers of Japan' together. Several newspaper editors instantly attempted to suppress it as disrespectful. MacArthur, confident and relaxed in battle dress with no tie, towered, hands on hips, over a small man with thick pebble glasses in a cut-away morning suit, whose arms were held stiffly by his side. Hirohito had a slight facial tic, and a twitch in one shoulder. He was a shy and self-conscious person who had had no contact whatsoever with the common man: when the Emperor passed, his people had been compelled to bow themselves to the ground, and windows which might give a view of his progress from above were boarded up. Now he was required to make small talk – and soon became known as 'Ah-So San', because he could rarely think of anything else to say. (He was not always helped by his interlocutors. 'One young woman worker in the fertilizer plant was apparently unable to believe that the Emperor was talking to her. Hirohito was forced to take his leave when the woman failed to answer his questions although he was standing less than two feet from her.'

Mark Gayn, deeply critical of the Imperial institution and disposed to dismiss its humanisation as 'an act of political face-lifting,' nevertheless felt sorry for the Emperor himself – 'a tired, pathetic little man compelled to do a job distasteful to him, and trying desperately to control his disobedient voice and face and body'. But the campaign gradually began to take effect, and by January 1947 Hirohito was being hailed by the press, one hopes to his satisfaction, as 'Nippon's First Down-to-the-Earth Sovereign' – 'the man of the year'.

10

Prescription for Peace: Rewriting the Constitution

Underlying American policy in Japan was the belief that democracy and aggressive war are mutually exclusive. The more monolithic a state becomes (the argument runs) and the fewer the hands in which power is concentrated, the easier it is to mobilise it for war. The transfer of sovereignty from the Emperor to his people was just one of a series of fundamental reforms aimed at making it impossible ever again to reconstruct Japan as a totalitarian and potentially aggressive state. These changes were incorporated in what was perhaps the Occupation's most valuable legacy – the new Constitution of Japan.

Under the Constitution, the people elected representatives to the Diet, which was now Japan's sole legislative body. The Diet also had the final say in determining the state's budget, and firm control over the Cabinet, which exercised the executive powers of the state. For the first time in Japan's history, the majority of Cabinet ministers had to be elected and ultimately responsible to the people. The rule of the unelected few was gone forever – with one interesting, if temporary, exception. SCAP itself had the power to bypass both Diet and people by directly instructing the Cabinet to issue a 'Potsdam Ordinance' – in other words, a measure to implement the provisions of the Potsdam Declaration whether the Japanese people liked it or not. This was something of a blunt instrument – hence a new verb which crept briefly into the Japanese language: 'potsudamu', 'to bulldoze' – and the power was used, with great circumspection, only when the order came straight from Washington. Otherwise all policymaking was within the scope of the Diet, and the electorate was kept informed of how its interests were being represented through the press and by daily 15-minute radio discussions of the Diet's proceedings – an extraordinary change from the militarists' secretive and wholly authoritarian style of government.

The architects of the new Constitution also felt it crucial to create an external check on the government machine, and established an independent judiciary. Judges were no longer the servants of a government ministry; on the contrary, they had the power to review all legislation drafted by the government and passed by the Diet, to ensure that it was consistent with the new Constitution. In this they resembled their American counterparts rather than British courts, which do not have the right to question acts of Parliament. (In 1948 SCAP flew members of the Japanese Supreme Court to the United States to observe American justice in action in such centres as Washington and New York, Cheyenne and Laramie, and to collect 'information of value in improving the dignity, efficiency, and independence of the Japanese judiciary as a genuine third branch of government'.)

Local government too was to be freed from central control. Under the militarists, the influence of the Home Ministry had extended right down to village level, spreading its repressive feelers over every family in Japan through a network of spies and agents – the military police, the thought police, and the neighbourhood associations or *tonari gumi*. Now the Japanese people were to be encouraged to take charge of their own lives in every possible way – to elect their own local government officials, to oversee the running of their own local police forces, free of central interference except in a national emergency.

The Constitution incorporated a 'bill of rights' which was progressive by the standards of most western democracies and truly revolutionary in Japan (though in some fields the reforms certainly rested on a basis of earlier Japanese efforts). The freedoms already heralded in the Civil Liberties Directive – speech, thought, religion, assembly and the press – were entrenched for all time by the Constitution, and discrimination on the grounds of race, nationality, creed or political opinion was outlawed. Universal adult suffrage was introduced, and primogeniture abolished. Most striking perhaps were the changes in the status of Japanese women; not only were they given the vote, they were given the right to choose their own husbands and to sue rather than be sued for divorce, plus equal inheritance, property and parental rights.

Giving people more control of their own destinies was not only a precondition of democracy, it was also seen as a giant step towards demilitarisation. (In particular, the enfranchisement of women was expected to have a softening effect upon foreign policy.) This shows great faith in human nature: but the new Constitution also included what was intended to be the ultimate legal safeguard against Japanese militarism – the famous Article 9, in which the Japanese nation, with America breathing stertorously down its neck, declared its formal intention of laying down its arms for all time.

'Aspiring sincerely to an international peace based on justice and order, the Japanese people forever renounce war as a sovereign right of the nation and the threat or use of force as means of settling international disputes.

In order to accomplish the aim of the preceding paragraph, land, sea, and air forces, as well as other war potential, will never be maintained. The right of belligerency of the state will not be recognized.' It was an extraordinary promise to make and one it was to prove impossible to keep.

After Article 9, the feature of the new Constitution which has been most hotly debated in Japan is the question of its origin. Was it in any sense home-grown, as it purported to be? When it was first submitted to the Diet, MacArthur claimed, 'The Government Draft now before the Diet is a Japanese document and it is for the people of Japan . . . to determine its form and content'. Or was it, as its critics have always insisted, an alien invention imposed arbitrarily and even illegally on a defeated nation by temporary rulers convinced that what was good for America was good for the world?

It might be thought that to rewrite the Constitution would have been considered no more high-handed than any of the other changes made by SCAP under cover of the polite fiction that the Japanese government was setting its own house in order. In fact it was more than ordinarily important that constitutional reform be presented as a Japanese initiative. Many Americans involved in the Occupation, both in Washington and Tokyo, suspected that in carrying out reforms over and above those mentioned in the terms of Japan's surrender, America was on shaky ground, morally and legally*. Political philosophers have long debated whether the victor in a war has the right to alter the political structure of the loser – and most have concluded that, other than in wholly exceptional circumstances, he does not. (Michael Walzer, for instance: 'The outer limit of what can legitimately be sought in war . . . is the conquest and political reconstruction of the enemy state, and only against an enemy like Nazism can it possibly be right to reach that far. . . . The right does not arise in every war; it did not arise, I think, in the war against Japan'.)

There was much in international law, and in the codes of behaviour to which most Western nations publicly subscribed, to suggest that in changing the Japanese constitution the Americans would be assuming wider powers than were usually conceded to an occupying force. The Hague Convention of 1928 precludes tampering with the political machinery of an occupied country.

---

* Alfred Hussey, for instance, expressed concern as to whether the Occupation as a whole had been *ultra vires*. George Blakeslee too felt Japan had the right to protest any action taken outside the terms of surrender.

The Atlantic Charter of 1941 proclaimed America's commitment to the right of all peoples freely to determine their own form of government. The international law of belligerent occupation declares that the sovereignty of an occupied country is only temporarily suspended and the occupying power should not seek to maintain its influence in perpetuity.

It might seem that because Japan had surrendered unconditionally, its sovereignty was no longer protected by laws and agreements such as these – that America had the right to do with Japan precisely what she chose. But the Japanese hotly denied (and continue to deny) that their surrender had in fact been unconditional. What was the Potsdam Declaration, they argued, if not a statement of the conditions of surrender? What had the crucial negotiations immediately preceding Japan's acceptance of the Potsdam Declaration been about if not the conditions on which Japan was prepared to surrender? America's subsequent bold assertion in the United States Initial Post-Surrender Policy that surrender had been unconditional was no more than a 'Stalin – New Dealer Trick' – the reference being to Stalin's suggestion that the Allies should agree to milder (ie. conditional) terms in order to achieve the surrender, 'but once we get into Japan to give them the works'. There were many Americans who felt the Japanese had a point.

In general moral and legal terms, therefore, if America was to preserve its image as a stern but fair victor, and if the Japanese were to be persuaded to accept the new constitution, it had to be presented as Japanese-originated. There was, too, a specific practical reason – a question of immediate tactics in America's relations with her Allies – for concealing the fact that the new constitution was to all intents and purposes an American document. Constitutional reform was one of the few areas in which America was specifically required, under the Moscow Agreement of December 1945, to consult the Far Eastern Commission before taking action. MacArthur saw FEC involvement (which entailed Russian involvement) as a real threat to the country's freedom. To forestall Soviet interference, he had to produce a constitution for Japan before the first meeting of the FEC; but to avoid repercussions, he had to pretend that he had done nothing of the sort – that the reform was in fact the outcome of the Japanese government's own efforts. The importance of maintaining this public façade is suggested by the fact that years later Alfred Hussey, one of the Government Section officials most closely involved in the reform, was advised by the CIA against writing about the Occupation, and in particular about the way in which the Constitution had been brought into being. Their reason was presumably that at that stage of the Cold War – it was then 1956 – disclosure of America's methods could only benefit the Soviets.

Hussey was himself sensitive on the subject. In 1958, two years after the Japanese government had set up a special commission to investigate the origins of the Constitution, the members of the commission asked to interview the principal American officials, Hussey among them. He promptly wrote to several of the others suggesting that they align their accounts, omitting certain elements of the story and stressing that the draft constitution had been freely accepted by the Japanese people.

It had indeed been examined, debated and finally passed by the Cabinet, the Privy Council and the Diet, and some amendments, not all insignificant, had been permitted by SCAP*. But on the day the Constitution was finally put into effect, Shimizu Cho, the Emperor's constitutional advisor and the chairman of the Privy Council which had approved the draft, drowned himself. He wanted, it was said, to defend the national polity of Japan; but only in the spirit world would he be free to fight. Over the events which led up to the submission of the new Constitution 'to the people', the Japanese had little or no control.

MacArthur's original intention had undoubtedly been that the Japanese should carry out their own reform. Certainly in the period immediately after the surrender various different Japanese groups were studying the possibilities of constitutional change, in anticipation of American demands. The Foreign Ministry, unprompted, had produced two separate documents by the first week in October 1945. Small unofficial groups of lawyers and academics were exploring the likely implications for the Constitution of the Potsdam Declaration. And the Emperor himself had expressed interest in the subject to his advisors, among them Prince Konoye, Deputy Prime Minister in the first Occupation Cabinet.

This probably explains why Konoye reacted with such alacrity to what he took to be an invitation from MacArthur to review the Constitution, and set up a committee for that purpose in mid-October. He was, however, a far from ideal figurehead for reform – much too deeply implicated in Japan's military aggression for the American public's taste, having been Prime Minister three times between 1937 and 1941. It was not long before SCAP disassociated itself from his efforts – prudently, as it turned out, since six weeks later he was ordered to present himself at Sugamo Prison for incarceration as a suspected war criminal.

* They included the substitution of two Diet chambers for one, the deletion of a provision for the nationalisation of land ownership, and the deletion of the Diet's right to review Supreme Court decisions.

In the interim a more respectable body had been appointed to investigate the Constitution under the leadership of Minister of State Joji Matsumoto. Untainted by militarism, positively liberal by pre-war standards, his committee nevertheless gave no indication of being any more willing than Konoye's to make fundamental changes to the Meiji Constitution of 1889. This, Matsumoto held, had been distorted and needed merely to be restored to its original form, not replaced; it certainly would be neither necessary nor desirable to tamper drastically with the powers of the Emperor, who was to remain the unchallenged head of state, 'supreme and inviolable'.

Hopes that the Japanese were going to reform themselves along the right lines were fading fast – and in the meantime MacArthur was told of forthcoming instructions from Washington which went far beyond anything Matsumoto's committee was ever likely to propose. The American government's directive, SWNCC 228 (which was notified to MacArthur on December 13, 1945, officially received by him on January 9, 1946) was specific enough to clear him of personal responsibility for devising and foisting fundamental structural change on Japan. Well before Japan was defeated, the planners had taken some measure of constitutional reform almost for granted, and since the beginning of the Occupation it had continued to be discussed in depth within the State Department. (The Department's representative in Tokyo, George Atcheson, had conferred frequently with Konoye, as well as keeping Washington informed of unofficial Japanese proposals for change.) Now MacArthur was formally advised of Washington's wishes. He could, of course, have enlightened Matsumoto's committee as to what it was expected to achieve*. But this might have drawn attention to the existence of a unilateral American directive. So instead he chose to pursue his own 'informal' researches in parallel, actively blocking contact between SCAP and Matsumoto.

On February 1, 1946, the press carried reports of the Matsumoto Committee's provisional conclusions, which were, as expected, inadequate. Later that day General Whitney, head of Government Section, prepared for MacArthur a memorandum on the extent of his authority to proceed with constitutional reform. He made it quite clear that MacArthur must act fast if he wished to implement the provisions of SWNCC 228 without Allied interference. 'Your authority to make policy decisions on constitutional reform continues substantially unimpaired until the FEC promulgates its own policy decisions on this subject' – but the first meeting of the FEC was only three weeks away.

---

* He had been specifically advised by Atcheson to convey the contents of SWNCC 228 to the Japanese as guidelines.

Whitney also produced a fine piece of sophistry to explain that once the FEC was fully operative, it would have no come-back against any constitutional reforms that had already been enacted *provided* these could be passed off as originating with the Japanese. The FEC would be within its rights to object (through its Tokyo arm, the Allied Council for Japan) to MacArthur himself issuing orders on constitutional reform. But 'it is my opinion that the word "order" in the Charter of the Allied Council is used in the sense of compulsion and would not embrace a mere approval by you of constitutional reform measures submitted to you by the Japanese government'.

On February 3, 1946, MacArthur ordered Government Section to prepare its own draft constitution as quickly as possible. For one frenetic week, behind closed doors, a steering committee consisting of Charles Kades, Alfred Hussey and another Government Section officer, Milo Rowell, spurred on and coordinated the efforts of working groups in nine different subject areas. SWNCC 228 provided their basic frame of reference; but MacArthur had also given Whitney a list of three specific points he personally wished to see included. The Emperor was to remain the head of state but responsible to the people, and all vestiges of the feudal system, including the peerage, were to be obliterated – so far his instructions were in line with Washington's. And war as a sovereign right of the nation was to be abolished: this, the first appearance in writing of what was to become Article Nine, was not even hinted at in SWNCC 228.

Otherwise the drafters were free to use their discretion in their choice of material. None was an expert in constitutional law and each had his (or her) individual sources of inspiration. Charles Kades, trained as an attorney, kept remembering snatches of Lincoln's *Constitutional History of New York*. One of the officers working on the Emperor's altered position within the state and his relationship to the people had a keen interest in the French Revolution, and drew on his memories of the writings on the Abbé Sièyes on the concept of *volonté nationale*. Another junior officer produced from the library of Tokyo University a compendium of the pre-war constitutions of Europe; from this came fragments of the fundamental laws of Yugoslavia, Czechoslovakia and Estonia.

On February 13, 1946, with time growing short, Whitney set out with Kades, Hussey and Rowell to secure the Cabinet's agreement to the SCAP draft. So extraordinary were the methods he used that immediately after the meeting his three lieutenants drew up a memorandum to preserve them for posterity. Signed by all three jointly, this remarkable 'Record of Events' contains far more descriptive detail than the average official document, all of it revealing and some of it compromising.

At 10 a.m. the Americans arrived at the house of Shigeru Yoshida, then Foreign Minister, where they found Yoshida, Matsumoto, Jiro Shirasu (Yoshida's secretary) and Mr. Hasegawa of the Foreign Ministry sitting round a table littered with papers relating to the Matsumoto draft. 'General Whitney sat with his back to the sun, affording best light on the countenances of the Japanese present who sat opposite him.' He immediately 'throttled' discussion of the Matsumoto draft by declaring that it was 'wholly unacceptable to the Supreme Commander as a document of freedom and democracy', and instead handed over fifteen copies of the SCAP draft for their consideration. 'At 10.10 o'clock General Whitney and the undersigned left the porch and went out into the sunshine of the garden as an American plane passed over the house. After about fifteen minutes Mr. Shirasu joined us, whereupon General Whitney quietly observed to him: "We are out here enjoying the warmth of atomic energy"' – an unbelievably crude reminder of America's ultimate sanction, but one which Whitney himself regarded as a choice 'psychological shaft'.

Back in the house, at 10.50, Whitney explained to the Japanese representatives the main principles of the SCAP draft and the necessity of adopting them forthwith as their own. He reinforced his arguments with two unmistakable threats. If the Cabinet chose to reject the new Constitution, they would increase the chances of the Emperor being tried as a war criminal. And, with the first postwar election approaching, SCAP would put its proposals directly to the electorate, which would certainly ruin the present government. 'The Supreme Commander has been unyielding in his defence of your Emperor against increasing pressure from the outside to render him subject to war criminal investigation . . . but, gentlemen, the Supreme Commander is not omnipotent. He feels, however, that acceptance of the provisions of this new Constitution would render the Emperor practically unassailable. He feels that it would bring much closer the day of your freedom from control by the Allied Powers. . . . He is determined . . . that the principles [contained in the draft] shall be laid before the people – rather by you – but if not, by himself. . . . General MacArthur feels that this is the last opportunity for the conservative group considered by many to be reactionary, to remain in power; that this can only be done by a sharp swing to the left. . . . I cannot emphasise too strongly that the acceptance of the draft Constitution is your only hope of survival.'*

* In a meeting within Government Section some time between 4.2.46 and 6.2.46, Whitney claimed that MacArthur had empowered him to use both the threat of force and force itself.

The effect of these tactics on Yoshida and his colleagues was, not surprisingly, stunning. 'The face of the Foreign Minister was dark and grim and his expression did not change during the balance of the conference while General Whitney talked . . . [He] gazed intently at General Whitney with an occasional side glance that swung until it would reach the eyes of one of the undersigned, when it would immediately shift back', and all the while he rubbed the palms of his hands slowly back and forth along his trousers. 'The face of the interpreter [Shirasu] remained a complete blank during the entire proceedings. However, it was observed that he was having physical difficulty in speaking and constantly wet his lips. . . . As General Whitney rose to depart he asked Mr. Shirasu for his hat and gloves. Mr. Shirasu, who is normally a very calm and debonair person, was so flustered that he first started for an ante-room near the entrance of the house and then, remembering he had placed our caps and gloves in the library adjacent to the sun porch, rushed back again, procured General Whitney's cap and gloves and showed visible indication of extreme nervousness as he handed them to General Whitney.'

It seems more than likely that the men who went to the trouble of recording these details, besides being aware of the drama of the occasion, were ashamed – not of the Constitution itself, in which they had implicit faith, but of the methods employed to make it law. In particular it was the threats against the Emperor – against the man, not just the institution – which Hussey in 1958 still wanted Kades and Rowell to conceal from the Japanese Commission on the Constitution. (As he pointed out, 'It is extremely unlikely that the existence of the Memorandum of Events prepared later that day by the three of us who accompanied General Whitney is known to the Japanese or, for that matter, to more than a dozen Americans'.)

The new Constitution contained much that has been of great and lasting value to Japan. The drafters were indeed, as they felt themselves to be, working hard and unselfishly in the best interests of the Japanese people. As a later Japanese Prime Minister, Tetsu Katayama, observed, although it *was* imposed by SCAP, it was imposed on reactionaries, and welcomed by those who truly believed in the new democracy it embodied. But not everyone accepts that the end justifies the means: and to that extent the origin of Japan's Constitution is its principal weakness. For those who object to specific constitutional provisions – Article Nine, for instance – the fact that it can be accused of being an alien imposition provides an excuse to call for revision of the Constitution as a whole, and thus places in jeopardy the whole body of Occupation reform.

PART THREE

JAPAN ON TRIAL

11

Savage Apes

Japanese officer's diary entry for March 29, 1943: 'This will be something to remember all my life. If ever I get back alive it will make a good story to tell. . . . Our commander . . . told us personally that, in accordance with the compassionate sentiments of *bushido*, he was going to kill the prisoner himself with his favourite sword. So we gathered to observe this.' The prisoner, a pilot of the Australian RAF, was brought out at dusk, his head shaved, and was made to kneel in front of a bomb crater by Japanese soldiers with fixed bayonets. 'He remains calm. He even stretches out his neck and is very brave. When I put myself in the prisoner's place and think that in one more minute it will be goodbye to this world, although the daily bombings have filled me with hate, ordinary human feelings make me pity him. The commander has drawn his favourite sword. It is the famous *Osamune* sword which he showed us at the observation post. It glitters in the light and sends a cold shiver down my spine. He taps the prisoner's neck lightly with the back of the blade.' At this point the Australian gestured to the officer to do the job with one cut – a bravely calculated affront to the officer's dignity in front of his men, since by *samurai* tradition to fail to decapitate with a single stroke is the sign of a poor sword or a poor swordsman. Having readied his sword, the officer 'then raises it above his head with both arms and brings it down with a sweep. . . . All is over. The head is dead white, like a doll. The savageness I felt only a little while ago is gone, and now I feel nothing but the true compassion of the *bushido*. A senior corporal laughs loudly. . . . Then a superior seaman of the medical unit takes the chief medical officer's sword and, intent on paying off old scores, turns the headless body over on its back and cuts the abdomen open with one clean stroke'.

Controlled ritual executions of this type were at one end of the scale of Japanese atrocities during the Greater East Asian War, which at the other end descended into bestiality. Captured Allied soldiers were used as bayonet dummies, live targets for rifle drill, sword and karate practice. Prisoners-of-war were starved, tortured, denied medical care and worked to death in countless Japanese prison camps; twenty-seven per cent of all prisoners in Japanese hands died. Throughout the Japanese Empire, from New Guinea in the south to Manchuria in the north, civilians were beaten, raped, their possessions looted, and countless thousands indiscriminately massacred. Women were forced into prostitution organised by the Imperial Japanese Army, which also conducted a huge narcotics operation to help fund its war effort. At sea, struggling survivors of torpedoed warships, merchantmen, and submarines were machine-gunned. Prisoners of the Imperial Japanese Navy were thrown to the sharks, or taken to the Navy's secret interrogation centre at Ofumi and tortured to death. Allied nationals were used in scientific and medical experiments – to develop poison gases and bacteriological weapons; to evolve techniques of surgery without anaesthetic; to discover cheap substitutes for drugs the Japanese no longer possessed – camphor, for example, was injected as a trial substitute for penicillin.

Though the Rape of Nanking and Japan's other iniquities in China during the 1930s were well known, full details of atrocities against Allied personnel were slow to emerge. The Red Cross, for example, was denied access to many prisoner-of-war camps, and the Japanese refused to supply any information on their prisoners to the Allied governments. After the surrender, many camps were discovered in South East Asia and Japan which had previously not been known to exist, and judging by the number of prisoners still unaccounted for, several other camps may have existed which were never found.

In addition, such information as the Roosevelt and Truman administrations possessed, they kept from the American public. This was partly from a genuine fear of reprisals. After the furious calls for vengeance for the murders of three of the fliers captured after the Doolittle Raid on Tokyo in March 1942, the Japanese had promised that in future *all* captured airmen were now assured of 'a one-way ticket to hell'. And there was also a tendency to keep the American public's attention focused on German atrocities, reflecting the grand strategy of World War II – to defeat Germany first.

Nevertheless, occasional disclosures were seen as a tonic to the war effort. Record sales of War Bonds followed both the news of the Doolittle murders and the official report on the Bataan Death March – the forced march in April 1942 of 65,000 American and Filipino prisoners across Luzon in tropical heat. During the week-long trek without water, food, rest or medical attention, the column was decimated, the death total soaring to over 8,000 as Japanese soldiers bayoneted and shot stragglers, and buried alive those too weak to continue; a further 28,000 survivors of the March died in prison camps during the next seven weeks.

The news was released in America in January 1944, and brought American hatred of the Japanese to a new peak. Throughout the year both Senate and Congress endorsed speeches calling for revenge on the perpetrators of atrocities such as these. In opinion polls some eighty-eight per cent of Americans demanded that their commanders be punished as well; and President Roosevelt warned neutral countries against giving asylum to 'Tojo and his gang', should they try to go to ground.

Tojo and 'his gang', the principal conspirators in Japan's military aggression, were eventually to be brought before a special Nuremberg-style tribunal convened by MacArthur in Tokyo. This was an international court made up of justices from eleven Allied nations and was known as the International Military Tribunal for the Far East (IMTFE). The rest, from generals and admirals down to private soldiers – the 'minor' war criminals who were not seen as part of the warmongering conspiracy – were tried in the capitals of Asia by military tribunals convened by each Ally under its own military laws. Each Allied nation followed its own war crimes policy within either its own sovereign territory or colony, or its own command area. The French, for example, held trials in Saigon; the British in Kuala Lumpur, Singapore and Hong Kong; and courts were also established by Australia, Canada, China, Holland, India, the Philippines, New Zealand and the United States. (Russia, only in the war with Japan for a week, also held atrocities trials, suitably timed for maximum propaganda effect.)

The Japanese apparently committed atrocities wherever they set foot. Hundreds of thousands of non-combatants (prisoners-of-war or civilians) were maltreated or died in Japanese hands in contravention of the rules of war. During the war a centre for collating alleged war crimes had been set up in Chungking by the United Nations War Crimes Commission; and by the end of the war, extensive lists of defendants were available with accompanying evidence, mostly in the form of sworn testimony. Nevertheless, only 5,700 Japanese were ever brought to trial. (Of these 4,405 were convicted and 984 sentenced to death.) Quite clearly, a large number of war criminals, major and minor, for a variety of reasons escaped trial.

It was not always easy to track down the wanted men. Even in Portuguese Timor, where Allied nationals had been on the scene, investigators found it hard to penetrate to the truth – partly because they suspected these very expatriates, now eager to wine and dine the conquerors, of complicity in Japanese crimes.

Arresting the criminals as their troopships docked in Japan *en route* for demobilisation, should have been far simpler. But the British Admiralty complained to the Foreign Office: 'In a number of cases our efforts to bring perpetrators of crimes against British ships to book are being frustrated, first by the unsatisfactory behaviour of the Second Demobilisation Bureau (until recently the Navy Ministry) which fails to carry out certain of SCAP's directives, and secondly by the listlessness of the U.S. authorities in dealing with these evasions. The reason for the evasions would seem to be that the officers of the Bureau are reluctant to take action on anyone who could be induced to give away evidence unfavourable to themselves. This apparently leads to their conniving in the disappearance of the wanted men, who they allow to go underground and then report that there is no trace of them.'

In other cases, the Allies themselves gave immunity to known war criminals. Informants were one such group – those ready to betray fellow war criminals or Japan's military secrets. It was by giving immunity to men who had experimented with the lives of Allied nationals that the United States acquired Japanese research into bacteriological warfare. The promise of immunity – or conversely the threat of arrest – was also used to secure cooperation with SCAP reforms; the Emperor himself may well have benefited from a deal of this kind.

But the limited number of war crimes trials was due principally to the Allied decision to call a halt, somewhat arbitrarily and artificially, in 1949. In the three years during which war crimes trials were held, the pendulum had swung from the craving for retribution to compassion born of political expediency. Forty years on, in the calm of hindsight, it may seem axiomatic that all war criminals should have been apprehended and tried. But the late 1940s was a period of rapid and confusing change, its moral climate far more volatile and ambiguous. This is graphically illustrated by the British decision not to prosecute a Japanese naval officer already in custody, who had unquestionably been responsible for the machine-gunning of 600 British prisoners-of-war trying to stay afloat after the sinking of their transport ship. Speaking in the House of Commons on October 28, 1948, Winston Churchill expressed the prevailing sentiment: 'Revenge is, of all satisfactions, the most costly and long drawn out; retributive persecution is, of all policies, the most pernicious. Our policy . . . should henceforth be to draw the sponge across the crimes and horrors of the past – hard as that may be – and look, for the sake of all our salvation, towards the future'.

In Japan, 'minor' war trials in respect of individual atrocities committed against Allied personnel were held at Yokohama under the aegis of the U.S. Eighth Army. Where the victims were not all American, the relevant nation was invited by the U.S. Judge Advocate General to join in the prosecution. Over 1000 suspects were tried at Yokohama; 200 were acquitted, while 124 were sentenced to hang and 62 to life imprisonment. The shortest trial – that of prison guard Matsuo Okubo for brutalising inmates at his camp – lasted about four hours, the longest more than ten months. This was the Kyushu University case in which 22 defendants, including one woman, were found guilty of performing experimental operations on eight American fliers at the University clinic. Four of the offenders, one a Lieutenant General, were sentenced to hang. The death penalty was also imposed at Yokohama on three generals and six officers of the Western Army who beheaded some seventeen Allied airmen in the tense hours after the Emperor broadcast his surrender rescript. The first of the Yokohama condemned was hanged on March 5, 1946 – almost six weeks before the International Military Tribunal for the Far East was convened in Tokyo.

*　　*　　*

It was, of course, inconceivable that war crimes trials should not have been held in Japan. But the fact remains that such trials did not form an integral part of the original Occupation strategy. Throughout the war there had been a permanent dichotomy between the public's thirst for retribution and the planners' enthusiasm for reform. As far as the Yokohama trials were concerned, there was no inconsistency; the trial machinery was simply an extension of existing military legal procedure, and the trials conducted there (though they were occasionally accused of miscarriages of justice) did not disturb the natural progress of the Occupation reforms. SCAP and the courts at Yokohama could and did co-exist without undue friction.

At first the IMTFE in Tokyo too seemed unlikely to impede the progress of the Occupation. Indeed, it might have had positive value for the reformers as a model of democratic justice in action, a monument to the futility of militarism, a goad for arousing a sense of national war guilt which would guide the future course of Japan towards peace. But promise became nightmare as the Tokyo trial turned into a bloated Frankenstein's monster that lived and grew for almost two and a half years, threatening the Occupation with its presence, capable even now of souring its memory.

The problem was not that the Japanese war leaders were put on trial, but the basis on which they were tried. Had Tojo and his companions been tried at Yokohama, as other senior military officers were, for crimes within the U.S. military tribunal's jurisdiction, scarcely a ripple would have disturbed the surface of Japan. The difficulties all stemmed from the fact that the State Department felt it necessary to stage a second Nuremberg Tribunal in the Far East.

The Nuremberg Tribunal took the particular form it did because the Allies wanted more than a simple show trial, at which the Nazi leaders would pay publicly for their crimes. They wanted besides, with a single grandiloquent gesture, to outlaw aggressive war. From one angle, Nuremberg can be seen as a judicial prop to the United Nations; both were products of a concept of universal peace and brotherhood which had itself blossomed in the warmth of an extraordinary surge of post-war idealism, a sense that the forces of Evil had at last been conclusively defeated. Liberals of many countries shared the fervour, but the real dynamo was America – the richest and most powerful nation in the world, at the peak of her material wealth and moral righteousness. In the heady atmosphere of victory there seemed nothing to stop the Americans from taking the individuals who had led the enemy nations to wage aggressive war on the world, putting them on trial, and punishing them for this, the most heinous of all crimes.

But the liberal crusade, spearheaded by Henry Stimson, the veteran U.S. Secretary of War, had, it emerged, more emotional weight than legal authority. The conventional legal wisdom of the 1940s regarded international law as stemming from something more tangible than the opinion of right-thinking Americans. International law was not simply a matter of what 'ought' to be, but what had actually been established by agreement, practice or custom. It was precisely this solid basis of established law which was lacking in both the Nuremberg Tribunal and its oriental clone, the IMTFE.

In vain American liberals pointed to the 1919 Covenant of the League of Nations, to treaties like the 1928 Kellogg-Briand Pact under which sixty-five countries had renounced war as an instrument of national policy, in order to argue, in the legal purists' own terms, that the Nuremberg Tribunal had the support of international law. Their arguments were never wholly convincing, even to themselves, and were never wholly accepted. From the start there was widespread doubt that 'aggressive war' was actually a crime at international law. Consequently, the most important of the prosecution charges, the *raison d'être* for both the Nuremberg and Tokyo trials, was gravely flawed from the outset.

Stimson and the others were not unaware of the legal deficiencies of their case. But in their eyes the end justified the means. The principles of 'Stimsonianism' demanded that not just individual warmongers but war itself be condemned. 'An orderly world requires a single durable structure of world security, which must everywhere be protected against aggression: if aggression were permitted to go unpunished in one place, this infection would lead to a general destruction of the system of world order.' And if the 'punishment of aggression' required a stretching of the existing law, then so be it.

But not only was aggressive war not seen as a crime at law before Pearl Harbor, neither was it regarded as possible to attribute responsibility for acts of war to specific individuals. Up until Nuremberg, war was seen as an 'act of state'. Nevertheless, in their Charters both the Nuremberg and Tokyo tribunals were empowered to try 'Crimes against Peace' – the doubly flawed concept of individual responsibility for aggressive war. And thus the defence lawyers at both trials were able to score heavily with their arguments that these charges were *ex post facto*, based on law made after the acts had been committed. This kind of argument may have a surreal ring to it when the crime in question is World War II, but it served to sow doubts in the minds of both the German and the Japanese publics, creating an indelible image of the trials as 'victors' justice'. These charges, it was claimed, were simply self-serving inventions of the victorious Allies – and Axis cynicism became all the more pronounced when the United Nations itself later rejected the Nuremberg formula.

That body-blow was, however, in the future. In the autumn of 1945, the problem facing the State Department was simply that of establishing what to do with the major Japanese war criminals. There is an irresistible correlation to be made between the decision to retain the existing Japanese government structure, and the emergence of the IMTFE. The State Department's press analysts reported widespread criticism of U.S. policy toward Japan as 'too soft', and likely to maintain, even increase the power of a reactionary élite. In August 1945, 67% of Americans wanted the Japanese in general, and war criminals in particular, treated with extreme harshness: a show trial of 'Tojo and his gang' would seem to have been the obvious answer.

The decision to follow the Nuremberg precedent appears to have been made by SWNCC after Dean Acheson had discussed the question with the principal architect of the Charter of the Nuremberg Tribunal, Associate Supreme Court Justice Robert Jackson. Acheson pronounced, 'It is most important that the procedure and principles of the tribunal, as well as the definition of crimes, should harmonise with those adopted for the prosecutions in Germany.' Conceivably the planners were simply aiming at consistency in their crusade to outlaw aggressive war. But it is equally tempting to suppose that they were attempting to suppress doubts about the legitimacy of the charges used at Nuremberg by the simple expedient of repeating them. The argument seems to have been that, *ex post facto* or not, if the charges were upheld by a second international court, they must be valid.

The implication is irresistible: the IMTFE was brought into being for reasons other than the Japanese situation itself. The OSS had raised several fundamental objections against this kind of major international trial. Nevertheless, there is little evidence that in the days between the raising of the 'Nuremberg in Tokyo' proposal and its acceptance, anyone in Washington actually worked through the ramifications.

No one assembled all the elements to see if they would cohere into a working whole, no one made any systematic effort to answer the basic questions. What was the precise period of history which the trial would have to investigate? Would the charges that seemed to suit the Nazis so well really suit the proponents of Japanese militarism, in so many ways a phenomenon without parallel? Did the evidence actually exist, in truth as opposed to wartime propaganda, to substantiate the kind of charges the Allies had in mind? Could a tribunal composed of at least ten nations* operate efficiently as a unit and serve the ends of justice? – and here the planners might have considered the plethora of different languages, legal backgrounds and court prosecutors likely to be involved, and the difficulty of the Japanese language itself with the inevitable burden of translation. Would a high-profile prosecution based on what was essentially Anglo-American law serve any purpose in the context of the unique society of Japan? And finally, given the need to insulate the Emperor from criticism at least until the Occupation was a going concern, how was it proposed that the Tribunal pick its way round the central figure in the saga of Japanese militarism?

These blisters took time to rise. In the very short term, the IMTFE held promise of usefulness in the campaign for psychological demilitarisation. Besides, no one had an opportunity to object; by the time the Occupation was securely under way, SCAP found itself confronted with a *fait accompli*.

---

* The ten nations were the signatories to the Instrument of Surrender, which included South Africa. In the event, South Africa dropped out of any involvement in the Occupation.

12

A Creature of International Law

The British made jokes about Joseph Berry Keenan, President Truman's choice as Chief of Counsel to head the prosecution of the major Japanese war criminals. According to the British Associate Prosecutor, the man who should have been the dynamo of the prosecution was 'unable to distinguish black from white unless blended in the same bottle', an aphorism aimed both at moral and alcoholic weaknesses. A Foreign Office representative in Tokyo suggested they try to have him investigated by the Congressional Committee on Un-American Activities, 'though by my experience of American lawyers, they would find nothing un-American about his behaviour'.

In his day Keenan had been a ferocious and effective force in the American criminal courts. He had successfully prosecuted Machine Gun Kelly and other gangsters and, as a member of a Senate Committee in the early 1930s, had drafted tough Federal legislation against kidnappers and racketeers. After his success as Assistant Attorney General, Criminal Division, he had gravitated into national politics where he had performed personal service for President Roosevelt in securing Congressional finance for Presidential schemes.

In 1945, as far as the American public was concerned, Keenan was still good box office. His gang-busting persona fitted the hoodlum image of the Japanese militarists projected by Allied propagandists. But in all other respects – professionally, physically, intellectually – he was unsuited to head an international prosecution, particularly one in a remote Asian country. By 1945 he was nearing retirement, suffering from high blood pressure, and his alcoholism was out of control. 'Keenan often has to be put to bed before dinner', ran the reports, and after less than six months in Tokyo he was carted back to the States to dry out.

Assigning him to the Tokyo trial may have seemed a convenient way for Truman to remove an embarrassment from Washington.

Certainly it appears that Keenan was never intended to be anything other than a figurehead. Seconded to him were two lawyers of extremely high calibre – John Fihelly, chief of the Criminal Division, U.S. Attorney General's Department, and regarded as the best trial lawyer in the U.S. Government service; and John Darsey, who had been a personal representative of the U.S. Attorney General at Nuremberg. It was Darsey who suggested to Keenan that Fihelly was the right attorney to mould the prosecution into a 'cohesive machine', a suggestion 'made with the thought that you will not – with all of the overall problems which you are burdened with – be in a position to concern yourself with the mechanics of the trial'.

But they all underestimated Keenan. Apart from his recuperative visits Stateside, he stuck it out from start to finish, despite protests from his staff to MacArthur to dismiss him. He still had ability – a colleague remembers him as a 'genius' in his way; and though he was barely concerned with the 'mechanics of the trial' – he had, for example, neither drafted the indictment nor had he read it before it was approved, and he was convinced that the trial period commenced in 1931 instead of 1928 – he nevertheless dominated the prosecution. He provided the rhetoric, pushed his stocky figure into the limelight at every opportunity and had force of personality enough to treat the senior British prosecutor, King's Counsel and Bencher of Gray's Inn, as an 'office boy'.

Despite his obvious failings, Keenan does also seem to have been sincere about his mission. He shared the Stimsonian vision of a peaceful world order and from the beginning he urged upon his staff the righteousness of their cause. 'What would it mean to civilisation today if we were to adopt what Mr. Justice Jackson properly called "sterile legalisms" as a defence to Hitlers and Mussolinis and Tojos and the like, deliberately engaging in wholesale murder and destruction, not alone today upon soldiers under arms but on infants and aged people, spreading death and ruin and destruction in churches and hospitals and orphan asylums . . . If these war criminals were not punished, and by that I mean the individuals who caused these acts, after all we have been through it would be an open invitation to mankind to begin it all over again and again.'

Keenan arrived in Tokyo on December 6, 1945 with a staff of 39 attorneys, stenographers and clerks. Next day he had a long meeting with MacArthur (at which MacArthur's Chief of Staff counselled him against bringing *ex post facto* proceedings) and on December 8 a new SCAP section – the International Prosecution Section – was created, with Keenan at its head. Established within the official framework of SCAP GHQ, the IPS started work, and on December 9 John Darsey issued a series of memoranda to the attorneys getting the prosecution under way.

One of the first tasks was to draft the Charter and Rules of Procedure of the International Military Tribunal for the Far East. It is perhaps surprising that the prosecution should have been involved in the creation of the court which it was to serve and in particular in the defining of the crimes it was empowered to try, but this was more a product of expediency than of deliberate injustice. When the Tribunal was eventually brought into existence it was not part of the International Prosecution Section, nor was it part of SCAP. It was, like the Nuremberg Tribunal, a creature of international law, an anomalous body brought into existence for a defined purpose, and with defined powers by the authority vested in the Supreme Commander.

Six attorneys were entrusted with the job of drawing up the Charter, and by December 20 they had produced a draft. It is perhaps an indication of how the IPS itself viewed its task that the draft Charter gave the Tribunal only the power to try 'Crimes against Peace'. In the minds of these IPS attorneys, the Tokyo trial was a one-issue case: did Japan commit acts of aggressive war against the Allies? However, this limited jurisdiction did not suit Keenan, nor the British, nor the State Department. They all wanted the Tribunal to be empowered to try charges of maltreatment of Allied civilians and prisoners-of-war. As the British put it: 'Otherwise public opinion might be dissatisfied; more especially as many people think that a Crime against Peace would scarcely justify a sentence of death'.

But what seemed a simple and politically wise extension of the International Military Tribunal for the Far East's jurisdiction bore in it the seeds of the trial's inordinate length. The trial would now not only comprise crimes against the *ius ad bellum* – laws relating to the commencement of war – but also raise a whole, entirely separate range of charges relating to the *ius in bello*, the way in which the war had been conducted. The scope of the enquiry, the burden of evidence, and the work-load on the shoulders of all concerned were doubled or even tripled.

But the problem was not simply an increase in the volume of work. The inclusion of the *ius in bello* provided fresh ammunition for those who alleged that the victors were making up as they went along the laws under which they would try the vanquished. The definition of *ius in bello* the IPS took, as it took much else, from the Nuremberg Charter. At Nuremberg, the Tribunal's jurisdiction covered so-called 'conventional crimes' (viz. crimes defined by conventions and treaties such as the Hague and Geneva Conventions) plus a new category of criminal behaviour called 'Crimes against Humanity'. This latter group was much wider in scope than conventional war crimes – deliberately so, as it was intended to catch *all* atrocities and not simply those defined by international agreement. The roots of Crimes against Humanity have since been traced back to fifteenth-century natural law, but in the 1940s jurisprudential opinion considered charges under this head to be as much *ex post facto* as Crimes against Peace.

MacArthur promulgated the IMTFE Charter on January 19, 1946, but was obliged to amend it on April 23 following a Far Eastern Commission directive which demanded that *all* its members should sit on the Tribunal. The State Department had wanted to keep the Philippines out of the trial, and since it had given as its reason the fact that the Philippines was not a signatory to the Instrument of Surrender, India had also been ruled out. However, both the Philippines and India were members of the FEC, and these two nations joined the others: the principal allies – America, Britain and Russia; the Commonwealth countries – Australia, Canada and New Zealand (but not South Africa, which had dropped out); and the two other colonial powers – France and Holland. The only other Asian representative besides India was China – the Nationalist China of Chiang Kai-shek. Burma was permitted to attach a prosecutor to the British team, but none of the other Asian countries which had suffered at Japanese hands – Malaya, Thailand, Borneo, Korea, Vietnam – was allowed a voice. In many ways the Tribunal was the last bastion of colonialism.

The Tribunal was criticised for including only nations who were judges in their own cause: Japan was not represented, and nor were neutral countries. Perhaps in anticipation of this apparent injustice, the Charter contained several provisions specifically designed to give the accused a 'fair trial'. They were given, for example, the right to be represented by counsel of their own choice, but they were not protected against the possibility of unfair evidence being introduced. On the contrary, the Charter expressly denied the defendants even the most basic safeguards that are to be found in American and British courts.

In particular, the Tribunal was instructed to 'admit any evidence which it deems to have probative value' and not to be 'burdened by technical rules of evidence'. This meant that the court was expected to accept a wide variety of essentially dubious evidence, including hearsay and unsubstantiated documents, simply because it appeared to be genuine. At first sight, for a trial intended to impress the Japanese with democratic justice in action, this seems poor strategy. But need it have meant injustice? Not necessarily, according to the Tribunal which later tried Admiral Toyoda. 'To do otherwise in a war crimes trial is impractical . . . To be restricted to the commonly accepted judicial rules would soon result in encountering a great blank wall of silence – many guilty of the foulest crimes against humanity would escape.'

Keenan put forward a different justification. 'In domestic prosecutions we have the investigative agencies such as the FBI of our own country, Scotland Yard of London etc. Society can afford to impose severe restrictions upon the type of evidence to be received in such domestic prosecutions because society doesn't suffer by so doing. . . . However, when you haven't got any such army working along with the acts of the malefactor – and such acts for Japan go back over a period of fifteen years and extended ultimately 5000 miles in one direction and 5000 miles in another – sheer commonsense demands that in all justification society as such is entitled to certain protection and therefore there ought to be more latitude given in presenting evidence. . . . I hope we were not too zealous – we tried not to be – in not for a moment losing sight of the necessity of doing in our humble way whatever we could to bring about the end of this scourge of war.'

Keenan seems to have assumed that the prosecution had some responsibility not to exploit lax rules of evidence. The Toyoda tribunal, however, felt that 'the safeguard against errors of justice must rest . . . largely within the competence of the Tribunal itself. . . . Hearsay, opinion, secondary, even tertiary evidence will be most carefully weighed and evaluated to the best of the ability of the members before it is allowed to influence decisions in any degree whatsoever.' Far from being merely a device to guarantee convictions, therefore, the lenient rules of evidence provided scope for a display of magnanimous impartiality. But it was not to be. The Japanese people were only to experience 'Kriegsrecht', the right of war – which in this case was the justice of the victor.

Keenan was probably grateful for any leeway the Tribunal might allow him in the matter of evidence. Amidst a sea of devastation and growing misery as the first winter of the peace set in, the expatriate attorneys had to start from scratch to build a case against the leaders of a nation whose modern history was a closed book to the world. In an alien culture whose language they could not speak, with minimal backup, without established procedures or indeed relationships – most of the attorneys were strangers to each other – and before the eyes of the world, they had to prosecute 'Tojo and his gang', and do it quickly.

The International Prosecution Section gradually evolved an Investigation Branch staffed by famous FBI men of the pre-war era – like 'Pop' Nathan and Roy Morgan, members of the team who tracked down John Dillinger. Though their presence preserved the gang-busting image, Keenan could perhaps have picked more suitable allies. The sophisticated modern counter-intelligence capacity of the FBI would have been more useful to him. The IPS was out to prove political and ideological responsibility for the

Pacific War, not to track down person or persons unknown. Nor did it need the gangbusters' skill in ensnarement. The major Japanese war criminals did not, like the Nazis, try to go to ground: on notification of arrest they either presented themselves to the American authorities for incarceration, or committed suicide. General Honjo and Prince Konoye, both closely connected with the Throne, took their own lives – and Tojo had tried hard to do the same. When U.S. Military Police arrived at his house to arrest him, he shot himself in the chest at the spot where he believed his heart to be. He missed, however, because his heart was curiously elongated, and punctured a lung instead. A U.S. doctor with MASH experience quickly patched the sucking wound, front and back, and B-type blood commandeered from the arm of a U.S. mess sergeant saved Tojo's life. (General Eichelberger visited Tojo in hospital a few hours after his suicide attempt. As the General drew near, Tojo – very pale, believing himself at the point of death – gasped apologies for all the trouble he had caused the General. 'Do you mean tonight', Eichelberger asked, 'or for the last few years?')

The devastation in Japan not only impeded work but was also responsible, it appeared, for a dearth of documentary evidence. In Keenan's words, 'The Japanese pointed out where the records had been lodged, and those buildings didn't exist anymore'. But the true picture was neither as simple nor as honest as that.

There is clear evidence of widespread systematic destruction of documents by the Japanese military and bureaucracy following the surrender. The Sixth Air Force staff, for example, ordered: 'Intelligence reports (especially intelligence reports regarding POWs) shall be burnt entirely. . . . Personnel documents shall be burnt except those concerning the dead. . . . All top secret documents not written in currently used code shall be burnt'.

On June 2, 1947, after some eighteen months of effort, the Investigation Branch announced that it had information dealing with 'the burning of documents by the Foreign Ministry, by the War Ministry and by the army, and by the police on instructions from the Home Ministry'. Investigator R. H. Larsh, enthused by this discovery, minuted his boss, Edward P. Moynaghan, Chief of the IPS Investigation Branch: 'Because the entire picture of the wilful destruction of Japanese government documents is not completely clear, I intend to learn who were the top persons who directed the destruction by burning . . . Despite the fact that most of the actual testimony in the record [IMTFE transcript] concerning the burning of documents was given by members of the Foreign Ministry, the situation of that Ministry's destruction of its records is the vaguest of all and most full of questionable statements'.

His investigation seems to have borne fruit. In a candid letter from the Foreign Office, Takajiro Inoue admitted: 'With reference to the informal talks I had the pleasure of having with you the other day, would you kindly allow me to rectify the following point? I stated, at that time, that no official meeting took place in which a decision was reached as to the burning of the official documents belonging to the Archives Section. That statement was not correct. I now recollect that a meeting of all directors and section chiefs of the Secretariat did take place at the end of June or the beginning of July 1945. I myself, as Director of the Economic Affairs, attended that meeting and all officials present agreed that any important documents deposited with the Archives Section should be burnt at the right moment'.

The fact that SCAP was ruling Japan indirectly meant that Keenan was obliged to maintain protocol in the acquisition of most documents. At the start he was forced to ask the Central Liaison Office to supply him with the material he needed. The IPS was later able to obtain documents more directly, but this itself became a problem. Under the by-line 'Bulldozers rather than filing clerks', a representative of the IPS Documents Branch told *Time* magazine, 'At first I listed all incoming documents. Then they came in so fast that I listed only incoming bags. Then crates of bags. Now I just list the rooms they're in.'

As the momentum of investigation built up, documentary evidence – treaties, research memoranda and the like – also poured in from Allied government sources; the United States passed over the records of its Embassy in Nanking, and Nazi archives were culled for incriminating material.

Surprisingly the war crimes suspects themselves often proved willing sources of information. Koichi Kido, the Lord Keeper of the Privy Seal and the Emperor's right hand man throughout the war, gave his diaries to the IPS. These were of immense value to the prosecution as they gave a factual day-by-day insider's account of the progress of Japanese politics from 1937 onwards. Nevertheless, when Kido was indicted and convicted partly on the basis of his own diaries, he was outraged: 'This now famous diary was used by the prosecution to further its theories and was disregarded by the prosecution when it proved an obstacle to their aims and ambitions . . .'.

Interrogations were equally valuable. The Charter of the IMTFE was quite specific that 'all purported admissions or statements of the accused are admissible'; there was to be no nonsense about reading the war criminal his rights. Tojo is a case in point. He was interrogated by John Fihelly on over fifty occasions, some 124 hours in all, before being charged, and defence counsel was present during none of these interviews. Roughly twenty hours of this material was used against him, and constituted a major factor in his conviction. (As one prosecutor has remarked, it really did not matter what defence Tojo put up during the trial, once Fihelly's interrogatories were lodged.)

But, unlike Nuremberg, there was simply not enough pertinent documentary evidence to plug all the gaps in the prosecution's case, so the IPS needed to find witnesses. In some respects this was easy. The Allies could supply experts on military and economic matters, and a parade of mutilated and abused civilians and Allied personnel would testify to atrocities. But where other aspects of the case were concerned, particularly the secret day-to-day activities of the Japanese leadership, it was virtually impossible to find anyone of high enough rank to be of use.

One source who could have been of enormous value was Prince Konoye. He had been at the centre of events from the early 1930s on (in the Cabinet, three times as Prime Minister, and as President of the House of Peers) and he had strong personal ties with the Emperor. He was also a weak and vacillating character, as soon became apparent when he was confronted by Allied interrogators. One American general who had cause to interview him on several occasions described him as 'a rat who's quite prepared to sell anyone to save himself and even went so far as to call his master the Emperor "the major war criminal"'.

But the night before Konoye was due to report to Sugamo prison and deliver himself to the American authorities, he took poison, leaving a note explaining that he could not 'face the humiliation of being tried by the Americans'. On the face of it this is reasonable enough – but it fails to square with the circumstances surrounding his arrest.

In the first place, it is not clear – despite the fact that he was being arrested – that anyone actually intended to put Konoye on trial. Chiang Kai-shek wanted his name removed from the Chinese list of war criminals, presumably because Konoye had attempted to put an end to the fighting in China; and the British never had him on their list at all. One contemporary source – John Fihelly's report on his investigation into Konoye's suicide – suggests that even the Americans had no real intention of trying him as a war criminal. Conceivably, his arrest was aimed primarily as a warning to the Matsumoto Committee then engaged in drafting a new Constitution for Japan. If Konoye, a royal Prince, was not immune from attack, then they might be led to assume that no one was safe, not even the Emperor himself – unless, of course, in the meantime the Japanese showed themselves eager for reform. This was the threat which Whitney was to spell out so crudely two months later.

Why did Konoye not take these factors into account? Why should someone of his timid and indecisive disposition have taken

[112]

such bold and final action before he had even been indicted? The answer may be that suggested by Harold Henderson, a senior official in CIE. Henderson claimed to have relayed to Konoye a verbal message from MacArthur. The precise wording of this message Henderson would not repeat; but he hinted that Konoye may have misconstrued it, and that 'it may have had something to do with his death'. MacArthur's utterances were often obscure, sometimes deliberately so, and it is perfectly plausible that Konoye should have misunderstood him, perhaps reading into the General's words a direct threat of imminent prosecution.

Nevertheless, this does not entirely explain his suicide. All the evidence suggests that Konoye would have cooperated with the prosecution. His personal secretary, for instance, went out of his way after Konoye's death to be helpful; Keenan had him specially listed as a 'Confidential Informant' of the highest importance. Given the Japanese emphasis on loyalty, the secretary was presumably following Konoye's lead. And Konoye himself must have had the potential for using the information he possessed as a bargaining tool: in his case, even if he had been prosecuted successfully, the death sentence would have been highly unlikely. So difficult is it to understand why he should have taken his own life, the possibility arises that he did not; there was no shortage of people at every level of the Japanese government who would have preferred Konoye not to testify.

Whatever the truth may be, had he been willing to cooperate Konoye would certainly have been a better proposition than the character on whom the prosecution were forced to rely instead. Keenan's star witness was a man whom *Life* alluded to as 'sybaritic and unwholesome', a description which turned out to be a masterpiece of understatement.

When General Ryukichi Tanaka first presented himself, he seemed too good to be true. He had been a high-ranking officer in the Kwantung Army until 1939 and had then been promoted to the War Ministry in Tokyo. Even his stated motive for cooperating with the Allies was beyond reproach: Tojo, he said, had put him in a mental asylum for expressing the view that the war could not be won. As far as supplying incriminating evidence was concerned, he did a remarkable job. Virtually all the defendants suffered at his hands. He testified, for example, that Tojo had been in favour of brutal treatment of prisoners-of-war, and that far from being surprised to have been appointed Prime Minister, as he claimed, he had let it be known that unless he received the appointment, 'it would be difficult to control the army'.

But years of FBI training made Roy Morgan a little suspicious of Tanaka. His investigations (conducted because, as he explained to

Keenan, he felt it would be better if 'prior to trial . . . we know of General Tanaka's condition') cast considerable doubt on Tanaka's value as a witness. Morgan checked the asylum story, and found it inaccurate. Tanaka was admitted not on Tojo's orders, but after he had suffered a serious mental breakdown. And his medical record (even in the opaque IPS translation) would make the average lawyer hesitate to accept those portions of his testimony which were uncorroborated. Tanaka was suffering from 'isomunia' and 'anamnesis' (insomnia and amnesia). 'Since six months, observed physical exhaustion and iso-munia. These symtons [sic] grew worst, feeling of anxiety and unrest, palpitation and feeling of strong pressure in the breast. Since two weeks sense of fear due to the old syphilis for paralysis specially noticed. Syphilis past treatment. Blood and cerebrospinal fluid: Wass-erman tests negative. Family History: mental disease disposition positive. Father and grandfather committed suicide.' Morgan then found the doctor who had written this report, who told him that Tanaka's condition had been 'manic depressive'. The diagnosis of two other doctors who had actually treated Tanaka was 'melancholia caused by involution. . . . They stated that on his discharge from the hospital they did not believe he was entirely cured; but that with the passage of time he would return to be as normal a person as he had been prior to his first breakdown'.

By 1946, Tanaka's mental health appears to have been a matter of serious concern to the U.S. attorneys who had to deal with him. All three doctors had advised that if Tanaka 'were put under mental strain or pressure there was a great possibility of a relapse', and in at least one IPS interrogation where Tanaka was used to confront a suspect, the IPS took the precaution of forewarning the suspect to 'be gentlemanly' with him.

There is also a strong suggestion that Tanaka was primarily motivated by spite: it was patently obvious at the trial that he was 'out to get' some of the defendants. The IPS appears to have been well aware of this possibility from the start. The same accused who was asked to 'be gentlemanly' with him was also asked whether Tanaka had any reason to feel enmity toward him.

That the IPS should have been prepared to recruit a man like Tanaka displays a certain cynicism of outlook. That the pros-ecution should have been reduced to using him reveals the paucity of the evidence at their disposal. They must have badly needed his testimony – otherwise why take such an obvious risk? Had he broken down in court at the hands of a less than 'gentlemanly' defence lawyer, everything he had said would have been discre-dited. Apart from the impact this would have had on the pros-ecution's chances of conviction, in *this* of all trials, where justice had to be seen to be done, it would have meant disaster.

[114]

13

Crimes and Criminals

In the late 1980s there is an element of fantasy in the image of Americans and Russians shoulder to shoulder in a foreign court room confronting aggression. But the Tokyo trial was a genuinely international prosecution. The Allied nations were represented by some of their most eminent attorneys – among them Arthur Comyns Carr KC from England, with Christmas Humphreys as one of his juniors; Govinda Menon from India, with Krishna Menon as his junior; Dr. S. A. Golunsky from Russia, a jurist and diplomat who had attended the conferences of Dumbarton Oaks, Yalta and Potsdam. With Americans like Fihelly and Darsey, they formed a largely non-partisan cabal of legal excellence to lead the prosecution.

The majority of the trial's lawyers, however, were American. Some were very young, like Robert Donihi and Solis Horwitz, for whom the trial was both an early mark of distinction and a baptism of fire. The others were a broad cross-section of Federal and State attorneys on temporary secondment to the IMTFE – among them Mrs. Grace Llewellyn Kanode, the first woman prosecutor in a major war crimes trial.

Despite the enormous scale of the prosecution it was undertaking and the large staff it employed (at the height of its activities, 277 Allied nationals and 232 Japanese), the IPS was organised very simply. The Investigation and Documents Branches, staffed for the most part by non-lawyers, were collators of relevant material for the Legal Branch. The lawyers prepared and presented the prosecution case, under the co-ordinating eye of the Administrative Branch. This was led by Eugene Williams, to whom Keenan (doubtless to Darsey's fury) had entrusted 'overall supervision of the presentation of the entire case'. The system proved efficient, and despite constant rivalry between the cliques centred around Darsey and Keenan, the IPS remained flexible and responsive to the changing demands of the case.

[115]

From time to time the organisation regrouped, and once the prosecution phase had given way to the defence, it shrank in size as lawyers went home and the volume of work dropped. But from the preparatory weeks through to the final summations, one constant was the task of processing the evidence which increasingly piled up at the IPS's door. Whatever the language in which it was written, from Mongolian to French, every document – diary, letter, book, speech, interrogation report, treaty, memorandum – which might contribute the most trifling detail to the panorama of Japanese aggression had to be scanned and, if of probative value, analysed. Over 12,000 documents were processed in this way. Points of relevance were indexed and cross-referenced and made readily accessible to the attorneys.

Over the months, the IPS built up an impressive library of digested source material. This ranged from the voluminous 'Decisions of Imperial Conferences, Liaison Conferences, Privy Council Meetings, Cabinet Meetings, Four Ministers Conferences, Five Ministers Conferences, Senior Statesmen's Meetings, Imperial War Plans Council, Joint Conferences, Miscellaneous Conferences' prepared by IPS attorney Joe English (ex-Professor of Law at the University of Scranton, Pennsylvania) to 'Special Studies' on a variety of relevant topics from the 'Introduction of Shinto Religion in Manchuria' to 'Laws of War: treatment of bandits, irregulars and guerrillas'.

As an overall plan for the proceedings took shape, teams of attorneys were detailed to pull together the various strands of this diverse material and prepare small segments of the evolving prosecution case. John Darsey, for example, headed a team of five to brief 'Manchurian Military Aggression 1931–45'; Judge Hsiang, the Chinese Associate Prosecutor, a team of four for 'Narcotics in China and elsewhere 1932–45'; Valentine Hammack, former Assistant U.S. Attorney for the Northern District of California, a team of three (which included Robert Donihi) for 'Preparing Japanese Opinion for War – education, political organisation, assassination and threats, and police coercion'.

At the same time individual attorneys were assigned long-term watching briefs over specific defendants; each was instructed to ensure that his particular subject was properly implicated in the overall case, and to prepare to cross-examine him if and when he took the stand in his own defence. Generally the attorneys who had interrogated the prisoners in Sugamo were given this task – and there was considerable anticipation at the prospect of John Fihelly's joust with Tojo.

By the spring of 1946, the IPS found itself torn, as Keenan noted, between the need to hurry, so that the Tokyo trial could be held 'when psychologically most effective', and the desire that 'procedure should be sound'. It did not take the prosecution long, however, to resolve the dilemma in a manner entirely satisfactory to itself and distinctly unfair to the defence.

The IPS decided that psychological advantage was paramount, and chose to start before it had finished amassing all the evidence it believed to exist. By the end of the defence phase, nearly two years after the IPS had originally begun work, a wealth of extra incriminating evidence was available, and the IPS asked for the opportunity to 'rebut' the defence case. In the teeth of an outcry from the defence that this would effectively constitute a retrial, the court granted the request. The well-greased IPS machine was thus allowed to present its carefully prepared rebuttal evidence, while the Tribunal allowed the defence only ten days to prepare its surre-buttal of the new evidence. The Charter is quite silent on the matter of submitting additional evidence in this way: justice lay in the hands of the judges.

The main obstacle to the swift processing of evidence was the dearth of translators available to the IPS. Out of a total staff which by January 1946 had swollen to seventy, only five could read Japanese, and Keenan had no option but to request the Japanese government to supply fifty or so English-speaking Japanese nationals – 'Hobson's choice', as he put it. Eventually some two hundred Japanese nationals were employed on the staff of the IPS, which may have contributed to the constant breaches of security that plagued the trial; the British list of proposed defendants, for example, was leaked to the press almost as soon as it was notified to Keenan.

The swamp of translation difficulties was to swallow up prosecution and defence alike. Turning Japanese into English, and vice versa, with the precision of nuance required by lawyers is virtually impossible. Japanese as a language bears no relation to English or any other European language, and the process of translation is more like describing a picture in words – creating an equivalent, not a replica. Not only is it difficult, it is also particularly time-consuming. In a tone of near-desperation the head of IPS translation, after trying to explain to uncompromising attorneys why accurate translation of one page of double-spaced foolscap took one linguist two days, concluded by warning, 'Unless reasonable time is allowed for translation (*days* or *weeks* not hours) the language division will be forced either to delay the court proceedings or to turn out a succession of rush jobs that will embarrass the prosecution by not holding up in court'.

In the face of such difficulties, the Associate Prosecutor from England, Arthur Comyns Carr KC, found his first few weeks in

Tokyo a time of intense frustration. 'This is a frightful job you have let me in for', he wrote to Attorney General Sir Hartley Shawcross, whose representative he was. 'I have already been here as long as you said the whole trip would take, and there is no sign of the proceedings even beginning. On arrival I found the Americans with a huge staff engaged in an enormous research with a stack of documents which have never even been listed or translated.'

Carr was a senior and highly responsible lawyer. He quickly realised that rather than allowing himself to be simply a cog in a machine designed by Keenan, in the British and international interest he must assert himself and take a leading role in the prosecution. Perhaps because Keenan had effectively neutralised Darsey and Fihelly by appointing Eugene Williams as Chief Administrator, or perhaps because the Associate Prosecutors from the Commonwealth countries formed a commanding English law bloc, Carr was able to dominate the juristic aspect of the prosecution. He drafted the Indictment, served on the Evidence Committee, and wrote the legal argument in the prosecution's summation speech (a speech the New Zealand judge described as 'too clever to have been written by Keenan'). He also analysed the first 1500 of the IPS documents, and (up to the last moments) was responsible for two important defendants – Kido and Togo. Undoubtedly he was the most impressive figure in the Tokyo prosecution, and by taking charge of the Indictment he went straight to the heart of the entire trial.

The Charter marked out the areas of law in which charges might be brought – but it was the Indictment that defined the acts and omissions falling within the court's jurisdiction over which the case was actually fought. Altogether there were 55 charges – though not all were brought against all the defendants. The charges were divided into three related groups. The first group, Counts 1 to 36, spelt out the Crimes against Peace that the defendants were alleged to have committed over a seventeen-year period, from January 1, 1928 until the moment of the official surrender on September 2, 1945.

Count 1 was the most important in the Indictment, and it makes remarkable reading. It alleged that each of the accused had, for some or all of the time, been part of a conspiracy extending over seventeen years to secure 'the military, naval, political and economic domination of East Asia and of the Pacific and Indian Oceans and of all countries and islands therein and bordering thereon'. This was a breathtaking charge. For a lawyer schooled in the domestic criminal courts of London, whose natural habitat was the Old Bailey, it represented a quantum leap into the unknown. It also brought out a lawyerly sense of caution, and in Counts 2, 3 and

4 Comyns Carr divided up the conspiracy for domination between Manchuria, China, and the rest.

Count 5 stands on its own at a tangent to Count 1, alleging a conspiracy for world domination – this time in league with the Nazis. Allied propagandists had been stressing the Nippon–Nazi link throughout the war, but it was Comyns Carr who suggested its inclusion in the Indictment, simply because he had discovered valuable relevant evidence, including a statement by the Japanese Foreign Minister Matsuoka 'assuring Hitler that he would bring Japan into the war with the United States'. Comyns Carr was to fail with this Count; by one of the eccentricities of American justice the defence were able to procure a statement refuting the charge on behalf of 'Tojo and his gang' from Secretary of State George Marshall himself.

Still within the Crimes against Peace section, but dropping allegations of conspiracy, Counts 6 to 17 charged all of the defendants individually with having 'planned and prepared' wars of aggression against each Allied nation plus Thailand. Counts 18 to 26 charged some or all of the defendants with 'initiating' wars of aggression against these same nations in turn (with the exception of the Netherlands, which had declared war on Japan first). Counts 27 to 36 charged some or all of them with 'waging' aggressive war against the twelve.

Comyns Carr's purpose in making Counts 6 to 36 specific, each one restricted to a single nation or association of nations, was obviously to avoid the defendants being acquitted because they had been able to defeat part of an over-ambitious charge. He need not have worried. The Tribunal was perfectly prepared to do his work for him, and where the Indictment was too extensive, the judges pruned the charges to meet the prosecution's proof. For example, the IPS failed to prove the entirety of Count 1, finding it impossible to establish that the accused had conspired to secure 'military, naval, political and economic domination' of America, as the charge had implied. But the Tribunal backtracked: 'We do not think the conspirators ever seriously resolved to attempt to secure the domination of North and South America. So far as the wishes of the conspirators crystallised into a concrete common plan, we are of the opinion that the territory they had resolved that Japan should dominate was confined to East Asia, the Western and South Western Pacific Ocean and the Indian Ocean, and certain of the islands in these oceans. We shall accordingly treat Count 1 as if the charge had been limited to the above object'.

Not only did Comyns Carr minutely sub-divide the Crimes against Peace counts, he also provided in the Indictment an entire alternative set of charges – Counts 37 to 52. In March and April

1946, the legitimacy of *ex post facto* charges such as Crimes against Peace had been questioned, at Nuremberg and elsewhere, in a way Carr may have regarded as threatening. In a series of Counts which displayed courageous and creative draftsmanship, he provided the Tribunal with an unimpeachable fallback by charging the defendants with murder and conspiracy to commit murder.

His line of reasoning was that murder is the intentional killing (and this includes the issuing of orders to kill) of a human being without lawful justification. If a war is begun without lawful justification the deaths that result must be murder, and those who give the orders, murderers, plain and simple. So in Count 39, for example, it was alleged that 'the defendants . . . by ordering, causing and permitting the armed forces of Japan to attack the territory, ships and airplanes of the United States of America, with which nation Japan was then at peace, at Pearl Harbor, Territory of Hawaii, on the 7th December, 1941, at about 0755 hours (Pearl Harbor time), unlawfully killed and murdered Admiral Kidd and about 4,000 other members of the naval and military forces of the United States of America and certain civilians whose names and number are at present unknown'.

Counts 53 to 55 combined conventional war crimes and Crimes against Humanity charges. It is interesting that, as the British had predicted (and as was the case at Nuremberg), none of the defendants – even those convicted of Count 1 – was hanged unless *also* convicted of responsibility for atrocities.

The Indictment – which took ninety man-days simply to translate – represents a heroic endeavour on Comyns Carr's part, given the limited time available to him and the chaotic conditions of Japan so soon after the surrender. Some charges could not in the event be proved: out of the aggregate 217 charges adjudicated by the Tribunal, only 132 were proven. There was over-ambition in the scope of the conspiracy alleged in Count 1. There were simple mistakes – confusion between 'Togo' and 'Tojo', for example; the Japanese Central Liaison Office regarded the Indictment as full of errors. And there is also an unpleasant suggestion of deviousness in the charges relating to the U.S.S.R. Comyns Carr wrote that for reasons which the Russian prosecutor would 'doubtless understand, I have not included Counts for "initiating" and "waging" war against the U.S.S.R.' in 1945, since it was the Soviet Union which had attacked Japan in the last days of the war, in breach of their mutual neutrality treaty.

But though Comyns Carr can take the credit for getting the prosecution off the ground, he need not be held solely responsible for these defects in the Indictment. The other Associate Prosecutors had ample opportunity to review it, and they were not slow to criticise. Pedro Lopez, Associate Prosecutor for the Philippines, writing on behalf also of the French and Dutch Associate Prosecutors, carped at the 'repetitiousness and long-windedness of the Indictment' and condemned Comyns Carr for failing to include charges of setting up puppet governments or, more seriously, 'any charge against atrocities committed on the civilian population'. Lieutenant Colonel Brabner Smith, who had been Keenan's special assistant in Washington in the early 1930s and was again his right-hand man in Tokyo, was so alarmed by the document that he wanted the Associate Prosecutors 'who officially approved the present form of indictment' to take responsibility for it rather than Keenan. Smith claimed that the Indictment violated Article 9a of the Charter which provides that 'the indictment shall consist of a plain, concise and adequate statement of each offence charged'. It omitted 'violation of international law and the rules of war by Japan as a military occupant'; it alleged crimes which 'are not crimes under the Charter', such as economic domination (on this the Tribunal was later to rule in Comyns Carr's favour). Smith concluded that it had all 'the principal defects of the Nuremberg Indictment . . . without the justification that the Indictment, being an historical document, should set forth as a clear picture for the public an outline of the vicious activities of the war criminals which it is intended to prove'.

This last point raises wider issues, which Comyns Carr would quite properly have regarded as none of his concern. The Indictment is a complex legal document and, despite the narrative introduction which he was forced to incorporate, concentrated effort is required to understand it. It is the work of a lawyer, not a propagandist. Reviewing Japanese editorial comment on the Indictment, British Intelligence concluded that 'the Japanese people do not understand the nature of the imputed guilt' and that though the Indictment might appear to Western minds to be devastatingly complete, 'it is doubted if it will ever be understood by the more simple Japanese who start with different conceptions of life, death and personal conduct'. Thus, viewed from the perspective of the demilitarisation of Japan, this key document in the trial was clearly an opportunity missed.

Technical criticisms apart, the Indictment has some puzzling features, not least Count 1. Why for example did the IPS think it suitable in the Japanese context to allege conspiracy? And why go as far back as January 1, 1928 to find the starting point for the conspiracy? This imposed a huge burden of proof on the prosecution at a time when it was under heavy pressure to expedite matters. The conspiracy charge appears to have originated in 1944 with a proposal put to Henry Stimson, U.S. Secretary of War. But when he supported its use, he did not have Japan in mind, but rather the Nazi state with its rigid pyramidal structure, Führer at the top – the idea being to select one or more individuals from each level of the Nazi organisation and present them as *representative* of a larger group of conspirators. Stimson was a lawyer by training, and this was a simple legal device to achieve a spread of guilt wider by implication than the number of defendants in the dock.

But the Japan of the 1930s and 1940s was very different from Nazi Germany. Between 1928–1945 there were 17 different Cabinets in Japan; under the Meiji Constitution the division between the civilian and military command functions was absolute; and there was no comparable pyramidal state structure. As Comyns Carr himself put it: 'The whole Japanese situation is infinitely more complicated than the German for the purpose of a prosecution, as all the politicians, soldiers and sailors were all squabbling and double-crossing one another all the time'. If there was a conspiracy it was far from obvious where it was located, since the defendants at Tokyo, unlike those at Nuremberg, did not immediately appear to be linked to any specific group or organisation outside the trial. Consequently, the IPS seemed at times simply to be declaring its faith in a far-fetched theory of history rather than presenting a systematic case against a representative group of defendants.

At the time, the resonances of truth in the prosecution's allegations were muffled, and many have now become inaudible. Few historians subscribe to the contention that the war was the outcome of a conspiracy between persons known or unknown. Undeniably in each phase of Japanese military history from 1928 onwards she appears the aggressor: she struck at Manchuria, at China, at Pearl Harbor, Hong Kong, Kota Baru, following decisions made by her military and political leaders. But the causes of war were tangled in a complex web, woven over decades, of action and interreaction with the West, with Russia and with China – a morass of economic, national and imperial factors. In any event, in practical historical terms the weeks immediately following the war were hardly the time to determine its causes. As Carl J. Friedrich wrote: 'Few thoughtful Americans would argue that the state of general information concerning Japan would enable them to reach a wise decision at this time'.

The credibility of the prosecution, and ultimately the judgement in its favour, was undermined by the fantastic claims made under Count 1. What is puzzling is that trial lawyers of the quality of those within the IPS apparently failed to recognise the fundamental insecurity of their case. They were not obliged to make such sweeping claims: it might have been easier, for example, to sustain the charge of conspiracy over a shorter period. Comyns Carr himself pointed out that it was not until the summer of 1936, under the premiership of Hirota, that 'a national policy was adopted which really comprised the whole of the conspiracy as found by the Tribunal and as it ultimately developed in action'.

With 1936 as its base, the Count 1 conspiracy would still have incorporated the China Incident, the Russian/Manchurian border incidents and the Pacific War, as well as the redirection of Japan proper along the path of total war. The earlier and lesser incidents could readily have been covered by simple charges of planning, preparing, initiating and waging 'aggressive war', and the atrocities charges could also have been extended back as far as necessary. It would have made little difference to Allied public opinion, particularly since several of the accused – most notably Tojo himself – were not alleged to have joined the conspiracy until after 1936 anyway, being previously of too low a rank to influence policy measurably.

In all probability, the dating of the conspiracy rested on the evidence that was – or was believed to be – available. During the period of drafting the Indictment the IPS appears to have believed that it could produce conclusive proof of conspiracy as of 1928 – and here it seems to have fallen foul of one of Japanese history's major red herrings, the so-called 'Tanaka Memorial'. This was allegedly a document produced in 1927 by the government of Prime Minister Giichi Tanaka setting out a programme of conquest for Japan – first Manchuria, then the whole of China, South East Asia, India and Australia. But whether it ever actually existed is still not entirely certain; the majority think not.

MacArthur, however, believed the Tanaka Memorial to be a reality (as did Hollywood: in *Blood on the Sun*, James Cagney was sent to Japan to retrieve it). When Joseph Ballantine visited Tokyo in May 1946 he found the staff of the IPS feverishly ransacking the Japanese Foreign Office and General Staff archives for the original of the infamous document. Their desperation was no doubt fuelled by the fact that by then the Indictment had already been lodged in court, served on the accused, and broadcast to the world. Soon after Ballantine's visit, however, it seems to have dawned on the IPS that this vital piece of evidence might be a chimera. *The New York Times* of May 5, 1946 reported Ichiro Hatoyama as challenging MacArthur's view of Japan's past and explaining that the Memorial was a Chinese forgery. This was supported by Ballantine, who told the IPS quite simply that the Memorial was a hoax and had never existed. According to him, the lawyers then stopped looking.

If the Tanaka Memorial was originally a mainstay of the IPS case, it would help to explain not only the seemingly reckless sweep of Count 1, but also one of the few recorded displays of personal vindictiveness by an IPS lawyer against a defendant at the IMTFE. Comyns Carr pursued Hirota with an unprofessional obsessiveness that was surprising in a King's Counsel of his eminence. But remove the Tanaka Memorial from the case, as the IPS were forced to do, alter the focus of the conspiracy charge to 1936, and Hirota – then the Prime Minister – moves squarely into the centre of the conspiracy. If Comyns Carr had failed to secure Hirota's conviction, the foundations of the case which he had constructed in the Indictment would have been shaken, and even Tojo himself might have escaped.

The process of selecting defendants went in tandem with the drafting of the Indictment, and was begun by John Darsey on December 9, 1945. He instructed eleven counsel, including Donihi and Horwitz, to identify those war criminals 'who have contributed in a substantial and material way' to Japanese aggression. This was a far harder task than they, or the public at home, had been led to believe by allied wartime propaganda. They were dealing not in moralising generalities and absolutes of good and evil, but in the kind of guilt that is susceptible of legal proof in court. And as Darsey readily acknowledged, 'very little concrete evidence indicating the guilt of any of the suspects is presently readily accessible'.

Selection, which continued until April 1946, was not in any sense mechanical. The final list of defendants emerged slowly from a constant toing and froing among the Associate Prosecutors, in which several forces appear to have been at work. The Indictment made its own demands. Count 1 necessitated that the accused be leaders – but as Japan, unlike America, is a gerontocracy where seniority and age are necessarily connected, many of the obvious candidates, particularly those from the early years of the conspiracy, were no longer available. Some defendants were included in order to peg out the principal incidents of the seventeen-year period under scrutiny. Since the IPS had decided to try violations of both the *ius ad bellum* and the *ius in bello*, the number of such incidents was swelled by the major Japanese atrocities; the persons 'responsible' for the Rape of Nanking, naval atrocities, atrocities in the Philippines and others had to be included. And since the prosecution was alleging a conspiracy, every group that could have been involved had to be represented – military, political, diplomatic, economic and ideological.

Apart from some obvious candidates – Tojo himself and possibly the Emperor's chief advisor, Kido – the final list of defendants seems to have been largely a product of horse-trading. It was decided upon, subject to MacArthur's approval, by majority vote among the Associate Prosecutors (Keenan counting as the U.S.

Associate Prosecutor for this purpose); in the event of a tie, the prosecutor nominating had the casting vote. Twenty-six of the defendants were chosen by only nine of the Associate Prosecutors. India did not participate in the selection process, as Govinda and Krishna Menon had both contracted smallpox in Delhi; and the Soviet Union's representative was delayed by MacArthur's refusal to allow Soviet frigates to dock at Yokohama. The Russians did, however, manage to insist that two additional accused (both notably anti-Communist) be added to the list, giving an assurance – misplaced, as it turned out – that there was sufficient evidence to convict.

Had there been more time in which to prepare its case, the IPS might well have ended up with a different selection of defendants. Clearly the prosecution could only indict war criminals whom they believed they could successfully convict under Count 1. It is standard practice among prosecuting agencies in criminal cases to insist on being reasonably certain of a person's guilt before charging him; there was no inherent injustice in the IPS's attitude. But at the Tokyo trial the presumption of guilt was taken to extremes, because the consequences of failure to convict were too serious to contemplate. In April 1946 the IPS did not yet have all the evidence available, and in some cases its assessment of guilt was flawed.

In deciding whether any particular defendant was sufficiently incriminated, the prosecutors weighed five separate sources of evidence against him: his own admissions during interrogations; documents on file relating to him; information about him in the special study 'Conferences before the Emperor'; Kido's diary entries about him; and finally Ryukichi Tanaka's accusations against him. Tanaka's involvement even at this early and obviously crucial stage indicates the degree of influence he wielded over the Tokyo trial, and raises the distinct possibility that he used it for his own rancorous ends.

It is perhaps unfair to be overly critical of the eventual list of defendants. The hands of the IPS were tied by the need to keep the number of accused within manageable proportions. At the same time they were convinced that there would be other trials. One might complain that there was no representative of the *zaibatsu* among the accused, whereas at Nuremberg a member of the Krupps family had been indicted. But at the start of 1946 the IPS had not gathered enough evidence to tie the *zaibatsu* into the conspiracy; this was treated as a separate exercise, and as late as October 1946 Keenan was talking to the press about a second trial that would definitely include *zaibatsu* defendants.

In some ways, the first list of defendants was perhaps *more* impressive than might have been expected. By choosing men who during the course of their careers had held more than one high position in the military and/or government, the prosecutors achieved a wide coverage of public office. Four of the accused, for example, had been Prime Ministers; four had been Foreign Ministers; five Army Ministers; two Navy Ministers; three Home Ministers; and so on.

Nevertheless, when an enterprising *Newsweek* reporter took to the streets with photographs of the defendants, only three out of the twenty-eight were consistently identified by the public. This suggests the difficulties facing those who wished to exploit the IMTFE as a propaganda tool in the demilitarisation campaign. The accused were not swept into the dock at Tokyo by a wave of righteous anger among the Japanese. The Japanese people did not recognise their leaders as evil (as the Germans were to turn against the Nazis), nor even as having done wrong. As Shidehara stated in the November–December 1945 session of the Diet, those responsible 'had committed serious blunders', but had had no intention of betraying their country. It was perhaps foolish to require the Japanese to make the same moral judgements that one might expect in a Western Christian context; this point is discussed later. Equally significant was the observation by the OSS that whatever their feelings toward the trial, the Japanese preferred not to allow it to become a divisive issue. Any shock and guilt the trial may have provoked 'gradually became subordinated to the belief that under foreign control national unity was essential for speedy reconstruction of the country'.

The Indictment did arouse interest when it was published in full in the newspapers – but reactions to the choice of the accused was mixed. The defendants seemed to many to be old and forgotten men – Hirota, for example, had been retired for eight years – and in any event it is not in the Japanese character to brood over the past for its own sake. Some people thought that those selected were unlucky; others were less forgiving. A cartoon in *Yomiuri Monthly* depicted children playing 'court': as one of the little boys is pushed, struggling, towards the Bench, the 'Chief Justice' admonishes him, 'If you do not like to be a war criminal, you should remember that we always let you be the important general when we played war'. Uppermost, however was a widespread sense of relief: the indictment did not name the Emperor.

14

The Shadow of the Emperor

The failure to indict the Emperor dealt a fatal blow to the demilitarisation potential of the Tokyo trial. The overtly political nature of the decision destroyed the trial's credibility as a display of equality under the law – and for many Japanese at least, the old men in the dock became victims, even martyrs, rather than villains brought to justice. With Hirohito beyond the prosecutors' grasp, the IMTFE became largely an irrelevance in people's day-to-day lives, and public interest in the trial waxed and waned with its intrinsic entertainment value – reaching fever pitch only in the minutes preceding the expected confrontation between Tojo and John Fihelly.

The Emperor's absence also had a marked effect on the conduct of the trial. The IPS faced the challenge of presenting a conspiracy case without either casting aspersions on the Emperor or openly declaring him immune from prosecution – and found it a nightmare, as every avenue of argument seemed to lead directly or tangentially to the Throne. The defendants, however, did not want the Emperor implicated either, and at moments the trial acquired a surreal quality as accusers and accused joined forces to thwart the President of the IMTFE, Sir William Webb, in his obsessive search for proof of the Emperor's war guilt. (At the end of the trial, Webb publicly denounced the failure to indict the Emperor, by challenging the severity of the sentences passed on others in the absence of 'the leader in the crime'.) On one occasion, for instance, Tojo had given testimony which reflected badly on the Emperor, to Webb's obvious glee. That evening according to Seiichi Yamazaki, Keenan's private secretary, Keenan, Ryukichi Tanaka and Yamazaki himself arranged through the Imperial Household to have Tojo contacted in his prison cell (possibly by Kido). There, presumably without the knowledge of his American defence counsel, he was persuaded to amend his testimony.

Hirohito was not even to be called as a witness. This did nothing to ease the task of the defence lawyers, and the manifest injustice

to their clients – even though by their silence the defendants con-
nived at it – eventually proved too much for some of the American
attorneys to bear. In a *cri de coeur* John G. Brannon, Kido's lawyer,
wrote to MacArthur: 'These Japanese defendants . . . with their
almost holy reverence for the Emperor of Japan balked and utterly
refused to consider the idea of calling him as a witness. To me now,
after more than two years of association with the accused and their
[Japanese] attorneys a better understanding of this psychology is
afforded. But while I have perhaps only a feeble knowledge of their
sacred feelings, I have yet to lay claim to comprehension of the
legal reasoning which would prompt the prosecution to predicate
the case against the defendant Kido on the theme of deceit,
treachery and trickery toward the Emperor of Japan without producing the then head of state to testify whether such misconduct
by this most intimate advisor had actually been perpetrated upon
him'.

Given the obvious potential damage to the credibility of the
IMTFE, the Japanese people's loss of interest, and the outrage
offered to public opinion throughout the world – why then was the
Emperor not indicted? There is no simple answer to this question.
For example, his immunity does not seem to have been the product
of any positive policy decision reached in Washington before the
Occupation began. On the contrary, America anticipated the day
when Hirohito *would* be put on trial. On November 29, 1945, the
Joint Chiefs of Staff ordered MacArthur not to delay in collecting
evidence since 'the United States Government's position is that
Hirohito is not immune from arrest, trial and punishment as a war
criminal. . . . It may be assumed that when the Occupation can
proceed satisfactorily without him, the question of his trial will be
raised'. But for the time being, in accordance with the Basic Initial
Post-Surrender Directive, the Americans were to rule Japan
through the existing government structure and no positive action
was to be taken against its nominal head.

In retrospect, there seem to have been two decisive stages in the
shielding of Hirohito – the first, the period of greatest upheaval
and reform in the early months of the Occupation; and the second,
the trend towards conservatism in its later years. (By 1951 any
prospect of Hirohito's indictment seems to have vanished; formal
Notes presented in that year by the Soviet Union to America and
Britain proposing the trial of Hirohito as a war criminal were
simply ignored.)

MacArthur spelled out the reasons, all of them eminently practical, for maintaining Hirohito on his throne during the opening
stages of the Occupation, in a top secret message to the Joint Chiefs
of Staff on January 25, 1946. 'Destroy him and the nation will disin-

tegrate. . . . Civilised practices will largely cease, and a condition of underground chaos and disorder amounting to guerrilla warfare in the mountainous and outlying regions will result. I believe all hope of introducing modern democratic methods would disappear and that when military control finally ceased some form of intense regimentation probably along communistic lines would arise from the mutilated masses. . . . It is quite possible that a minimum of a million troops would be required which would have to be maintained for an indefinite number of years. In addition a complete civil service might have to be recruited and imported, possibly running into a size of several hundred thousand. An overseas supply service under such conditions would have to be set up on practically a war basis embracing an indigent civil population of many millions. Many other most drastic results which I will not attempt to discuss should be anticipated.' Nor, at this point, did it seem possible to compromise by removing the man but preserving the institution – arranging for Hirohito's abdication, and the accession of a new Emperor to the throne. The political after-shock would still have been too great a threat to the delicate processes of disarmament and constitutional reform that were preoccupying SCAP in the early months of 1946.

Pressure on the IPS to act swiftly and the herculean efforts of Comyns Carr to complete the Indictment with despatch worked in the Emperor's favour, and the deadline for the selection of defendants passed without Hirohito ever having been in danger of being named. Comyns Carr told Sir Alvary Gascoigne in strictest confidence that the Emperor had not been indicted because in a vote by the Associate Prosecutors the majority had been opposed. But this was window-dressing; even had the majority approved, there seems little chance that MacArthur would have sanctioned his inclusion. In any case, as far as the British were concerned, indicting the Emperor would have been 'a capital political blunder'; and the Russians, who had trumpeted Hirohito's war guilt in the media, made no mention at all of including his name among the accused after they arrived in Japan.

Once the immediate need to secure peaceful surrender and the safe establishment of the Occupation was past, it might seem that there was no good reason why Japanese public opinion should not have been manipulated in favour of Hirohito's abdication. A new Emperor could have been installed and, after a suitable cooling-off period, Hirohito brought to trial – outside Japan, possibly at Pearl Harbor.

But still the Allies vacillated, producing a confusing variety of arguments to justify the inaction which cumulatively guaranteed the Emperor's survival. One was a sense of obligation under the terms of the Potsdam Declaration. A great deal of hard work had gone into drafting a provision which would hint to the Japanese that they might keep their Emperor, without alerting public opinion at home to the politically explosive fact that the Emperor, in the short term, was to be preserved to save Allied money and effort. The Japanese had taken the hint with alacrity, and now, as MacArthur's Military Secretary pointed out, to put Hirohito on trial after having made good use of him 'would amount to a breach of faith. . . . The Japanese feel that unconditional surrender as outlined in the Potsdam Declaration meant preservation of the state structure, which includes the Emperor'. The fact that the U.S. Office of War Information had deliberately refrained from castigating the Emperor in the propaganda it aimed at Japan during the war only strengthened Hirohito's position.

In any event, SCAP would have been hard pressed to find an effective substitute through whom they might as successfully exploit the prestige of the Imperial institution. Crown Prince Akihito, Hirohito's direct successor, was still a boy and would need a Regent – and the list of possible candidates for that post among the Imperial family was short and unpromising. (The most obvious candidate, Hirohito's brother Prince Chichibu, was ill, and had in the mid-1930s been deeply implicated in rightist plots.) Besides, Hirohito had much to recommend him for the future, a young man still with the prospect of a long reign in front of him. The British were particularly hopeful: 'It is a fact that the Imperial House of Japan had a long tradition of respect for our own Royal House. . . . If the Imperial House can transform itself into a genuine constitutional monarchy on the British model, its continuance will suit our interests.'

Ultimately, however, the key to Hirohito's survival was MacArthur. On September 27, 1945, the Emperor had made his first visit to MacArthur's headquarters. As they sat cosily before a log fire, in the manner of American presidents past and present, Hirohito declared, 'I come to you . . . to offer myself to the judgement of the Power you represent as the one to bear sole responsibility for every political and military decision made and action taken by my people in the conduct of the war.' This was a brave gesture and one, though perhaps Hirohito did not know it, to which MacArthur was guaranteed to respond sympathetically. Six days later, his Military Secretary produced a memo: 'From the highest and most reliable sources, it can be established that the war did not stem from the Emperor himself. He has personally said that he had no intention to have the War Rescript used as Tojo used it.'

The International Prosecution Section unquestionably obeyed the orders it had received from the Joint Chiefs of Staff to gather evidence on the Emperor's war guilt; there are discernible traces in the IPS files of enquiries which continued at least until March 1946. But two months before that MacArthur had made up his mind. On January 25, he made his views clear to the JCS, views that were to remain unchanged throughout the Occupation. 'I have gained the definite impression from as complete a research as was possible to me that [the Emperor's] connection with affairs of state up to the time of the end of the war was largely ministerial and automatically responsive to the advice of his counsellors.' This cannot have been based on anything much more substantial than his own intuitive assessment of Hirohito's character; but it was decisive.

Whatever the ultimate reason for Hirohito's non-indictment, the question remains – did MacArthur leave a war criminal on the throne of Japan? Again, this is difficult to answer. The question turns in part on the interpretation of 'war criminal'. Certainly as far as the IMTFE proceedings were concerned, had Hirohito joined 'Tojo and his gang' in the dock, it seems probable on the basis of the evidence produced that he would have been convicted. Webb, who as President of the Tribunal naturally had great influence, considered him guilty beyond doubt. Perhaps even more significantly, Comyns Carr wrote to the British Attorney General on January 2, 1948: 'Incidentally, the defendants, if they have done nothing else, have proved the guilt of the Emperor pretty conclusively.'

But this assessment, made without cognisance of the evidence the Emperor might have adduced in his own cause requires closer examination. In terms of gaining a conviction at the IMTFE, the evidence which has emerged in the decades since the war would only have confirmed Comyns Carr in his belief in the Emperor's guilt. This reflects, however, less on Hirohito's moral turpitude than on the way in which Comyns Carr himself had framed the charges. Given the central position of the Emperor from 1928 onwards, it would have been impossible for him to escape a conspiracy charge where 'a defendant may be guilty of conspiracy even though he did not authorise or actually participate in the perpetration of the ultimate unlawful act . . . as long as he failed expressly to withdraw from the evil combination'. Equally, no minister (and this included the Emperor, as head of state) could be acquitted of responsibility for atrocities, even if he were not directly charged with the duty of looking after prisoners-of-war, unless he had 'satisfied himself' that a proper system had been established for the purpose, and thereafter 'had no reason to suspect' that it was not being properly carried out.

To point out that the criteria for judging guilt were very strict is not, however, to subscribe to MacArthur's view that Hirohito should be absolved of all responsibility. Evidence currently available indicates that Hirohito did have a degree of power in government; he gave orders on occasion which were obeyed; his opinion inevitably carried weight; and the Imperial institution was used with his knowledge as sanction for actions that were often deplorable. Defendant Hata testified, for example, that following the Doolittle Raid, the Imperial General Staff obtained Imperial approval for the promulgation of a law – contrary to the rules of war – permitting the death penalty for Allied airmen who attacked the Japanese home islands or territory under Japanese control.

But Hirohito was not a leader. In many respects his position was similar to that of the *zaibatsu* families: at worst he was no more than a collaborator, and often an unwilling one. And in mitigation of even this guilt, several factors can be identified which combined to push him further down the path of collaboration than he would ideally have liked. He had a strong sense of duty, and regarded his position under the Meiji Constitution as genuinely that of a constitutional monarch; so when faced with a unanimous decision by his ministers he felt himself obliged to grant it Imperial sanction. Should he have considered opposing or modifying a decision, he was at the mercy of his acolytes – men like the Marquis Kido – to whom he necessarily turned for information and advice concerning the outside world. In a real sense, power in Japan lay behind the throne.

He had another reason for his compliance, beyond the experience of the West. In traditional Japan, the concept of family extended back from the living into antiquity, and forward from the living into infinity. The Japanese in the 1940s still had a very strong sense of other-worldliness, and tended to order their conduct in accordance with what they saw as their duty both to their ancestors and to their progeny. One ancestor in particular weighed heavily on Hirohito's mind – the Emperor Meiji. It was Meiji who had given Japan its Constitution; and under Meiji's rule Japan took its first steps towards empire. In the process, hundreds of thousands of Japanese lives were sacrificed, and according to Shinto doctrine each one had become a 'nation-protecting *kami*', worshipped at the Yasukuni Shrine. Hirohito could hardly betray his ancestor and the *kami* by acceding to Allied demands in the weeks before Pearl Harbor that Japan give up the territories won at such a price – demands which in any event his advisors told him were unjust.

Nevertheless, on balance he seems to have been a restraining force. Could he have done more in standing up to the militarists? MacArthur once told Sir Alvary Gascoigne over lunch that he had asked Hirohito, 'Well, if you felt so strongly against war, why did you not step up to the microphone and pronounce an Imperial Rescript against it?' Hirohito had replied by saying that no Emperor of Japan had ever been known to act against the opinion of his advisors. 'If I had taken such action in 1941 I should most certainly have had my throat cut.'

The suggestion that Hirohito was afraid of death is misleading. His *samurai* upbringing and strong sense of duty directed him to do what he thought was right and not merely what was expedient. If he did deliberately manoeuvre to stay alive, it may well have been because he had reached the same conclusion as the Allies about his successor – who in 1941 would have been Prince Chichibu. Given that the Imperial institution was to continue, Hirohito was the best man for the job. In the context of Hirohito's obligations to his ancestors, his decision to end the war in the face of army opposition and surrender the fate of the Imperial institution to the Allies in fact showed remarkable courage. As Chairman of the Privy Council, Baron Hiranuma, remarked: 'His Majesty, the Emperor, is responsible to his Imperial ancestors. Therefore, it is the Emperor's grave responsibility if the Imperial family lineage is threatened.'

Leaving questions of guilt and justice to one side, Hirohito at liberty probably was, and is, a stronger force for peace than the example of Hirohito executed beside Tojo, Hirota and the others could ever have been. Beneath the mild, inoffensive, 'human' facade cultivated so assiduously for him by SCAP and the Imperial Household, there seems to have lain a genuine commitment to peace, which may have played an important part in forging the national consensus that has so influenced the course of post-war Japan. Trite though his public statements of the Occupation period may sound in translation to the 1980s, in their context they undoubtedly carried great force with his people. In Hiroshima, on the eve of the sixth anniversary of Pearl Harbor, the *New York Times* reported: 'Emperor Hirohito, standing at the site of the atomic bomb blast that flattened this city, today broke all precedent by delivering a brief and unexpected address to 40,000 wildly cheering citizens . . . standing alone and unattended on a raised platform where he could look out over the heads of his subjects to the spot where the Japanese shrine to the atomic bomb stands. . . . "I cannot but feel very sorry for the disaster that this city suffered. I believe, however, that we must construct a peaceful Japan keeping this disaster deep in our memory. We must work to continue the rebuilding of our country, and to contribute to world peace".'

The early years of Hirohito's reign may always be something of an enigma, and the failure to try him has robbed history of vital insights into pre-war Japan. How he might have defended himself can only be a matter for speculation; but some inkling appears in a document he gave to Sir George Sansom, visiting Tokyo in January 1946 as the British nominee to the FEC. Sansom, on official business, had felt it wiser to refuse an invitation from the Emperor to discuss 'certain matters' alone and in private. So Hirohito put his message in a letter, a private communication between individuals whose sincerity there is little reason to doubt. 'I did my utmost to avoid war. Things, however, came to such a pass for reasons of internal affairs that we very reluctantly opened hostilities against your country, with which Japan has long maintained most friendly relations ever since the time of the Emperor Meiji, and where, during my memorable visit, I was given a most cordial reception by the Royal House, the pleasant recollections of which I have always cherished. It is a matter for sincere regret that you should have suffered from great loss of life and property caused by this war.

I signed my name to the Declaration of War with heart-rending grief, repeatedly telling General Tojo, the then Prime Minister, that, while recalling the memories of my happy days in England, I should be obliged to do that with much regret and reluctance.

I earnestly desire to carry out the terms of the Potsdam Agreement faithfully, and to make every effort to rebuild a better nation dedicated to peace and democracy.'

15

The Case for the Prosecution

Note:
1. No smoking in court at any time.
2. Use of cameras in courtroom is prohibited except by accredited photographers.
3. Spectators leaving at any recess forfeit right to return to courtroom for that session.
4. AM spectators must be seated not later than 0915.
   PM spectators must be seated not later than 1315.
5. Pass will be surrendered to Military Police on request.
6. Use only the headphone provided at your seat. Do not tamper with this equipment.
7. When judges enter courtroom stand and remain silent.

* * *

The judgement of history is nowhere as harsh as in the field of stage and opera design. What is past is cliché. So it is perhaps unkind to stigmatise the packaging of the IMTFE as melodrama. At the time, the symbolism inherent in the choice of the Japanese War Ministry Building as the venue for the Tribunal may have seemed apt and striking rather than simply naive – though even contemporary commentators remarked on the larger-than-life quality of the courtroom SCAP built for its juristic offspring. The high-ceilinged chamber at the heart of the building, the coruscation of massed flags behind the over-high Bench irradiating the source from which justice would descend, seemed, as *Time* put it, more suited to 'a Hollywood premiere'.

But this citadel of virtue was soon under siege. The air-conditioning did not work and the hot court went on strike. The simultaneous translation technology functioned only in fits and starts; and perhaps more seriously from the point of view of theatre, stage management had forgotten to dress the principal actors for their parts. At the grand opening, on May 3, 1946, into a courtroom ablaze with film crews' Klieg lights which bounced and flickered off the high polish of ubiquitous mahogany panelling, shuffled the accused – 'a miserable-looking lot, dressed in the non-descript clothing which the Sugamo Prison authorities had pre-scribed for inmates. . . . Certainly the trial would have been a different affair had the accused been dressed in morning clothes or immaculately pressed uniforms, with medals, polished boots and other trappings of the military. As it was . . . the group looked like a gathering of ordinary old men'.

The rhetoric of Keenan's opening address had the same off-centre quality. 'This problem of peace', he intoned, 'which has ever been the desire of the human race, has now reached a position of [sic] the crossroads. For the implements of destruction that we already know of, even in what might be called a primitive develop-ment, have reached such proportions that only the human imagin-ation at its highest development is fit to cope with the realities. Our question, Mr. President, at the crossroads is now literally an answer: "To be or not to be".'

From bathos, the proceedings quickly degenerated into pure comedy. The defendants were seated below the judges and to their right in two long rows, one behind the other. Directly behind Tojo sat Shumei Okawa, the principal surviving military ideologue, whose brain, unbeknownst to the Allies, was slowly being eroded by syphilis. As Okawa's counsel was later to explain, an Indian couple at this moment entered the Visitors Gallery and Okawa, seeing them, called out 'Indien, Kommen Sie'. As he spoke, he banged on the table he imagined was before him. Unfortunately the hard surface off which his slap resounded was Tojo's bald head. The courtroom, hearing the first report, was transfixed, only to collapse in disrespectful laughter as Okawa repeated the ges-ture. Ultimately, Okawa was to be saved by American penicillin; but by this time the charges against him had long been dropped and he became a free man, released unconditionally from the asy-lum in which SCAP had incarcerated him, seven days after Tojo's execution.

William Sebald, who was to succeed George Atcheson as the State Department's official representative in Japan, was so disen-chanted by the first day's proceedings that he attended no more of the 419 days on which the court was to sit: 'I was not in sympathy with the theory that the victor should try the vanquished for deeds which, in the context of international law at that time, were not crimes, however abhorrent or deplorable they might have been from the viewpoint of philosophical concepts of right and wrong. . . . My feelings on this point were strong; so strong, in fact, that I felt uneasy throughout this first theatrical court session and I never returned to the courtroom.'

*   *   *

On June 13, 1946, after a prelude during which each of the defendants had pleaded not guilty to each of the charges in turn, the prosecution began in earnest. The IPS lawyers approached their task not count by count, nor working chronologically through the events under scrutiny from 1928 onwards, but by breaking down the subject matter covered by the Indictment into a number of major themes and presenting them in as neat a sequence as the state of preparation of the evidence would permit. The prosecution case was cumulative; by the end of it the aim was to have assembled a full and rounded picture of the iniquities listed flatly in the Indictment, a picture from whose midst the defendants could not be extricated.

The charges concerned individual responsibility for acts of state, so in the initial phase it was for the prosecution to explain how the Japanese government had been organised and how it operated, to demonstrate how the accused were implicated by virtue of the offices of state they had held. In the second phase, each conspirator's path to power within this government structure was described, and how he used this power to indoctrinate and manipulate the Japanese people into acquiescing in the militarists' grand design. It was this apparatus of propaganda, censorship, physical coercion and centralised educational control which, even as the prosecution described it, was being dismantled by SCAP.

Ryukichi Tanaka came into his own in the next two phases with intimate descriptions of the conspirators' pursuit of their aggressive plans – first against Manchuria, which they transformed into Manchukuo ('The Land of the Manchus'), a puppet state under the Army's control; and then against China proper, which the Imperial Japanese Army invaded in 1937. The rapacious exploitation of China and the Chinese people for Japan's gain formed the subject of the fifth and sixth phases, which were followed by the phases in which the prosecution discussed the episodes leading up to the Pacific War.

One such phase was devoted to exploring how Japan adopted a total war ideology after 1936, channelling all her industrial, economic and manpower resources into building a state ready for modern warfare. (This phase naturally brought the *zaibatsu* question to the forefront. The prosecution's expert witness went no further than to say, 'The so-called *zaibatsu* group always spear-

[137]

headed Japan's industrial expansion during the last few decades', but Keenan announced grandly to the press that there might well be trials of other Japanese leaders including members of the *zaibatsu* families 'not necessarily after the end of the present trial'.) At this point the prosecution also dealt with military preparations for war, including the training for the surprise attacks of December 7, 1941, and the ordering of military currency for use in occupied South East Asia. The prosecution described how between 1936 and 1941 the army swelled from 250,000 to 2,100,000 men; in the process discipline and morale were inevitably dislocated, paving the way for the unrestrained brutality the Japanese armed forces were to show during the war.

Diplomatic preparation – the allying of Japan with Germany and Italy – was the subject of a different phase, and German documents from Nuremberg provided a useful source of evidence. The trial produced its own minor diplomatic incident when the French prosecutor, presenting evidence of Japanese aggression against France and Indo-China, insisted on addressing the court in French – straining the court's translation facilities, and irritating the President, who was later obliged to assure the court that no discrimination against France had been intended.

The French gave way to the Russians who presented their phase of the case from 8 to 21 October. The Russian Associate Prosecutor Golunsky irritated everyone, particularly the Japanese public, by harking back to the Russo–Japanese War of 1904–5 (a war Japan was justly proud of having won) and drawing a parallel between Pearl Harbor and the sneak attack by the Japanese on Port Arthur, Russia's main naval base, in 1904. He reopened the border disputes of 1936 and 1938 which the Japanese regarded as having been settled at the time, and produced secret documents relating to Japanese plans for the invasion of Siberia – though the defence claimed these were no more than routine yearly tactical exercises for the training of staff officers.

Golunsky also worked hard to implicate the *zaibatsu* in war preparations. In this he echoed the current Japanese Communist Party propaganda, which raises the question of whether there was co-operation or communication between the JCP and the Russians at the IMTFE; the CIA was to report traces of 'liaison' between the Russian judge and the Japanese communists. The Russian phase was followed by evidence on Japanese aggression against the United States, the British Commonwealth and the Netherlands, including an account of how the decision to go to war was actually reached.

The systematic presentation of the prosecution case concluded with the counts of Crimes against Humanity and conventional war crimes. Technically, this was a difficult phase for the prosecution. After the Nuremberg judgement, they recognised the difficulty of proving that the defendants had conspired to order or authorise others to commit atrocities. Thus the crimes charged were essentially acts of omission, which could only be proven by a series of tortuous evidential steps. The prosecution had to establish successively that atrocities were committed; that each defendant charged owed a duty of care to those who had suffered; that he had known or should have known of their suffering; that he had failed either to stop the atrocities or prevent their recurrence; and having so failed, had stayed in office.

The Tribunal's findings on Tojo's personal involvement in atrocities – a vital factor in the decision to hang him – illustrate the type of case the prosecution had to build. 'Tojo was head of the War Ministry which was charged with the care of prisoners-of-war and of civilian internees in the theatre of war and with the supply of billets, food, medicines and hospital facilities to them. He was head of the Home Ministry which was charged with a similar duty towards civilian internees in Japan. Above all, he was head of the government which was charged with continuing responsibility for the care of prisoners and civilian internees.

'The barbarous treatment of prisoners and internees was well known to Tojo. He took no adequate steps to punish offenders and to prevent the commission of similar offences in the future. His attitude towards the Bataan Death March gives the key to his conduct towards these captives. He knew in 1942 something of the conditions of that March and that many prisoners had died as a result of these conditions. He did not call for a report on the incident. When in the Philippines in 1943 he made perfunctory enquiries about the March but took no action. No one was punished. His explanation is that the commander of a Japanese Army in the field is given a mission in the performance of which he is not subject to specific orders from Tokyo. Thus the head of the government of Japan knowingly and wilfully refused to perform the duty which lay upon that government of enforcing performance of the Laws of War. . . .

'Statistics relative to the high death rate from malnutrition and other causes in prisoner of war camps were discussed at conferences over which Tojo presided. The shocking condition of the prisoners in 1944, when Tojo's Cabinet fell, and the enormous number of prisoners who had died from lack of food and medicines is conclusive proof that Tojo took no proper steps to care for them. The Tribunal finds Tojo guilty . . .'

It has been argued persuasively – particularly in the cases of Koki Hirota and Mamoru Shigemitsu who were both convicted of acts of

omission – that the Tribunal showed a fundamental lack of understanding of the relationship between the civilian government and
the military in the field. Nevertheless, the Tokyo Tribunal has
established a precedent which imposes a strict duty of care on the
individual members (civilian and military) of the government of a
nation at war. If they fail in it, they may pay with their lives. It was
this duty of care which Bertrand Russell's mock tribunal found
certain American leaders to have breached during the Vietnam
War.

Tacked on to the end of the prosecution's presentation was a
'catch-all' phase in which evidence newly discovered was
adduced. At last on January 24, 1947 the IPS rested its case. To the
lawyer, the methods by which a prosecution of this magnitude is
assembled are of the utmost fascination – but the Japanese public at
large was neither legally trained nor remotely familiar with the
ways of Anglo-Saxon jurisprudence, and the prosecution seems
wholly to have failed to capture their imagination. In vain had Keenan instructed his team to avoid 'that type of droning testimony
that causes the attending public and the newspaper men to lose
interest'.

All attempts to inject life into the proceedings were frustrated by
Sir William Webb who forbade the IPS lawyers to colour their submissions for public consumption. Colonel Morrow, in charge of
the China phase of the prosecution case, was one unfortunate
victim of Sir William's wrath. His over-ripe description of the Rape
of Nanking – 'Sadistic mobs of soldiers spelled a tale of horror without parallel since the days of Attila the Hun' – proved too much for
Webb. 'These inflammatory statements which have been indulged
in by Colonel Morrow certainly tend only to antagonise the Tribunal. We are being treated as a jury, not as eleven sober judges. . . .
To take only two examples: what witnesses would be called upon
to testify that the Chinese soldiers fought as they never fought
before, and the Japanese behaved worse than Attila the Hun?
Those may be the facts but they don't intend to prove them. . . . I
repeat, we resent being treated as a jury. We are judges and we are
going to be treated as such.'

By the end of June 1946, the *Stars and Stripes* had already judged
the Tokyo Trial to have deteriorated into a 'second rate show', and
the people for whom the IMTFE had been so expensively staged
stopped coming. There were, of course, the loyal few. Lady Webb
was a regular; Mrs MacArthur dropped in occasionally, though her
husband never appeared; Mrs Cramer, the wife of the U.S. judge,
'never missed a day'. Nor, segregated in the 'Japanese Nationals'
section of the Visitors Gallery, did the daughters of defendant Koki
Hirota. Their mother had committed suicide shortly after their

father's arrest, and month after month they sat watching as their father allowed the prosecution's allegations to go unanswered, refusing to take the stand to give evidence on his own behalf.

Joseph Grew, who had been America's ambassador in Tokyo for much of the period covered by the trial, numbered Hirota 'among the best type of Japanese. . . . If I had the pick myself, I know of nobody whom I would have more gladly chosen to head the government with American interests in view'. When Hirota's sentence of death was announced a petition of thirty thousand signatures was quickly raised by his daughters from among the people of his home town. Since the trial he has become a martyr, a victim of the combative form of Anglo-American justice which, at least in the hostile air of Tokyo, made no allowance for men who failed to defend themselves.

Hirota's conviction on atrocities charges is generally seen as a consequence of the court's unwillingness to grasp the total inability of any civilian minister to control the military in the Japan of the 1930s. Historians, on the whole, agree with Hirota's own account of his purpose in accepting the premiership in 1936, in the days following the military's attempted *coup d'état*: 'The military are like an untamed horse left to run wild. If you try to stop it head on, you'll get kicked to death. The only hope is to jump on from the side and try to get it under control while still allowing it to have its head to a certain extent. Of course, it's a hard job to jump on without stirrups, and since you're riding bareback there's no telling when you'll get thrown off. But somebody has to do it. That's why I've jumped on.'

No one knows why he failed to contest the prosecution's view that he was the 'principal figure' in the second phase of Japanese aggression against China. To Richard Storry there was 'something moving and mysterious about Hirota's adamantine poise and reticence during the trial and afterwards. He reminds me of a dignified Roman senator, or perhaps an ascetic Mandarin of Imperial China'.

As the trial progressed, however, Hirota, with the eye of a professional diplomat, must have taken some comfort from the hash the prosecution was making of the proceedings as far as its potential value as an instrument of propaganda and political advantage was concerned. The promise the Indictment gave of huge labours for the IPS was fully redeemed, and the prosecution did not rest its case for a full eighteen months after the start of the Occupation. The Allies were driven to despair by the amount of time the trial was consuming. MacArthur told Sir Alvary Gascoigne that he was 'worried to death' about it, and though both he and President Truman had urged the IPS to accelerate the prosecution, 'it had proved impracticable to do so on any scale as each country concerned was bent on having its full share in the revelation of Japanese barbarity' – in particular Australia and the Philippines. 'The General felt strongly that this unduly long session would result in the Tribunal defeating its own end. As it was, the American press carried practically no news regarding it, and also public opinion from Japan and America was not interested.' With the defence phase yet to come, MacArthur gloomily anticipated a long delay before final judgement, and condemned the manoeuvres of the 'American shysters' acting for the defence, who in his view were already playing for time.

In fact, the Tribunal had from the outset submitted to pressure to speed the proceedings, to a degree which badly damages any claims it might have had to impartiality. The Charter had created the IMTFE 'for the just and prompt trial and punishment of the major war criminals in the Far East'. Although Webb expressed the view that the trial should be fair rather than speedy, and MacArthur reported to the Department of the Army that it was 'impossible to bring pressure upon the court for greater expedition in this matter', there is clear evidence that the Tribunal did recognise a need for haste, and responded to it in ways prejudicial to the accused.

In the first week of the trial, the prosecution asked that at its discretion the evidence of Japanese-speaking witnesses be given in affidavit form only, without the witnesses themselves having to appear in court. The process of extracting evidence by question and answer – evidence which had to be translated and was then subject to cross-examination – ate up the court's time, and the IPS pointed out that without this concession the prosecution case could last into 1948. The Tribunal granted the request though, as Webb said, 'not without grave misgivings'. These were well-founded: the ruling denied the defendants the fundamental right to challenge the witnesses in court, to cross-examine them and give the court some measure of the credibility of their testimony. In addition, in both the prosecution and defence phases, such witnesses as were required to appear in court were compelled to submit in advance an affidavit containing their evidence – so that translation time would be saved – and cross-examination was restricted to the matters raised in the affidavit. Both factors worked against the defence, the former putting an intolerable burden on their translation facilities which were much more limited than those of the prosecution, and the latter shielding the witnesses from potentially revealing questions on other areas within their competence.

Shortly after the prosecution phase closed, the Tribunal convened a tripartite conference with prosecution and defence to discuss ways of speeding up the trial. Webb suggested, for example, that the time available for the defence of each individual accused should be fixed at two days. Ben Bruce Blakeney, speaking for the defence as a whole, made their discontent plain: 'It was of course our friends of the prosecution, not we, who drew this Indictment. . . . 55 counts, covering 17 years of time and half a world of space. It was they who put in evidence running the gamut from the celebrated and portentous fire-cracker incident at home to the theft of Mrs. Wang's pig in Far China', all of which the defence were going to have to rebut.

The Tribunal, however, was unsympathetic, and responded with various new devices for saving time. Most significantly, it tightened up the rules on the nature of the evidence it would accept. A 'best evidence' rule was introduced – which meant that dubious or unproven evidence of the type which had been readily accepted in the prosecution phase was turned down when submitted by the defence. And the Tribunal claimed the right to reject evidence which it regarded as irrelevant to the case. This latter point was to be hotly contested, and perhaps demonstrates most graphically why, in the interests of justice, a nation should not be judge in its own cause.

It is fair comment on the trial as a whole to say that it revealed how Japan acted between 1928 and 1945, but not how she was acted upon by other nations. As E. H. Norman, the Canadian representative on the Allied Council for Japan, put it, 'For obvious political reasons, it was impossible to examine and analyse the internal events in such countries, for example, as China or the U.S.S.R. in the years in which Japan was directing various forms of aggression or intrigue against them'. Much evidence that might have had value to the defence was simply unavailable to them, hidden by the Allied nations, and when the defence did try to build an argument on the basis of another country's activities, the Tribunal refused to countenance it. In June 1947, rebutting the charges that Japan had planned and waged war against Russia, Ben Bruce Blakeney argued that on the contrary, it was Russia and not Japan which had displayed aggression. It was, after all, the Soviet Union which had broken the Neutrality Pact with Japan and invaded Manchuria. However, in the view of the Tribunal, evidence on the Russian entry into the Pacific war was irrelevant.

The Tribunal also refused to hear defence arguments to the effect that Japan's action in Manchuria and China had been motivated by the threat of Chinese and Soviet communism. Among the submissions rejected by the Tribunal on this count were Sir Winston Churchill's 'Iron Curtain' Speech of March 1946 and President

Truman's remarks in Congress on the worldwide threat of communism. And on April 29, 1947, the Tribunal handed down a blanket ruling that evidence relating to the existence of communism in China and the Soviet Union was inadmissible; Webb said that the 'existence or spread' of communism was not 'relevant'.

The court lost considerable credibility by its attitude. Outside the courtroom, political reality mocked these judicial pronouncements. America and Russia were squaring up to each other in the opening rounds of the Cold War and fear of the imminent outbreak of World War Three was real and prevalent among the Japanese. In his affidavit, Tojo rubbed salt into the wound, claiming that Japan had 'made the prevention of communism the common essential policy among the independent states in East Asia . . . and at the same time herself a barrier against world Bolshevization. The present condition of the world two years after the end of World War II eloquently tells how important these barriers were for the peace of the world'.

The argument that such evidence was 'irrelevant' – irrelevant, that is, as far as *this case* was concerned, and in the strictly legal sense – proved increasingly hard to sustain. The defence consistently attempted to pursue an embarrassing and destructive line of argument to the effect that the Allies had behaved equally badly in the war. Had not America broken the international laws of neutrality with the lend-lease arrangement with Britain? Had not Russia invaded Finland? And partitioned Poland in a cosy agreement with Hitler? And most tellingly as far as the Japanese were concerned, had not the Allies risen to the acme of barbarism at Hiroshima and Nagasaki? The Tribunal might sustain prosecution objections to such leading questions, and refuse to admit the supporting evidence, but lasting damage was done. It did no good to point out that the Allies were not on trial, because the implication was that they ought to have been. Japan was not the only villain, simply the only loser.

16

The Case for the Defence

Looking back over four decades to the Tokyo trial, now that the rancour of war has receded, one question remains hard to answer. How far did the Allies owe a duty of care to the accused – a duty to ensure they had a proper defence? Did they owe 'Tojo and his gang' an equal chance, a fighting chance, or no chance at all?

All the cards were in the Allies' hands. They determined the law and procedure; they drew up the charges; they chose the defendants; they began the trial when it suited them; their representatives alone sat on the Bench. In the circumstances, was it just to incarcerate the war criminals from the autumn of 1945 until the end of April 1946 without bringing charges against them? to interrogate them without either Japanese or Western-trained lawyers present, and then use the results of these interrogations in evidence? to construct the powerful machine of the IPS, well-greased with American money and the pick of legal brains from the Allied nations, without making similar provision for the defence?

Anglo-American criminal trials are as much about winning and losing as they are about justice, and with all these disadvantages, it is hard to see how the defence at Tokyo could have done other than fail. Left to fend for itself against overwhelming odds, in the end it proved disorganised, inefficient and ineffectual.

At the beginning of the defence phase, the Chief of Defence Counsel, Dr. Somei Uzawa, made a national radio appeal to the Japanese people. In it he described the defence's critical lack of 'funds, communications, lodgings and food', and he asked not for sympathy but for practical help. The response appears to have been nil. Instead, the attorneys ended up contributing 1,000 yen and the defendants 10,000 yen each to a central pool to pay for translators, clerical help and the services of witnesses. (By March 1947, the defence was indebted to a local hotel 'in an amount of seven or eight thousand yen in respect of witnesses brought to Tokyo'.) Eventually Webb persuaded SCAP to arrange for the

Japanese government to pay senior Japanese counsel 1,800 and juniors 1,500 yen per month. But the fact remains that as a legal machine the defence could never bulk as large as the IPS, purely through lack of funds. Its most serious disadvantage was perhaps its shortage of translators, crucial in the preparation of court documents. After the Occupation, Japanese counsel were to claim that given another ten million yen ($30,000), none of the defendants would have been hanged.

There were also American lawyers, paid by the U.S. government, acting for the defendants – but their involvement was characterised by bitterness and frustration. The Charter contained a range of provisions which seemed to offer scope for a fair defence – the French judge, for one, was confident it would be possible. Following up these provisions, the General Secretary of the Tribunal, Vern Wallbridge, established an International Defence Panel – a team of American lawyers to assist and advise Japanese counsel. This scheme was destroyed in embryo on the day the Indictment was lodged in court, when Webb ruled that the only counsel to be heard before the IMTFE would be those formally appointed in writing by the accused. Six of the original panel expressed their outrage at the injustice of isolating the defendants in this way by resigning their positions. One of them, Valentine Deale, complained bitterly: 'To expect Japanese defendants to care adequately for their own defence in an Anglo-American trial prosecuted by lawyers skilled in criminal procedures was an absurdity which cannot be justified by legalistic verbiage about the right of defendants to conduct their own defence. The fact of the matter was that if the accused before the Tokyo tribunal were to receive a fair trial, it would be because of American counsel assigned to them by American authority.'

The Japanese lawyers appointed by the accused tended to bear out Deale's opinion. Even the Japanese press criticised them for their ineptitude, and the American lawyers who eventually replaced the original International Defense Panel quickly came to realise that the Japanese counsel 'did not know what the trial was about. Japanese lawyers as a group were thoroughly unacquainted with Anglo-American legal procedure. They did not know what it meant to make a real defence for their clients. A prevailing idea of the duty of a criminal defence attorney was, figuratively speaking, to put flowers gracefully on his client's grave'. Moreover, they were 'too polite and courteous to stand up against the Australian judge who presided over the court'. (Early in the trial Webb had dismissed one Japanese effort at cross-examination as 'a waste of time'.) But however out of touch the Japanese lawyers may have been, they were nevertheless in charge; and the incoming team of

Americans was obliged to co-operate in the Japanese strategy of defence – a strategy which sometimes bore little relation to the merits of the case.

After the six early resignations, other attorneys were brought in from the States, though by July 1946 three of the accused still had no U.S. representation. It is alleged that among the lawyers who volunteered to defend the Japanese war criminals, there was a handful of carpet-baggers who were out for what they could get and behaved despicably towards the relatives of the accused. Certainly the turnover of personnel was suspiciously high; but there were also some extremely idealistic and enterprising young men – mid-Westerners for the most part – who stayed throughout the trial and whose personal courage and dedication to the cause of justice went far both to illuminate and to redeem the fundamental inequities of the IMTFE. Owen Cunningham, former head of the Des Moines College of Law, was typical: 'I am not, and never have been, an advocate of the Japanese cause, but a defender of the legal rights of one defendant involved. My role was to see that justice as understood in Anglo-Saxon countries was fairly and impartially administered.'

Cunningham expressed the bitterness of the U.S. defence attorneys at the handling of the Tokyo proceedings in a speech that was to have him debarred from them. He railed against the 'erroneous presumption of guilt rather than innocence [which] prevailed throughout the whole trial' and considered that the 'prosecution was bent on conviction, not justice, fairness and the inalienable rights of man. The prosecution was not a branch of any permanent system of law enforcement, but created for the occasion with no code of ethics to guide its conduct, emphasising the dangers which arise from a political prosecution accountable to no authority and whose sole purpose is conviction'.

There was an element of suicidal bravery in the decision to volunteer for the defence – the U.S. War Department, for example, had said it would 'frown on any American counsel in the Army appearing for the accused', and the volunteers could also expect a degree of opprobrium from friends and colleagues back home. They showed their courage from the start of proceedings by arguing that a tribunal comprised solely of representatives of victor nations could be neither 'fair, legal nor impartial', and specifically challenging certain judges on the grounds of 'personal bias and prejudice' – Webb, for example, because he had headed the official Australian inquiry into Japanese atrocities in New Guinea; the Philippine judge, Delfin Jaranilla, because he had actually been a participant in the Bataan Death March. As for the Soviet judge, Major Ben Bruce Blakeney for the defence argued that Russia should not be represented at all because it 'has itself conducted armed aggression in Asia and in Europe, has been adjudicated guilty, and for its guilt has been expelled from that very League of Nations upon the Covenant of which the prosecution now so heavily relies' – words which the Soviet Associate Prosecutor asked Keenan to have struck from the record.

Nor was the American judge immune. The original appointee, John P. Higgins, had resigned on July 12, 1946, apparently hounded out not by the defence but by Keenan. In his place MacArthur appointed Major General Myron C. Cramer, former Judge Advocate General. The defence protested this appointment on principle – firstly because Cramer had already missed too much of the testimony; secondly, because the Charter did not confer power on MacArthur to make substitutions; and thirdly, on the personal ground that Cramer had previously given legal opinion on related matters – viz. internal American responsibility for the failure adequately to defend Pearl Harbor.

All these challenges failed, among other reasons because the Tribunal did not at that time regard itself as qualified to question the source of its own authority – namely MacArthur's power as Supreme Commander. There seems to have been some disagreement among the American defence counsel as to whether or not they should question MacArthur's power to create the Tribunal in the first place. Owen Cunningham recalled: 'The defence contended from the very beginning that General MacArthur had no authority to set up the IMTFE. I wanted to make a legal test of the General's authority but my associates urged that it be postponed. At that time he was having trouble with the Russians. There was a question whether it was within our function to test the political wisdom and policy of the trials, or whether our only purpose was to defend before whatever court the accused were arraigned. I yielded to the appeal to patriotism.' In January 1947, however, the gloves came off and Hirota's U.S. counsel tried to challenge MacArthur's jurisdiction – only to have the motion dismissed by Webb as 'political harangue'.

The defence were not afraid to upbraid the judges on their frequent absences from the court. The Charter of the IMTFE, unlike that of the Nuremberg Tribunal, made no provision for alternate judges; when any member was absent, there was simply less than a full complement. This produced inconsistency in the rules of evidence, what was admitted depending largely on who was sitting that day. (Webb was on one occasion to acknowledge, 'I would be deceiving you if I said decisions did not turn on how the court was constituted from time to time'.) The defence maintained a constant barrage of criticism of the Bench in this respect, and with some justification. By Owen Cunningham's calculations, an aggregate of 466 judge-days was lost to the court: Röling and McDougall (Netherlands and Canada), 14 days each: Cramer (U.S.A.), 28 days, after arriving two months late; Bernard (France), 32 days; Zarynov (U.S.S.R.), 37 days; Jaranilla (Philippines), 38 days; Lord Patrick (Britain), 43 days; Mai (Nationalist China) and Northcroft (New Zealand), 49 days each; Webb (Australia), 53 days; Pal (India), 109 days. Lord Patrick regarded the absences of Webb and Pal as 'the gravest blot that had yet stained the honour of the court'.

American counsel were also extremely enterprising in the type of evidence they sought to gather on their clients' behalf. They were assisted by the Operations Division of the War Crimes Section at the Pentagon, and through it obtained books (including Joseph Grew's *Ten Years in Japan* – 'We are proposing to use hundreds of excerpts from this book'); copies of treaties; newspaper articles (including 'recent Herbert Hoover article on America's provocation of Japan prior to Pearl Harbor attack'); official reports and documents (such as the Nuremberg court transcript, the Congressional Hearings on the Pearl Harbor attack, and Cramer's opinion on internal responsibility); and more *recherché* information – 'an agenda of West Point Studies 1928 to date', and 'official document outlining the duties and responsibilities of a Chief of Staff in the U.S. Army'.

Through the Pentagon, defence counsel were also able to obtain affidavits from many leading Americans – among them Grew himself, Joseph Kennedy, and the Secretary of State, General George C. Marshall. This last affidavit was Owen Cunningham's idea, and is one of the more remarkable documents of the trial. In it General Marshall explained his view that there was no evidence of 'close strategic co-operation between Germany and Japan' – a view which Cunningham buttressed by flying to Nuremberg to interview leading Nazis, including von Ribbentrop. With this affidavit he defeated Count 5 of the Indictment virtually single-handed. To Comyns Carr's chagrin, and perhaps to the surprise of a world educated by Allied propagandists, the Tribunal's findings were that 'although some of the conspirators clearly desired the achievement of these grandiose objects, nevertheless there is not sufficient evidence to justify a finding that the conspiracies charged in Count 5 have been proved'. (Cunningham had also obtained from General Marshall a second affidavit dealing with 'U.S. military preparations and the sending of reinforcements to the Philippines in 1941' which was to form part of the Japanese self-defence argument, but the court for its own reasons refused to admit this document.)

In a case of this magnitude, however, while individual enterprise and industry could achieve isolated success, without long-term co-ordinated effort directed to specific ends, no fully effective defence was possible. For all its cliquishness, internecine axe-grinding and Keenan's unreliability, the IPS was an efficiently administered machine. It pursued defined targets, and possessed the advantages of having drawn the charges to suit its evidence, and having had a long pre-trial period of preparation with unlimited access to official support services. The defence, under-financed, started its preparations late, short of legal, linguistic, and clerical staff, and lacking firm leadership. It was also handicapped by the fact that whilst from the prosecution's side the accused formed a group of conspirators, and major portions of the prosecution evidence related to the group as a whole, to the defence they were individuals, each out to defend his own separate life and liberty – a fragmentary and more complex process.

The defence position became increasingly untenable as the prosecution heaped up incriminating evidence around it. Defence counsel never achieved anything approaching a state of absolute readiness to make a complete case, and were continually obliged to halt the court proceedings while they scraped together evidence and arguments simply to meet the demands of the next phase. On February 3, 1947 – one week into the defence phase – the court granted a twenty-day recess; on March 25 a seven-day recess; on June 19 a recess lasting until August 4. The Tribunal was naturally sceptical of the need for these interruptions, and ultimately a committee of judges was invited to investigate for itself. The committee's report of March 1947 revealed a lamentable state of confusion. Where the IPS had 200 translators, the defence shared 72, 'of whom they say four or five only are competent'. Out of 2000 documents which the defence proposed to submit in evidence, only 300 had been processed. Few of the Japanese defence counsel spoke English, so conferences with American attorneys were both laborious and fertile ground for misunderstandings. And 'conflicting interests and personalities . . . have prevented the appointment of heads of several departments'.

In the opinion of Lord Patrick, the defence 'will never be anything else but in a mess. They will blunder on, asking from time to time for a short spell to enable them to get ready for presentation the next part of their case. They have no organisation which would have the authority to reject unessential and irrelevant evidence, so they waste their time and clutter up the machinery of translating and copying evidence with the preparation for presentation of the most irrelevant stuff, which this tribunal rejects when they present it. Their only system is to take every topic in the long history on which the prosecution has touched, and where the prosecution has said 'yes' to attempt to establish 'no', or make a most protracted and utterly fulsome apologia for Japan's acts'.

What is perhaps disappointing is the judges' total lack of concern over the fact that justice was clearly not being done. The Tribunal displayed, in the words of the New Zealand judge, nothing more than the worry that 'there may easily be a complete breakdown, as a result of which the defence counsel will say in a body either that they cannot go on with, or that they are being prevented from presenting, their defence, leaving the case to be concluded with a declaration to the world that the trial has been unfair'.

To a large extent, the problems of the defence were compounded by the court's refusal to accede to their motion at the end of the prosecution's case that at least some of the charges had clearly not been proven. Given that the Tribunal was ultimately only to consider ten out of the fifty-five counts originally advanced (mainly for reasons that must already have been obvious by the end of the prosecution phase), some of the charges could and should properly have been struck out before the defence started to plead.

In presenting its case, the defence had to take account of the fact that each accused had separate interests, and at points these interests could, and did, conflict. Consequently, though there was a general defence phase concerning matters of law, fact and interpretation common to all defendants, there was also an individual defence phase where each accused pursued his own objectives at the expense of the others.

The common ground included several fundamental points of law which are now thought to weigh quite heavily in the defendants' favour, but at the time were rejected by the Tribunal. (It should be said that in arguing points of law, as opposed to handling cross-examination, Japanese counsel, particularly Harvard Law School graduate Kenzo Takayanagi, were extremely effective.) Among these points were the contentions that the charges of 'Crimes against Peace' and 'Crimes against Humanity' were *ex post facto*; that international law recognised no individual liability for acts of state; and that the concept of conspiracy was solely a device of Anglo-Saxon jurisprudence, and did not then exist at international law.

In dealing with the evidence relating to the common ground, the defence ordered its presentation to correspond roughly with that of the IPS. Within this framework, defence counsel set out to challenge, counter-balance or reinterpret the prosecution's evidence. They disputed, for instance, the prosecution account of how the Japanese government worked, an account designed to highlight the conspiracy motif, by pointing out that between 1928 and 1941 there had been no less than fifteen cabinets. This suggested a degree of change and discontinuity which would have made an effective conspiracy far harder to sustain, and the defence claimed this single fact seriously undermined the prosecution's argument – an argument which Tojo characterised as 'unthinkable to persons of reason and intelligence'.

Not all the defence's contentions, however, were this cogent. As to the fate of Allied prisoners-of-war, they claimed on their clients' behalf that 'shipping losses' had been responsible for the failure to supply adequate food and medicines. To explain the active mal-treatment of prisoners, they wheeled in the Pope's representative, the Apostolic Delegate to Japan. He chose to inform the Tribunal that in order to arrive at an 'impartial judgement' on the treatment of prisoners-of-war, they must consider 'that the Japanese do not have that idea of prisoner that a long Christian culture had given us'. He himself had visited more than thirty prisoner-of-war camps and found the condition of prisoners' quarters and clothing to be the same as that of the 'common people' of Japan.

In explaining why Japan had gone to war against the Western Allies in 1941, the defence largely followed the line of Japanese wartime propaganda: that Japan had been driven by economic blockade and military pressure to fight a 'war of self-defence'. The contention was that in reality hostilities had already begun before Pearl Harbor – and the lawyers cited in evidence U.S. aid to China, the fortification of Singapore, troop reinforcements in the Philip-pines, and the progressive restrictions on international trade which culminated in the freezing of Japanese external assets and the total oil embargo of July 1941. The question was 'not who had lit the fuse which had started a major conflagration, but who had lit the *first* fuse'.

Here the defence profited from the post-war public outpouring of war stories, reminiscences, score-settling and soul-searching in which some of the Allies had indulged. In the Congressional Enquiry into the events leading up to Pearl Harbor, they struck an unexpectedly rich vein. In arguing that the Allies were already act-ing against Japan before December 1941, they found most helpful, for instance, the Enquiry's account of the 'secret American-Dutch-British conversations held at Singapore in April 1941', and in parti-cular the British revelations that by April 1941 they were organising guerrilla forces in China and 'subversive activities, sabotage and corruption in Japan and in Japanese-occupied territories'.

Predictably, the defence expended great effort in justifying the bombing of Pearl Harbor before war had been declared – and in the end produced an explanation which the Tribunal appears to have accepted as plausible. The official declaration of war, the defence claimed, was of such secrecy and importance that it could be typed out in Washington only by one particular senior diplomat – whose typing was both so bad that he had to retype it and so slow that by

the time the declaration was presentable, Pearl Harbor was ablaze.
Well before the defence reached the end of the evidence relating to
the defendants as a group, Comyns Carr was in paroxysms of rage.
He cabled the Attorney General: 'The defendants have now
finished their general case, which they ought never to have been
allowed to present, as most of it has been a sheer waste of time.'

As the defence moved into the individual phase, undignified
dissension and mutual recriminations broke out in the ranks of the
accused. The Army blamed the Cabinet, and *vice versa*, and the
Navy, which had been skilfully keeping clear of the mêlée, was
dragged down by defendant Muto's disclosure that the Navy had
in fact 'requested the Foreign Office to delay delivery of Japan's
final Note to Mr. Cordell Hull'. Each accused naturally tried
hardest to rebut those portions of the prosecution's evidence
which related specifically to himself. Matsui denied that the
Imperial General Staff had planned the Rape of Nanking. Doihara
was stated to have been 'surprised' when Hitler decorated him
with the Grand Cross in 1941 (presumably as a token of his contribution to the development of the Axis). Araki said that parts of his
speeches had been quoted out of context and did not represent his
real attitude. Koiso, Tojo's successor as Prime Minister, argued
that the 'fighting speeches' he had made were 'what any man in
the same position would have had to make', but his 'real intention'
had been to 'try to conclude hostilities by negotiation'.

Not all the accused spoke in their own defence; several, as Owen
Cunningham recalled, refused to take the witness stand 'because
they did not care to be subjected to the extensive, as well as abusive, cross-examination'. The experience of the first few – they
went in alphabetical order – might well have been a deterrent to the
others. Hashimoto, for example, was bullied into admitting that in
January 1941 he had advocated seizing control of the Pacific and
dominating continental Asia as far west as the Persian Gulf.

But beginning with Kido, the accused discovered an unwitting
ally in the Chief of Counsel for the Allied Nations. 'Keenan', wrote
Comyns Carr to the Attorney General in despair, 'who has
behaved fairly decently since his return, has now started to display
the cloven hoof. He suddenly announced his intention the other
day of cross-examining, himself, one of the accused (Kido) who
has been assigned to me by him from the beginning. Of course, I
don't personally care whether I cross-examine a particular accused
or not: the trouble is (a) this man is a rather important and difficult
case, requiring a great knowledge of detail which he can't possibly
acquire in the time and would be incompetent to handle if he did,
and (b) his obvious reasons are (1) he wants to prevent the British
Commonwealth from figuring too prominently in the case, and

[153]

(2) he wants to develop a row he has started with Webb, the President, over the question of the Emperor's responsibility, about which both parties have already made some pretty injudicious remarks, and are likely to make more, neither being at all discreet. For the first of these reasons and personal spite, he has also taken away from Quillam, of New Zealand, another accused and handed him over to a newly arrived and perfectly incompetent American, who again knows nothing about it. . . . He has also taken another rather important accused away from a probably incompetent Filipino, and given him to a certainly incompetent, though very pleasant, American. The case is thus in danger of being finally reduced to a laughing stock, if it wasn't already.' Two weeks later, on October 21, 1947, he lamented, 'Everything has worked out even more disastrously than I anticipated. . . . As a result of the way the case is now being handled I anticipate a number of acquittals or disagreements'.

But the most important defendant, Tojo himself, had yet to take centre stage, and in the wings waited John Fihelly. As he waited he prepared himself for what promised to be the single most important cross-examination of his life. In many ways, the success of the IMTFE as the spearhead in the campaign for the psychological disarmament of Japan would depend on his being able to crack her wartime leader and humble him in the public mind.

17

Tojo's Defence of Japan

'A *samurai* who is not prepared to die at any moment will inevitably die an unbecoming death. But a *samurai* who lives his life in constant preparation for death – how can he conduct himself in a despicable manner? One should reflect well on this point and behave accordingly.'

Hagakure, the teachings of Jocho Yamamoto.

The persistent efforts of the defence counsel to discredit the IMTFE on legal and moral grounds were brought to a triumphal conclusion by Hideki Tojo. His personal evidence took only seven days of the court's time – three days of reading out his affidavit and four days of cross-examination – but in that time, he won the propaganda war. His victory was the final irony for the Allies, who had hoped to see militarist Japan dragged through the dirt.

It was not as though the Japanese attorneys made any effort to conceal their intentions. Several of them had had pre-war connections with the military, and had already defended army officers and civilian ultra-nationalists involved in the political violence and murder of the 1930s. Tojo's personal counsel, Ichiro Kiyose, had defended the young army officers responsible for the full-scale *coup d'etat* attempt on May 15, 1932, in the course of which Prime Minister Tsuyoshi Inukai and several others had been assassinated. Now Kiyose wrote in the *Seikai Shunju* (Political and Economic Review) of his 'determination to make clear to the world that the Manchurian and China incidents, as well as the Pacific War, were not begun with an aggressive intention and that Japan did not outrage the spirit and basic meaning of the treaties which were concerned with military moves'. In his radio appeal for funds, the Japanese Chief of Defence Counsel informed the nation that 'Japanese lawyers needed aid in order to prove that circumstances forced Japan to go to war'. And Yutaka Sugawara, a director of the Japan Lawyers Association, went one stage further in an article in the *Horitsu Shimpo* (Law Journal): 'We, as the lawyers of Japan, must make a desperate attempt so that the judges will not misunderstand the position of the nation and the Emperor. . . . Let us remember that we are here as lawyers *for the defence of Japan* as well as for the twenty-eight defendants.'

In striking this forceful and dramatic note, the defence was playing to its only strengths. In the legal battle they may have struggled along in the wake of the prosecution, hamstrung by lack of funds, facilities and time. But to be successful in the propaganda war, they did not need a large efficient organisation; with Tojo more than willing to sacrifice himself for the cause, they were a formidable force.

Critics of Masaki Kobayashi's four-and-a-half hour documentary 'Tokyo Trial' (released in the U.S.A. in 1985) complained that in it Tojo figures as a national hero. The truth is that at moments during the proceedings, he came close to becoming one. He started slowly. At first his own people ridiculed him for his ignominious failure to shoot himself in the heart; and skilful SCAP press photographs of Tojo in prison, warm and eating from a full rice-bowl, did nothing to endear him to an impoverished nation facing the harsh winter of 1945/6. He also suffered humiliation at the hands of individual Americans – an army dentist who inscribed 'Remember Pearl Harbor' on his bridgework; a young military policeman who clogged his earphones with chewing gum.

Slowly, however, Tojo pulled back. With time, the débacle of his suicide attempt receded, and his own carefully cultivated reserve stood out amongst the undignified mutual recriminations of his fellow-accused. He also had several pieces of luck – not least the timing of his appearance. Because the accused were called in alphabetical order, his turn to testify came towards the end of the defence phase, giving him virtually the last word. And by the time he took the stand, on December 26, 1947, the Japanese were beginning to tire of the American presence. Even MacArthur was feeling that the Occupation had rather 'shot its bolt', and the time was ripe for a Japanese triumph.

Two rules of procedure also worked to Tojo's advantage. The first obliged him to present his evidence as sworn testimony in writing three days before it was read out in court – so he was given every opportunity to make a formal written statement of the Japanese militarists' case. And the second prevented the prosecution from using more than one lawyer to cross-examine him. The chances of a single attorney being well enough prepared to unsettle a man who had done more than most to shape modern Japanese history were surely slim. At Nuremberg the American prosecutor, an Associate Justice of the Supreme Court, had been humiliated by Hermann Goering, and Tojo must have had hopes of his forthcoming encounter with Fihelly.

Tojo's other major assets were his own and his counsel's intellectual abilities. The Imperial Army was a rare phenomenon in Japanese society in being a genuine meritocracy: it was the best men, in army terms, who, like Tojo, rose to the top – men who, though often of humble birth, were invariably of the highest mental capacity. And Ichiro Kiyose was a formidable ally. A law graduate of Kyoto Imperial University, he had studied in Germany, France and England before taking his doctorate. Whilst making his name as one of Japan's leading attorneys, he had also entered politics and was for a time Vice-Speaker of the House of Representatives. Together the two of them fashioned Tojo's testimony – the sword with which the Tribunal's achievement would be dismembered.

Tojo's affidavit is a quite remarkable document. With it he achieved two ends. He created for himself the *persona* of an honest, loyal patriot, sincere in his duty and his love for the Emperor; and, with closely-reasoned but simple arguments, he justified Japan's pre-war policy. By the rules of their own show trial, the Allies were trapped into permitting a public apologia for militarism.

The affidavit calls to mind, no doubt deliberately, one of the great men of Japanese modern history, Aritomo Yamagata. The image Yamagata liked to project of himself was that of the uncomplicated fighting man – 'I am merely a soldier'. He was in fact a great statesman, under whom Tojo's father had served; he was also the only man in Japan before Tojo to have held simultaneously the posts of Prime Minister, War Minister and Home Minister. To evoke his memory was to buttress securely all Tojo's assertions of sincerity – a concept which for the Japanese is of extreme significance. The *shushin* textbooks of the 1930s taught, 'We must be sincere in everything we do. Our personal conduct will then naturally become just and we shall become men of virtue'. In some of the political *causes célèbres* of the 1930s, where the defendants had been able to convince the court of the purity of their intentions they escaped virtually unpunished – even those who had committed murder and attempted to overthrow the state. Nor – and this was of more importance as far as the Tokyo trial was concerned – did they incur the opprobrium of the Japanese people. Undoubtedly, the success of Tojo's affidavit was predicated on the general belief that he had acted in good faith in his service to the nation. No matter what he had done, what suffering he had brought upon the people, according to the Japanese system of values he was less to be blamed than admired, for in the face of all that had befallen him he had displayed the fundamental virtue of sincerity.

Against this background, the affidavit painted a skilful picture of peace-loving Japan provoked by the Allies. 'That I had any pre-conceived notion or plan for aggression', wrote Tojo, 'is entirely without foundation, and so far as I know no member of that Cabinet held any such belief.' It had been the United States which had frustrated Prince Konoye's peace initiative to President Roosevelt in August 1941 by holding out for agreement on every one of the most critical and hotly-debated issues. It was the U.S.S.R. which had broken the Neutrality Pact. 'Never once was an unfriendly act directed against the Soviet Union, despite the pressure exerted by the Germans.' Tojo denied that Japan had made any preparations for war, pointing rather to the Allies' own 'military encirclement' of Japan through a web of treaties and understandings, and their rapid consolidation of their military strength. He cited the pre-war increases in U.S. naval and military expenditures – $51 million to increase aircraft production; $3 million for 'strengthening the defence' of the Hawaiian islands; the lengthening of the terms of military service for U.S. forces; the installation of the Eastern Military Command in the Philippines under MacArthur – and underlined his conclusion heavily: 'It was clearly discernible that the U.S. was exerting itself feverishly in military expansion.'

And while the Allies prepared for war, he continued, they did everything possible to cripple Japan economically. 'Japan relied upon America and Britain for the major portion of her imports of essential materials. Once these were cut off, the very existence of the nation was endangered.' All this preparation and pressure, Tojo explained, was to force Japan to pull her troops out of China, and he candidly recalled what his reaction had been at the time: 'If we swallow the American demands, totally giving up the stationing of our troops in China and withdraw them wholesale, what will ensue after that? Not only would Japan bring to naught those sacrifices and those efforts paid for in the course of the China Incident of more than four years standing, but also Chinese contempt for Japan will ever expand if we retire from China uncon-ditionally because of United States duress. Relations between Japan and China will grow worse, coupled with the thoroughgoing resistance against Japan maintained by the Communists. . . . Repercussions at our loss of prestige will be keenly felt in Manchu-ria and Korea. Moreover, difficulties confronting the American–Japanese negotiations are not confined to the single question of evacuation, but include also the recognition on our part of the said four fundamental principles – interpretation to be placed on the Tripartite Pact, non-discrimination of international commerce, and many other matters. Viewed in this dim light, a compromise with

The imagery of Japanophobia, still current: octopus tentacles sucking South East Asia dry. Wartime propaganda poster by Pat Keely – 'The Indies Shall be Freed – Work to Achieve This'. (*Imperial War Museum*)

Japanese soldiers celebrating victory on Christmas Island.
(*Imperial War Museum*)

Surrender ceremony aboard U.S.S. *Missouri*: MacArthur at the microphone looks on. (*Imperial War Museum*)

The press photograph that outraged traditionalists: MacArthur and Hirohito at the American Embassy in Tokyo, September 1945. (*Associated Press*)

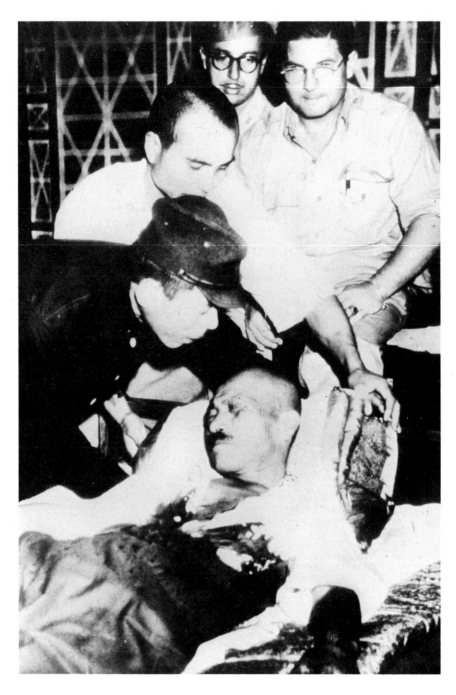

Tojo's life being saved shortly after his suicide attempt.
(*Imperial War Museum*)

The ruined Imperial War Ministry Building, 1945 by official British war artist James Morris. (*Imperial War Museum*)

The defendants at the IMTFE inside the restored War Ministry Building: Tojo front row of dock, fifth from left, Shumei Okawa directly behind him in white. (*Associated Press*)

Japan learns to jitterbug – geisha and G.I. in Tokyo, 1946.
(*Associated Press*)

Japan rearms: Pacific War veterans marching in the 1952 inauguration
parade of the so-called National Security Force. (*Associated Press*)

The Ron-Yasu axis: President Reagan and Prime Minister Yasuhiro Nakasone outside the Oval Office. (*Associated Press*)

U.S. Marines on exercise beneath Mount Fuji. (*Associated Press*)

Yukio Mishima, dressed in the uniform of his Shield Society, haranguing members of the Self-Defense Force in the moments before his ritual suicide. (*Associated Press*)

the U.S. became too insurmountable to apprehend.' There was, besides, the insuperable obstacle of American intransigence. 'Japan had made concessions to the U.S. to almost unbearable limits so that the negotiations might be successfully concluded, and yet the U.S. showed no signs of responding to them and that government did not move an inch.' Tojo accused the U.S. of 'waging an economic war against Japan while at the same time keeping herself out of actual war' – placing herself in a position 'to reap the fruits of victory over Japan without resorting to an act of war'.

By the autumn of 1941, he declared, Japan's predicament was fast becoming desperate, resolvable only by desperate measures. 'If Japan could not solve the fatal situation by means of diplomacy, then there would be no way remaining for her but to take up arms and break through the economic and military barrier flung around her.' And the sooner the better, as the odds against Japan were lengthening all the time. 'There was a danger of an exhaustion of liquid fuel and, on the other hand, during the second half of the following year the strength of the American navy would be vastly augmented.' Reasonable weather, too, was essential for the plans the Japanese had in mind – 'The High Command considered that the month of November was the most conducive time for a successful operation; December possible but difficult; and in January quite impossible of performance'.

Tojo ridiculed the suggestion that Japan had ever sought world conquest. Even the Triple Alliance with Germany and Italy was considered 'solely as a means of defending this country against the onslaughts of the "Have" nations, and to find a way to survive under the prevailing international situation'. In the war Japan waged on the U.S. and Britain, attack was simply the best form of defence. 'It was apparent that we could not be too hopeful of winning against the two greatest powers in the world. Japan had no alternative but to advance to the Pacific and Indian Oceans, holding up strategical points, occupying regions for military resources and repulsing enemy attacks to the best of our ability and spirit to the last ditch.' (Tojo's biographer has suggested that Tojo's estimate of the power of this spirit, when set against America's spiritual poverty, was hopelessly unbalanced, distorted by the railway journey he had made across the United States whilst returning from Germany in 1922. 'He observed a country, in contrast with Germany, rich and apparently untouched by war. He saw a people, compared with the formal Teutons and his ultra-formal countrymen, casual to the point of being undignified, thoroughly unmilitary and uninhibitedly dedicated to the pursuit of material prosperity. This brief and superficial encounter left him with convictions which were to prove as fatal for him and his country as his uncritical admiration of Germany. America might be materially strong, he concluded, but lacked the spiritual strength of the Japanese; a dangerous opinion in itself but the more so in one who held as an article of faith that purpose plus hard work would inevitably prevail over mere material factors'.)

At the heart of the Pacific conflict, Tojo argued, was the Allies' grave misunderstanding of Japanese policy on the Asian mainland – whose main thrust was to make the prevention of communism common policy among the independent states of East Asia. The European Allies resented, too, Japan's efforts 'aimed at the liberation of the countries of East Asia from the intolerable position or status of colonies and semi-colonies under the control of the Powers, so that they might secure identical freedom with other racial states'. 'Asia for the Asians' was resonant propaganda in a world where colonialism was dying on its feet.

Within the mainstream of his justification of Japan's actions, Tojo took time to clear up other matters outstanding. Despite appearances, he maintained, there had been 'no design what-soever to camouflage Japan's intention, if any, to start war'. He pointed out that in any case 'the American authorities had succeeded in deciphering our secret code and knew our decision before it was presented to them'.

As for the issue of the Emperor's guilt, Hirohito bore no respon-sibility for war. In one skilful paragraph, Tojo depicted His Imperial Majesty as totally reliant on the advice of the military and the Cabinet, a man of peace who yet recognised that Japan had no choice but to fight. He described how he broke the news of the government's decision for war to the Emperor in the late afternoon on November 2, 1941. 'While presenting the submission I could see from the expression of His Majesty that he was suffering from a painful sense of distress arising from his peace-loving faith. When His Majesty had listened to what we had to submit, He was grave and thoughtful for some time and then with a serious air of concern He declared, "Is there no way left but to determine, against our wishes, to wage war against America and Britain in case our effort in American–Japanese talks should fail to break the deadlock?" Then He continued, "If the state of affairs is just as you have stated now, there will be no alternative but to proceed in the prepar-ations, but I still do hope that you will further adopt every possible means to tide over the difficulties in the American–Japanese negotiations." I still remember quite vividly, even today, that we were awe-stricken by these words.'

And then, in a conclusion worthy of Yamagata himself, Tojo faced up to what in his mind was the principal point at issue – the responsibility not for starting the war but for losing it. 'I feel that it devolves upon myself as Premier. The responsibility in that sense I am not only willing but sincerely desire to accept fully.'

Tojo was not content simply to have his affidavit read into the court transcript, to be submerged by the weight of material generated by almost two years of proceedings. One day, no doubt, it might be exhumed and re-examined, and a Confucian society places great stress on the writing of history – but Tojo had more immediate ends in view. He requested permission from SCAP and, incredibly, received it, to publish his testimony before taking the witness stand. This demonstrates a remarkable lack of political acumen on the part of the censors. (They later showed that they had learned from their mistakes when they suppressed, without the slightest hesitation, the dissenting judgements given by members of the Tribunal itself.) It enabled Tojo to launch the most cogent defence of pre-war Japanese militarism and the most scathing attack on SCAP's reforms to be heard in public during the whole Occupation period. (Where the censors did, however, draw the line was the Foreword written by the 'Tokyo Trials Research Society', crude and strident where the affidavit was reasoned and calm.) When SCAP realised its error, it tried desperately to halt distribution of the affidavit, but it was too late.

On the day Tojo was due to take the stand, December 26, 1947, the queues started forming outside the old War Ministry Building in the bitter cold before dawn. Ticket touts established a thriving black market in Visitors' Gallery passes, and by the start of proceedings there was not a vacant space in court. The Allies had finally achieved their aim – the entire interest of the nation was for the moment focused on the trial proceedings. But the Japanese people were eager not for another recital of their war guilt, that would hardly have been human nature, but, secretly, for the sight of a Japanese hero, victorious in single combat.

For the first two days the public was disappointed. The court's time was devoted entirely to the reading of Tojo's affidavit into the record, punctuated by a few direct questions from the other defence counsel, and while the crowd saw Tojo on the stand, he was not locked in conflict with John Fihelly, but smiling at friends and photographers, and signing autographs for American souvenir hunters. Nevertheless as the reading drew to a close, the pressure on Tojo – and on Fihelly, for all his courtroom experience – must have been intense. Both knew just how much was riding on the outcome of the cross-examination. Tojo must have felt a certain unease, because Fihelly knew his opponent and the strengths and weaknesses of his case better than anyone. Despite its confident tone there were enough false premisses in the affidavit to give a skilful cross-examiner scope for inflicting serious damage. But as Tojo settled himself, waiting for the duel to begin, there was an extraordinary interruption.

Exactly what happened is still unclear; Comyns Carr and Owen Cunningham, for example, differ significantly in their accounts. The crux, not in dispute, was the already existing court ruling that only one counsel might cross-examine a witness. As Comyns Carr tells the story, Keenan decided on the spur of the moment to take over the cross-examination of Tojo – the suggestion being that he could not bear the thought of someone else garnering all the credit and the attendant publicity. He may have seen it as a way of redeeming the case as a whole, and his conduct of it in particular; he may have had in mind Justice Jackson's Nuremberg humiliation at the hands of Hermann Goering and determined to prove himself the better man. Whatever the reasons for his intervention, the results were catastrophic: Fihelly, in despair, simply stood up and left the courtroom.

Owen Cunningham, on the other hand, has recorded that Keenan approached him before the cross-examination and asked whether the defence would object to his addressing a few preliminary questions to Tojo, after which the defendant would be turned over to Fihelly. The defence had no objection, and Keenan duly rose and put his questions. It was when he informed the Bench that he would like to hand the cross-examination over to Fihelly, that Webb, having conferred with his colleagues, announced: 'Only one counsel for each party may cross-examine a witness. . . . A majority of the Court is against you, Mr Chief of Counsel. You will not have the assistance of Mr Fihelly. A majority of the Court has intimated to me that it is opposed to your application being granted, and I have announced the results.' If the Bench had wanted vengeance on the man who had grandstanded the prosecution, bullied colleagues and witnesses alike, and abused his power before them for the preceding two years, they could not have found a revenge more devastatingly complete.

The transcript of the trial itself inclines more to Comyns Carr's account. Keenan asked the Bench if he might put some questions to Tojo and, with the express agreement of both defence counsel and Tojo himself, then hand over to Fihelly. On a poll, the Bench refused, and Keenan – who at that point still had the option of simply letting Fihelly proceed – went ahead regardless.

Keenan may have been surprised by the court's decision, but his innate toughness came to his aid. Ill-prepared, with Fihelly gone from the courtroom, he nevertheless set about his task in characteristic style. 'Accused Tojo, I shall not address you as General because, as of course you know, there is no longer any Japanese

Army.' Tojo, no doubt, could hardly believe his luck. He may have had a grudging respect for Fihelly, but he had Keenan's measure and felt only contempt for him. Over the next four days he scored heavily in every exchange, in the process doing much to sustain his affidavit. He showed the greatest dexterity in turning Keenan's questions against him. When Keenan asked, 'I suppose you know that the President of the United States is the highest authority of that Republic?', Tojo replied: 'I know it in the same sense that I know that the Emperor of Japan is the highest authority in Japan'. Again – Keenan: 'Of course, it is obvious, is it not, that the Vichy Government was under the control of the Hitler Government; you know that, don't you?' Tojo: 'I was well aware of the fact that the Vichy Government was operating under German occupation, but I consider the Vichy Government as the legitimate government of France. It is just as the present Japanese Government, operating under the American government, is the legitimate government of Japan'. If the Bench's intention was to see Keenan humbled, then Tojo more than obliged. And in the process obliged himself: Sir Alvary Gascoigne reported that in private, Japanese observers praised Tojo for having stood up to his accusers 'like a true Japanese'.

MacArthur had foreseen the possibility of Tojo emerging triumphant, despite Fihelly's skill; it had been the Supreme Commander's suggestion – and he was later to say that he had actually given orders – that there should be no cross-examination at all. After the débacle, his worst fears realised, MacArthur met Sir Alvary Gascoigne. The general effect of Tojo's defence on the Japanese public was, he admitted, 'probably profound'.

18

Judges and Judgements

'What fatally flawed the moral basis of the Tokyo trial was the post-war acts of the nations that had judged Japan, including the United States and the Soviet Union: the despatch of combat troops to Hungary, Czechoslovakia, and Afghanistan by the Soviet Union, to Vietnam by the United States, and to Egypt (the Suez Canal) by Britain and France . . . In addition to these acts of aggression, the United States has more or less continuously intervened militarily in Central and South America, while the Soviet Union continues to maintain within its own boundaries a harsh system of suppressing dissidents, a system that includes incarceration in concentration camps. Such acts have turned the Allied powers' boast that the Tokyo trial was "civilisation's justice" into the sheerest hypocrisy.'

Yasuaki Onuma, 1984

*   *   *

The last great sea battle fought broadside against broadside was off Jutland in 1916, between England and the Kaiser's Germany. Technically, in the sense that the Germans scurried back to port, the Royal Navy won the engagement, but not without the heavier loss. Despite the best that British armour-plating could do, the occasional German shell hitting a cruiser's gun-turret set off a chain reaction which sent fire down the ammunition lift straight into the ship's magazines. Had the Tokyo defence but known it, with virtually their first salvo they achieved this kind of lucky hit – not on the prosecution's case, but on the Tribunal itself.

The fundamental design flaw of the IMTFE, if one might call it that, was that the judges differed radically in their attitudes towards the basis of their appointment. This was not simply a question of nationality, though naturally the legal system in which each had been raised had its effect; it was more a matter of personal philosophy. Not every judge, it seemed, regarded himself as bound to apply the law of the Charter of the IMTFE – nor even accepted the Charter as an accurate reflection of international law.

'When I got out here', wrote the British judge, Lord Patrick, to the Lord Chancellor, 'it was early apparent that a considerable number of members of the Tribunal . . . were inclined to think that they could accept the appointment and still apply to the trial a conception of law at variance with the law as declared in the Charter. They had no good answer to the argument that apart from the Charter, and their appointment to act under it, they had no jurisdiction to sit in Japan or pronounce any judicial order there, and that the Order which appointed them (issued by MacArthur as Supreme Commander) declared that their duties and responsibilities were set forth in the Charter. They were inclined to think they could accept a mandate, being minded to defeat its primary purpose. I confess the point of view seems to me to involve rank dishonesty.'

Strictly speaking, of course, Lord Patrick was right. Those judges who accepted appointments under the Charter with every intention of disregarding its law were guilty of deceit towards the governments which had nominated them and towards the Supreme Commander. The question is, however, whether the dishonesty could be justified as the exercise of a conflicting moral imperative. A man who felt strongly that the IMTFE Charter was illegal, given the opportunity to act by his government, might secretly determine to oppose the will of the Tribunal as a matter of principle.

This seems to have been the attitude of the Indian judge, Mr Justice Radhabinod Pal – though the pure moral stance he adopted on the grounds of jurisprudence was more than a little compromised by what seemed to the Foreign Office at least to be an obvious political motive. In 1946, India was on the verge of independence. A strong pan-Asian movement had developed, alongside what Nehru called a 'clean slate' policy of forgiving and forgetting the events of the war; and opposition to this 'colonialist' tribunal on which so few Asian nations were represented would reap a rich political harvest. Between the extremes of Pal and Patrick stretched a maze of conflicting opinion, and it was here that the defence's shells struck home.

In its opening address, the defence moved that the Indictment as a whole be dismissed because aggressive war was not a crime at international law, nor could there be individual responsibility for acts of state. This was a direct challenge to the basic premises on which both the Nuremberg and Tokyo tribunals were founded, and an implicit denial of the validity of the Charters under which they had been set up. At that time neither Pal nor the Philippine judge, Delfin Jaranilla, had arrived in Tokyo, so it was only the nine judges present who agreed after much debate ('a long collieshangie', as Lord Patrick called it) to dismiss the defence motions – in effect asserting that they recognised the law of the Tokyo Charter.

Their decision to dismiss was announced in court, and it seemed the defence salvo had bounced off the armour. But the judges had agreed only on the decision itself, not their reasons for it, and much uncertainty remained as to the precise authority of the Charter, uncertainty which was extremely damaging in an area of such fundamental importance to the Tribunal's credibility. In Patrick's view, the waverers could, at the time of the ruling, have been persuaded to commit themselves to a single unified judgement if one had been prepared to which they might put their signatures. But President Webb, whose responsibility it was, could not be induced to prepare such a document before hearing the outcome of the Nuremberg trial, which would obviously reflect on the law of the Tokyo Charter.

The Nuremberg judgement was delivered on September 30 and October 1, 1947, and shortly afterwards, Webb circulated to the other judges a version of the reasons for dismissing the defence motion which brought Lord Patrick, writing confidentially to the Lord Chancellor, to the verge of hysteria: 'It is an extraordinary document. It justified the declarations of law in the Charter largely upon the ground that they were in accord with the so-called "Law of Nature". It contained *twenty pages* of quotations from such writers as Aristotle, Polybius, St. Paul, Ambrose of Milan, St. Augustine, Isidor of Seville, Thomas Aquinas, Ayala, Molina, Suarez, Grotius, Vattel, Sylvester Maurus, Colonna, John Gerson, and a host of others. It omitted to notice that the "Law of Nature" of the Greeks, of the medieval Catholic writers, of the early writers on International Law, of the modern neo-Kantians, all differed radically in content. It turned out that he had not prepared it. It was prepared by a young Australian devil [junior barrister] in his office, by a young American woman in his office, and by a Catholic lecturer in Saint Sophia University here. It is incredible but the fact.'

Webb was resentful at the rejection of his rationale – 'a not very good student's essay', in the opinion of New Zealand judge, Erima Northcroft. In its place Webb provided five alternative grounds for dismissing the defence motion, which had the effect of cancelling each other out. These too were howled down, and eventually he plumped for the view that the Charter was valid simply because Japan, by the Instrument of Surrender, had agreed to the Tribunal's jurisdiction. As Patrick pointed out, such an opinion was 'valueless for the future because it is based on that special contract'.

Worse, Webb's ineptitude provoked the other judges into writing their own opinions for and against the decision to dismiss the defence motions.

In the New Year of 1947, as Lord Patrick reported, the Bench was in disarray. Australia, in the shape of Sir William Webb, still saw the Allies' contract with Japan – the Instrument of Surrender – as the source of the Tribunal's jurisdiction. Britain, Canada and New Zealand regarded the Charter as expressing valid international law. The Soviet judge – who could not speak English – agreed with the British, but was also insisting on having 'a lot of fulminations inserted about the dastardly attack by the fascist nations'. The French judge – who also spoke no English – held that 'there is no law whatever, international or domestic, save such as proceeds from "le bon coeur"', whatever that might mean in practical terms. And the Dutch judge, Röling, had just circulated a statement to the effect that the law of the Charter was *not* valid. He had asserted, according to an indignant Lord Patrick, 'that aggressive war was not a crime according to international law and is not now, and that there is not in any event individual responsibility for acts of state. . . . Yet he voted for the opposite result'.

Mr Justice Pal, in a 260-page statement, expressed the same view as the Dutch judge as regards aggressive war and individual responsibility – a position, as Patrick pointed out, which he had quite clearly held ever since he was first appointed. 'So why the Government of India ever nominated him, and why Great Britain insisted on India being represented on this tribunal – America objecting – it is difficult to see.' As for the Philippine judge, 'appointed at America's insistence, since we insisted that India must be represented', he 'just doesn't understand. He has twice voted on incidental matters, by his own confession, for the view directly opposed to that he intended. It is not lack of English, it is lack of grey matter with him'.

The divisions amongst the judges were widened by Webb himself. He was in many respects blood brother to Keenan – domineering, abrasive, with a genuine talent for alienating his colleagues. (He was also quite prepared to alienate Keenan: when the latter was a few lines into his Closing Address, Webb turned to one of the other judges and remarked, *sotto voce* but with his microphone on, 'This is dreadful.') He treated his fellow judges as members of a jury – or worse. He verbally abused both the Chinese and New Zealand members, to their profound indignation; the New Zealand judge at one point asked to be recalled. In the courtroom, Webb alone had a microphone; and he generally sat alone in chambers to deal with interlocutory proceedings, including important questions of evidence.

Matters appear to have come to a head at the Canberra Conference in 1947, when the Prime Minister of New Zealand complained directly to the Australian Prime Minister. In October Webb was summoned home, ostensibly because of 'important proceedings' forthcoming in the Queensland Supreme Court which required his involvement. (Webb himself told his colleagues confidentially that it was because 'Australia had lost interest in the trial'.) He departed on November 7, 1947, leaving MacArthur with a serious problem. It was clearly too late in the proceedings to replace Webb with a newcomer, so the Presidency would have to pass from Australia to one of the other nations. The next most senior judge was Northcroft; but MacArthur thought him unsuitable in view of 'the insignificance of New Zealand as a world power', and offered the post to Lord Patrick. Patrick, however, was suffering from a recurrence of the tuberculosis which he had contracted in a German prisoner-of-war camp in the First World War, and he refused. According to Sir Alvary Gascoigne, this 'dumbfounded' MacArthur, who felt 'he should have risked sudden death in court rather than turn down the appointment'. Ultimately MacArthur pulled rank on the reluctant U.S. judge, General Myron Cramer, and ordered him to replace Webb – admitting later to Sir Alvary that from the standpoint of experience and knowledge of jurisprudence, Cramer was not a suitable incumbent, but MacArthur 'thought he would do well nevertheless'.

Cramer, however, was only appointed 'Acting' President. MacArthur had no intention of allowing Australia's 'deplorable' recall of Webb to go unchallenged; it was, in his view, a disgraceful shelving of international responsibility and it appears that – to the chagrin of the other judges – he personally engineered Webb's return to Tokyo, having him back on the Bench by December 15, in time for Tojo's cross-examination.

After the defence rested on January 12, 1948, there followed a period of rebuttal by the prosecution, drawing on new and valuable sources of evidence, and a desperate 'surrebuttal' by the defence. Closing arguments began on February 11: Owen Cunningham later recalled the fury of the defence attorneys at having their final arguments 'edited by a committee of judges before we were permitted to deliver them in court. They didn't want us to say anything they didn't want to hear. They certainly butchered my final argument, but as it turned out it made very little difference'. After affording each defendant the chance to submit 'evidence in mitigation' – this despite the fact that officially they had not yet been judged, so that strictly speaking there was nothing to mitigate – the Tribunal adjourned to consider its verdict.

The date was April 16, 1948, twenty-three months after proceedings had commenced, and the task the judges faced was daunting. The court had sat on 417 days, during which they had heard oral evidence from 419 witnesses and received in evidence affidavits and depositions from another 779, together with 4336 exhibits (documents, maps, diaries and other papers). The transcript of the trial ran to an estimated 9,500,000 words – over 48,000 mimeographed pages, with the exhibits totalling another 30,000 pages. So it was not until November 4, 1948 that the Tribunal resumed to give its verdicts and to be, for a week, the centre of national attention. Though Webb's *persona* was familiar, and both Northcroft and Patrick had taken their turns at the single microphone, as far as the watching public was concerned the dark-suited, black-gowned judges had hitherto been merely the supporting cast. Now, briefly, the spotlight was upon them.

Psychologically, it was an important moment. The points scored by the defence were fading in people's minds. A wise, trenchant, and above all unanimous judgement, accompanied by just sentences, might have smothered the ferment of discontent that had frothed throughout the trial. But as had come during the course of the trial to seem inevitable to those behind the scenes, no single judgement was handed down. Instead there were six – the trial remaining a political disaster to the end. The first of the six judgements was the composite judgement of the majority. Then came separate but essentially concurring opinions from Webb and Jaranilla, who also put their names to the majority judgement; partial dissents from Bernard (France) and Röling (Holland); and, to all intents and purposes, total dissent from Pal. None of the minority judgements was read out in court.

The majority judgement was signed by the representatives of eight countries – Australia, Britain, Canada, China, New Zealand, the Philippines, the Soviet Union and the United States. It ruled on questions of law and fact, and handed down the verdicts and sentences. All the defence motions on points of law were dismissed; in particular, the eight upheld Lord Patrick's view that the Charter was soundly based because it was an expression of international law as evidenced in the Kellogg-Briand Pact of 1928.

Röling, in his separate judgement, came for all practical purposes to a similar conclusion – that the law of the Charter was binding on the judges – but through a different line of reasoning. He opposed the Patrick view because he considered aggressive war to have become a crime only in 1945, with the international agreement under which the Nuremberg Tribunal had been set up. Nevertheless he regarded victorious powers as having the right to 'counteract elements constituting a threat to . . . newly established order'; and if they chose to exercise that right by judicial means rather than by political action, then they were entitled to do so. Röling regarded 'crimes against peace' as a judicial device to achieve valid political ends – not valid international law, but a valid method of exercising political rights.

At the end of the day, only two of the judges saw the Charter as grounded in natural law; only two really reflected the original Stimsonian belief that aggressive war was to be punished and outlawed because it was *by nature* a crime, that the new world order was to be shaped primarily by moral arguments. The two were Webb, who repeated in his separate judgement the gist of his ill-fated earlier attempt to rebut the defence motion by reference to the 'Law of Nature'; and Bernard of France, who argued that aggressive war 'is and always has been a crime in the eyes of reason and universal conscience'. (This belief was challenged outright by Pal, speaking with the voice of the prevailing positivist philosophy of law: 'Any distinction between just and unjust war remained only in the theory of the international legal philosophers'.)

The majority judgement also dismissed the suggestion made by the defence that 'conspiracy' was merely a legal device of Anglo-American law. From the facts of the case, the majority concluded that a conspiracy dating back to 1928 to initiate and wage aggressive war was by any standards clearly proven. Pal took issue with this finding precisely because it had been reached by inference from the evidence. In his view there were various alternative hypotheses that might be drawn from the same facts by putting them in 'their proper perspective' – which for him was 'the Britanno-centric world order, the development of communism and the world opinion of Soviet policy, the internal conditions of China, the China policy and practice of other nations and the internal condition of Japan from time to time'. He was not suggesting that these alternative hypotheses were any more watertight than the conspiracy theory – simply that because conspiracy was not the *sole* legitimate inference, it was not proven.

Among the alternatives he presented was the suggestion that Japanese policy might be explained in terms of the rise of communism in China – a view which has since been repeatedly cited by the far right in vindication of Japan's war leaders. Pal hedged what he was saying with qualifications, making it clear that he was only offering hypotheses; but in the circumstances it was a dangerous game to play. It is hard to believe that he failed to recognise the openings he was making for the old guard – though he would not necessarily have been gratified to know that upon his death in 1967 a memorial service would be held for him in Tokyo by an association of the relatives of convicted war criminals.

The majority judgement is over 1,200 pages long and covers in great detail both the evolution of the conspiracy and the history of Japanese atrocities in the Second World War. After reviewing the broad scope of the evidence, the questions of law and interpretations of fact, the majority gave its verdicts on each of the defendants – which came, after so massive a trial, almost as an anticlimax. The accused, with the possible exception of Tojo, seemed puny and insignificant in comparison with the colossal crimes discussed. Their ranks had dwindled: two had died, Okawa had been discharged on grounds of insanity, and three others were in hospital dying of cancer. As the twenty-two remaining waited to hear their fate, they made a pathetic target for judicial wrath on so grand a scale.

And the fact of Allied disunity made itself nowhere more plain than in the matter of the sentences to be imposed. SCAP prudently forbade publication of the full texts of the dissenting opinions – but though the Japanese were denied the reasons for them, the conflicting conclusions reached by the judges as to guilt and sentencing could not be kept secret. The front page of the *Nippon Times* of November 13, 1948 exposed the schisms. 'Tojo And Six Others Are Sentenced To Hang; 16 Draw Life; Shigemitsu Is Given 7 Years'; 'Sentences Held As Too Lenient' (by Jaranilla); 'Full Acquittal On All Charges Asked By Pal'. The *Nippon Times* went on, 'Webb Names Emperor As "Leader in the Crime"', and reported his suggestion that since the ringleader had gone unpunished it would be wholly inappropriate to hand down any death sentences on men who were essentially lesser criminals. Bernard urged that all the accused be acquitted, on the grounds that the procedure of the IMTFE had been invalid, and Röling, too, wanted five, including Hirota, acquitted of all charges.

There was enough in a few short paragraphs in the *Nippon Times* to make any pretence of righteous unanimity pointless. 'Justice Pal considered threadbare the prosecutors' contention on negotiations preceding Pearl Harbor' – and Pal was quoted as saying: 'The evidence convinces me that Japan tried her utmost to avoid any clash with America, but was driven by the circumstances that gradually developed to the fatal steps taken by her. . . . Everything at least on the Japanese side seems to have been done with sincerity'.

At this point, with a lemming-like display of fair-mindedness, SCAP permitted Tojo to release a further statement to the press. He took his opportunity with *samurai* bravado: '"I do not want clemency", Tojo tells his attorney', ran the headline. 'At the beginning of the trial, I was worried that the responsibility of the Emperor might be questioned. I feel at rest now that the doubt has been cleared. From the beginning I was ready to take the entire responsibility for the war, but regrettably others were brought into the trial. . . . If you ask my opinion about the trial I can only say it is a victors' trial.'

The court adjourned *sine die*. There were to be no more trials of major war criminals, and virtually all those prominent Japanese who had been arrested were now safe from prosecution. Keenan went home to a public eulogy from President Truman, and Comyns Carr was recommended for the Chairmanship of the Monopolies Commission and a knighthood. Robert Donihi, a veteran of both Nuremberg and Tokyo prosecutions, ran for Congress, while defence counsel Blewett and Furness prepared for a further major case on behalf of a Japanese defendant. Röling went on to a career in the International Court of Justice at the Hague; Lord Patrick, dying from a recurrence of tuberculosis aggravated by the heat and humidity of the Tokyo summer, went home in the hospital ward of a British troopship. Sir William Webb continued as a Justice of the High Court of Australia, never to be budged from his view that Hirohito should have been hanged.

The sentences, in accordance with the Charter and the FEC directive, had still to be confirmed by MacArthur, after he had consulted the other Allied nations. With the approval of a majority, he announced his decision in a radio broadcast on November 24, 1948. The short statement was a public relations masterpiece, managing to be both sincere and politically effective. He catered to the wishes of the Allied publics by altering the sentences not at all: the seven sentenced to death would hang. He also contrived to preserve in the Japanese public's eyes the image of Olympian detachment which he had maintained all through the trial. He said his duty was 'utterly repugnant' to him, which, judging by contemporary descriptions of his demeanour on the day of the decision, was true; and avoiding all discussion of the culpability of the convicts he prayed that 'an Omnipotent Providence may use this tragic expiation as a symbol to summon all persons of good will to a realisation of the utter futility of war – that most malignant scourge and greatest sin of mankind – and eventually to its renunciation by all nations. To this end on the day of execution I request the members of all congregations throughout Japan of whatever credo or faith, in the privacy of their homes or at their altars of public worship, to seek Divine help and guidance that the world keep the peace lest the human race perish'.

*   *   *

It was generally expected that the 'tragic expiation' would be made on December 8, 1948, the seventh anniversary (Japanese time) of

Pearl Harbor; MacArthur rarely wasted the opportunity for a fine symbolic gesture. But the drama was far from over. On November 29, 1948, seven of the defendants (including Hirota, but not Tojo) appealed to the United States Supreme Court for leave to apply for writs of *habeas corpus*; if leave were granted, they would apply for the writs to be issued against MacArthur and others in Japan. (A writ of *habeas corpus* by a person detained in custody requires his custodian to appear in court to justify detention of the person as lawful: in this case MacArthur would effectively be required to testify before the U.S. Supreme Court as to the validity of the IMTFE Charter and his right to hold the defendants under it.) The first hurdle the applicants had to cross was that of establishing whether or not the Supreme Court had jurisdiction to hear their applications. On December 6, by a 5:4 vote, they were permitted a preliminary hearing on December 16 – which effectively ruled out Pearl Harbor Day as the date for the hangings, since MacArthur obviously had to grant a stay of execution pending the hearing.

In the interim one of the judges broke ranks. (He 'refused permission to use his name', but was believed, from some of the sentiments expressed, to be Bernard – though in places the syntax of the interview reads more like the impeccable English of an Indian with a public school education.) In the belief that he was 'morally justified', he revealed the details of the voting on the sentences. 'Actually there was a close vote in five cases in which the death penalty was proposed.' The vote on Tojo's execution, for instance, had been only 7:4 in favour. But the real shock was the case of Koki Hirota, whose death sentence was supported by no more than six of the eleven judges. These revelations, Sir Alvary Gascoigne reported, were 'most unfortunate', coming at a time when there had just been a flurry of 'ill-judged' press reports suggesting that the Supreme Court was going to examine not merely the constitutionality (under American law) of General MacArthur's action in establishing the IMTFE, but also the proceedings, judgement, and sentences. 'The publication of a statement that death sentences were only decided by a narrow majority, coming on top of such inaccurate reports, will add to the existing confusion in Japanese minds and may create suspicion that the guilt of the accused was not clearly established and that the legality of the trial was not above question.'

In the event, on December 20, 1948 the Supreme Court denied the seven applicants permission to file for *habeas corpus*. (Politically speaking, this was just as well, since MacArthur, feeling that the appeal was based on a 'complete misunderstanding' of his 'international status', had said that should a writ be granted, he would 'neglect' it and refer it to the FEC, 'who would know well enough how to deal with it'.) So now there was nothing to stop the executions going ahead at the earliest practicable moment – and they took place just after midnight on December 23, 1948.

No advance notice was given, lest anyone should try to interfere; in secrecy the corpses were taken for cremation and, on instructions, the ashes were scattered to the wind. However, one of the Japanese defence counsel was later to reveal that he had arranged with the crematorium attendants to rescue a few of the remains. These were kept carefully hidden until the end of the Occupation, whereupon they were returned to the families. In the years that followed, repeated efforts were made to rehabilitate Tojo and others in the public mind; eventually they received the ultimate reward of loyalty – enshrinement as 'nation-protecting *kami*' at Yasukuni with the rest of Japan's war heroes.

This, however, was in the future; at Christmas 1948, the trial seemed at last to be concluded. But one of the U.S. Supreme Court judges, Justice William Douglas, while concurring in the rejection of the seven defendants' application, had promised to give his reasons for so doing at a later date. On June 27, 1949, he published them; and among his comments, many of them critical, may perhaps be found an epitaph for the IMTFE. 'It took its law from its creator and did not act as a free and independent tribunal to adjudge the rights of petitioners under international law. As Justice Pal said, it did not therefore sit as a judicial tribunal. It was solely an instrument of political power.'

19

Alien Soil

Behind the scenes, as the IMTFE drew to its inevitable conclusion, the Allies surveyed their handiwork with pessimism. The Foreign Office labelled the trial 'a political failure', and the OSS felt its intended effects upon the Japanese to have been achieved 'only to a limited degree'. Sir Alvary Gascoigne observed 'little evidence of genuine resentment of the actions of the criminals, except insofar as they were "unsuccessful" from Japan's point of view'.

One wonders if they can seriously have expected the judgements to produce a better return. Except at theatrically compelling moments, the Japanese public had displayed only apathy towards the IMTFE. The trial's many unfairnesses, its weaknesses in procedure and, from an international perspective, weaknesses at law had not gone unremarked; and these flaws were the more glaring when set against the standards of justice prescribed for the Japanese by the bill of rights in the new Constitution.

Then, the IPS attorneys had conducted themselves as lawyers, not propagandists, leaving Tojo centre stage to present his message of 'self defence against colonial aggression'. Only victor nations sat on the Bench, many of them colonial powers with far longer records of imperialism than Japan – and they allowed the colonies they were intent on regaining no place among the judges. Many Japanese believed that the Allies had their own charges to answer, in this, and as regards the Pacific War. The prosecution had failed, in most people's eyes, to prove Japan's sole responsibility for starting the war; and in what followed, America in particular bore its share of guilt – Hiroshima, Nagasaki, and the incessant incendiary and napalm raids on the residential areas of Japan's cities, towns and villages.

If the Allies had hoped to engender a sense of collective liability and contrition for the war among the people of Japan, their overall strategy was poor. By exonerating the Emperor and, in effect, the *zaibatsu*, they isolated the militarists as the 'guilty' element in

Japanese life and made them the sole scapegoats. The roots of evil in Japan lay not in any national predisposition to aggression, it seemed, nor in the way Japanese society was structured, but with a handful of individuals who had 'deceived and misled the Japanese people' – this was the suggestion of the Potsdam Declaration itself.

But a still more fundamental problem was the question of what Anglo-American law could be expected to mean in a Japanese context – and this, of course, has wider implications for the Occupation as a whole. What chance of survival did western democratic ideas have in an Eastern anti-democratic setting?

Criminal courts working in the western common law tradition are not courts of morals, but the law they apply generally reflects and interacts with the morality of the societies in which they have evolved. This kind of connection between law and morality still does not exist in Japan. In the West we expect the criminal law to fulfil our expectations of an abstract and universal justice; but to the average Japanese in the 1940s the criminal law was simply a coercive bludgeon in the hands of authority, not the servant of society as a whole. Despite SCAP's reform of the Japanese criminal law and procedure along American lines (and about eighty years' previous experience of a French-based legal system), as late as 1968 one authority concluded that 'for a long time yet modern law [in Japan] may very well remain a mere "veneer" behind which the traditional ways of acting, thinking and living will be perpetuated'.

Social controls in Japan exist within the group, and are not dependent on the external authority of the state working through the criminal law, or transcendent laws of morality derived, as in the West, from religious teachings. The group possesses its own value system, its own internal code of behaviour – essentially Confucian – which is self-sufficient, so the members of the group do not depend on, or share, the type of universal principle espoused by western societies. There is a huge gulf between the Christian conscience, operating in obedience to a complex of universal moral laws, a conviction of absolute good and absolute evil, and the Japanese ethical code based on their sense of obligation – which corresponds roughly to an awareness of the demands of filial piety. So the Allies' blithe assumption that they would be able to arouse in the Japanese mind a sense of 'war guilt', as Christian America might understand it, was hopelessly misplaced.

But can this lack of anything resembling a western Christian conscience among the Japanese be used to explain their barbarity in the Second World War? Are they a 'cruel' race? The causes of Japanese atrocities were never investigated either by SCAP or by the IMTFE or the tribunals at Yokohama – which was perhaps just as well, since prevailing theories were, in retrospect, little more than puerile.

Writer (and one-time captive of the British) Yuji Aida considered that at the root of Japanese mishandling of prisoners-of-war lay a lack of experience in tending livestock; and behind the frenzied murders was a lack of direct experience of shedding blood, since animals were rarely slaughtered in Japan, the national diet consisting essentially of rice, vegetables and fish. Two American wartime anthropologists concluded independently that 'because Japanese infants were forced to control their sphincters before they had acquired the necessary muscular or intellectual development, they grew up filled with suppressed rage. As adults, the Japanese were able to express this rage in their brutality in war'. The British Foreign Office in February 1945 also subscribed to the infantile repression theory: 'Their behaviour after defeat in the Philippines, when all restrictions had clearly gone by the board, was typical; it was strictly comparable to that of a disappointed child who, losing his temper and with it all control, smashes his toys and kicks his companions or anyone near him'.

But other sociologically-based explanations are more plausible – Masao Maruyama's suggestion, for instance, that the hierarchical structure of Japanese society was to blame. Oppression tends to be transferred: the stronger bullies the weaker, who in his turn finds someone weaker still to persecute. Those at the bottom of the family hierarchy have only the cat to kick, so to speak; and soldiers at the bottom of the army heap vented their outraged feelings on the 'lesser races' of Asia.

Other aspects of Japan's group society also seem to have been conducive to wartime savagery – forms of social behaviour which were common to civilian and soldier alike, but took on a new and horrible dimension under the special stresses of battle.

The emphasis on loyalty, for example, was near-obsessional and of particular relevance to the treatment of prisoners. For the soldier, this meant loyalty to his Emperor unto death – nothing less. The fighting man who surrendered showed himself unwilling to pay his due; he earned the utter contempt of his peers, and his family was notified that he no longer existed. Hardly surprising, then, if the Japanese soldier viewed enemy captives in the same light – as worthy only of disdain and indifference. In the Japanese scale of values, they were better dead.

Equally dangerous was the erosion of a sense of individual responsibility – a natural consequence of life centred firmly on the group. It was endemic throughout Japan's consensus-oriented society – but lack of accountability might seem to have had its most hideous results on the battlefield. The individual had nowhere to look for guidance but to the group, and no external reference against which to assess the group's decision, no basis from which to oppose it. There was only one single source of morality, from which the group as a whole derived its code – and that was the Imperial institution. Because the Emperor was worshipped as a deity incarnate, his orders automatically conferred righteousness on the actions he demanded. There was a general feeling at this time that 'Japan was by its very nature unable to do wrong'; and an official 'Report on the Mentality of Japanese War Criminals' held in Malaya and Singapore found the prevailing emotion to be one of bewilderment. 'Some of them write to their families that they do not even know what crimes they are supposed to have committed.'

But though one may identify aspects of Japanese society which might explain the commission of atrocities, are they the whole or even partial explanation? Characteristics such as an exaggerated stress on loyalty and a diminution of the individual will are hardly unique to Japanese society. They are to be found, in fact, in all armies – and soldiers only commit atrocities when certain circumstances prevail. This is something which America, so vocal about Japanese 'frightfulness', had painfully to acknowledge after the experience of Vietnam. Here, in conditions quite similar to those of the Pacific War, G.I.s were discovered to have committed atrocities, widespread and ferocious, which were directly comparable with Japanese war crimes. Atrocities in Vietnam were no more the consequence of traits in American society than those committed in the Pacific War were products of Japanese society.

Knowledge of the excesses in Vietnam prompted much American heart-searching and a great deal of research into the nature and origins of atrocities. And this suggested that outbreaks of savagery have less to do with the society from which the perpetrators are drawn than with what happens to them after they have left that society and been inducted into the army. There are several categories of atrocity, but that of 'indiscriminate violence' – i.e. atrocities *not* committed under orders – best illustrates the potentially disastrous effect of turning civilian into soldier, and explains why soldiers in Vietnam and the Pacific War were victims of the military system that made them, and the circumstances in which they found themselves.

'Indiscriminate violence' occurs when three factors are present. Firstly, when the soldier's civilian instincts have been destroyed. Any army forms a sub-culture within society, with its own rules and standards; these it is the aim of Basic Training to instil, at the expense of all the soldier previously knew and believed. It is essential for the army to teach him unquestioning obedience – but the cost is his individuality, initiative, and self-reliance. As his surroundings become more dangerous, until at last on the battlefield they are life-threatening, he becomes more and more dependent on authority, and voluntarily relinquishes responsibility for his own actions.

Then – and here the comparison with Japanese society ceases – the soldier's inhibitions against killing are broken down. Techniques of killing are taught easily enough; the psychological willingness to take human life has to be developed more gradually. On the positive side, the military values of 'duty', 'honour', 'glory' are deployed to justify the killing – backed up by a system of medals and promotions which rewards success in it. More negatively, army life has a generally brutalising effect, which seems to be regarded as part of a necessary process of 'toughening up'. But most potent of all is the inculcation – or perhaps simply the encouragement – of racial hatreds. The enemy is made out to be less than human – a 'gook' or 'Hun' or 'kike' or 'slope' or *gaijin* or 'dink' – and the killing becomes easier.

The third factor in the commission of indiscriminate atrocities seems to be the collapse of military discipline. This creates a situation where soldiers who are by now psychologically and morally weakened to the point of dehumanisation can indulge impulses they would normally be able to control – impulses existing within military sub-cultures everywhere. They give way to the desire to loot, to rape, but above all to the desire to take revenge, for the lives of others and, in a life-threatening situation, for their own lives.

This combination of regimentation, brutalisation, racism deliberately fomented, and the collapse of discipline throws light on what happened in Vietnam just as surely as it explains events in the Philippines in the last weeks of the war, when Japanese soldiers, cut off and without hope, spread carnage.

In other words, it is not enough to point to 'the nature of Japanese society' as an explanation of Japanese atrocities. If Japanese society was predisposed towards brutality, this was not through any unique racial or cultural characteristic but because it was the epitome of a *militarised* society. Not merely Japan's soldiers but her civilians too displayed many of the traits of armies everywhere.

But to say the nature of Japanese society is not in itself relevant to the committing of atrocities is not to say that it was irrelevant to the failure of demilitarisation. Japanese society was in important ways utterly antipathetic to the Western democratic ideas the Americans were attempting to import, as they were beginning to realise by the time the IMTFE drew to its disappointing close.

What the Americans felt themselves to be offering the Japanese was opportunity, and the conditions of liberty and equality in which to pursue it. But this was a programme which drew all its inspiration from American society and, more important, needed the cultural milieu of the West in order to thrive. The Japanese did not see individual self-interest as paramount – on the contrary, they distrusted it profoundly. They were not psychologically equipped to strike out on their own, to regard themselves as equals, to make utterly independent decisions, and compete with each other, and nor was their society equipped to cope with the phenomenon of 'democratisation'. To achieve the original objectives of the Occupation, the Americans needed a fundamental revolution in Japanese society, but were scarcely equipped to engineer it.

SCAP, of course, was able to ensure that the laws of Japan – which to the legalistic West seemed to be the scaffolding of society – were altered as befitted a democracy; this was achieved with military efficiency. But once it was done, the mass of the population was left to wallow uncomprehending in the wake of change, while a handful of CIE Information Officers worked desperately to explain the innovations and give meaning and coherence to the term 'democracy'.

The monthly schedules of the Information Officers give a clear picture of the volume and variety of new ideas the Japanese were expected to assimilate. The 'Political Affairs' Information Officer, for example, was pursuing in November 1948 the themes of 'local government; civil liberties; Illegal Property Transactions Committee; Judicial Affairs Investigation Committee; Habeas Corpus Act; Inquest Prosecution Law; activities of Prosecutor General's Office'. New that month was 'the meaning of the civil service', a topic given top priority jointly with 'War Guilt'. The 'Economic Affairs' Information Officer, on the other hand, was particularly concerned 'to make farmers and fishermen understand the importance of industrial democratisation'. He had to make clear to 75,000,000 Japanese (most of them poor and many of them under-educated) the significance of the creation of a stock market to absorb the shares released by the dissolution of the *zaibatsu*, and explain the nature of a prospectus, and where one might be found, plus the knottier points of the new Securities and Exchange Law 'designed to protect securities investors against nefarious practices'.

To make matters worse, the Information Officers were in direct and constant competition with the Japanese Communist Party, which by 1948 the CIA reported to have embarked upon a strategy of 'peaceful revolution through the Diet system', mobilising the masses not merely through propaganda but by involving itself in their economic problems, labour disputes and educational policies. By 1949 the JCP was able to command ten per cent of the voting population, a solid core of opposition to the Occupation, and the Information Officer seemed to divide his time between persuading the people of Japan not to listen to the Communists' siren song nor, at the same time, to participate in the thriving black economy.

Amidst the daily grind to find food, work and shelter, swamped by a deluge of libertarian reforms based on a concept which even Americans found it hard to define, the reaction of the Japanese was often to draw tighter into the group. During the Falklands War British army psychiatrists noticed that the soldiers were better able to cope with the stresses of their situation than was the contingent of war correspondents they had taken with them – and their explanation stressed that while the journalists were in competition with each other, the soldiers were a mutually supportive unit. It is, however, only a short step from mutual support to mutual dependency. Loyalty is the all-important virtue in Japanese society, and dependency is the other side of the coin: between them they constitute the glue which holds the group structure together.

In the hierarchical culture of Japan, this psychological tendency manifests itself in pseudo-parent/child relationships, loosely known as *oyabun* (parent or boss)/*kobun* (child or follower) relationships. The *oyabun*, the 'father', provides help and advice to his *kobun*, who in return gives his loyalty and performs services for the *oyabun* whenever called upon to do so. In 1970 Chie Nakane, the Professor of Social Anthropology at Tokyo University, expressed the view that 'most Japanese, whatever their status or occupation, are involved in *oyabun/kobun* relationships'.

This type of feudal relationship is anti-democratic and clearly rules out individualism in the sense that the 'follower' is almost entirely subject to the influence of someone else. It does, however, offer the reward of emotional security, and in the stressful times of the Occupation the *oyabun/kobun* pattern in society appears to have become ever more pronounced.

What was usually a loose behavioural pattern could become highly formalised when money was involved. In pre-war days, powerful *oyabun* – labour bosses, landowners, gangsters – collected small armies of *kobun*-retainers, who were often required to pledge their allegiance in initiation ceremonies involving the mingling of blood or other ritualistic gestures. Amidst the post-war chaos, there were advantages for the unemployed and the demobilised soldier in belonging to one of these feudal groups; they were almost invariably exploited, but they were secure.

Circumstances were ripe for the proliferation of *oyabun*-controlled empires. The Americans themselves needed efficient, readily-available workforces, and the labour bosses could meet their every need. Most of the barracks and U.S. Army installations in Japan dating from the 1940s and 1950s were built by 'indentured' labour of this kind – and thus the U.S. Army unwittingly perpetuated and fuelled the very tendencies the SCAP civilians were trying to eliminate.

By the time the war ended, a vast black market economy already prevailed in Japan. Farmers and fishermen, foresters and factory workers sold produce to illicit dealers, who sold it on outside the rationing system. As Japan's defeat began to seem inevitable, theft and widespread looting in the cities swelled the supplies of commodities in circulation, and at the surrender most stockpiles of Imperial Army and Navy supplies passed into private hands. The Occupation merely perpetuated wartime conditions in this respect: rationing was subverted and with the advent of the American dollar and the British pound, a new market in illegal currency deals boomed. Allied soldiers provided rich pickings for the Japanese criminal *oyabun*, who both stole from them and kept them supplied with prostitutes, gambling dens and souvenirs. Willoughby and G-2 grew agitated, with some reason, about the undue influence they believed *oyabun* to possess over some of SCAP's decision-makers. The simple power structure within SCAP and the absence of checks and balances provided a wealth of opportunities for the corruption which was, and still is, a significant feature of Japanese public life.

The exploitation of American weaknesses was, however, the least serious aspect of the problem. The *oyabun* possessed huge wealth, and with it they bought power amongst their own people. The police and judiciary were honeycombed with their corrupt and willing *kobun*; in the new 'democratic' Japan, officials elected at the local level tended somehow to be local *oyabun*, and at the national level, politicians looked to the big-time *oyabun* for their campaign funds. (SCAP was well aware that the Liberal Party, for instance, was a major recipient of 'hot' money.)

It was, however, through the *oyabun*'s overtly criminal activities that SCAP first became aware of the system. The Public Safety Division reported a major protection racket involving market stallholders; the ESS complained of labour bosses exploiting mineworkers in Hokkaido; Government Section recognised the 'clannish and clandestine combination of bosses, hoodlums, and racketeers' as 'the greatest threat to American democratic aims'. But it was not until September 1947 that a 'round-table' of concerned SCAP sections convened to compare notes.

Almost at once they realised that as far as direct preventive action went, they were helpless: the system was endemic in Japanese life, too deeply entrenched in government, police, judiciary and the economy to be simply stamped out by force. The only possible solution was a long-term one – an information campaign, conducted jointly with the Japanese government, pointing out to the Japanese people the threat which the *oyabun/kobun* system posed to their newly-found democratic way of life.

Fatally, however, before the campaign was officially under way, the story was scooped by a perspicacious American journalist, Howard Handleman, and splashed in the press in a series of sensationalist articles. 'Bootblacks and cabinet ministers are involved', Handleman wrote in November 1947. 'So are farmers and politicians, fishermen and gangsters, *geisha* and construction contractors, judges and murderers. . . . It provides strongarm men and, if necessary, killers, for the political bosses, who in return supply immunity from the law, freedom of action and other official favours.'

In much of what he said, Handleman was right; but he gravely over-wrote the story, welding the diffuse *oyabun/kobun* system into a 'hidden government'. 'Ten of General MacArthur's agencies', he proclaimed, 'have been working on the problem of learning the identity of the men who control this country.' This was a direct challenge to MacArthur – and it goaded him into the wrong reaction. It was, it seems, the first the Supreme Commander had heard of the *oyabun/kobun* scourge. His first response was to call a Sunday conference at which he proposed a flat denial of Handleman's allegations, until it was explained to him that there was too much truth for comfort in what Handleman had written, even if the conclusions to which he had jumped were wrong. In the days following, G-2 accused Government Section of having leaked the story deliberately; and the focus of the *oyabun/kobun* problem shifted from positive action to public relations.

Suddenly Government Section and CIE found their plans for an anti-*oyabun/kobun* propaganda campaign 'disapproved'. In the words of the message passed down from 'higher echelons', 'We would look awful fools to publicise the fact that we are now taking action on something that should have been done a long time ago'. By the New Year of 1948 public mention of *oyabun/kobun* was taboo, and the propaganda campaign had been shelved indefinitely. For some at the top of the SCAP hierarchy, possibly even MacArthur himself, it was more important to protect the image of the Supreme Commander in the eyes of the American people than to build true democracy in Japan.

PART FOUR

UPROOTING IDEALISM

20

From Enemy to Ally

In the closing months of 1945, at the instigation of the China Crowd, America had let loose a tidal wave of change upon Japan. Through willing hands in SCAP, with the vigorous if selective support of MacArthur, virtually every aspect of Japanese life was entered and rearranged – from the Imperial institution to the educational system, from commerce and industry to forestry, public health, entertainment and religion.

But the flood failed to carry all before it. By 1947 the suspicion was growing that, to some degree at least, Japanese society was impervious to change. In some areas the Japanese people were indifferent, even hostile to reform; in others the reform measures themselves were impractical, superficial or simply doomed in the face of overwhelming odds. Occasionally SCAP's well-intentioned gestures backfired badly.

The purge, for example, besides being dubious on moral grounds, was quite easily evaded. Then liberalisation of the labour laws had worked greatly to the advantage of the Japanese Communist Party; to conservatives in Japan and America, the Communists seemed to be everywhere – marching, meeting, speaking, publicising, making the most of their new-found democratic rights. Most seriously, SCAP's economic programme, if such it could be called, was in disarray.

The practical difficulties involved in dismantling the *zaibatsu* networks were already making themselves felt. But more urgently, the Japanese economy had totally failed to recover from the ravages of war. On the contrary, inflation had soared wildly and the food situation was one of permanent crisis; purely on humanitarian grounds MacArthur had been obliged to authorise large-scale relief shipments. America faced the prospect of staving off Japan's financial ruin indefinitely through emergency aid, with no return on the investment – a burden the American taxpayer was increasingly unwilling to bear.

However, when a fresh initiative finally came, its objective was not to prop up the ailing reform programme but to replace it. Washington issued new instructions for Japan, which contradicted MacArthur's original brief on almost every point, and to some degree reintroduced into Japanese society several of the salient features of militarisation. The shift, and the reasons for it, lie at the heart of Japanese/American relations in the post-war period.

That America should sooner or later alter its course was to some inevitable. In a secret discussion memorandum dated May 16, 1945, the Office of Strategic Services for example faced up squarely to 'Factors Generally Limiting U.S. Ability to Achieve Objectives'. Some of them applied specifically to Japan – 'vitiating effect of United States racial prejudice', 'distortions or cumulative defeat of policy due to U.S. inexperience in foreign or colonial administration', 'possible unwisdom of policy due to general inability . . . to understand Japanese psychology, demographic and economic problems'.

But the OSS went on to list more universal shortcomings. At the root of the irresolution in American policy lay the 'conflicting pressures' inherent in 'the American constitutional framework'. The individualism so noticeably lacking in Japan bred in America competition, factionalism, unbridled self-interest, lobbying, pressure groups. Operating within a political and economic system in which the only constant is the fact of change, these factors, as the OSS concluded, made 'consistency and effective application of policy uncertain'.

There is clearly truth in the OSS observations. But as far as Japan was concerned, the specific catalyst of change in the context of the Cold War was the convergence of American vested interests, economic and military, behind the once-defeated but still surviving Japan Crowd. The policies which Joseph Grew and others had put forward while the Pacific War still raged now found sympathetic ears in a divided and economically stagnant world.

Even while the tide of China Crowd reform was at its height, the Japan Crowd's philosophy made sense to American big business and military strategists alike. Japan should be rebuilt as quickly and efficiently as possible. American dollars should be poured into a mould of right-wing political stability and *zaibatsu*-led economic recovery. And, some added, the fallen enemy should be picked up, greeted as friend and ally, and rearmed.

*　　　*　　　*

The first chill of the Cold War spread quickly from Europe to Asia. In February 1945, seven months before the Occupation began,

America had agreed at the Yalta Conference that in return for its entry into the Pacific War, the Soviet Union could annexe the Kuriles, a chain of small islands no more than five miles off the northern coast of Japan. The 'Allies' were in future to agree on little else. Within a fortnight of Yalta, Russia had violated its commitments in Poland and Rumania, where it insisted on maintaining puppet governments, and was systematically stripping large areas of Eastern Europe of industrial equipment.

In May 1945, Grew urged Truman to abrogate the Yalta accord, or at least delay Stalin's intervention in Asia. At the Potsdam Conference in July the American representatives, fully aware of Russia's intention to 'turn' Germany, expressed profound misgivings as to the wisdom of 'letting Russia in' to the war in Asia at all. Some believe that the atomic bombs dropped in August on Japan were more truly aimed at the Soviet Union, a warning gesture to forestall invasion by the Red Army. One historian has called the explosion at Hiroshima 'the first shot in the Cold War.'

If in fact it was, it failed to deflect the Russians for long. Two weeks later they were firmly entrenched in North Korea, and, despite agreeing to respect the 38th parallel, were infiltrating and trying to communise the South before the Americans could establish themselves there. One American observer warned the Secretary of State, 'There is little doubt that . . . several parades and demonstrations in Seoul have admittedly been Communist-inspired . . . It is possible that well-trained agitators are attempting to bring about chaos in our area so as to cause the Koreans to repudiate the U.S. in favour of Soviet "freedom" and control.'

Even the Japanese were aware of US/Soviet tensions in 1945. On the day of the Surrender, naval officers who flocked to Tokyo calling for continued resistance to the American invaders were calmed by Rear-Admiral Tomioka Sadatoshi with the words 'With the end of World War II, there is sure to be a confrontation between democracy and communism, that is between the U.S. and the Soviet Union. In the rift between them Japan can find a chance to regain its feet'.

In October 1945 the U.S. initiated a study of atomic warfare which included plans for bombing twenty sites in Russia and Russian-controlled areas. In November, General George Marshall travelled to China with aid for Chiang Kai-shek's Nationalists in their struggle against the Chinese Communist Party, reflecting American fears that Russia would intervene with a view to establishing a second Soviet Republic in Asia. In January 1946 Truman stormed, 'I'm tired of babying the Soviets. . . . Unless Russia is faced with an iron fist and strong language, another war is in the making'. In February, in a speech in Moscow, Stalin claimed that the causes of World War II were 'the dynamics of capitalist imperialism'; a peaceful international order, he announced, was no longer possible, and Russia should treble the production of iron and steel for munitions. This, in the eyes of one observer, amounted to 'a declaration of World War III'. And it was in March 1946 that Churchill declared the 'Iron Curtain' to have descended across Europe.

So, while in Tokyo Government Section prepared the new Constitution for Japan, CIE worked on 'clean' textbooks, and the purge entered its first phase, in the outside world the struggle for advantage which would thenceforth dominate American foreign policy had already begun.

In this context Russia's intentions towards Japan had never been in any doubt as far as MacArthur was concerned. In November 1945 he met Field-Marshal Alanbrooke, who recorded in his diary: 'He became most interesting about the Russians. According to him they were at present interested in converting Manchuria, and Korea if possible, into Communist states with some form of allegiance to the Soviet Union, as has already been done to Mongolia. He felt certain that they would also attempt to convert Japan into a similar subject country so as to be able to use Japanese manpower at a later date for operations in the Pacific.'

This was why MacArthur so strongly resisted Russian participation in the administration of Japan, and vehemently disapproved of the setting up of the Far Eastern Commission, with its obvious potential for Soviet disruption, in December 1945. He never ceased to complain of Russian interference in the day-to-day running of the Occupation, confiding to Sir Alvary Gascoigne his mistrust of the activities of the Russian Mission in Tokyo. It was, he said 'a state within a state', comprising more than five hundred 'men of Moscow', remarkably over-qualified for the jobs they nominally held – chauffeurs with degrees in applied mathematics, gardeners who specialised in telecommunications, and so on.

With every turn of the screw in East/West tension the strategic importance of Japan, poised on the frontier of the Communist world, increased. In the event of renewed war in the Pacific, from Japan it would be possible to oversee the Pacific trade routes and dominate the exits and entrances to the Yellow Sea and the Sea of Japan, controlling the approaches to Asian ports from Shanghai to Vladivostok. Possession of Japan in the days before the development of intercontinental ballistic missiles would secure America's outer defence perimeter, pushed beyond her home waters during the Pacific War, at a line stretching from the Philippines, Taiwan and Okinawa in the south through Japan and on to the Aleutians and Alaska in the north.

Should the Japanese archipelago fall to Russia, on the other hand, it would form the crucial link in a chain of Soviet offshore defences from North Korea to the Kamchatka Peninsula from which all the American Pacific bases could be threatened. In the event of China succumbing to communism and aligning herself with Russia – and for years all but the most optimistic in Washington were to take it for granted that all Communist countries would naturally coalesce into a single bloc – it would be doubly necessary to secure Japan*. Should the kind of technical expertise and industrial potential shown by Japan in the war years be combined with the limitless manpower and raw materials of the Asian mainland, the United States faced the menace of a truly formidable warmaking complex.

In economic terms too, the allegiance of Japan was critical. The American economy was in increasing danger of stagnating through lack of overseas markets for the output of its immense industrial capacity. Other nations were for the most part in desperate financial straits, their economies in ruins, and were unable to earn, by exporting to America, the dollars with which to pay for the goods America needed to sell. There was in effect a 'dollar gap'; and Japan was a crucial component of America's strategy for bridging it in Asia, as were the recipients of Marshall Aid in Europe.

In order for Japan to be re-established as a buyer of American goods, she had first to be rebuilt as a maker and seller of her own – and this entailed guaranteeing her access to raw materials. 'The security interest of the United States in the Far East', wrote one adviser, 'short of military action, hinges on finding and securing an area to complement Japan as did Manchuria and Korea'; and the obvious area to choose, now that Korea and Manchuria were potentially closed to Japan in Communist hands, was South East Asia. America's aim was to integrate the economy of the South East Asian region with Japan as its industrial hub, and tie the whole firmly into the western economic and monetary system.

This was in effect a recreation of the Co-Prosperity Sphere, and the attendant risks were high. 'Economic penetration is the first step', warned William Macmahon Ball, 'political domination the second'. To American strategists in the late 1940s, however, to have risked the alternative – the possibility that the resources of the

---

* In March 1948 the CIA reported the existence of a Japanese Communist Party document entitled 'Important Directive concerning present world conditions'. This referred to a directive from what was called 'the Far East Cominform' to the effect that all communist parties in the Far East should coordinate and intensify their activities so as to distract attention from Europe.

Pacific region might fall into Communist hands and be lost to the western economy – would have been folly.

*   *   *

Japan could no longer be seen in isolation; she was now an interlocking part of the American world picture. The world had changed almost out of recognition in the years since Pearl Harbor. America's foreign policy as a whole had been forced to change in response – and the way in which it changed had dramatic repercussions for Japan.

Economic supremacy and the way the spoils of war were divided had projected America into a leading role in that post-war world. But the burden of these new responsibilities imposed a considerable strain on Washington's antiquated foreign policy-making apparatus. It was in partial response to this problem that Congress passed the Truman administration's National Security Law in April 1947, creating the National Security Council (NSC) and its intelligence source, the Central Intelligence Agency, to centralise, co-ordinate and unify American policy in the realm of national security.

The principal significance of the NSC was that its scope was global. Gone was the compartmentalisation of foreign policy by geographical area which had spawned the China Crowd/Japan Crowd divisions. The NSC was also a considerably more powerful policy-making body than SWNCC or any of the other organisations it superseded. Besides the Joint Chiefs of Staff and the Secretaries of the Army, Navy, Air Force and State Department, its members included the newly-created Secretary of Defense and both the President and Vice-President. It was a new forum, with unrestricted power to make new policy – or, if it chose, to reappraise policies that had previously been considered and discarded.

The Japan Crowd, for instance, though frustrated by the China Crowd in the final shaping of the directives to MacArthur, had never lost sight of their objectives, and in the intervening years had found powerful support amidst the mêlée of conflicting interests in Washington. The formation of the NSC was in fact just part of a thoroughgoing reorganisation of foreign policy making whose overall effect was to reinstate firmly the original thinking of the Japan Crowd.

Their policies had already been given a boost at the start of 1947 when Truman began to surround himself with a new team of foreign policy advisers. Most were professional soldiers or business men, a few were career diplomats; what united them was the belief that confrontation with the Soviet Union was inevitable, and that Japan could be a useful ally.

The team included James V. Forrestal, Secretary of the Navy and one of the earliest voices raised against Soviet aggression; General William H. Draper, who had played a crucial part in opposing the payment of reparations and the deconcentration of big business in occupied Germany, which he saw as America's most valuable potential ally in Europe; John Foster Dulles; Averell Harriman; and a middle-ranking foreign service officer named George P. Kennan.

Kennan had first made his mark in February 1946 when as *chargé d'affaires* in Moscow he sent home a long telegram full of forebodings about Soviet intentions. This report (which he elaborated in May 1947 in *Foreign Affairs*, concealing his identity by signing the article simply 'X') was to form the core of the American Cold War strategy. Cooperation with Russia, Kennan stated, was no longer possible – the watchword of the future was 'containment'. In essence, containment meant meeting the Soviet threat wherever it should arise. The principal threat, however, was not perceived to be the Red Army, but economic and political weaknesses within war-shattered countries like Japan and Germany which could be exploited to the Soviet Union's advantage. 'Containment', therefore, should not take the form simply of military confrontation, but of restoring these and other potential allies to something like their former political stability and economic strength. This was the philosophy behind the Marshall Plan in Europe – 'altruism serving strategic ends', in the words of one observer – and it was now to be applied to Japan.

As early as February 1947 the State Department's Division of Japanese and Korean Affairs produced proposals for an 'economic crank-up' of Japan – an end to curbs and restraints, and the beginnings of positive planning to restore Japan to self-sufficiency and a central position in the Asian economy.

In March 1947, SWNCC (in its last months before the NSC took over policy control) embarked on a full-scale reassessment of policy, analysing the role that each and every country was likely to play in economic terms in the conflict between Russia and America. In May, Dean Acheson, then Under-Secretary of State, made a speech in Mississippi calling for 'the reconstruction of those two great workshops of Europe and Asia – Germany and Japan – upon which the ultimate recovery of the two continents so largely depends'. The appointment of George Kennan in the same month to head a new group – the Policy Planning Staff – within the State Department 'both affected and reflected the changing direction of policy' in Washington.

In January 1948 Kenneth Royall, Secretary of the Army, speaking in San Francisco, described America's objective as being to develop a self-sufficient, democratic Japan able to stand up as a 'deterrent' to any future 'totalitarian war threat'. This confirmed a major shift in policy signalling that Japan and not Nationalist China, increasingly beleaguered by Mao Tse-tung's forces, was to be America's bulwark against communism in the Far East. In March 1948 Kennan himself visited Tokyo to discuss Washington's shifting attitude to the Occupation with an increasingly puzzled and indignant MacArthur. Hot on his heels arrived a group of American corporate executives headed by William Draper, now Under Secretary of the Army, advising against any further interference – negative, that is – in Japanese industry.

And finally, in October 1948, the National Security Council gave substance to the sentiments of Forrestal, Kennan, Royall and Draper, and issued a major policy statement on its wishes for the future of Japan. With this directive, known as NSC 13/2, the National Security Council effectively cancelled the instructions of 1945, and the Occupation entered a new phase.

MacArthur was ordered that no more reforms were to be 'pressed' upon the Japanese government, and pressure to enforce existing measures was to be relaxed, particularly where political reform had been achieved at the expense of economic recovery. The priority now was reconstruction; Japan was no longer to be punished as an enemy, or even reformed for her own good, but pushed ahead as an ally with all the strength at SCAP's disposal. As a bitterly frustrated William Macmahon Ball pointed out, 'Seldom can a defeated nation have had such an important role allotted to it so soon after its defeat'.

In practical terms in Japan the repercussions of Washington's seeming change of heart were felt most forcefully in four areas. These were economic policy, labour relations, political liberties, and disarmament; and in each of these areas many of the main aims set out in the BIPSD of November 1945 were aborted.

MacArthur had originally been instructed: 'You will not assume any responsibility for the economic rehabilitation of Japan or the strengthening of the Japanese economy'. Now, however, America poured in technical assistance and advice, and dollars with which to buy the basic commodities that Japan so desperately needed to fuel her industries.

In all this, speed of recovery was of the essence, and any policy which seemed likely even temporarily to impede the return to economic normality was ruthlessly jettisoned. In effect this meant the end of the attempt to dissolve the *zaibatsu*. No-one had ever alleged that the *zaibatsu* were inefficient, merely that their domination of Japanese trade and industry was inequitable. But now efficiency was prized more highly than economic democracy.

Washington's change of heart put the Americans embarrassingly out of step with the Allied policymakers in the Far Eastern Commission. In May 1947 the FEC issued its Directive 230, confirming the deconcentration policies sketched in the BIPSD. MacArthur never wavered in his support for these policies, and ignoring all signs that opinion in Washington was rallying behind the *zaibatsu*, he virtually compelled the Japanese Diet to pass the Deconcentration Law legalising the destruction of 'excessive concentrations' of wealth in December 1948.

It proved, however, a hollow victory, because Washington and not SCAP was to decide what was 'excessive'. Indeed, the members of the Deconcentration Review Board were selected by William Draper, with the sabotage of the German deconcentration programme already to his credit. 'I am certain', he remarked, 'they will be men who will not interfere with production'; and before long the Board had reduced the number of target companies from 325 to 30. When the programme finally petered out altogether, only nine corporations had been dissolved.

The Anti-Monopoly Law was also watered down, and unfair methods of competition more narrowly defined, permitting a variety of trade restraints and other practices which to outside observers seemed blatantly monopolistic.

Those *zaibatsu* unlucky enough to have been disrupted either through liquidation of their holding companies or the dispersal of their subsidiaries re-formed more or less rapidly, coalescing this time around banks. New *zaibatsu*-style conglomerates developed, helped no little by the fact that the Americans chose to distribute their 'priority production' aid among a small number of large firms. And finally cartels and price-fixing revived, under the auspices of the Ministry of International Trade and Industry (MITI), formed in 1949 to oversee Japan's re-entry into world markets.

Also at an end, naturally, were the attempts to impose industrial limits. Aid now poured into industries previously restricted because of their military potential – steel, coal, iron, ship-building. The reparations programme was halted with only a fraction of the earmarked plant and machinery having been transferred. And as for the purge of business leaders, it was over almost before it had begun. As Royall had said in San Francisco: 'There has arisen an inevitable area of conflict between the original concept of broad demilitarisation and the new purpose of building a self-supporting nation. . . . We cannot afford to sterilize the business ability of Japan'.

In another respect, too, the *zaibatsu* were let off the hook during this period. Their grip on Japanese industry had looked like being seriously weakened by the development of an independent labour movement; in the latter years of the Occupation that grip was to tighten again, as SCAP apparently turned against the unions it had created. Many take January 31, 1947 as the cross-roads – the evening on which MacArthur publicly ordered trade union leaders to call off the General Strike they had planned for the following day, declaring 'I will not permit the use of so deadly a social weapon in the present impoverished and emaciated condition of Japan'.

MacArthur's instructions from Washington were only to prevent strikes that appeared to interfere with military operations or directly endanger the security of occupation forces. It is unlikely that the proposed General Strike would have done either of these things, and in the eyes of many Japanese workers this was a grave betrayal, the beginning of a slide towards reaction which culminated in the National Public Service Law 'encouraged' by SCAP through the Diet in December 1948. This law withdrew the right to strike from all government employees – one third of all trade union members and arguably those most likely to exercise their rights, among them railwaymen, teachers, post office workers and miners. Bitterly opposed at the time, the National Public Service Law undoubtedly paved the way for sterner moves by the Japanese government between 1950–1952, and helped shape a repressive policy towards the labour movement which persists to this day.

In banning the General Strike, MacArthur was visibly dropping his pose of political neutrality by preserving in power the Yoshida administration, a government perceived both in Japan and in Washington to be selfish, incompetent and reactionary. Arguably he was also contravening another provision of the BIPSD: 'Changes in the direction of modifying the feudal and authoritarian tendencies of the government are to be permitted and favoured'.

For many, then, particularly on the left, SCAP's determination to clean up Japanese politics was called into question. There were other signs. The purge of ultra-nationalists lost much of its impetus at this stage. MacArthur was ordered by NSC 13/2 to inform the Japanese government that no further extension of the purge was envisaged; in various areas, in fact, it was to be lifted or relaxed.

Several categories of 'relatively harmless' purgees were automatically to be declared re-eligible for public office – Tojo's 1942 nominees for the Diet, for example – and other cases were to be re-examined on their individual merits. (It was at this point that most big business purgees returned to public life, and with them a principal source of Liberal Party funds.) The volume of appeals against designation swelled, as did the proportion of purgees reinstated. In fourteen months, the first Appeals Review Board had rehabilitated about 150 appellants, less than 10% of the total; the second and third boards reinstated respectively 30% and 90% of those who asked. In 1951 the decision to depurge by categories cleared 177,000, leaving a mere 8,710 in limbo at the end of the Occupation. There was, moreover, no specific provision in the Peace Treaty to make the purge perpetually binding. Its legal basis – the terms of the Potsdam Declaration accepted by Japan at the surrender – had expired, and it was revoked in its entirety the day after the Treaty was signed.

'There must be eliminated for all time the authority and influence of those who have deceived and misled the people of Japan. . . .' Within ten years of the Potsdam Declaration most of the deceivers, as designated by SCAP, were back in public life. In October 1952, 139 former purgees were elected to the House of Representatives. In 1954, Ichiro Hatoyama, whom SCAP had felt to require an individual purge memorandum, became Prime Minister; his Cabinet contained eleven other purgees.

At the same time there had been growing pressure for the release of convicted war criminals, whom many were no longer afraid to hail as true patriots. In 1958 the new Prime Minister was Nobusuke Kishi, who had been held from 1945 to 1948 in Sugamo, awaiting trial as a Class A war criminal. He had been Minister of Commerce and Industry in the Tojo cabinet which declared war on the U.S. – for which he was purged by SCAP – and was accused by his political opponents of having financed his career on the proceeds of army raw materials channelled on to the black market after the surrender. Okinori Kaya, less fortunate, had been sentenced in 1948 to life imprisonment by the IMTFE; by 1963 he was Justice Minister.

The apparent softening of mood towards the pre-war right in the later years of the Occupation was cast into sharp relief by a conspicuous hardening of attitude towards the left. From 1948 onwards, the purge machinery survived principally as a weapon to be used against Communists. This had been made possible by a subtle shift in the criteria for designation. Originally the targets had been those with militarist sympathies. Then, in attempting to apply the purge to 'excessive concentrations' of wealth, SCAP had gone beyond its demilitarisation brief and extended the range of 'undesirables' to include those displaying 'anti-democratic traits'. By the late 1940s 'anti-democratic' was construed almost exclusively to mean 'Communist'.

With McCarthyism gathering momentum in the States, MacArthur authorised the Yoshida government to move against Communists in the public sector at the end of 1949. Without recourse to the formal purge procedures, over ten thousand suspected subversives were removed from government service, the media and the educational system; and subsequently industrialists were able to dislodge an equal number of union activists from the private sector. As tension mounted in Korea, Communist activity in Japan became increasingly unacceptable, and on June 6, 1950, two and a half weeks before the official outbreak of the Korean War, MacArthur took direct action and ordered the purge of the entire central committee of the Japanese Communist Party. The following day he removed the editorial staff of *Akahata* (Red Flag), the Party's official organ, and by the end of the month the paper had been suspended altogether as 'an instrument of foreign subversion'.

The 'Red Purge' was a project rather more to the taste of General Willoughby and G-2 than the original purge had ever been, and American counter-intelligence staff co-operated wholeheartedly with the Japanese government in identifying suspects. British representatives in Tokyo commented disdainfully on the 'anti-Communist hysteria' Willoughby had managed to whip up, aided by pamphlets originally intended for the American market but now translated into Japanese and widely distributed. The work of the U.S. Chamber of Commerce, they bore such inspiring titles as 'How to Spot a Communist', 'The Communist in Labor Relations today', and 'Communism: a World Threat'.

The efficiency of the Japanese surveillance system also increased dramatically. The Special Investigation Bureau had always had something of a right-wing complexion. It had operated less than vigorously against ultra-nationalists, being staffed largely with ex-members of the thought police who had quit their jobs promptly enough after the surrender to avoid being purged themselves. But between 1948 and 1952 its staff grew from 150 to 1,700, and it acquired a new chief – Mitsusada Yoshikawa, an anti-Communist crusader since the time of the Sorge/Ozaki Russian spy trial in 1941. (Yoshikawa was later to testify in the U.S. against Americans, before the McCarran Committee investigating the leftist members of the Institute of Pacific Relations.)

Most startling of all, perhaps, was the apparent about-turn on the subject of disarmament. Barely four years after inducing the Japanese to incorporate in their Constitution a pledge to renounce war and arms forever, MacArthur was ordering Yoshida to establish a 'National Police Reserve' of 75,000 men, to be equipped and trained by America, as a means of preserving internal security. Two years later, under heavy American pressure, this force was expanded to 110,000 and combined with an embryo navy into a National Security Force armed with tanks and heavy artillery. By 1954 Japan possessed its own Self-Defense Forces, air, sea and land, which despite Article 9, the peace pledge, were nevertheless authorised to defend the country against external attack.

21

Continuity in Change

What did America really hope to achieve in Japan? The loftiness of the original charter, the high-flown language of most of the public pronouncements and the unashamed idealism of some of the reforms gave the impression in the early days that SCAP was trying to build the perfect state. MacArthur's men were, it seemed, attempting to transplant the finest American virtues into soil where they could flourish without restraint, so that ultimately a new Japan, characterised by pacifism, intellectual enlightenment and political and economic equality, could be triumphantly restored to the community of nations.

For their pains, the Americans of that generation have been sharply criticised, first for making the attempt – a mark of sentimental utopianism and rampant ethnocentricity – and then for abandoning it when it no longer suited their purposes. The charge is capriciousness, and at first sight it seems justified. Certainly many of the policies of the later years bore little resemblance to the programme outlined in the 1945 directives.

Is it really accurate, however, to say that America deviated from its true purpose in Japan? To have devised an idealistic programme of reform and then performed a complete *volte face* and abandoned it would indeed have been discreditable. But supposing American actions in Japan between 1945 and 1952 were *not* contradictory after all but, taking the long view, ultimately consistent? Then American intervention in Japan appears in a rather different and even less attractive light.

The truth of the matter is that some of the most valuable elements in the original programme, SCAP neither reversed nor even modified. Land reform, improvements in the social and legal status of women, innovations in public health, reform of the legal system all survived and prospered. In fact, critics of the 'reverse course' are really only talking about three main areas where American policy did seem abruptly to change from radical to conservative – political life, economic policy and military rearmament.

Even here, however, there is an underlying continuity in American thinking. This may clear America of the charge of inconsistency, but lays her open to a rather more serious indictment. To accept the policies of the later Occupation years as the logical outcome of earlier plans is tantamount to saying that America, or at least the pre-eminent American policymakers, never genuinely intended to reform Japan, nor, which is of more relevance, fully to demilitarise her.

*   *   *

Never during the planning stage or the first eighteen months of the Occupation was there any consensus in Washington that Japan should be restored to the international community as a free agent. The China Crowd alone appeared to believe that Japan could and should be treated as though she existed in a vacuum – that there was scope for the free play of idealism. Far more common was the view that Japan's reconstruction was meaningful only as it fitted into the American post-war scheme of things. Even the US Initial Post-Surrender Policy of August 1945 described America's aim as being to bring about in Japan 'the eventual establishment of a peaceful and responsible government which will respect the rights of other states and *will support the objectives of the United States*' (our italics).

As one might expect in the aftermath of a major war, most policymakers were acutely sensitive to the pressures of the international environment – and here the overwhelming consideration, even before the war had ended, was the threat posed by communism in general and the Soviet Union in particular. In this context it was imperative that Japan be brought back into world affairs at the very least as a neutral, and preferably on America's side. Henry Stimson neatly summarised the view of the pragmatists. 'We are there', he wrote, 'for the primary purpose of our future self-protection against possible aggression. We are not there to create an ideal state.'

In these circumstances it seems more extraordinary that any of the China Crowd's idealism should have found its way into the original directives to MacArthur. And in fact the China Crowd had perhaps won the immediate planning battle only to lose the war. However radical individual policies – *zaibatsu* dissolution, rightwing purges, labour liberalisation – may have been, they were implemented within a framework that was entirely incompatible with the overall philosophy of reform.

The China Crowd's hopes of dislodging Japan's entrenched conservatism were really shattered not in 1947 or 1948, but in August 1945, when Japan surrendered without being invaded and America finally decided to work through the existing system, preserving the Emperor and much of the *status quo*. This was a victory for the Japan Crowd that was to prove more significant in the end than the China Crowd's temporary triumphs on individual issues. 'By retaining intact two of pre-war Japan's privileged élites, the Imperial institution and the bureaucracy', writes Herbert Bix, 'the Truman administration insured that the formal democratisation of Japan would take place within the conservative framework of the old régime. The American plan for post-war Japan was thus highly conservative from its inception.'

This conservatism was in fact apparent from the start in several areas where America's critics have deplored a 'reverse course' – labour relations and the purge, for instance. In neither case were SCAP's policies ever intended fundamentally to alter the *status quo*. Political freedom in Japan was always to be limited to what was consistent with maintaining a pro-American (which is to say decidedly anti-Communist) government in power.

So it is artificial to depict MacArthur's prohibition of the General Strike, say, as a bolt from the blue. The ban was of course highly dramatic – issued at the last moment and reducing the union leaders to public tears of frustration and despair – but it was hardly unexpected. Within weeks of introducing the first labour reforms in 1945, MacArthur was attempting to regulate the way in which the unions used their new freedom.

In April 1946 the Japanese government's food distribution system was showing signs of collapse, and, largely at the instigation of Socialist and Communist-led unions, the Japanese people began to experiment with the new political weapon of mass demonstrations. That year at least a million people participated in May Day marches. On May 14 a furious crowd denouncing inequalities in food rationing tried to storm the Imperial Palace grounds. On May 20 a group of thirty unionists, headed by Communist leader Kyuichi Tokuda, forced its way into the Prime Minister's residence and staged a sit-down protest. Hours later MacArthur issued a public warning: 'The physical violence which undisciplined elements are now beginning to practise will not be permitted to continue'.

SCAP's attitude towards even non-violent unionism, if politically motivated, was demonstrated quite clearly in mid-1946 by its support of management against workers in a major press dispute. The Japanese press had been among the first sectors of industry to unionise, and by the end of 1945 most papers were under worker control and well to the left. The union at the *Yomiuri Shimbun*, whose proprietor Matsutaro Shoriki was conspicuously right-wing, was the first to go on strike. SCAP's Labor Division had some sympathy with their removal of Shoriki; he had, after all, refused to print the photograph of Hirohito with MacArthur, or permit any reference in his paper to the hoarded goods scandal or *zaibatsu* war guilt, and he was later to be arrested as a suspected major war criminal. They could not tolerate, however, the Marxist beliefs of the triumphant new editor and union representatives, and when the *Yomiuri* workers took industrial action again, the police were used to break the strike and replace the old editorial staff.

In August 1946, just twelve months into the Occupation, MacArthur issued a warning that strikes threatening Occupation objectives would be forbidden. Two months later the unions planned an 'October offensive' which was to take the form of a staggered strike of the major unions – press, miners, electrical workers and others – staggered precisely because they anticipated that a General Strike would be prohibited. Even then SCAP intervened. Major Imboden of CIE visited the offices of the *Asahi Shimbun*, whose support was critical to the success of the press strike, and persuaded its union members to withdraw. MacArthur himself deterred the electricians: according to Sir Alvary Gascoigne, MacArthur said he had 'recently threatened to imprison certain of the electrical workers for causing inconvenience to the Occupation by cutting off the current and they had immediately "piped down"'. On October 25, 1946 Gascoigne concluded, 'In the event of any serious threat of a general strike, the General would step in openly to stop it.'

Thus when the ban came on January 31, 1947 it was the outcome, predictable and predicted, of a year of working at cross purposes. SCAP did not 'betray' the unions which it had created, because it had never intended to create the kind of unions these had become.* Labour policies in America had evolved primarily to deal with unions in private enterprise, and what the planners had envisaged in Japan was a similar type of 'economic' union, which would concern itself principally with wages, hours and working conditions. But what actually developed were highly politicised organisations on the European model, prepared and eager to use their bargaining power to exert political pressure.

The politicisation of the unions was largely, if not wholly, the

---

* Justin Williams Sr. also points out that MacArthur balanced the ban on the General Strike with an order to Yoshida to call a general election for the House of Representatives – an election which led to Yoshida's replacement by a Socialist.

result of radical and especially Communist influence. It appears that both the planners in Washington and SCAP in Tokyo at first seriously underestimated the potential strength of communism in Japan – it was perhaps too hard to reconcile with the stereotype picture of the average Japanese as a rabid ultra-nationalist, fanatically devoted to the Imperial institution. They granted a good many freedoms – the release of all political prisoners, for example – apparently without considering the implications for the development of communism.

But whatever the Basic Initial Post-Surrender Directive of November 1945 may have had to say on the subject of civil liberties, it was never the intention of the majority in Washington that the Japanese should be free to choose communism. The more radical members of the China Crowd who helped to shape the BIPSD may have seen the right to espouse communism as coming under the heading of freedom of opinion. John Emmerson, for example, wrote: 'We could not deny freedom to Communists because they were Communists. If we believed in the system we preached, we would have to take the risks.' But the mainstream of American policy was that Japan was to be democratic, with a 'peacefully inclined and responsible government' – and on both of these counts communism failed to qualify.

From one point of view it was the Communists who ultimately sabotaged hopes of fostering a genuine liberal democracy in Japan. With total freedom of action, America might, through its attack on the extreme right, have given moderate forces a breathing space to reorganise and re-emerge after almost two decades of repression. But with the left-wing threat increasingly apparent, America could not take the risk of leaving, even temporarily, a political vacuum into which communism might flow. Instead of the revival of 1920s democracy for which the planners had hoped, SCAP found itself permanently obliged to sponsor the continuation of arch-conservatism.*

Against this same background, the way in which the purge developed is also quite coherent. It is claimed that SCAP not only put it into reverse, with the depurge of the militarists, but also twisted it out of shape to serve a new policy of anti-communism. In fact, provisions for using it against Communists had always existed. Included in the BIPSD as ineligible for public office were all

---

* And to support a government which the Americans themselves perceived to be hostile to their reforms. The CIA reported in 1948, 'The leadership of the Democratic Liberal Party is ideologically opposed to many occupation-instituted reforms, and there are indications that during the tenure of the Liberal-led Yoshida cabinet the government sought to minimise the effects, if not the implementation, of these reforms'.

persons 'who manifest hostility to the objectives of the military occupation'. As might be expected in the aftermath of war, attention was focused initially on the warmongers – among whom the Japanese Communists could hardly be counted since most of them had spent the war in jail. But in 1947 that programme was practically completed and the militarist threat was receding – while the Communist threat, equally obviously, was not.

The 'Red Purge' was actually the more moderate of two possible countermeasures – the other being the total abolition of the Japanese Communist Party, which Willoughby loudly demanded. At the height of union violence on the railways in July 1949, MacArthur seriously considered it. Instead he seems to have decided to give Yoshida his head in purging the public sector. The manner in which Yoshida accepted this decision almost suggests that the Red Purge was a sin of omission by SCAP rather than one of commission – a failure to restrain the man who was to propose the creation of an Un-Japanese Activities Committee. 'My government', Yoshida stated firmly, 'would prefer to conduct the anti-Communist campaign on its own initiative and on its own responsibility. In the interest of Japanese-American relations I do not wish to see your headquarters involved directly in our fight with the Communists.'

So in its championship of the conservative government in Japan against Communists, wherever they showed themselves, America displayed unmistakable continuity of purpose. But what of the lead item in the China Crowd manifesto – economic democracy and the dissolution of the *zaibatsu*? Nowhere perhaps was the reformers' downfall more obvious than in the sabotage of the deconcentration programme in favour of the economic 'crank-up'.

But, equally, on no other issue were the China Crowd more isolated at the outset from mainstream American policy. No other single element of the reform programme provoked anything like as much comment and hostility in the States. Even before the BIPSD was drafted, while *zaibatsu* deconcentration was just an academic issue being thrashed out in the pages of left-wing publications, opposition to it was growing – not merely in the ranks of the Japan Crowd, but in American industrial circles and, for different reasons, among military strategists.

The *zaibatsu* themselves were all too aware of the schizophrenia among American planners on the subject of deconcentration and this might well explain their singularly successful use of delaying tactics in the early years of the Occupation. They evaded SCAP's regulations, sent envoys over MacArthur's head to Washington and New York, and showed themselves perfectly willing to let the economy fall apart, for the time being at least, under the twin scourges of inflation and the black market. America, they felt, was at heart more for them than against them, and it was only a matter of time before she made her true feelings known.

The 'new' policy had in fact taken root before the war was even over. Economic rehabilitation had been the aim of the Japan Crowd virtually from the earliest days of planning. In July 1943, Robert Fearey produced a paper on 'Japanese Post-War Economic Considerations' in which he argued that far from scaling down Japan's foreign trade or industrial potential, America should vigorously promote them. He had in mind the fact that before the war Japan had provided the third largest market for American goods in general, and certain producers – America's cotton growers, for instance – were heavily dependent upon this outlet.

Men like Joseph Grew saw the best hope for the Japanese economy in reviving pre-war trade patterns in a concentrated economy under a cooperative financial élite. The original instructions to MacArthur recommending deconcentration and the purge of business leaders were issued only after Grew and his supporters had resigned or been dislodged. Even out of power, however, they maintained their opposition to the policy of punitive reform. Ultimately they were to see their ideas prevail not because of the practical difficulties in which the deconcentration programme found itself, though these provided excellent ammunition, but because the Japan Crowd philosophy coincided with the interests of military strategists and the American business community.

Some of the leaders in domestic business circles, the *zaibatsu's* American counterparts, patently feared that SCAP's deconcentration programme might be used as a blueprint for similar action against themselves. The Edwards Report had spoken, after all, of the campaign against the *zaibatsu* as part of an 'international attack upon arbitrary exercise of economic power'. Primarily, however, American business leaders resisted deconcentration in Japan because, as MacArthur explained in 1948, it ran counter to their own post-war plans. 'The big Wall Street combines and other large commercial interests in the States which had before the war traded with the *zaibatsu* in Japan were now looking towards the day when they might be able not only to trade with a "revamped" *zaibatsu* . . . but also partially to control them.'

It appears to be left-wing orthodoxy that since World War II America's foreign policy has been shaped not by Congress or public opinion, nor even by the military or the bureaucracy in Washington, but by the leaders of big business, the so-called 'corporate élite'. According to this analysis foreign policy has not been a defensive response to an ever-present Soviet threat, as is usually claimed. It has been a sustained initiative towards expansion, which is crucial if the multinationals are to secure the new markets they need to survive. And it has been dictated by the members of the corporate élite, who dominate the strategic policy-making agencies (the State Department, the Pentagon, the Treasury, the CIA and so on), who pack the special committees and task forces heavily relied upon by successive Presidents, and who control the media and other means of shaping opinion.

Though this theory is polemical and politically-based, it has considerable appeal in relation to the immediate post-war period – and especially where policy-making for Japan is concerned. Here a significant proportion of the men Truman chose for his advisers, and appointed to the highest policy-making positions, did come from the upper echelons of the so-called 'power élite' – men like John Foster Dulles, from the law firm of Sullivan and Cromwell; Averell Harriman and Robert Lovett, both from the investment house of Brown Brothers Harriman; James Forrestal, from the investment house of Dillon Read.

'What I have been trying to preach down here', commented Forrestal, 'is that in this whole world picture the Government alone can't do the job; it's got to work through business. . . . That means that we'll need to, for specific jobs, be able to tap certain people.' As the first Secretary of Defense, Forrestal was able to 'tap' a former vice-president of Dillon Read, William Draper, as Under Secretary of the Army; and he had already invited yet another Dillon Read partner, Ferdinand Eberstadt, to draw up the plans for reorganising the defence establishment which formed the basis of the National Security Act of 1948.

Men like Forrestal, Draper and Harriman may not have been furthering the interests of their own particular corporate concerns in Japan, but their presence in influential positions created a climate which was highly favourable to the business lobby in general.

There was concrete evidence of this lobby at work. A few of the commercial giants chose to make their wishes for Japan known at first hand. The President of Westinghouse, for example, put in a plea to the War Department against the deconcentration of Westinghouse's trading partner Mitsubishi Kenki K.K. A Vice-President of the B. F. Goodrich Company wrote to the Chief of the Anti-Trust and Cartels Division of ESS appealing against the indiscriminate application of the purge to Japanese business. 'Our interest in resuming our former business relations and making any additional investment in Yokohama Rubber Company is dependent on being associated with competent and responsible Japanese nationals.'

In general, however, *Newsweek* was the mouthpiece for big business throughout the Occupation. The magazine had been founded in 1937 by among others Vincent Astor and Averell Harriman, whose father had been one of the boldest of the 'robber barons' of the 1870s and 1880s, making his fortune in the Union Pacific Railroad Company. In 1947 Harriman's brother was a director and Astor Chairman of the Board of *Newsweek*.

The Foreign Editor, Harry F. Kern, was a personal friend of Harriman's and a dedicated supporter of Japan's recovery, having sympathised with Japan even during her years of imperial expansion in the 1930s. The Tokyo correspondent was Compton Pakenham who had spent some of his earliest years in Japan and, in the words of one critic, 'looked upon most indicted war criminals in Tokyo as childhood playmates'. Between them they crafted a series of vitriolic *Newsweek* leaders against SCAP's economic policies, in particular the purge of experienced managers and the dissolution of sound and successful commercial enterprises.

Kern and Pakenham also tried to intervene directly on behalf of the *zaibatsu* in relation to an official exchange scheme to bring Japanese students to the States, by setting up a committee and offering its services to the Department of the Army in an advisory capacity. Daniel Imboden of CIE voiced the suspicions of many SCAP reformers: 'A *Newsweek* man, Kern, and the evil Packingham [sic], have suggested forming an advisor group for Japan. . . . When, as, and if many great men and women of the American *zaibatsu* class join in this great work of being advisors . . . it is not too much to believe that this advisor group might find it convenient and in the public interest to offer a strata of recommendations that seek to integrate the disintegrated *zaibatsu*.' More coherently the head of CIE, Donald Nugent, relayed the warning to the U.S. Chief of Staff: 'It is the belief of Major Imboden . . . that the so-called *Newsweek Committee* . . . would attempt to influence student selection to the end that sons and daughters of *zaibatsu* families would be given first (and perhaps sole) consideration.'

The *Newsweek Committee* was in fact a small unit within a larger organisation, the American Council for Japan, which acted as a forum for the discontent with SCAP's reformist policies expressed so forcefully in *Newsweek*. Kern and Pakenham were central figures in the American Council, but it also attracted leading members of the Japan Crowd – Joseph Grew, Eugene Dooman and Joseph Ballantine – which was steadily regaining its wartime influence, though no longer in the State Department. (For example, Ballantine's advice had been sought by George Kennan while the latter was preparing a major Policy Planning Staff study on Japan in August 1947; Ballantine counselled depurge and reconstruction.)

The multi-faceted American Council met in the offices of a New

York attorney named James Kauffmann – and it was Kauffmann who, as much as anyone else, was to be responsible for sabotaging finally the deconcentration programme. He had been for many years a lawyer in Tokyo, representing American interests in Japan – firms like General Electric, Westinghouse, Ford, National Cash Registers, Otis Elevator and Dillon Read – and in August 1947 he was commissioned by members of the American business community to report on SCAP's activities in the economic field.

Somehow, while it was still being discussed in secret by the Allied representatives at the Far Eastern Commission, he obtained access to FEC 230, in which the original deconcentration policy was reaffirmed, and drew on it to devastating effect. In his report he claimed that SCAP was pursuing policies that were 'socialistic and 'unAmerican', policies which made investment in Japan 'unadvisable'. That the economy remained precarious, 'much to the delight of several hundred Russians who are attached to the Soviet Embassy in Tokyo', was due, he believed, to the ineptitude and eccentricity of the men in charge of its stabilisation. 'The high command in Japan has failed to take advantage of the services of experienced business men which have been offered. It has accepted the advice of mediocre people and listened to the siren song of a lot of crackpots . . . Not only financial institutions, but all business is to come under the knife of the economic quack.'

Kauffmann in turn leaked FEC 230 to *Newsweek*. (For this MacArthur prohibited his return to Japan, but the ban was soon overturned by Secretary for the Army, Kenneth Royall.) He then took care to deliver copies of his Report not only to his employers but also to the Treasury and the Pentagon – where, to some at least, its contents will not have come as much of a surprise.

The Army, in fact, paid close attention to the American Council for Japan, being much in sympathy with its aim of rehabilitating the Japanese economy. For strategic reasons the military preferred to see Japan strong and from the beginning were opposed to the reductionist strategies of the China Crowd. For financial reasons they preferred to see Japan self-sufficient: as GHQ SCAP was a field command, the Pentagon was responsible for the Occupation budget, and was anxious to keep to a minimum the drain on the American taxpayer. And the Army, too, had its overlap with the corporate élite.

To continue the left-wing thesis, army policy has in modern times been determined to a significant extent by commercial interests. 'Business', it is said, 'is both a fount and magnet for the Military Establishment. Business careers are now part of the aspirations of thousands of military officers, while key businessmen and their lawyers continuously pass in and out of major bureaucratic posts in the Defense Department and national security agencies, usually remaining long enough to determine key policies and then return to business.' Mutual back-scratching keeps military and business circles firmly locked together.

Again this is polemical – but again the theory sheds light on the methods by which the China Crowd's policies, and the deconcentration programme in particular, were defeated. The role played by General Draper in the demise of FEC 230 illustrates the left-wing theory very neatly. Draper, a senior investment banker, was taken from the army reserve to become a General in 1940, and stayed on in the Department of the Army after the war had ended. By 1949 he was back in private life. But in the interim he had played an exceptionally important part in engineering the collapse of the deconcentration programme and, incidentally, the waning of MacArthur's power in Japan. (It is perhaps more than a coincidence that many, including Harry Kern, pictured Draper taking over from MacArthur as Supreme Commander.)

Draper discussed Kauffmann's findings with him before the Kauffmann Report was released. He then used the Report to orchestrate his attack. It was Draper who persuaded *Newsweek* to savage the deconcentration programme in December 1947 on the basis of FEC 230 – of which, thanks to Kauffmann, *Newsweek* had a copy, though it was still officially classified. And it was Draper who persuaded Kern to send a further copy to Senator William Knowland of California, who used it to denounce SCAP in the Senate. (Draper had previously endeared himself to Knowland by drafting a programme for credits to make California's cotton surplus available to Japanese mills.) Draper had already taken the precaution of circulating a memorandum sent to him from Tokyo by a 'confidential' source apparently within SCAP, a 'Mr. Wm. W'; this denounced MacArthur as vain, unscrupulous and dishonest, interested in Japan only as a springboard to the presidency.* The coalescence of military and commercial interests which Draper typified form the backdrop – unobtrusive but all-important – to the evolution of the policies ultimately expressed in NSC 13/2.

*   *   *

If American policy changed course, then, it did so virtually before the Occupation had even begun. America's true aim in Japan was

---

* The antipathy was mutual: in January 1948 MacArthur snapped at Draper, 'The answers to the present economic problems do not lie in . . . the coddling of war guilty and their associates merely because affiliated with American interests'.

deflected not in 1947 or 1948, but in 1945 when promises were made in its name, and ideals pursued vigorously for a few months, to which only the China Crowd and liberal elements in SCAP really subscribed. George Kennan wrote later that the original directives on the occupation of both Japan and Germany had 'reflected at many points the love for pretentious generality, the evangelical liberalism, the self-righteous punitive enthusiasm, the pro-Soviet illusions, and the unreal hopes for Great Power collaboration in the post-war period which . . . had pervaded the wartime policies of the Allied powers.' But the war was over, and the group which had espoused these values and ensured their enshrinement in the Basic Initial Post-Surrender Directive for Japan immediately lost power and was replaced at the helm by other groups more genuinely representative of American post-war aspirations.

The Basic Initial Post-Surrender Directive itself, the highwater mark of reform, acknowledged its own impermanence. 'This directive does not purport finally to formulate long-term policies concerning the treatment of Japan in the post-war world. . . . Those policies and the appropriate measures for their fulfilment will in large measure be determined by developing circumstances in Japan.' It might more prophetically have read 'developing circumstances in Washington', where Franklin D. Roosevelt, who had been at least partly responsible for the moral tone of wartime pronouncements, had been succeeded by Harry Truman.

Truman may have been a Democrat, but he was encumbered from 1947 on with the first Republican-dominated Congress since 1930. He was also cast in a very different mould from FDR, and he surrounded himself with different advisers. New Dealers like Henry Wallace soon left his administration, and the men of the China Crowd were dispersed. Theodore H. White, who had himself visited Yenan in the heady days of 1944, was to report in 1953: 'The basic burden of the reporting of the China Service in the critical years (1944–9) was that in the inevitable clash between the Chinese Communists and Chiang Kai-shek, Chiang would be the loser. This correct judgment has resulted, however, not in honor either collectively or individually to the China Service. China has gone Communist. In some fashion the men of the China Service were held responsible. The China Service, therefore, no longer exists. Of the 22 officers who joined it before the beginning of World War II, there were in 1952 only two still used by the State Department in Washington.'

By 1947 members of the Japan Crowd were already filtering back into positions of influence. Business leaders, who supported so much of the Japan Crowd philosophy, had a commanding voice – some said *the* commanding voice – in international affairs. And perhaps most importantly, the military was assuming a far more prominent role in foreign policy planning. The State-War-Navy Coordinating Committee (renamed the State-Army-Navy-Air Coordinating Committee in 1947) had already become, in Justin William's description, 'a peacetime mechanism by which the armed services intruded deeply into the precincts of the State Department'. When SWNCC/SANACC was itself superceded by the still more influential National Security Council, the process was carried a stage further.

And the new/old policy of restoring Japan's strength which these factions favoured – 'new' in contrast with the initial instructions, 'old' when traced back to Japan Crowd planning – met with ever-decreasing resistance in Tokyo. Many of the more liberal of the Occupationaires had resigned or been replaced or transferred within months of their arrival – Ken Dyke, overall head of CIE; Robert Berkov, head of the CIE press division; Theodore Cohen, head of the Labor Division. Others like Charles Kades hung on, only to leave in 1948, bitterly disappointed by the reflorescence of conservatism in Japanese political life after the brief flirtation with socialism in 1947.

MacArthur too was perhaps not the leader he had been in 1945. He continued to defy Washington's instructions when they ran counter to his own inclinations, but in real terms his power to stem the tide was waning. He said himself to Sir Alvary Gascoigne that 'while he retained the fullest control of everything in Japan, he did not feel that he was so "potent" as he had been where the Allied powers were concerned, and particularly was this so as regards his own country'.

This was not, as some suspected, a result of increasing age. MacArthur was sixty-eight in 1948, but in Gascoigne's opinion, he was 'good for at least another five years of hard work, and although there are various rumours afloat about him suffering from some obscure disease which makes his hand extremely shaky [the head of SCAP's Public Health and Welfare Section observed 'definite signs of Parkinson's disease'] I have had it on the quiet from his medical advisor that he is as sound as a bell. When the lift is out of order in his Headquarters (a not unusual occurrence) he leaps up the six flights of stairs and arrives at the top as cool as a cucumber, followed by a very out of breath orderly officer'.

MacArthur's position in Tokyo was in fact deliberately undercut. His persistence in pushing on with the original reform programme made him, in the eyes of the new men in Washington, the biggest single threat to the security of Japan, and Kennan and Draper joined forces to take him out of the game.

To some extent he played straight into their hands. On March 17,

1947, during an unscheduled press conference, he announced that he felt the time was ripe to grant Japan her independence*. In so doing he united all those who for a variety of reasons opposed him. The Department of the Army felt it was far too soon to cast Japan adrift to take her chances with the Soviet Union. The State Department was anxious to modify 'the broad influence exercised on foreign policy by U.S. military governors in the defeated Axis countries' – in other words to bring men like MacArthur under civilian control. All were suspicious of his presidential ambitions, which by now were an open secret, and the eventual fiasco of his bid for the Republican nomination did nothing to improve his credibility.

In this climate it was not hard to persuade Truman that MacArthur's unilateral control of the Occupation should be broken. Kennan's visit to Tokyo in March 1948, as the first major State Department official to visit occupied Japan, with the Draper Mission hot on his heels, was an augury of things to come. Increasingly, as special 'advisory' missions from the States followed one another in quick succession, control of the Occupation was exercised directly from Washington. Gradually MacArthur lost the power to protect the reforms he had originally introduced – and among them was Article 9 and the renunciation of war.

It is Article 9 which in all this is the enigma. For unlike the other radical reforms which circumstances (and vested interests) conspired to conquer, the renunciation of war did not originate with the China Crowd. And this raises an important question. If America, or at least a pre-eminent group of American policymakers, was determined from the outset to rebuild Japan as an ally, who persuaded the Japanese to lay down their arms for all time? Who, contrary to mainstream American policy, genuinely wanted to demilitarise Japan in perpetuity?

---

* He planned to repeat his call for restoration of sovereignty. On 14.4.47 he told Gascoigne he was 'preparing to make a further public statement stressing the necessity for an early peace with Japan . . . a more "carefully prepared" one than the pronouncement which he had made on the 17th March, and which will be directed at the *people* of the United States. Above is extremely secret as General MacArthur has not informed his own Government'. He appears, however, to have been discouraged.

22

'An Honest Mistake:' The Origins of Article 9

In 1945 Japan's military machine lay in ruins – her soldiers dead or demobilised, their weapons confiscated and destroyed, their leaders in prison or excluded from positions of authority. In 1946, the new SCAP-drafted Constitution attempted to make this state of affairs permanent by enshrining in Article 9 a renunciation of war and arms for all time. Nevertheless, in 1952, when the Occupation ended, Japan had standing forces of more than 110,000 men armed with American equipment, and was under heavy pressure from American Secretary of State John Foster Dulles to triple her military strength. By 1953, Vice-President Richard Nixon was describing Article 9 as 'an honest mistake'.

On the question of disarming Japan, as on so much else, America appeared to have undergone a change of heart. But once again the 'reverse course' was simply a coming to prominence of ideas which had been present from the start. In this case it was the ideas of American military leaders who, even before the Japanese had been defeated, had seen in them valuable allies for the future. To find military men arguing for armaments is hardly surprising; what is less obvious is who their opponents were. Few disagreed that Japan's defeated war leaders should be removed, and her existing military power destroyed. But from disarmament for the immediate present to permanent pacifism – the proposition that Japan should *never*, for any purpose, rebuild her armed forces – was a long step; and to this day America seems uncertain as to how that step (now much-regretted) was taken, or who took it.

The idea of Japan's renouncing war does not seem to have come from Washington. During the Pacific War the planners, China and Japan Crowds alike, may fleetingly have considered such a gesture, under the influence of the Atlantic Charter; as late as June 11, 1945, a SWNCC discussion document – SWNCC 150 – provided for 'to the extent possible, the permanent disarmament and demilitarisation of Japan'. But, perhaps more significant, in the OSS's hard-headed 'Working Outline for Analysis of Policy Issues Regarding Japan' of May 1945, pacifism was not among the options listed. The planners were indeed invited to consider 'principles of disarmament'; but simultaneously they were required to assess 'time required for rearmament'. And by the time it came to issuing specific guidelines to MacArthur for use in drafting the new Constitution, Washington apparently took for granted the revival of Japan's military establishment. Why else should SWNCC 228 have insisted on the future supremacy of the civilian branch of government 'over the military'? Total disarmament belonged, it seemed, to the perfect state which, as Stimson pointed out, America was *not* trying to achieve.

Nor, on the other hand, does Article 9 seem likely to have originated with the Japanese. None of the Japanese drafts for the new constitution in the spring of 1946 admitted the possibility that postwar disarmament might be permanent. On the contrary, the proposals of the official committee headed by Joji Matsumoto included explicit provision for armed forces and national conscription. (Matsumoto was in fact one of Article 9's most outspoken opponents, making a spirited last-ditch attempt to have the provision removed from the body of the Constitution into the preamble, where it would have had virtually no legal force.)

Charles Kades did once suggest that the Emperor may have been the author of Article 9. Hirohito had said, after all, in September 1945 that 'the solution of the problem of peace will lie in the reconciliation of free peoples, both victor and vanquished, *without recourse to any armaments*'. And in the New Year's rescript with which he was supposed to have renounced his divinity, he also mentioned the prospect of building a new Japan 'through thoroughly being pacific'. But these sound rather more like pious hopes than serious proposals to amend the Constitution.

Similarly, it is hard to attribute anything firmer than generalised aspirations for world peace to Baron Kijuro Shidehara, Prime Minister of Japan at the time the Constitution was drafted. According to the 'authorised' version of the birth of Article 9 – the account given by MacArthur in his *Reminiscences* and parroted by Whitney and Willoughby in their books – it was Shidehara who made the suggestion that Japan should formally renounce war, at a meeting with MacArthur on January 24, 1946. (The meeting's main purpose was for Shidehara to thank the Supreme Commander for a gift of penicillin which had speeded his recovery from a serious illness the previous month.) This story, however, should probably be regarded as part and parcel of the contention that the Japanese were responsible for drafting their own Constitution – in other words, as a diplomatic fiction designed to minimise the extent of America's interference.

Those who knew Shidehara best felt that such an action would have been distinctly out of character. While as a declared pacifist he undoubtedly would have desired the universal renunciation of war by all the nations who had so recently suffered from it, this was a very different matter from suggesting that Japan should adopt a policy of unilateral disarmament – and permanently enshrine that policy in the Constitution. His son has insisted that he was a 'realistic idealist' who had no patience with 'illusory idealism'; and Shidehara is on record some weeks later as having challenged MacArthur on the practicality of Article 9 – 'You seem to emphasise moral leadership, but there will be no followers'. Certainly, if he did feel the renunciation of war was necessary, it is odd that he should have failed to mention it to Matsumoto so that it could be incorporated in the Japanese draft constitution.

It has been suggested that in attributing Article 9 to Shidehara, MacArthur was simply shifting responsibility for an action which, by the time he wrote his memoirs in 1964, was generally considered to have been an error. More charitably, others believe that there was a straightforward failure in communications. Shidehara might well have suggested that all *references* to the military be deleted *from* the Constitution (references such as those the Matsumoto Committee persisted in making) – while MacArthur understood him to suggest that all *military* should be obliterated *by* the Constitution. Most likely of all, however, is that on more than one occasion, in the hope of persuading MacArthur to be lenient in his treatment of the Emperor, Shidehara made vague and inspirational remarks about the desirability of an end to war. These remarks MacArthur escalated and translated into positive action because they accorded so well with what he and Government Section already had in mind.

Interestingly, Government Section, in its official account of the drafting of the Constitution, makes no mention of the supposedly crucial role played by Shidehara. Some of the GS staff most intimately involved in the drafting undoubtedly felt that if Shidehara *had* brought forth the idea of renouncing war, it had sprung from seeds which they themselves had planted. It was Kades, for example, who on the way to one meeting with Shidehara had casually suggested to Whitney a rescript renouncing war, on the lines of the one renouncing divinity; during the meeting Whitney passed the notion on to the Prime Minister. Certainly the senior staff of Government Section seem the most plausible originators of Article 9, idealists as many of them were. Alfred Hussey, who wrote an early draft of the Article, was a man of consciously high principles, rather resented by the more pragmatic in SCAP as puritanical and doctrinaire. Charles Kades, who wrote a later draft, frequently expressed his admiration for earlier treaties renouncing war. Courtney Whitney, described by Roger Baldwin (head of the American Council for Civil Liberties) as in some respects a 'surprising liberal', furiously resisted any attempts to moderate the force of the disarmament campaign. Any one of them could have initiated the idea.

But whatever the source, it was MacArthur who translated wishful thinking into concrete political action by including the gist of Article 9 in the notes he handed to Whitney with the request that they be included in the Constitution. 'War as a sovereign right of the nation', he wrote, 'is abolished. Japan renounces it as an instrumentality for settling its disputes and even for preserving its own security. It relies upon the higher ideals which are now stirring the world for its defense and its protection. No Japanese Army, Navy or Air Force will ever be authorized and no rights of belligerency will ever be conferred upon any Japanese force.'

These notes, whether they were written directly by MacArthur or dictated by him to Whitney (and it is now impossible to tell, as the original document has mysteriously disappeared), leave no doubt as to MacArthur's intentions – total, unqualified and permanent disarmament. Both the notion and the wholeheartedness with which he espoused it are in character. Incongruously enough for a professional soldier, he had long expressed pacifist sentiments. Roger Baldwin remembered, 'He said that tho war was his business, and that the sound of the bugle was the first memory of his childhood, he hated it as the scourge of mankind.' It is easier, of course, to prescribe sacrifice for others than for oneself; but MacArthur was to advocate the outlawry of war again, in America, and in circumstances where he could be accused of no ulterior motives. So sweeping a gesture appealed to his love of the broad principle, the lofty ideal; it was also a natural corollary of his Christian missionary zeal.

Article 9's birth then is to be laid principally at MacArthur's door – and a puzzle is solved. When so many prominent Americans were anxious to reconstruct and fortify Japan as quickly as possible, who else would have engineered a move that seemed destined to weaken her in perpetuity but MacArthur – a man who was never afraid to be out of step. 'A sound idea cannot be stopped', he had declared, and he made quite sure that this one was carried through on a wave of his idealistic fervour. (According to Frank Rizzo, one of the GS staff involved in the discussions of the SCAP draft constitution, the renunciation of war was a 'given', strictly non-debatable.)

MacArthur had, besides, two purely practical arguments with which to persuade the Japanese of the wisdom of accepting Article 9.

Most importantly, it was a means of guaranteeing the safety of the Emperor – Theodore McNelly explains: 'The main argument for abolishing the Emperor system was that it might again be exploited to support militarism and aggression, but a radical disarmament proposition would largely negate that argument'. In addition, it was a means of pre-empting a plan then being debated in the FEC for a control commission on which all four major powers, including Russia, would be represented; this commission would monitor demilitarisation in Japan for a period of twenty-five years. Better, one might argue, to short-circuit this type of interference by foreswearing arms 'voluntarily'.

But MacArthur did not succeed in bringing Article 9 into being completely intact. While his original notes were still under discussion within Government Section, Kades deleted the provision that 'Japan renounces [war] as an instrumentality . . . *even for preserving its own security'*, on the grounds that it was unrealistic. This removal of the explicit prohibition of war as a means of self-defence opened the way for a crucial amendment which was made to Article 9 during its passage through the Diet. Hitoshi Ashida (then chairman of the Constitutional Amendments Committee for the House of Representatives) introduced a further change in the wording so that arms were now renounced specifically as a means of settling *international disputes* – the implication being that as a means of self-defence, they were permitted.

Ashida was taking advantage of the way Article 9 had been drafted by the Americans. It fell into two parts – the renunciation of *war* as an instrument of diplomacy, and the renunciation of *arms*. Almost everyone subscribed in principle to the former – a notion which had long been bandied about as part of the currency of international diplomacy. The Kellogg-Briand Pact of 1928 had attempted to outlaw aggressive war – and though visibly ineffective, most notably in World War II, the Pact was still technically in force*. More recently, under the United Nations Charter of 1945, fifty signatories had again renounced war in very similar terms.

But the renunciation of war as a means of settling disputes did not necessarily entail the total renunciation of the right to maintain armed forces for any purpose whatsoever. That was an extra and separate undertaking – and Ashida's amendment was designed to make it clear that the Japanese people espoused the former, but not the latter: that in years to come Japan *could* rearm in its own defence.

---

* Whether the Kellogg-Briand Pact had actually succeeded in making aggressive war a crime at international law was doubtful, as the controversy over *ex post facto* charges at both Nuremberg and the IMTFE made clear. See Chapter 11 above.

It is probable that this seriously compromised version of MacArthur's original Article 9 reflected more accurately the mainstream of American policy: Japan was to lose the immediate capacity to attack America, without being deprived altogether of the future right to bear arms. Such an outlook would not have been without precedent. The tradition of the Founding Fathers, after all, was anti-militarist without actually being pacifist. The Fathers were opposed to the permeation of society by exclusively military values and the keeping of a larger standing army than was actually needed, with the attendant risk that this force might be used for political purposes. But they were not opposed to the mere existence of an army, provided it was under strict civilian control and used exclusively for defence; the opposite of militarism was (and is) *civilianism*, not pacifism. This attitude was also embedded in the Charter of the International Military Tribunal for the Far East. Japan was being put on trial for waging 'unjust' war – the implication being that other wars, and other armies, might be considered just.

MacArthur, it would seem, was almost alone among the policy-makers – in Washington, in SCAP and in the Japanese government – in wanting to construe Article 9 as an absolute ban on war and arms. Government Section accepted the Ashida amendment in the full knowledge that it paved the way for defensive rearmament. And a *New York Times* leader on proceedings in the House of Peers in late August 1946 was headlined 'Japan's Arms Ban Held Transitory – Constitutional Debate Reveals Belief That Commitment May Lapse Later On'.*

But in 1946 a total renunciation of war appealed irresistibly to the Japanese people – and world opinion too demanded a gesture of this kind ('A pacifist from an enemy country is always esteemed'). No political leader wished to be seen publicly to be undermining or weakening the moral stand. Even Yoshida, anxious to preserve Japan's new image as a peace-loving nation, stood up in the Diet to defend Article 9, rather unexpectedly, as an absolute ban: 'It is an obvious fact that most modern wars have been waged in the name of the right of self-defence of the nation. Thus I believe that to recognise a right of legitimate self-defence is . . . to provide a rationale for provoking war.' Ashida's amendment, therefore, had

* *NYT* 29.8.46. 'Japan's aspirations to obtain admittance . . . to the United Nations organisation and thereupon to claim the right to rearm defensively are becoming increasingly clearer. . . . There is increasing evidence that a certain section of Japanese opinion . . . regards the proposed Constitutional provision renouncing "forever" the maintenance of an army, navy or air force, as a temporary expedient. Force of circumstances . . . may eventually force its revision'.

to be oblique, offering a loophole but not a damagingly obvious one. As Theodore McNelly points out, 'The politicians and statesmen who draft these documents are frequently aware of . . . ambiguities and deliberately tolerate or create them for practical purposes.'

In this way the foundations were laid for the deceit and double standards which have characterised Japanese defence policy since the war. Thanks largely to MacArthur, Article 9 became law: but it hardly reflected the wishes of the majority of American policy-makers. And it came into being with birth defects which have been progressively exploited to permit America's original intentions for Japan to prevail in part at least.

23

The Dragon's Teeth: Willoughby's Embryo Army

Some Americans, of course, saw no need for the Ashida amendment. To them, Article 9 was simply an irrelevance. On the day following the official surrender, some forty-eight hours after setting foot in Japan for the first time, Major General Charles Willoughby set to work to rebuild the Japanese army, and nothing was to deflect him from his course.

MacArthur's empire in Japan was a somewhat schizoid organisation divided roughly between military and civilians, with an ever-widening fissure between the two camps. Their outlooks and methods of approach were entirely different, and their priorities irreconcilable, as Alfred Hussey explained: 'The instructions from Washington . . . were generally speaking in very unspecific terms, and there was a constant battle that went on between GHQ, Far East Command and GHQ, SCAP – that is the military security forces against the civilians who were responsible to MacArthur for the political decisions that would put Japan back on its feet and make Japan an Asian democracy.' What Hussey does not mention is that there were also bitter feuds between the military and civilian officials *within* SCAP, the former doggedly resisting the reformist tendencies of the latter.

Willoughby was the leading representative of the military mind, and in a position to make its influence felt. As a prominent member of the 'Bataan gang', he was close to MacArthur, and one of the principal beneficiaries of the Supreme Commander's tendency to infiltrate favoured military cronies into essentially civilian administrations. Thus he held a dominating position both in the military hierarchy (as head of Far East Command's G-2/Intelligence Section) and in the civilian command structure (as head of SCAP's own G-2, with effective control also of the Civil Intelligence special staff section). This spread of power enabled him closely to co-ordinate the entire American intelligence operation in Japan. The Civil Intelligence Section comprised both a policy-making body and an operational agency with a large field staff; Willoughby referred to it as 'a sort of FBI' for security surveillance. When it was first set up its attention was ostensibly directed towards the ultra-right; but it was also used from the start to detect and suppress left-wing subversion and by the end was almost exclusively devoted to that purpose. The investigative units of the Far East Command Counter-Intelligence Corps were spread throughout the prefectures, working in close collaboration with the military police on law enforcement and the preservation of public order.

It was this operational network which gave Willoughby his main advantage and a useful lever to employ against the civilian staff sections of SCAP. The latter made policy, but on the whole had no personnel of their own in the field to implement it, and so had to rely on Willoughby's operatives. For instance, while the purge of ultra-nationalists was at its height, although Government Section was making the policy, Civil Intelligence Section was in charge of its enforcement.

This division of responsibility became significant when, as frequently happened, Willoughby's views were at variance with those of the civilian sections of SCAP. He collided most often with Government Section under General Whitney, his arch-rival for MacArthur's attention. Whitney was a consistent champion of the demilitarising reforms set out in the original instructions to MacArthur. He favoured, for example, the purge of business leaders and the decentralisation of the police – both of which Willoughby opposed, regardless of the social and ethical principles involved, the one as a wilful waste of experienced manpower, the other as an obstacle to efficiency.* (Willoughby's views were shared by most military men in Japan. Major J. C. Milligan, for instance, a former Pennsylvania fire chief, now head of Public Safety and Rationing in a military government team, was indignant at the havoc wrought by the purge amongst the local police. 'I'm no reformer. My job is to maintain public safety. I don't care what the guy's politics are as long as he does a competent job.')

Whitney was himself a military man, a near-millionaire, and a convinced anti-Communist, but he appeared positively revolutionary beside Willoughby – MacArthur's 'loveable fascist'. This was the man who called General Franco the second greatest general in the world, and on his retirement from the U.S. Army in the

---

* Nor was Willoughby entirely happy to destroy confiscated Japanese weaponry. He alleged that Russia did not destroy the arms it seized in Manchuria, but preserved them and later supplied them to the Chinese Communists, tipping the balance in their favour in the civil war.

1950s became one of the dictator's advisers. In 1939 Willoughby had, besides, written approvingly of Mussolini's adventures in East Africa. 'Historical judgement, freed from the emotional haze of the moment, will credit Mussolini with wiping out a memory of defeat by re-establishing the traditional military supremacy of the white race.' As his critics pointed out, 'Had a Japanese written this sort of opinion about the Japanese "race", he would have been purged by the Occupation'.

To many of his colleagues he was known as 'Baron von Willoughby'; he was German-born, his real name Charles von Tscheppe-Weidenbach, and the stereotype of a Prussian officer – very tall, ramrod-straight, autocratic, intellectually powerful, fine-featured, arrogant, prone to sudden rages. In many respects Willoughby was himself the epitome of the kind of militarist the Occupation was dedicated to destroying in Japan. He gave absolute priority to a single strategic imperative – the fight against communism – and had little patience with abstract moral theory or reformist ideology (like many of his juniors in military government, who were wont to dismiss the directives and supporting rationale they received from the staff sections as 'more crap from SCAP', wholly out of touch with day-to-day realities in the field).

He set great store by military-style discipline, and deplored its destruction in Japan where its stabilising influence could have been invaluable. It was Willoughby and G-2 who wished to preserve military penal codes within the Japanese army until all troops were finally demobilised, Government Section who felt they should be abolished because they permitted 'the retention of authority by ex-officers over ex-soldiers within Japan' – a serious impediment to psychological disarmament. Perhaps most significantly, Willoughby believed implicitly in the solidarity of the military caste. Before the war many American professional soldiers had had links with their Japanese counterparts within the ruling oligarchy. During the war, despite being enemies, in a curious way they were bound even closer, as Willoughby put it, by 'years of intimate combat association'. Now in the aftermath of war Willoughby and many like him were finding that in important respects they had more in common with the remains of the Japanese military hierarchy than with the American civilians in Tokyo.

Indeed, Willoughby deeply distrusted those on his own side who had different priorities – men more concerned, as he saw it, with social reforms and vague human rights than with Japan's security and, ultimately, the security of America. Early in the Occupation the military General Staff attempted to take over the work of Government Section; in the face of furious resistance from

Whitney, Hussey and Kades, they failed. But as the campaign against left-wing subversion intensified in the States, so Willoughby was increasingly able to use his intelligence organisation to effect against American 'radicals' in Japan. By January 1947 he had already investigated and circulated reports on men like Thomas Bisson. In June 1947 'at a time when Washington, apprehensive of Communist infiltration into government offices, required a thorough security investigation of all Army employees', Willoughby established a full-blown 'Loyalty Desk' within the Far East Command. While it also examined the credentials of Japanese witnesses and lawyers for the IMTFE, its principal targets were prospective entrants to SCAP and those already inside the organisation, with special reference to 'leftists and fellow-travellers . . . hired in the States and unloaded on the civil sections of GHQ'.

Willoughby's investigations were co-ordinated with those of the FBI at home. He received reports from the States on the past activities of SCAP employees, and the list of grounds for suspicion lengthened: involvement with American organisations designated as questionable – the Institute of Pacific Relations, the Washington Book Shop, the American League for Peace and Democracy, and so on; Russian contacts; association with the 'Red' press at home or in Japan; links with the Japanese Communist Party. Amongst the papers of Justin Williams, Chief of Government Section's Legislative Division, is a record (dated June 30, 1947) of a visit to the Division's Captain Richard Brown by a major in Civil Intelligence Section. He asked about General Whitney's role in the purge. He queried the relationship between two officers in different divisions, whom he described as 'leftists': did G. . . . 'run' T. . . . or vice-versa? He demanded of Brown whether Government Section staff knew that G-2 held files on them; and he made his exit claiming that Government Section was trying to 'tear down the Japanese government, weakening it to the extent that any -ism, viz. communism, can assume power'.

American military police, it seemed to some in Government Section, had become deeply implicated in the Japanese police's violations of civil liberties – the suppression of labour demonstrations, arrests without warrant, even the torture of prisoners. Now their combined forces, plus those of Willoughby's Civil Intelligence Section and Counter-Intelligence Corps, were used to keep watch on SCAP employees. One of the legal officers from a military government team told Alfred Hussey that CIS's Counter-Intelligence Division had ordered Japanese police 'to spy upon the activities of all American personnel who came into their area, and NOT TO LET THIS FACT BE KNOWN TO THE MILITARY

GOVERNMENT OFFICERS' (his emphases). The purpose of this surveillance was not only to monitor potential subversion, but also to accumulate evidence of minor breaches of Occupation rules which could then be used to remove officials whose 'attitude' Willoughby did not care for. The Deputy Chief of one ESS division was asked to resign for 'conveying U.S. supplies to a Japanese national' (a present, to a girlfriend, of rations worth less than $1.50), and for staying in a Japanese house for forty minutes after the curfew. Three other officers were dismissed without explanation and told that the charges against them were 'classified'. A rule was introduced to the effect that any employee could be removed for three offences against regulations so petty that it was hard to tell when they had been infringed. In a passionate outburst to Whitney, Hussey condemned G-2's campaign against those holding different political or economic beliefs, as destructive of all the Occupation stood for. 'Can we, who are denied our basic civil liberties by our own officials, persuade the Japanese of the worth of the doctrines we profess?'

The vendetta did not end with the Occupation. Some former SCAP liberals found it hard to get jobs in civilian life; Thomas Bisson, for instance, lost his post at Berkeley, and spent the rest of his working life teaching at a small mid-Western religious college for women. Others fell foul of Joseph McCarthy – and Willoughby enthusiastically supplied the Senator with 'substantiating evidence' of their guilt. (He was on occasion too zealous for his own good: in his anxiety to see the investigation of John Emmerson brought to a satisfactory conclusion, he got himself labelled 'a disgruntled person' acting 'without any first-hand knowledge' – and this by the head of his own Civil Intelligence Section.)

But Willoughby inflicted the most serious damage on the reformers' cause by virtually nullifying their efforts towards the disarmament of Japan. In 1964, while ill in hospital – not long in fact before his death – Alfred Hussey recorded on tape some of his reflections on the Occupation, intending later to work them up into a book. 'It was the Army that fought us', he remembered. 'They wanted to maintain the basic military establishment of Japan in order to fight communism. . . . General Willoughby himself told me in 1947 of a top secret order from the Pentagon to maintain the nucleus of the General Staff and to maintain the records of the Japanese Army and Navy. G-2 proceeded to do this, although it was directly contrary to specific orders from Washington to SCAP.'*

---

* Willoughby disobeyed orders again in 1950, when he worked to establish spy networks inside Communist China jointly with the KMT, 'regardless of official American policy.'

The order from the Pentagon has not been traced. But whether or not Willoughby was acting on instructions, he lost little time. It was not to be expected that the senior staff of the Imperial Japanese Army would pass into civilian obscurity without a struggle, especially since so few had actually suffered defeat in battle. As *The Times* commented on August 27, 1945, 'The way is . . . opened for the propagation of the myth, which proved so formidable a factor in the rise of the Third Reich, that the army had not been conquered, that the war was lost by poor civilian morale caused by the Allies' employment of an unfair weapon. . . . It will be strange indeed if the Japanese General Staff does not endeavour to "go to ground" as the German General Staff did in 1918.' In the event, there was no need for them to act furtively – or even independently.

In January 1946, 190 Japanese generals and admirals were still in place, exercising their former power openly and above board. Under the BIPSD, SCAP was permitted to retain the services of military leaders 'where absolutely required' for the attainment of Occupation objectives; and for such tasks as demobilisation and minesweeping round the Japanese coast, the 190 were given blanket exemption from the purge. At the same time, however, similar numbers were being secretly recruited for quite other purposes.

On August 19, 1945, a Japanese military mission had visited MacArthur's headquarters in Manila to learn the arrangements for the official surrender ceremony. Among its members was General Seizo Arisue, later to be responsible for the Americans' official reception at Atsugi. He recalled the mission being received by Willoughby, who entertained his military guests with a turkey dinner (so rich that it 'frightened our wartime stomachs'), and then improved the shining hour by enlisting them as prospective allies. On September 3, 1945, three days after his arrival in Japan, Willoughby renewed contact with Arisue. The two men had much in common. Each was the head of his country's military intelligence network; and Arisue shared Willoughby's social and political leanings, being an aristocrat and a fervent anti-Communist, who had provided one of Japan's closest links with Mussolini. In September 1945 Willoughby discreetly encouraged him to develop his own intelligence organisation within G-2. (Separate sections were devoted to gathering information on Russia, Manchuria and Korea; surveillance of the Japanese Communist Party; map-making and planning of transport routes and military strong points. These Japanese-American groups, formally dissolved at the end of the Occupation, were still operating covertly in the 1970s.)

Arisue was embroiled in two other ventures. At Willoughby's

urging he assembled another large body of senior Japanese officers, this time for the purposes of 'historical research', and set them to work on a series of monographs detailing Japanese operations in Manchuria and the Pacific. After this, they were invited to contribute to 'the MacArthur Histories', supplementing from the Japanese perspective an account of MacArthur's campaigns.

The 'Histories', later to have something of a chequered career, were in fact less important in themselves than as a screen behind which Willoughby might assemble the nucleus of a new Japanese army. In May 1946 the Japanese 'research team' was joined by Tokushiro Hattori – former private secretary to Tojo, Japanese military observer during Mussolini's Ethiopian campaign, staff officer with the Kwantung Army, and a leading figure in Japanese military intelligence. Hattori's mission in life after the war was to exploit the American-Soviet conflict to Japan's advantage. America, he was convinced, intended to launch a pre-emptive strike before Russia had a chance fully to recover from the war. Thus, sooner or later, it would be greatly in her interest to rearm Japan – and when that day came, Japan should be ready. With Willoughby's blessing, under cover of the historical research operation, Hattori built up his own prototype General Staff, a network of 50–60 officers spread throughout Japan.

A command structure was taking shape – but Willoughby had also to consider the rank and file. Several aspects of the demobilisation machinery operated by the Japanese under American military auspices worried Government Section. So many ex-officers seemed to be involved – more than 80,000 in January 1946, most of them in jobs which could equally well have been handled by civilians. And their approach to the problems of demobilised soldiers seemed unnecessarily to maintain and foster the spirit of militarism. It was Government Section policy, in accordance with the BIPSD, that military pensions (other than disability allowances) should be stopped, to eliminate the notion that soldiers received special treatment in Japan. Since all servicemen had made compulsory contributions to pension funds throughout their period of service, there was an element of injustice in this, and it added significantly to the distress experienced by 10 million veterans and their dependants. (Willoughby saw in it 'the hand of the Russians', forcing destitute ex-soldiers towards disaffection.) So the Local Assistance Bureaus set up to alleviate the distress served a genuinely humanitarian purpose. But they also enabled the central Demobilisation Bureaus to trace the whereabouts of every surviving soldier in Japan, and perpetuated the bonds of obligation between officers and their men.

In some cases chains of command were preserved intact as

whole units made the transition to civilian life together. A friend of Alfred Hussey, writing from the north of Japan, told him of a Local Assistance Bureau manned by one general, one colonel, one lieutenant-colonel, 7 majors, 20 lieutenants and 140 enlisted men, which was arranging (quite illegally) memorial services for war dead and funerals for their ashes – 'all Shintoistic, public and official – except on paper'. Even more conspicuous were the communal farms inhabited, owned and run exclusively by veterans. Japan's original mobilisation system had been organised on a territorial basis and military units were largely composed of men from the same region. Now when ex-soldiers applied through their Local Assistance Bureaus to work on the land, the tendency was to return them to their original garrisons. In the days following the surrender, a considerable proportion of the Imperial Japanese Army's assets had been hastily redistributed – property to the Finance Ministry, land to the Ministry of Agriculture. Thus the Japanese government was in a position to make available to the would-be farmers the land and buildings of the former arsenals and military installations, rent free, plus large quantities of military supplies. Scandalised foreign press correspondents, quicker to detect the abuse than the SCAP civilians (and certainly readier to do so than Willoughby's intelligence gatherers), reported the existence of communities run entirely on pre-war lines: positions within society determined by army rank, paramilitary drill and discipline, tanks used as tractors, and an education patterned on the 'Farmers for Manchuria' schools of the 1930s.

Willoughby had, in essence, preserved the means of remobilising Japan's armed forces. His principal tool was the documentation maintained by the demobilisation authorities: Hussey even alleged that a Central Records Office had been set up in Chiba Prefecture 'in which were collected, indexed, and cross-indexed the records of every man who had served in the Japanese military during the war and was still alive'. The militarist spirit was kept alight in small cells spread throughout the body of the nation. And the SCAP civilians seemed powerless to do more than protest: when civilian advisors in ESS pointed out the threat of resurgent militarism, G-2 simply sneered, 'The Russian Mission has displayed a critical interest in the Demobilisation Board, along similar lines of enquiry'. As for the one man with the power to control Willoughby and his Japanese henchmen, it is not clear whether MacArthur ever knew what was happening.

24

Unsheathing the Sword

If Alfred Hussey was right in alleging the existence of a secret order from the Pentagon to preserve the nucleus of Japan's armed strength, then Willoughby must be seen not simply as a reactionary maverick but as the advance guard of larger forces – which some two years later moved to the attack in earnest. It is not clear how closely the campaign was coordinated – how much Japan's eventual armaments owed to Willoughby's early handiwork and initiative, or how many of his original plans were thwarted by the State Department or Government Section, MacArthur or Yoshida, the Japanese public or the Far Eastern Commission. But in terms of bolstering Japanese military leaders' hopes of a revival, and establishing the whereabouts of trained military potential, much of the groundwork had been done under cover in Japan by the time rearmament began to be discussed above board in Washington.

The rearmament debate was bitter and protracted – and this time the opposing factions were not separate 'crowds' within the State Department, but the State Department itself pitted against the Department of the Army (and subsequently the Department of Defense). Military and civilians may have been at one on the necessity of rebuilding Japan economically; but the reconstruction of her independent military strength was another matter.

The consensus of opinion among civilian planners in Washington – leaving aside the views of the dwindling minority which felt that Japan should be excluded entirely from the international political scene – seems to have been that Japan should be aligned as an *unarmed* ally. America should render her harmless as a potential enemy; should deny her to Russia; should maintain its own troops in the home islands for the duration of the Occupation. Many felt that America might also prepare to defend Japan after the restoration of sovereignty, from bases within the country and from Okinawa, keeping open the option that *at some time in the future* Japan might rearm (though men like George Kennan would have preferred to see Japan adhere to Article 9 and remain an unarmed neutral indefinitely).

But as America's international position deteriorated from the unchallenged supremacy of mid-1945, the military began to insist ever more strongly on the recruitment of Japan as an *armed* ally. They disagreed vehemently with the State Department over the timing of the restoration of sovereignty to Japan. On political and diplomatic grounds, the State Department urged that independence be granted sooner rather than later. From the purely strategic point of view, the Department of the Army felt independence should be postponed as long as possible – certainly until America had secured a guarantee of the right to maintain bases in Japan, and possibly until Japan was in a position to defend herself. Rearmament, they appeared to suggest, might actually be made a condition for the restoration of sovereignty. Otherwise, even with American troops based permanently in the home islands, Japan might become a power vacuum destabilising the entire East Asian region.

America's capacity to defend her friends had, after all, declined. As troops were demobilised and not replaced, the U.S. Army dwindled from twelve million men in June 1945 to 1.6 million in 1947, and these of limited combat effectiveness. In the immediate post-war period the Department of the Army, with an eye to public opinion, was reluctant to recall men struggling to reintegrate themselves into civilian life. Strict ceilings had in any case been imposed on the defence budget; and after March 1947, conscription no longer existed. But the demands on American troops were multiplying – so rapidly in Europe that the Planning and Operations Division of the Department of the Army pronounced it 'mandatory that we employ only minimum forces in the Far East'. As far as Asia was concerned, the Truman Doctrine of 'containing' the Soviet Union was proclaimed at a moment when there were insufficient troops to back it up: in General Marshall's words, America was 'playing with fire when we have nothing with which to put it out'.

To enlist the support of indigenous forces in the areas which required policing must have seemed a natural solution to strategists in Washington. And despite Article 9, the rebirth of a Japanese defence capacity appealed strongly to many of their opposite numbers in Tokyo. By August 1947, three months after the Constitution with its pacifist provision had finally become effective, Harry Kern and *Newsweek* were reporting from Japan 'growing interest' in rearmament. The focus of this interest appears to have been Hitoshi Ashida. Having successfully insinuated the idea that Article 9 did not preclude the right of self-defence, he exploited the breach he had made by advocating, in a long memorandum, the establishment of a centralised 'paramilitary' force to ensure Japan's internal security against subversion and civil unrest. As to her defence against attack from outside, Japan should look to America for guarantees – in return for which America might be offered Japanese bases for her Far Eastern operations 'on an emergency basis'.

This was not the first rearmament proposal to come from the Japanese. On August 29, 1945 the government had decided 'informally' to try to maintain a police force of a quarter of a million men and a 'gendarmerie' of comparable size; and in November 1945 Arisue had discussed a similar suggestion with Willoughby. But the Ashida memorandum acquired extra weight through being presented in Washington by General Robert L. Eichelberger, commander of the U.S. Eighth Army in Japan, an early and consistent champion of Japanese rearmament. (The origins of the association between Ashida and Eichelberger are not clear, but it is interesting that both had connections with the American Council for Japan.)

There was no official response to Ashida's proposals, but it seems likely that they confirmed the existing trend in American strategic planning: as America's position in the Far East deteriorated – as a Communist victory in China became ever more probable and Russia strengthened its influence in South Korea – the balance began to tip towards the military standpoint. In mid-September 1947, the latest draft of the crucial 'U.S. Policy toward a Peace Settlement with Japan' contained a clear reference to the restoration of Japan's military power; and on February 2, 1948, Secretary of Defense James Forrestal ordered the Department of the Army to study the 'feasibility' of limited rearmament.

By that time the Soviet Union had detected signs that America was ready to condone or positively encourage rearmament. The Far Eastern Commission was even then putting the finishing touches to its policy statement on the demilitarisation of Japan, and the Russians seem to have been perfectly aware that this directive could not be going through at a more embarrassing moment for America. The Russian representative did all he could to draw attention to it – tabling a string of amendments with which no one else could be expected to agree, abstaining from critical votes, publicly questioning America's sincerity – in an attempt to bring into the open the growing contradiction between American intentions as expressed in the FEC, and United States policy in Washington. For his part, the American FEC representative was roundly condemned by the Department of the Army for failing to ensure that the embarrassing directive was shelved, and with it America's public declaration of support for a policy of demilitarisation 'when that policy is now being re-examined in the light of post-Occupation needs'.

In March 1948, during the visit of Kennan and Draper to Tokyo, Draper revealed a 'general trend in recent War Department thinking toward the early establishment of a small defensive force for Japan, to be ready at such time as U.S. occupation forces leave the country'. This was an idea which General Eichelberger was already discussing privately with Willoughby and his immediate superior, General Paul J. Mueller. (Eichelberger mused wistfully, 'Dollar for dollar there is no cheaper fighting man in the world than the Japanese. He is already a veteran. His food is simple'.)

All, however, acknowledged the danger of provoking Russia too far, and a Planning and Operations Division 'Military Survey' in April 1948 concluded, 'Establishment of Japanese armed forces would precipitate a situation [viz. open confrontation with Russia] which would require that the United States maintain more military forces in the Far East than have heretofore been allocated, and hence is not desirable from a military point of view *until the United States is committed to war*' (our italics) – that is to say, war with Russia, in which case there would be nothing further to lose. The safest course in the meantime, it was suggested, was to turn such forces as *were* legal in Japan into the basis for future rearmament: 'Even though created originally for the maintenance of domestic law and order, an augmented Civilian Police would be a vehicle for possible organisation of Japanese armed forces at a later date and could initiate manpower registration records.'

In the summer of 1948 the American Council for Japan hosted a luncheon for representatives of American big business, at which General Eichelberger put the case for Japanese rearmament: a force of, say, 150,000 troops would be sufficient to confront Russia with the prospect of a war on two fronts. This figure of 150,000 recurred in the American Council's paper 'American Policy toward Japan', released in the autumn of 1948. And it was finally enshrined in NSC 13/2, issued in October 1948 – where it took, however, the form of a 150,000-man 'national police force'.

While NSC 13/2 acknowledged, 'It may well become extremely important to our national security for Japan to be capable of providing some degree of military assistance to the United States, at least to the extent of Japan's self-defence', it was still too soon for America's official spokesmen to press for undisguised rearmament. But on September 3, 1949 a U.S. Air Force weather plane in the Pacific picked up signs of radioactivity slightly above the 'official alert' level. The Russians had detonated their first atomic bomb. This prompted a dramatic escalation in America's atomic energy programme, and ultimately the quantum leap to the thermonuclear device. In the meantime, however, with their nuclear superiority no longer unquestioned, the necessity for the Americans to maintain conventional superiority became immeasurably more urgent. In April 1950 an early draft of NSC 68 recommended a huge increase in defence spending and massive rearmament at home: and the pressure to recruit armed allies abroad intensified.

It is fascinating that during this period the principal opponents of Japanese rearmament, overt or covert, should have been MacArthur and Yoshida. Crudely speaking, MacArthur is best known to the general public of the 1980s as the hawkish military leader who promised the Philippines 'I will return!' and kept his word, and later urged the atomic bombing of Korea and the spreading of a belt of radioactive waste along the border with Manchuria. Yoshida was execrated throughout the last years of his political career as 'a lackey of the American cold-warriors', under whom Japan committed herself irrevocably to rearmament. But for five years the two of them, complementary if not co-ordinated, first prevented and later delayed and modified the growth of Japanese armed forces.

MacArthur agreed with only part of the Department of the Army's strategic planning for Japan. Obviously, she was to be secured against the Soviet Union. But this could be achieved, he felt, by air cover operating out of Okinawa, which his wartime experience had convinced him was the key to U.S. strategy in the Pacific, both in defence and in attack. From the beginning of the Occupation he acted on this belief. Field Marshal Alanbrooke, visiting him in November 1945, reported: 'Okinawa was truly a wonderful sight; hill tops had been removed and pushed into valleys, one trunk arterial road ran the whole length of the island with excellent sideroads distributed like ribs along its length. The island had become one vast aerodrome. . . . In the Pacific, with the new super-bomber now on the slips in America, we should be able to attack Russia from America after refuelling at Okinawa.' For some time MacArthur did not even envisage the possibility of permanent American bases in Japan, let alone the need for Japan herself to rearm. Over the years his interpretation of Article 9 relaxed slightly from the extreme stringency of his original 1946 notes; but in principle he was to oppose rearmament consistently from the Surrender until the outbreak of the Korean War.

Most simply, MacArthur believed that it would be morally wrong to undo an action – the introduction of Article 9 – which had obviously been beneficial in itself. The Japanese 'would not be willing to establish an armed force of their own unless we forced them into it. This we should not do'. It would, in addition, shatter America's credibility in Japanese eyes – 'Japanese rearmament is contrary to many of the fundamental principles which have guided SCAP ever since the Japanese surrender. . . . Abandonment of these principles now would dangerously weaken our prestige in Japan and place us in a ridiculous light before the Japanese people', undermining respect for the Constitution as a whole. Encouraging or compelling rearmament, in defiance of 'solemn commitments', would understandably alienate America's allies, especially in South East Asia whose people were still 'mortally fearful' of a resurgent Japan. And in any case, with her economy ailing, her supply of raw materials suspended and her merchant marine destroyed, Japan could never be reconstructed as more than a fifth-rate military power.

In June 1948, MacArthur was reluctant even to expand the existing police force to meet the figure of 150,000* – a move which he claimed would provoke a 'very explosive international reaction' – and even after receiving the formal request to do so in NSC 13/2, he continued quite successfully to stall. Small arms for the Japanese police requisitioned from America in December 1948 would not be finally delivered, he informed Washington, until early 1950. (They were in any case elderly cast-offs, many of which, according to Eichelberger, 'will not shoot'.) On March 1, 1949 MacArthur conjured up the image of Japan as 'the Switzerland of the Pacific'† : the thought of raising an army for the purposes of self defence he dismissed as 'premature'.

January 1950 brought an apparent change of heart: in his New Year's message to the Japanese people he announced that 'by no sophistry of reasoning' could Article 9 be taken as meaning that Japan had renounced 'the inalienable right of self-defense against unprovoked attack'. But in all probability this was designed less as a prelude to Japanese rearmament than to pave the way for *American* bases in Japan, then becoming a hot issue in the negotiations for a peace treaty: Japan, MacArthur was asserting, had not renounced the right to enlist the aid of her friends against her enemies. In June 1950 he was still protesting publicly that for Japan herself to possess an army would cause 'convulsions' in Australia, New Zealand, Indonesia and the Philippines.

Yoshida's reasoning, if not his motivation, was much the same.

---

* In Korea he was prepared to reinforce the existing police, but was similarly reluctant to create a South Korean army. For his hesitation he has sometimes been blamed for the unpreparedness of South Korea's armed forces at the outbreak of war in June 1950.
† MacArthur was fond of the analogy with Switzerland. It was one he had already used in 1936 when he said that by 1946 he would make the Philippines 'a Pacific Switzerland' – too well-defended to be worth attacking.

The economy would not stand it, and nor would the Japanese public – particularly 'the tender sex'. The threat of a revival of militarism – which he found personally repugnant, having spent a brief period in a military prison during the war – could have serious repercussions on the revival of trade in South East Asia. And he had a nagging fear – well-justified, as it turned out – that once Japanese armed forces were brought into being, America might require them to be used in Korea.

But as confrontation with the Soviet Union in Korea drew ever closer, MacArthur and Yoshida could avert the inevitable no longer. By the spring of 1950 even moderates in the State Department had abandoned hopes of genuine Japanese neutrality and accepted the need for 'limited' rearmament; and the outbreak of actual hostilities provided the occasion for final victory for the hawks. With America at war it was hard to deny that Japan must be reconstructed as a military as well as an economic ally. Henceforth MacArthur and Yoshida would be able to do no more than apply the brakes, moderate the excesses of the more fervent neo-militarists, and throw up a smokescreen by maintaining, in the teeth of the evidence, that the forces which had been brought into being were neither army nor 'war potential'.

Between June 21 and June 23, 1950, even before the Korean War officially broke out, MacArthur withdrew his opposition to the rearming of Japan. On July 8, 1950, thirteen days after the North Koreans had crossed the thirty-eighth parallel, he ordered Yoshida to create a 'National Police Reserve' of 75,000 men, using as justification the fact that he had had to withdraw four divisions of the U.S. Eighth Army for service in Korea at a time when Japan's external security was considered to have been jeopardised by the Sino-Soviet Pact of February 1950, and her internal security was threatened by the increasingly violent activities of the Japanese Communist Party. As never before, the argument ran, Japan needed at least to be able to contribute to her own defence.

MacArthur maintained stoutly that the National Police Reserve was no military force – that it was no more than an enlargement of the civilian police to bring it up to the level authorised by the Potsdam Declaration. He insisted that the Reserve would be under civilian control, and with Yoshida, thwarted an attempt by Willoughby and General Shepherd (the American Chief Military Adviser to the new force) to make Colonel Hattori its Commander. As far as his sponsorship of Hattori was concerned, Willoughby's original plans were confounded – and in this respect at least MacArthur and Yoshida unquestionably tempered the character of Japan's armed forces.

But the fact remained that this 'civilian force' had been created by

Potsdam Ordinance, without Diet approval: Justin Williams informed leaders of the Socialist Democratic and People's Democratic parties, 'The whole subject is totally and completely outside the sphere of politics and Diet discussion'. And this was a moment for which the Department of the Army had been preparing since early in 1948, when its Planning and Operations Division had written, 'The United States can provide, within 180 to 270 days after approval of a limited Japanese rearmament project, infantry-type weapons and the ammunition therefor. . . . Presently there is in Japan a pool of several million individuals with prior military experience who could rapidly be called into service for defense of the home islands'.

At the start the NPR was patently an American puppet force, dressed in American cast-off uniforms, housed in the barracks the American divisions had evacuated (where new Japanese troops had to cope with uncongenial American-style showers and lavatories), trained by American instructors who could speak little or no Japanese. But, as the P & O report had prophesied, its backbone was soon stiffened by an influx of veterans of the Imperial Army. Hussey suggests that the Americans simply went to the Central Records Bureau established by the demobilisation authorities in Chiba Prefecture and selected 'volunteers'. And as the purge was progressively abandoned in 1951, even the most senior ex-officers became available for service; the Japanese government wrote individually to three thousand, 'drawing their attention' to the opportunity available to them. The rifles and light machine-guns with which the force was initially equipped were soon supplemented with mortars, bazookas, and 'special vehicles' (otherwise known as light tanks). As yet the troops were mainly deployed to counter domestic unrest – in or near the major industrial areas which were the heartland of the Japanese Communist Party. But this was clearly, in Willoughby's words, 'the army of the future' – the first open violation of the spirit of Article 9, the thin end of the wedge.

And Japan did not have to wait long for the wedge to be driven in. By 1951 Yoshida was under acute and intensifying American pressure to expand Japan's embryonic armed forces – not from MacArthur, but from John Foster Dulles. Dulles had special responsibility for negotiating the peace treaty with Japan, and in mid-1950 he made Washington's wishes clear to Japan's Prime Minister. The Americans wanted to retain bases in Japan after independence; they wanted to see a far larger Japanese army – Dulles mentioned a figure of 350,000 men; and they urged Japanese participation in a scheme for collective defence which Dulles had devised for the Asian-Pacific region.

Yoshida had no intention of outraging future Asian trading partners by committing Japanese troops to operations outside the home islands; but his perspective on rearmament was beginning subtly to alter. His views on Article 9 were softening: in early 1950 he had conceded that Japan might have retained the right of self-defence 'without war potential' – which at that time meant roughly that Japan might resist attack, and recruit the aid of the Americans, but might not maintain permanent armed forces. (Over the next two years, his definition of 'war potential' was to become increasingly elastic, enabling him eventually to argue that standing forces were in fact permissible providing they did not have the potential for 'full effectiveness' in waging modern war.) More significantly, he had come to see American bases and a sharing of the responsibility for defence as part of the price to be paid for Japan's sovereignty, which was his principal objective.

During a second round of talks in January–February 1951, Yoshida (according to his Chief Cabinet Secretary Katsuo Okazaki) came to a private understanding with Dulles to establish in the near future something more closely resembling America's conception of a Japanese army. When Truman relieved MacArthur of his Far Eastern command in April 1951, a further barrier in the way of accelerated rearmament was demolished. The Peace Treaty which was signed by Japan and America in September 1951 and implemented in April 1952 – bringing the Pacific War formally to an end – made no explicit mention of rearmament, but it recognised Japan's 'inherent right of individual or collective self-defense' and stated that she might 'voluntarily enter into collective security arrangements'. In the accompanying Security Treaty – signed simultaneously – Japan was assured of, though not absolutely guaranteed, American defence against external attack. In return America secured the right to station forces in Japan indefinitely, at the same time expressing the 'expectation' that Japan would 'increasingly assume responsibility for its own defense'. On the first day of Japanese sovereignty Yoshida told the nation it could not be assumed that the security arrangement with the United States would continue forever. 'That is why we must undertake to build up a self-defense power of our own gradually . . . and go a step further to defend world peace and freedom in collaboration with other free nations.'

In August 1952 Yoshida established the National Safety Agency as a policy-making body in charge of Japan's defence. He insisted that it was to be under civilian control; but his choice of 'civilian' to head it was curious – Tokutaro Kimura, a purgee with intimate connections with the right-wing underground, who in 1950 had proposed the creation of a clandestine 'Patriotic Anti-Communist Drawn-Sword Militia'. The forces at its disposal were also larger: in

October 1952 the National Police Reserve was expanded to 110,000 men and combined with a modest navy into a National Security Force. Yoshida's protestations that this too was no more than a glorified police force became increasingly comic as field and heavy artillery and medium tanks made their appearance. The troops also started being deployed as an army, the more highly armed and mechanised units being concentrated principally in the northernmost island of Hokkaido with a view to repelling a Russian invasion.

In political terms, the National Security Force cost Yoshida dearly. In elections held during the month of its creation, the Liberal party lost dozens of Diet seats, as did the Japanese Communist Party which also favoured rearmament, mostly to the benefit of the Socialists who opposed it. But despite Yoshida's obvious discomfort, American pressure continued. Now that independence had been conceded, the lever for prising an increase in forces out of Japan was the promise of Mutual Defense Assistance. MDA, which Walter Lippmann called 'a diplomatic slush fund and military pork barrel', was primarily directed at strengthening indigenous military forces. But it also incorporated various forms of economic and technical aid which Japan was exceedingly anxious to secure. It was gradually made clear, however, that to qualify for the latter she must also submit to the former; before Japan could receive MDA, she must demonstrate that she was in official possession of an army and navy, and capable of resisting armed invasion.

The deviation from Article 9 was now beyond disguising – as was American interference. In September 1953 the *Yomiuri Shimbun* wrote angrily, 'It is America which destroyed our mighty army and navy and the munitions industry . . . even dumped research equipment [the drowned cyclotrons] into the ocean. It is also America which, with an air of importance, forced on Japan a silly constitution renouncing arms. . . . In short, it is America which made Japan such that it cannot meet the American demands of today. . . . If America wishes to have Japan as its true ally, it must first recognise its past errors.'

Two months later the *Yomiuri* found an American to oblige. Vice-President Richard Nixon, on an official visit to Tokyo, made several speeches emphasising that Soviet global ambitions were now focused in Asia, and impressing upon Japan the need for collective defence. Finally, after conferring by telephone with Washington, at a luncheon for the America-Japan Society on November 19, 1953, he explained publicly that Article 9 had been a mistake. 'It was an honest mistake. We believe now as we believed then in the principle of disarmament. We believe in peace. . . . But on the other hand, we recognize that disarmament under present world conditions by the free nations would inevitably lead to war and, therefore, it is because we want peace and we believe in peace that we ourselves have rearmed since 1946, and that we believe that Japan and other free nations must assume their share of responsibility of rearming since 1946. . . . It must be admitted that the primary responsibility for Japan's defense must rest upon Japan and the Japanese people.'

In March 1954 a Mutual Defense Assistance agreement was signed under which Japan promised to take 'all reasonable measures which may be needed to develop its defense capacities'. Four months later the Diet passed two laws which established Japan's armed forces as we know them today. The Defense Agency Law created in the Japan Defense Agency a *de facto* Ministry of Defence; and the Self-Defense Forces Law purported to legitimise the maintenance of permanent armed forces. There were still restrictions. The principle of civilian control was sacrosanct; service was to be entirely voluntary – conscription was ruled out; and the new troops were under no circumstances to be sent to serve overseas. But the Self-Defense Forces were larger again than the National Security Force – the army had now swelled to 130,000 – and still more heavily armed. And, as the name suggests, they were for the first time explicitly authorised to defend Japan against external aggression.

*   *   *

As constituted in 1954, the Self-Defense Forces had three branches: the army, or Ground Self-Defense Force, whose evolution from National Police Reserve to National Security Force to Self-Defense Force has already been traced; the Air Self-Defense Force, which was newly created in 1954; and the navy, or Maritime Self-Defense Force, whose rebirth, like that of the army, had been being planned, in collusion between Japanese officers and like-minded Americans, almost from the moment of the official Japanese surrender.

The maritime equivalent of General Arisue, and prime schemer on the Japanese side for the reconstruction of the navy, was Admiral Kichisaburo Nomura – Japanese ambassador to the United States at the time of Pearl Harbor, and the man most probably responsible for the lethal delay in Japan's declaration of war. Nomura anticipated Japan's rapid post-war expansion as a commercial maritime nation, perceived the need for a navy to support and protect this crucial trade, and was determined that this navy should be truly Japanese. While Article 9 was being reviewed by the Privy Council, of which he was a member, he furiously attacked it with the prescient question, 'Do you intend to revise this later, or will Japanese be forced to wear *American* uniforms?' At his instigation the documents division of the Second Demobilisation Ministry (formerly the Navy Ministry) became the nerve-centre of 'very confidential studies'. By day, the staff concentrated on the work for which they had been exempted from the purge – that is to say, the demobilisation of Japan's Imperial Navy; by night, they worked on secret plans for rebuilding it.

Parallel to Nomura's operation but not apparently co-ordinated with it, there was pressure from the Japanese government, supported by certain elements within the American military hierarchy, for expansion of the existing coast guard. In the seas around Japan fishing boats were regularly preyed upon and often seized by Chinese, Russian and Korean pirates; and Japan's long exposed coastline tempted both smugglers and illegal immigrants from Korea. An outbreak of cholera in Korea in the summer of 1946 made it imperative to halt the influx of refugees, and in September 1946 representatives of the United States Navy in Japan presented proposals for a preventive force of around 1000 men, preferably demobilised sailors, equipped with U.S. Navy surplus smallarms, including deck-mounted guns of up to 57mm in calibre.

The prospect of the reappearance of Japanese armed vessels on the high seas, manned by veterans of the Imperial Navy, horrified the reformers in Government Section. At a single stroke it would violate three treasured principles – demilitarisation, decentralisation of the public safety forces, and the purge – and in November 1946 MacArthur rejected the proposals 'out of hand'. But six months later they were revived and significantly upgraded, this time by Willoughby and G-2, and the best Government Section could achieve was a modification of some of the more extreme provisions. The result was the creation in March 1948 of a 10,000-man Maritime Safety Board (later renamed Maritime Safety Agency).

Government Section contrived to insert in the law bringing the Maritime Safety Board into being the clause: 'Nothing in this law shall be construed so as to permit the Maritime Safety Board or its personnel to be trained or organised as a military establishment or to function as such'. This was, however, a somewhat hollow victory, for the MSB was from the beginning as much a military force as its army counterpart, the National Police Reserve. It was based on an American model, the United States Coast Guard, which had itself been designated a military service since 1915; it was uniformed and armed, though the size of its vessels and calibre of its armaments were limited; in all its operations it was patently oriented to meet an external threat; and at the very least its personnel formed a training cadre for a fully-fledged navy.

The military effectiveness of the force was dramatically demonstrated at the end of 1950, when Japanese ships and sailors were sent to Korea on a mission which has remained until now the only overseas deployment of Japanese troops on active service since the war. The case was admittedly a special one. Following the successful amphibious landing at Inchon on the west coast of South Korea in September 1950, MacArthur wanted to launch another on the east coast to the north of the thirty-eighth parallel at Wonsan. But this stretch of coast had been very strongly protected with over three thousand magnetic and contact mines scattered over an area of four hundred square miles, and the only qualified minesweepers available belonged to the MSB. Between October 2 and December 10, 1950, forty-six minesweepers and twelve hundred Japanese personnel battled to clear the way for the assault: two ships were sunk, eight sailors injured, one killed. (Anxious to forestall public disquiet over the 'irregular' circumstances in which this man had met his death – under arms at a time when Japan officially had no armed forces and was not at war – an official of G-2's Public Safety Division visited his home and 'financially compensated' his father.)

Throughout this period of growth, Nomura had, like Arisue, been seeking American sponsorship. Capitalising on the 'traditional international camaraderie of naval officers' and on friendships he had made before the war, he acquired crucially influential allies. He already had contacts with the American Council for Japan. Now he cemented close links with Rear-Admiral Arleigh Burke, Deputy Chief of Staff to Admiral Turner Joy, Commander of the United States Navy in the Far East. In 1972, Burke described the blossoming of their relationship. 'I did not know many Japanese. In fact, I did not like the Japanese, for I had fought too long in too many battles against them. Still I wished to know more about their psychology. . . . Once a week Admiral Nomura explained Japanese history and philosophy to me. . . . Naturally during these conversations we discussed the future role of Japanese military forces. I believed both that no great nation could exist unless it had a suitable military force and that a nation should not overemphasise its military. Nomura and I exchanged ideas on what the military organisation of Japan should be.'

Admiral Burke's idea was that Nomura should assemble the ten most gifted officers from the former Imperial Navy as the nucleus of a reconstructed High Command. To this Admiral Joy added the information that America had just taken charge at Yokosuka of eighteen frigates previously held by the Russians under a lend-lease agreement: these vessels she might be prepared to make available to a future Japanese naval force. In February 1951 Nomura discussed with John Foster Dulles the prospects for a recrudescent navy. In April he formulated his plan: if America could supply, by loan or gift, the essential ships, weapons, and planes, Japan would furnish the men, their pay, and the support services – these needs to be met from the resources of a strengthened Maritime Safety Board.

In October 1951 America decided to offer Japan the eighteen frigates, plus fifty landing-craft. In March 1952 the limits on the size of the Maritime Safety Board and the tonnage of its vessels were lifted. By April a new Maritime Safety Force had evolved, with a good deal of assistance from Nomura; in August it was amalgamated with the army into the National Security Force. In January 1953 Nomura wept with pride as the first vessels were formally transferred to Japan; and by July 1954 when the Self-Defense Forces Law legitimised the *fait accompli*, many more had been handed over under the Mutual Defense Assistance Agreement to Japan's Maritime Self-Defense Force.

The Imperial Air Force found no champion comparable with Arisue or Nomura. Though it was reported that SCAP had allowed Japanese aviators to assist Chiang Kai-shek on Formosa in 1949, in general the ban on flying, and in particular the re-creation of an air force, was effective. It was not until July 1954 that the Air Self-Defense Force came into being as an independent entity. With the relaxation of SCAP's restrictions on war-related industries, however, Japan was permitted to start building aeroplanes again in 1952; and by 1953 the industry had multiplied sixty-five-fold.

The munitions industry as a whole had re-established itself even earlier. In December 1945 Edwin Pauley, the architect of the original reparations programme, had prophesied gloomily: 'I am inclined to think that the great corporations will take over the country in spite of our program of breaking up the *zaibatsu* and that it will be next to impossible to pry loose the machine tools which should be removed as a disarmament measure. If this happens, a most important sector of the Japanese war potential will remain functioning, integrated, and in the hands of those who ran it during the war.' With the final abandonment of reparations and the emphasis on renewing Japan's industrial strength, his prediction was realised. In American eyes, Japan's manufacture of munitions would solve two problems: Japan could substantially develop her export trade, at the same time meeting America's military needs in the region. As one patriot remarked, 'Strategically, having some of our war production capacity located just off Siberia is worth much thought.' In 1950 MacArthur proposed the reactivation of Japanese munitions factories, and by March 1952 the manufacture of weapons had been authorised unconditionally.

One further element in Japan's war-making potential developed significantly during this period. It was originally the Far Eastern Commission's desire that all atomic research in Japan should be halted. Japanese scientists, however, spurred by the over-whelming necessity of developing alternative sources of energy, maintained a constant pressure on SCAP – who were by no means reluctant to bend a little. The scientists were permitted a graduated and carefully monitored return to research on the peaceful uses of atomic power – while the Americans did their best to obscure this development from the Allies (including Britain, erstwhile partner in the Manhattan Project), with whom they might have to share the fruits. Japanese atomic research was by no means as advanced as America's own, but it might, for all they knew, have something to offer the Russians; and SCAP preferred to conceal the fact that certain materials – uranium compounds, thorium compounds, monazite, rare earth metals and others – were being confiscated and exported to the United States.

The decision to allow Japan to go nuclear is perhaps the best evidence of how quickly Japan's image had changed, in the minds of the strategic planners, from Enemy to Ally. To the civilian reformers and the non-American members of the Far Eastern Commission, who remained deeply suspicious of a resurgence of Japanese militarism, it would have seemed self-apparent that possession of nuclear power stations was a significant step towards the manufacture of a weapon which the Japanese might be prepared to use simply to exact retribution for Hiroshima and Nagasaki. But instead of a threat, Japanese research facilities were treated by America as a potential asset, as the title of an Army Department memorandum of mid-1948 suggests – 'The Use of Japanese Research Facilities as an Advanced Base in the Event of Acute Emergency in the Far East'.

PART FIVE

FOUR DECADES ON

25

Pressure to Rearm

The period of official American domination of Japanese affairs ended in 1952 with the former enemy now a favoured ally. With American help, an intensely anti-Communist government had been entrenched in Japan, the economy was accelerating, and gradually, discreetly, in violation of MacArthur's Article 9, armed forces were being assembled. By the mid-1950s Japan seemed set to become the bulwark against Communist expansion in Asia which America so urgently desired. But what progress has been made since then? Have American hopes been fulfilled? And at what cost? Has Japan remilitarised, as many claim, and is she now a threat to the region and the world?

*   *   *

Beyond question Japan has rearmed. In the 1960s and 1970s her overall defence spending multiplied by 500 per cent; in the past five years it has swollen again by forty-one per cent, a steeper rate of increase than America's own under Ronald Reagan, and currently Japan's defence budget is the eighth largest in the world. In the 1980s Japan deploys twice as many destroyers as America in the East Asian region, and more tactical aircraft than operate out of all the United States bases in South Korea, the Philippines and Japan put together.

The Self-Defense Forces now have an authorised strength of some 272,000 men distributed between the three services. The Ground SDF (authorised strength: 180,000 – roughly the same as the British Army, less than one quarter the size of the U.S. Army) consists of twelve infantry divisions and two composite brigades, one armoured division, one artillery brigade, one airborne brigade, one training brigade, one helicopter brigade and eight anti-aircraft artillery groups (low-altitude surface-to-air missile units). These formations are allocated to five armies – Northern, North-Eastern, Eastern, Central and Western.

The Maritime SDF (authorised strength: c. 46,000, as compared with a British Navy of some 70,000 and the U.S. Navy of well over 500,000) is targeted to possess four escort flotillas, ten divisions of anti-submarine surface ship units, six divisions of submarine units, two minesweeping flotillas (one each in the western and eastern waters of Japan), and sixteen squadrons of land-based anti-submarine aircraft units with about 220 combat aircraft to provide cover.

The Air SDF (authorised strength: c. 46,000 – slightly over half the size of the RAF, less than a tenth of the size of the U.S. Air Force) possesses about 430 combat aircraft, comprising air reconnaissance, air transport, interceptor, support fighters, early warning, and high-altitude surface-to-air missile units.

Today, by most international standards, the SDF constitutes a powerful military presence, modest in manpower but equipped with some of the most sophisticated weaponry in the world. And the upward trend continues: Japan's Mid-Term Defense Program 1986–90 states – 'Efforts shall be made to improve the air defense capability of the main islands and the capability to protect sea lines of communication in the waters surrounding Japan by improving and modernising equipment such as aircraft, vessels and surface-to-air missiles. At the same time, taking into account the geographic characteristics of this country, efforts shall be made to improve the capability to counter a landing invasion by modernising divisions, diversifying formations of divisions, and strengthening such capabilities so as to destroy the invading forces in the outer seas and coastal waters'.

Japan already possesses the F-15 fighter interceptor. As of 1984 she had on order such items as Chinook helicopters and the Hawkeye early warning system, and the most recent shopping list projects improvement of the existing HAWK (Homing All Way Killer) missile system, and the upgrading of Japan's surface-to-air missiles from Nike to Patriot. In the past, the SDF's weaponry came almost exclusively from the United States – as gifts, loans, the products of joint ventures or licensing arrangements, or as straightforward purchases. Often Japan served as a convenient outlet for equipment that in U.S. Army terms was obsolete. Now, however, while Japan still remains the world's major recipient of American-made weapons (taking fourteen per cent of all U.S. arms, ahead of such clients as Egypt, Saudi Arabia and Israel), she is keen to diversify and buy from European countries, not least in order to offset her huge trade surplus with the EEC. In 1985 she was considering buying tanks from West Germany and in 1984 had FH-70 155mm howitzers on order from Britain.

More important, Japan has her own rapidly expanding munitions industry. Japanese arms production, halted in 1945, was initially revived to supply American forces in Korea. War in Vietnam brought further demand, and Japan achieved her highest export figures to date in 1968–9. Now the aerospace industry is flourishing, almost ninety per cent of it given over to military production: work in military electronics, though a recent development, is accelerating, mostly in cooperation with foreign companies such as Philips, Siemens and Honeywell. Research in rocketry began in 1955 with the decision to add 'defensive' missiles to the Japanese armoury, and is now highly sophisticated. Indeed, Japanese launch systems are being hailed as a cheap and reliable competitor to NASA's shuttle programme for delivery of satellites.

So far, Japanese arms manufacture has been largely under American licence: the new Patriot missiles and most of the additional F-15 fighter-interceptors, for example, are being made in Japan under licence. But there is also full scope for the Japanese genius for adaptation-cum-improvements; from this point of view the defection of Victor Belenko, who landed his shiny new MiG-23 in Japan in 1976, was a distinct bonus. British arms exporters too have expressed bitterness at the Japanese practice of manufacturing clones of imported weapons. And in recent years Japan has been developing not merely her arms industry but her defence technology, and is making high-grade equipment of her own; some defence specialists boast of a ship-to-ship missile 'better than Exocet'. In the future she is likely to be pre-eminent in the fields of microelectronics, biotechnology, and fine ceramics, all with military applications.

As yet, Japan lacks a nuclear strike capability – which is not to say that the possibility has been overlooked. As early as 1970, 'small size nuclear weapons' for self-defence were mooted, and in the late 1980s Japan is beyond doubt a 'threshold state', with the potential both for manufacturing nuclear weapons and creating the necessary delivery systems.

Since being secretly revived during the Occupation, Japan's nuclear industry has flourished: currently Japan is the fourth biggest nuclear energy producer in the world (behind the U.S., U.S.S.R. and France), and by 1990 nuclear power will supply twenty-eight per cent of her total energy needs. For many years the industry depended heavily on foreign reactors and imports of enriched uranium, principally from America with assistance from Canada and Britain. Now, however, Japan is in a position to export her own atomic technology: in July 1985 Mitsubishi Heavy Industries signed an agreement with the People's Republic of China paving the way for the transfer of plant, components and nuclear fuel.

And, perhaps more significant for Japan's development of an independent nuclear weapons capability, she has built her first nuclear fuel reprocessing plant at Tokai-mura, assuring herself of a supply of plutonium. Plutonium is the material used in nuclear weapons, and unilateral use of the Tokai-mura plant appeared to contravene the Nuclear Non-Proliferation Pact. Japan is now also committed to replacing its light water reactors with fast breeder reactors, despite the fact that, because they complete the cycle of the nuclear fuel chain, they facilitate the creation of an independent nuclear capability and are considered to be a threat to the effectiveness of arms control.

Even without nuclear weapons, Japan has a good deal to offer as an ally. The SDF provides a 'denial force' capable of fighting at the very least an Alamo-style delaying action against invaders. Japan has a serviceable early warning system, and is ideally placed geographically for surveillance of the Soviet Pacific fleet based at Vladivostok. With ships, reconnaissance planes, observation posts and sea-bed sonar, the SDF monitors activity in the straits through which Soviet vessels must pass to gain access to the Pacific Ocean. In an emergency Japan could mine these straits, trapping the bulk of the Russian fleet in the Sea of Japan. And Japan has undertaken to defend sea lanes within a 1,000-mile radius of her shores, though it will be ten years before she has the necessary hardware to perform this task effectively.

In all these respects, the SDF has been useful to America in her efforts to secure the East Asian region. Since 1952 Japan's armed forces have evolved essentially within the context of the Security Treaty with America, and the Americans have done their best to tighten the bonds and draw the Japanese ever closer into partnership. They have encouraged Japanese reliance on American-made weapons, for example, and they present Japanese defence policy as wholly compatible with their own, even an extension of it. In June 1985 a Pentagon spokesman asserted that the United States saw Japan's forthcoming Mid-Term Defense Program 1986–90 as one component of America's own world strategy. Joint U.S./SDF exercises have been held, the first in November 1982; in 1984 joint manoeuvres were carried out in Hokkaido simulating the response to Soviet invasion. Studies have been made of the feasibility of joint defence of the sea lanes, and joint action in the event of renewed fighting in Korea.

Perhaps most significant, proposals have been made to integrate the command structures of the two forces, rather as the U.S. and South Korean armies are presently integrated. This has been fiercely resisted by those who fear it would dangerously erode Japanese freedom of action – placing her, in the view of one critic, in the same relation to Washington as Manchukuo once stood to Tokyo. Nevertheless, links are being forged. In 1984 a Central Command Headquarters was set up within the SDF, with direct links to its counterpart under the American Commander-in-Chief in Japan; and the SDF is acquiring compatible equipment which will enable Japanese ships and planes to communicate directly with American control centres.

But Japan's present value to America is dwarfed by her potential contribution to joint defence. She may be the world's eighth largest military spender, but her arms budget still represents no more than one per cent or so of her Gross National Product, while other economically significant countries earmark up to six times as much proportionately. The U.S.A., for example, spends around six per cent of her GNP on defence, Britain five per cent, and West Germany some three per cent. With this kind of budget, Japan could significantly lighten America's burden in the region. (It has been estimated that with a budget of even three per cent she could create a military force 'capable of facing the Soviet Union on its own'.)* In strategic terms, the Pentagon's frustration at the sight of such potential remaining unexploited is understandable, and America continues to push for a more generous Japanese contribution, a more wholehearted commitment, as she has done for almost forty years.

Recently, however, the character of America's pressure has changed, becoming more intense, with a different objective in view. In the immediate post-war years the disparity between American wealth and Japanese austerity meant that America could make only modest demands on her new ally. Japan was required to play no more than a passive role in the American strategy of containing communism, merely providing bases and facilities in the home islands and Okinawa, and securing herself against internal subversion.

But Japan's economic 'miracle' made her parsimony when it came to defence spending harder for the Americans to stomach; and with the relative decline of the U.S. economy, the Japanese were repeatedly accused of enjoying a 'free ride' at America's expense. (America, it is pointed out, currently spends on military research and development twice as much as the entire Japanese defence budget. And while Japan benefits from a bilateral trade

* Ikutaro Shimizu, a former anti-war leader turned rabid proponent of an independent nuclear-armed Japan, suggests that three per cent of GNP will buy – in addition to nuclear weapons – seventeen aircraft carriers, thirty-four anti-aircraft destroyers, eighty-five multi-purpose destroyers, 350 F-15 Eagle fighter-interceptors, and an increase in armoured vehicles from the present forty-eight to 200–300 per division.

surplus of around $50 billion, America is expending time, energy and money defending Japanese markets, Japanese sources of raw materials, and Japanese supply routes, in particular her access to oil from the Middle East.) Even before these recriminations soured the relationship, however, America was urging Japan to play a more active part. And now American demands are for collective defence, for a junior partner in Asia who will free American forces for action elsewhere. She wants Japan as a NATO-style ally, committed to attacking the United States' attackers even if not attacked herself, and defending the United States' friends.

The seeds of this policy can be seen as far back as 1951, in John Foster Dulles's 'Pacific Pact'. Since Japan's safety was dependent on the stability of East Asia, he argued, she should contribute to the defence of the entire region. And similar thinking lay behind America's encouragement in 1965 of normalisation of relations between Japan and South Korea. But it was not until the end of the 1960s that the trend in American policy, the unwillingness to carry the load alone, became clear. In November 1969 Nixon proclaimed the 'Guam Doctrine': from now on the United States expected her Asian allies to assume a larger share in their own defence. The American commitment, particularly in lives, could no longer be unlimited.

In the same month, Nixon issued a joint communiqué with Japan's Prime Minister Eisaku Sato. Its primary purpose was to announce the projected reversion of Okinawa to Japanese sovereignty; but in the process it linked Japan's security to defence of the anti-Communist regimes in Taiwan and South Korea. After the reversion of Okinawa in 1972, Japan also naturally assumed greater responsibility for the defence of the island as American troops were withdrawn. These strategic shifts were accompanied by a dramatic reduction in the number of American installations in Japan – from 2800 in 1952 to 125 in 1970.

The following decade made quite obvious the inadequacy of America's global capacity, and this had profound effects on the U.S.-Japan relationship. By the end of the 1970s America's influence had been or was being tested on every side – in Vietnam, in Central and South America, in Iran and the Middle East – and resources were simply being stretched too thin. In 1977 President Carter had alarmed Japan by announcing his intention of withdrawing 32,000 U.S. troops from South Korea; in 1980 he switched several warships based in Japan to the Indian Ocean to defend the Gulf. It was at this point that Defense Secretary Harold Brown was alleged to have said that America could offer South East Asia no assistance other than the nuclear umbrella, because of the gravity of the Middle Eastern situation.

The Reagan administration has made a sustained effort both to dispel the defeatism of the post-Vietnam era, and to reassure Japan and South Korea that America's commitment to the defence of the region is solid. But the fact remains that in the 1980s America needs the material help of her allies more than ever before. This is particularly true in the Asian theatre because of two visibly mounting threats.

Since the end of the Korean War, the Communist regime in the north has spent a high percentage of its GNP annually on building up its military strength, with the express intention of conquering the south. The Korean peninsula is now one of the most highly militarised territories in the world, and arguably the most dangerous. Secretary of State George Shultz and Secretary of Defense Caspar Weinberger have both warned of the imminent danger of war, basing their forebodings to a large extent on the instability of the region's dictator, Kim Il Sung. Kim has ruled North Korea ever since the Soviet occupation ended; he is now elderly, in deteriorating health, and his last remaining ambition is to reunify his country, by force if necessary. (If he does not do so, his son, it is feared, may be obliged to take up the cudgels in order to guarantee his dynastic succession.) What is particularly alarming is that neither Moscow nor Peking may be any more able than America or South Korea to predict or restrain the behaviour of a man who has been for years a law unto himself.

The Soviets themselves, of course, continue to pose the greatest threat to the security of East Asia, and the last decade has seen a massive arms build-up in the region. The rapprochement between the United States and the People's Republic of China engineered by Nixon in 1972 raised hopes that America had found an Asian counterweight to the Soviet Union. But since then China has hardly lived up to expectations, while the threat from the Soviet Union has substantially increased.

In the last ten years, Soviet ground forces in Asia have been boosted from thirty-one to forty-one divisions (370,000 troops) with improved firepower and mobility; military aircraft have advanced both in numbers (to 2,390) and in sophistication; intermediate nuclear weapons systems – 162 SS-20s and 85 Backfire bombers – have been introduced; and naval tonnage has grown by a third. These augmented forces have several objectives – to protect Vladivostok; to threaten China; to challenge American supremacy in South East Asia through the newly available bases at Cam Ranh Bay and Da Nang; and, since the late 1970s, to menace Japan.

In these circumstances, it is hardly surprising that American pressure on Japan to upgrade her armed strength is at an all-time peak. In this perspective, it is no exaggeration to say that the Americans are primarily responsible for Japanese remilitarisation, as far as rearmament is concerned. But they have not been without allies within Japan. And it is their great good fortune that this crescendo in their demands for increased spending and wider commitments coincides with the entrenchment in power of Yasuhiro Nakasone, the most hawkish Prime Minister since the Pacific War. For almost four decades he has championed a powerfully armed Japan capable of assuming major responsibility for her own defence.

In the eyes of the alarmists, Nakasone's career is a case history of the revival of militarism in Japan. After graduating in law from Tokyo University in March 1941, he served in the wartime Imperial Navy. For a short spell during the Occupation he worked as an Inspector for the Tokyo Metropolitan Police Board, until in April 1947, a few weeks before his twenty-ninth birthday, he was elected to the Diet. Here he attracted attention from the start as one of the most dynamic and determined of younger politicians, with outspoken views on 'the Japanese spirit', and law and order. And in particular he insisted on the need for rearmament, which in the immediate post-war context placed him well to the right of many of his colleagues.

Allegations of extremism cling to Nakasone. In 1950 he was registered as a member of the National Territory Defense Research Association, a group founded to promote national security against communism and to combat the conclusion of a 'defeatist' peace and unequal peace treaty. Though not itself classifiable as an ultra-nationalist society, the NTDRA had positive links with other groups which were. It has also been alleged that at one point in his early career Nakasone ran a distinctly militarist private school, with the motto 'Let us sacrifice ourselves for the Showa Restoration'. In the Diet he was a consistent critic of Article 9. From the outset he supported the Ashida interpretation which allowed for the possibility of arming in self-defence; and in the mid-1950s he attracted a good deal of attention by claiming that it was under *his* influence that Nixon had dismissed the pacifist provision altogether as 'an honest mistake'. Not surprisingly, Nakasone favoured constitutional revision. In the late 1950s and early 1960s he was a vociferous member of the Commission on the Constitution – and was still complaining about 'alien' laws in 1978. 'The process by which the Constitution was drafted,' he wrote, 'was dictated by GHQ. . . . [It] contains elements that are no longer in keeping with reality.'

As far as influencing national defence policy was concerned, Nakasone's first real opportunity came in January 1970 when

Prime Minister Eisaku Sato appointed him Director General of the Japan Defense Agency – the civilian body controlling the SDF. His appointment came at a crucial period in Japan's post-war defence strategy: within six months the US/Japan Security Treaty was due to expire, and though it would automatically continue for an indefinite period, from now on each side had the option of terminating it on one year's notice. Clearly it was open to Japan to consider the conditions on which she wanted the relationship with the United States to continue. Sato was dead set on securing the reversion of Okinawa to Japan – but to do so, Japan would have to convince America that she was willing and above all ready to assume the military responsibilities that went with the territory. Inevitably the defence issue would be brought into the public arena, and Sato wanted it considered in the most positive light possible. A firm posture had to be adopted, and Nakasone was certainly the man for the job. He went, in fact, rather beyond what was required of him. In October 1970, nine months after he had taken charge, the JDA issued Japan's first Defense White Paper – an act bitterly criticised as official recognition of an illegal defence establishment. A day later, it was followed by a draft Defense Build-Up Plan.

In their final approved form, however, neither the White Paper nor the Defense Build-Up Plan was as forceful as Nakasone had intended. His principal theme in preceding months had been the need for an independent defence capability – particularly in the light of the Guam Doctrine. The Security Treaty, he felt, should now take 'second place' to Japanese self-reliance. Military strength had in the past been Japan's only recourse, her only defence against victimisation. (This was the gist of a speech he had made three years before, in an ominous echo of Tojo's affidavit. 'Japan,' he claimed, 'which had become the champion of the coloured races, was encircled by the white man, and made the decision – we will not be defeated. And what was the final guarantee that poor tiny Japan would confront the white man? Military armament.') And military strength was no less necessary now – Nakasone's ambition being to see restrictions on Japan's conventional rearmament lifted.

In 1970, however, this was moving too fast, even for Sato, and Nakasone's proposals were significantly modified. The final version of the White Paper contained no suggestion that the Security Treaty was to be considered merely as a supplement to Japan's own efforts. There were, nonetheless, several features which disturbed the supporters of Article 9. Conscription was not explicitly ruled out; and the possession of nuclear weapons for defensive purposes, though 'undesirable', was not deemed to be illegal.

Before leaving the JDA in July 1971, Nakasone, perhaps as a final symbolic gesture or as a stand against hypocrisy, excised the peace dove from the coat of arms on SDF caps. When he became Prime Minister in 1982, his views seemed little changed. He was still calling for more generous spending on the SDF – Japan's defence had, he said, been 'carried out on the cheap' – and for a more significant Japanese contribution to the relationship with America to counter the charges of a 'free ride' for Japan.

His critics claim that during his time in office he has kowtowed unnecessarily to America. Certainly he has gone to great lengths to establish a close personal bond with the American President. The 'Ron/Yasu relationship' is regarded with some scepticism in Japan. (Both men, it is pointed out, have a misplaced confidence in their command of the English language. 'When Japanese reporters see the mouths of the Prime Minister and a foreign leader moving, they assume that communication on a high level is taking place. . . . Conducting diplomatic negotiations in broken English is hardly the best way to safeguard life and property. . . . There is nothing so dangerous as trade and defense commitments made in the context of a Ron-Yasu chat.') Nevertheless, the Ron/Yasu axis has seen Japan take responsibility for defence of the sea lanes up to a radius of 1000 miles from the Japanese coast, agree the transfer of arms technology to America, and join the SDI programme. During this period Nakasone's public utterances have suggested more clearly than ever before that Japan might be willing to regard the Security Treaty as a collective defence agreement. In January 1983, for example, he announced that Japan was ready to take control of the straits commanding the approaches to Russia's Pacific bases. He has also caused serious alarm in Japan by describing the country as an 'unsinkable aircraft carrier' – by implication, at America's disposal.

Against all this, of course, should be set the fact that in building up Japan's armed strength, whatever the reasons he may give the Americans in public, Nakasone is equally paving the way for autonomous defence – an ideal which, some argue, he has never abandoned. Beneath a surface veneer of 'internationalism', he remains a committed and uncomplicated Japanese nationalist.

This is clear from almost every stance he adopts on social and political issues – his right-wing posture on home affairs reinforcing the hawkish image his foreign policy has created. Japan, Nakasone feels, must be proud, must assert herself – 'A nation must shed any sense of ignominy and move forward seeking glory'. And if she is to attain a spiritual strength comparable with her material prosperity, she must look to her past – to the traditional values and institutions which once made her great.

Nakasone has got into trouble more than once for inadvertently revealing his belief in Japanese racial superiority. In September 1986 he remarked in passing to a meeting of the LDP that the average intelligence of the American was much lower than that of the Japanese, explaining that 'in America there are quite a few black people, Puerto Ricans and Mexicans'. Nevertheless, superior or not, the Japanese, in his view, have allowed their moral values to decline since the war. Nakasone favours both the teaching of ethics in schools, and firmer central control of education in general.

In this he is in full agreement with the views of Yukio Mishima. At one time, it has been alleged, his connection with Mishima was quite close, doubtless cemented by their common desire to see Japan armed to a level befitting her sovereign status. In the early days of their acquaintance Nakasone helped to launch Mishima as a political activist, giving him introductions to officers in the SDF which resulted in Mishima's private militia, the *Tate no kai* (Society of the Shield), being permitted to train at one of the SDF boot camps on the slopes of Mount Fuji, wearing army fatigues and using army equipment.

And like Mishima, Nakasone sees the Imperial institution as central to a moral revival in Japan. For the brand of nationalism he favours, in which the desires of the individual must be subordinated to the good of the state, he needs the Emperor once more as a focus. Nakasone's persistent efforts to restore the Throne to its former prestige reached a peak on April 29, 1986, when he seized the occasion of Hirohito's 85th birthday to stage official celebrations for the sixtieth year of the Showa era. (He was, of course, not oblivious to the effect his outburst of patriotism would have on the electorate. Strictly speaking, these celebrations should not have taken place until November 10, the anniversary of Hirohito's accession to the Throne. But Nakasone was due to stand for re-election in the summer of 1986, and was not prepared to risk letting the opportunity for so spectacular a display of loyalty pass out of his hands.)

Nakasone also appears to want to reforge the links between religion and the state which SCAP so carefully severed. He campaigned in the 1960s for government support of the principal Shinto shrine at Ise; and more recently he has been pressing for the revival of official state visits to the Yasukuni Shrine. Yasukuni is the chief *gokoku* or 'defending-the-nation' shrine, and as a champion of Japan's fighting forces, Nakasone is naturally anxious that suitable honour be paid to her war dead – even if these now include Tojo and the other leading Class A war criminals. 'Without such monuments of gratitude, who would be willing to lay down their life for their country?' – an interesting sentiment in the mouth of the chief executive of a country whose constitution renounces war.

In mid-1985, with the fortieth anniversary of the end of the Pacific War on August 15, 1945 approaching, Nakasone proposed that he and his cabinet should pay an official visit to Yasukuni. The Cabinet Legislative Bureau advised him that this might well violate the Constitution, but he was not deterred. There were precedents of a sort, as previous Prime Ministers had edged nearer and nearer to making the gesture. Takeo Miki had visited Yasukuni privately on August 15, 1975. Takeo Fukuda had gone as far as signing the Visitors' Book as Prime Minister. Zenko Suzuki had headed a group of Cabinet members. But all had kept a determinedly low profile.

This was not Nakasone's intention – though he did take the precaution of instructing ambassadors in 'sensitive' countries to explain Japan's motivation in reinstating official visits in this way. 'Japan had followed the path of peace,' he declared, 'with the keen awareness of the untold anguish it had caused to the countries of Asia. The official visit to the Yasukuni Shrine did not mean that Japan had changed its direction.'

What is perhaps most interesting about Nakasone is the consistency of his attitudes. Much of his present philosophy is to be found in a document he wrote over thirty-five years ago – a 'representation' he made to MacArthur towards the end of January 1951. Still bitterly humiliated by Japan's defeat, with the desire for revenge never far from the surface, he ranged over a wide variety of topics – the need for immediate restoration of Japanese sovereignty; the situation in Korea and the use of Japanese forces there; the inevitability of World War Three. He commented disparagingly on Japanese pacifism – 'The people who were so eager to defend their country before the war are now astonishingly negative toward war. It is for this reason that the Constitution providing for renunciation of war is bolstered, though in a vague atmosphere'. He weighed the pros and cons of neutrality for Japan. He criticised American carpet-bagging, and the apparent 'reverse course' in America's attitude to Japan, which had caused many Japanese to question American sincerity – 'There is some feeling that a convicted person who has not reformed completely yet, being necessary as a second in a scrap, has been made a co-operator on parole'. He warned of the growth of Asian nationalism, unintentionally underlining the point by his remarks on the state of Japanese national consciousness – 'Servility caused by the defeat and occupation has much spoilt morals fostered in two thousand long years. . . . The people who have no attachment to the culture and tradition of their own country are inferior people'.

And, with the National Police Reserve barely six months old, he deplored its semi-official status, its shadowy, slightly sheepish existence as a non-army. 'The salaried-man-like position of the member of the Force which has nothing to do with one's soul or the moral values is going to be deserted by the pure hearts of the youths.'

In the 'representation' Nakasone made or implied criticisms of American policy which MacArthur took seriously amiss. Justin Williams annotated his own copy of the document with the message 'Torn to pieces by the SCAP and hurled into waste basket'. In many respects this was shortsighted. In the shredded document Nakasone had signalled his support for a frank and open relationship, military and otherwise, with America. As he put it, 'I firmly believe that the rainbow bridge of idealism spanning over the Pacific Ocean must not be faded with clouds and mists'. He had also signalled his view of the alternative to alliance with America – namely, an autonomous defence capacity for Japan. 'The true defense of Japan . . . becomes possible only through combination of the liberty-loving peoples who are equal to each other. . . . The matter', he warned, 'is desired to be based on self-determination of the race.'

26

Remilitarised Japan

Rearmament does not by itself mean that Japan is remilitarising. For that conclusion to be drawn, many other indicators would need to be present in Japan today. The typical militarised society is by definition undemocratic, hierarchical, subject to centralised authoritarian control. It is aggressively nationalistic, xenophobic, and suffused with militarist values – glorification of war and the fighting man, and an exaggerated emphasis on loyalty, obedience and self-sacrifice. There are other significant symptoms – the unremitting upgrading of the armed forces, participation or dominance of the military in the political system, reliance on military strength to provide solutions to foreign policy problems, and so on. Beyond doubt some of these indicators exist or are developing in Japan. Across the spectrum of society – from politics to education, from business to entertainment – pointers to resurgent militarism can be identified. And projected against the backcloth of Japan's conduct in the Chinese and Pacific Wars, the lurid prophesies of the alarmists take on emotive force. It happened once; it can, and surely will, happen again. But what precisely are these indicators, and how accurate are the conclusions based on them?

*   *   *

To the observer steeped in western democratic traditions, the way Japanese political life is structured leaves a great deal to be desired. Since 1955 when Yoshida and Ichiro Hatoyama merged their separate conservative groupings, one single party, the Liberal Democratic Party, has held the reins of power. Indeed, one has to go back to 1947/8 and the socialist administration of Tetsu Katayama to find a government that has not been drawn from the right of the political spectrum. There has never been the two- or three-horse race characteristic of western democracies, and in Japan today there is still no single opposition party which provides a credible alternative to the LDP.

Complicating the issue, the 'hidden government' exposed by Howard Handleman in 1948 still persists, to the detriment of western-style individualist democracy. *Oyabun/kobun* ties unquestionably give the *oyabun* undue influence and the power to pre-empt his *kobun*'s democratic rights. When a senior and respected professor of economics, for example, was selected as a candidate for the Governorship of Tokyo, 'his first act was to run to his former teacher (*oyabun*), a very well-known economist almost eighty years old, to take advice on whether he should accept the offer or not. The press took this action as natural and anticipated the meeting of the two professors; the following day's newspapers carried pictures of the meeting and stressed the importance of the *oyabun*'.

The workings of paternalism among the electorate can obviously distort voting patterns. Equally, from the other side – among the elected representatives – the *oyabun/kobun* system is believed to be the root cause of the corruption, occasionally major, which is endemic in Japanese politics. The *oyabun/kobun* pyramid which stretches away below the political leadership down to the grass roots in the constituencies is a system of *reciprocal* obligations, and it imposes heavy burdens on those seeking to keep the loyalty of their power base. It was this kind of pressure which encouraged Prime Minister Kakuei Tanaka to accept a huge bribe (500,000,000 yen) for influencing All Nippon Airways' future planning in the direction of buying Lockheed Tristars. But where in the West corruption on this scale, once discovered, would force the politician out of public life, in Japan, even after his conviction by the Tokyo District Court in 1983 and four-year prison sentence, Tanaka's constituents voted him back in. They understood his circumstances.

The press, however noisy a watchdog of democracy it may seem to be, is essentially toothless. It was not until two weeks after the Tanaka/Lockheed allegations were first made that the national papers took up the story. Though in many respects admirably informative, in certain crucial areas the press is less than forthright. Above and beyond the general Japanese reluctance to express criticism in public, journalists on occasions practise automatic self-censorship – no revelations of politicians' activities 'below the navel', and nothing derogatory about the Emperor – and worse, on far more important issues they confer to reach a consensus about what should or should not be said, and how to say it. The complaint that 'Japanese newspapers are all the same' is quite often literally true. Journalists from different newspapers on permanent assignment to one particular ministry form a cabal and will collude with their subjects in the ministry and with each other to agree both fact and opinion – 'news management' of an obvious and potentially dangerous kind.

Democracy in Japan is further threatened by the political power of the business and civil service élites. Both the old *zaibatsu*, reconstituted in the later Occupation years, and the new industrial giants exert considerable influence on government policy. Electioneering is a very expensive activity in Japan, and big business input to LDP funds has played a vital part in keeping the party in power. The relationship is symbiotic: over the last four decades the LDP-dominated Diet has consistently adopted policies suitable for a merchant nation, passing – or retaining from the Occupation years – legislation conferring benefits and support for industry. Not least, the LDP has served big business by stifling or outmanoeuvring trade unions.

The business community's contribution to the conservative establishment is more than simply financial. Like the pre-war *zaibatsu*, today's giant corporations perpetuate traditional patterns in society – the very patterns on which militarisation thrived in the 1930s, the patterns which SCAP tried to destroy. The life-time's employment system has made the large company central to the existence of its employees, creating a closed social group akin to the extended family, the farming or fishing village, or the platoon of the Imperial Japanese Army. Within the corporation-group, the characteristic values of the Japanese collectivity prevail – loyalty, hierarchy (and the subordination of women within the hierarchy), obedience, conformity, consensual decision-making – the so-called 'system of irresponsibilities'. For the benefit of big business, students are kept under surveillance at university to identify and black-list trouble-making radicals and others likely to resist absorption into the collectivity. And to make quite sure of cooperation, new managerial recruits to large corporations are often compulsorily housed in dormitories while being indoctrinated with the company ethos.

Still less democratic and more indicative of a militarised society is the real and immediate power possessed by Japan's central civil service. This unelected, self-perpetuating élite sees itself as significantly different from the civil services of Britain or America: the mandarins of Kasumigaseki, Tokyo's Whitehall or Foggy Bottom, have a sense of mission, a conviction of their right to *make* policy, rather than simply executing the orders of the nation's elected representatives. Certainly, Japan's continuing economic success is regarded as due in large measure to the guiding hand of the bureaucracy, in the shape of MITI and the Ministry of Finance; and it is equally certain that few initiatives from the LDP or big business could succeed without bureaucratic approval.

Because of America's decision to settle for indirect rule, the bureaucracy survived the Occupation virtually unscathed, and to this day can be seen as providing continuity with the authoritarian government of the 1930s. As yet there has been no serious friction between notional master and its notional servant, government and the bureaucracy – but it is impossible to predict what would happen were the LDP to be ousted from pole position. Would the civil service obey the commands of a socialist administration – orders, perhaps, to disarm, since the Japan Socialist Party is committed to unarmed neutrality – or would Japan simply become ungovernable?

On this analysis, America may have removed Japan's military leaders, but ultimately, despite the good intentions of the China Crowd and the efforts of reformers within SCAP, the effect of the Occupation was to condone, even positively entrench the predominance of the conservative old guard. Towards its end, in fact, General Matthew Ridgway, MacArthur's successor as Supreme Commander, specifically empowered the Yoshida government to review America's handiwork to date and, if they so desired, to discard it. An Advisory Committee for the Reform of Government Orders was set up in 1951 for the 'rectification of excesses' – or as Yoshida put it, 'adapting democracy to actual conditions'. With the restoration of Japanese sovereignty, a genuine 'reverse course' began in earnest – a deliberate and systematic dismantling of the SCAP reforms of the early years.

The most obvious feature of the 'reverse course' of the 1950s was the progressive recentralisation of control and erosion of local autonomy. This caused most immediate controversy in the police force. But it is with regard to the children of Japan – the seeds of hope for a demilitarised future – that the turning away from Occupation values and back to the 'true Japan' has been most determined. By 1952 the organisational structure of Japanese education, revamped during the Occupation with a maximum of ambition and a minimum of material resources, was already showing the strain; and the Yoshida government was able to exploit the practical weaknesses in the SCAP measures to attack the content of education as well as its form.

The conservatives began by recentralising the system. The Ministry of Education was progressively strengthened at the expense of local autonomy, until in 1956 the locally elected school boards, which had not existed long enough to make any mark, were replaced by boards appointed centrally. This took care of many grass-roots activists for reform – and the Ministry similarly tightened its control over teachers who, on the evidence of their union's activities, were becoming ever more radical. In 1954 the

Yoshida cabinet passed 'education neutrality laws' prohibiting teachers to engage in any political activity, other than voting in elections, in or out of school hours, and forbidding any organisation (viz. the Japan Teachers' Union) to incite teachers to support political activity.

The closer the Ministry's supervision of the staff and system, the easier it became to regulate the content of the curriculum. One primary objective was the reintroduction of morals teaching. Even before the Occupation ended Yoshida was worrying aloud about the erosion of the true Japanese character and the decay of patriotism whilst all around communism was having its disruptive effects. Education, he declared, had become a security concern.

In 1951 his Education Minister Teiyu Amano drew up an 'Outline of Ethical Practice for the Japanese People'. This was both condescending and premature; Yoshida had misjudged the mood of the electorate and the 'Outline' was derisively rejected in the press. But in 1957 another Minister of Education, To Matsunaga, moved to the attack. 'It is necessary', he claimed, 'to hammer morality, national spirit and, to put it more clearly, patriotism into the heads of our younger generation.' He went on to denounce SCAP's education policies as aimed at 'the weakening of the Japanese race'; and by the following year, morals courses had been restored to the curriculum. It should be said that some observers see the new morals teaching, unlike the old *shushin* indoctrination, as 'harmless inspirational pap containing far less nationalism than *The Reader's Digest* but often resembling that magazine in general tone'. Nevertheless the trend towards reaction continues to worry liberals.

In 1966 the Central Council on Education issued 'Image of the Ideal Man', guidelines on personal and public values for use by education authorities in drawing up new courses; and there have been frequent calls for the revival of the Imperial Rescript on Education. The pre-war Japanese national anthem, the *Kimi ga yo* or 'Imperial Reign', was once described as 'a musical presentation of the Imperial Rescript', and during the Occupation it was condemned as feudal and banned from schools. In October 1947 one Japanese newspaper declaimed: 'The National Anthem expresses the prostration of the people before the feet of the Living God the Emperor. . . . It was written to help . . . the feudal class of Japan organise popular sentiments. . . . As long as the *Kimi ga yo* is the National Anthem and the people do not object to it, the democraticness of Japan will be suspect'. By the end of the Occupation it had fallen into disuse; but in 1978 in the revised 'Course of Studies' circulated to all schools by the Ministry of Education it was once more designated as Japan's national anthem. Twice a day, in some schools, pupils stand to attention to the strains of the *Kimi ga yo* as the national flag is raised and lowered.

In the most recent flurry over ethics and education, Masayuki Fujio (Nakasone's choice as Education Minister for a brief and controversial period in 1986) declared that 'Post-war education has ruined Japan'. By this he meant American-style education, which he felt had left the youth of Japan with a profound inferiority complex, and he called for the obliteration of the influence of the Occupation.

The most obvious manifestation of central control over the schoolchildren of Japan is the return to screening and standardisation of textbooks. For some years after the Occupation the authorisation system instituted by SCAP persisted in general outline: an Authorisation Committee and its specialist sub-committees, appointed by the Ministry of Education, continued to produce lists of approved books for schools to choose from on the basis of recommendations by teachers. But as the Ministry became increasingly suspicious of radicalism among teachers, and of 'undesirable' materials creeping into the classroom, especially in the realm of social studies, the system was brought under tighter central control. In 1956 the Ministry inserted full-time appointees into the screening committees; the number of manuscripts rejected by the social studies group in particular accelerated dramatically. In 1958 the power to recommend books to schools was withdrawn from teachers; and a standardised nation-wide curriculum, with which all textbooks had naturally to conform, was drawn up and made mandatory.

The effect was by now much as if the Ministry were actually writing the books itself, as it had during the war – and it was against this background that the notorious Ienaga case exploded. Saburo Ienaga is one of Japan's best-known historians, a peace campaigner and a crusader for academic freedom. In 1946 he was among those invited to contribute to CIE's first 'demilitarised' history textbook, *The Footsteps of a Nation*. On the basis of this contribution, he subsequently wrote a full-length history of Japan, which was approved for use as a school textbook in 1952. But by 1954 the Ministry was requiring 216 changes to be made. Ienaga's work, they claimed, failed adequately 'to recognise the efforts of Japanese ancestors'; it did not heighten awareness of what it was to be Japanese, nor did it try hard enough to foster affection for Japan. Specifically, the Ministry objected to Ienaga's assertions that the mythology concerning the Age of the Gods and the origin of the Emperor Jimmu had been deliberately fabricated to justify Imperial rule, and that the Imperial Rescript on Education and the use of the Emperor's portrait as an icon were devices manipulated to unite the nation. Ideas which had made him perfect for SCAPs purposes put him beyond the pale now.

Between 1954 and 1963 the book was submitted and rejected three times. Ienaga made a large proportion of the changes requested, but at the most significant he stuck fast, and took the Ministry to court, alleging state censorship in breach of Article 23 of the Constitution which guarantees academic freedom. Judgement when it eventually came was in Ienaga's favour, and in 1984 he filed another suit against the Ministry, claiming compensation of two million yen for mental anguish.

Japan is hardly unique in wishing to exclude 'antipathetic material' from its textbooks. Most nations have a tendency to emphasise their finer features and minimise 'negative behaviours', and this makes itself felt in what they allow their children to be taught. One scholar comparing the versions of World War II to be found in current history books of the Allied and Axis countries found a kaleidoscopic variety of interpretation. The Italian text, for instance, was inclined to suggest that Italy sided with the Axis in order to prevent Communist domination of Europe, and devoted considerably more space to the later years of the war than the earlier. Almost half of the West German text concerned resistance to Hitler, giving the distinct impression that, like the rest of the world, Germans were at war with the Nazis. (So unbalanced an account was it that the translator wrote asking if 'the other half' of the book had been lost.) There was no mention in it of the Final Solution, nor did the Russian text allude to the massacre at Katyn. The British account of the war made no mention of Roosevelt, nor the American work any reference to Churchill. Ex-President Marcos once remarked that Filipinos 'look with some sophistication' at the charge that Japan censors its textbooks – 'We realise that most of the big countries doctor histories to fit their requirements'. One has only to look, he added, at American accounts of Bataan and Corregidor which describe them as American engagements, failing to mention the countless Filipinos who died in defence of their homeland.

Natural bias is one thing, but in recent years it has been suggested that Japan's Ministry of Education is going too far in attempting positively to rewrite history. In 1982 a 'textbook scandal' broke out which threatened at the time to assume the proportions of an international incident, and still rumbles on. It started when a Japanese daily paper claimed to have evidence that the Ministry of Education was trying to conceal Japan's war guilt. In revised editions of history textbooks, the invasion of China in 1937 was said to have been described as an 'advance'; the Rape of Nanking explained as an 'abnormal happening' provoked by

Chinese resistance; and the deportation to Japan of one million Koreans for forced labour euphemised as 'implementation of the national mobilization order for Koreans'. As news of the alleged bowdlerisations spread, there were riots in Asian cities; three hundred Korean war veterans marched on the Japanese embassy in Seoul, and Japanese envoys seeking to explain the misunderstanding were refused entry to the country while the South Korean cabinet met for emergency discussions. China called it a plot to revive militarism, and delivered a formal protest, and the Japanese government was forced to apologise publicly and promise revisions to the textbook authorisation procedure.

At this point it was discovered that the original newspaper allegation had been inaccurate and that no such alterations had been made. But before dismissing the affair as a smear campaign against the ruling party, it is worth noticing an article published some ten years earlier by the *Asahi Shimbun* in which teachers complained that the textbooks from which they were teaching the history of World War II were no longer as candid as the earlier editions from which they themselves had learned in the 1950s. The episode which they chose to illustrate their point was the Manchurian Incident. In the 1956 texts the description ran: 'In order to find a way out of these acute domestic problems, Japan tried to monopolise Manchuria as an outlet for Japanese goods. . . . The Japanese army started the war in Manchuria in 1931 and established Manchukuo the next year'. In the 1974 texts it read: 'In 1931, due to an explosion on the railway near Mukden, the Japanese army began fighting with the Chinese army'.

It is also true that the Ministry of Education has issued guidelines to publishers on the terms to be used when discussing World War II; when describing Japanese atrocities, the Ministry advises, phrases such as 'abnormal circumstances' or 'the full truth having not yet been determined' might be suitable. (One of the indiscretions for which Masayuki Fujio was eventually sacked forty-nine days after taking office, was the suggestion that the Rape of Nanking was a figment, devised and perpetuated by Japan's enemies for propaganda purposes.) A yet more effective method of ensuring that young minds are not contaminated is to omit war-related questions from examination papers. In a system as exam-oriented as the Japanese, a subject which is never set is rarely studied.

Even more disturbing to some than possible government manipulation of the facts, is the suggestion that many historians – the professional interpreters and guardians of the past – are themselves adopting revisionist attitudes. Japanese intellectuals have tended this century to hold radical views, and many opposed militarism, even if during the war most preferred 'internal migration' to brave but futile defiance. During the Occupation, as militarist restraints were lifted and replaced by 'democratic' censorship, there was a brief flurry of outspoken criticism of Japan's war record, when even government publications acknowledged Japanese guilt. But it would have been unrealistic to have expected this to last; and a change in attitude can be traced as early as 1953.

In that year Yoshida's principal economic adviser, Hayato Ikeda, met America's Assistant Secretary of State for Far Eastern Affairs, Walter S. Robertson, to discuss the Mutual Defense Assistance programme and Japan's hopes of qualifying for aid by rearming. In the course of their conference, Ikeda and Robertson agreed 'to promote militarism among the Japanese people in a bid to increase public support for rearmament'. During the same period Education Minister Seigo Okana was declaring, 'I do not wish to pass judgement on the rightness or wrongness of the Greater East Asian War, but the fact that Japan took on so many opponents and fought them for four years . . . proves our superiority'.

Given this political climate, it is hardly surprising that books of a distinctly revisionist cast should have begun to appear – books like the 'Complete History of the Greater East Asian War' by Colonel Takushiro Hattori, the same Hattori whom Willoughby had hoped to see commanding the National Security Force. The title in itself was significant, since the use of the phrase 'Greater East Asian War' had been prohibited during the Occupation because of the implication that this was a war to liberate Asians from western domination. (It is perhaps worth noting that Japan's official history of the war years, published between 1966 and 1976, is entitled 'The Army and Navy Histories of the Greater East Asian War'.) Fusao Hayashi's even more positive 'Affirmation of the Greater East Asian War' followed a decade later; by which time nostalgia for the scarce blessings of wartime – comradeship, adventure, bravery and dedication – was beginning to cloud the memory and blur the national perception of war's realities. Even now in the 1980s, 'the war remains an undigested lump of myths, canards and alibis which distort the way Japanese see themselves, and, equally importantly, others'.

When in the 1970s Japan began to encounter open international hostility to her economic success, her response was to look hard at her relationships with other countries, past and present, and in particular 'to re-examine the Occupation period as the starting-point of her post-war history'. The time for gratitude, if it had ever existed, appeared to be over.

Critic Jun Eto resurrected the contention of the last wartime government that Japan's surrender had been conditional – a special agreement on the terms of the Potsdam Declaration – and that beyond the satisfaction of the Potsdam conditions America had had no right to interfere in Japanese affairs. Historian Takanori Irie advanced the peculiar argument that the new SCAP Constitution, like that of the Weimar Republic, had been drafted by a Jew (he had Charles Kades in mind) with a distinct 'antipathy to the state', and was aimed at destroying Japan as a nation. In the 1980s the Occupation tends to be cast as at best a giant exercise in brainwashing, ultimately doomed to fail. The Ministry of Foreign Relations' publicity booklet 'The Japan of Today', in its thumbnail sketch of Japan's history, does not mention it at all. This official account of the seven years following defeat runs: 'In August 1945 an exhausted and battle-weary nation accepted the surrender terms of the Allied powers and by Imperial edict the people laid down their arms. Seven years later, in September 1951, Japan signed the peace treaty'. And criticism is not always left to inference: a recent Japanese television documentary on the Occupation opened with a scene of multiple rape of a Japanese woman by a gang of G.I.s.

Many of the arguments presented with such skill by Tojo in his affidavit have resurfaced; and the IMTFE itself has been heavily attacked. Reviving the charges of 'victors' justice', Masayuki Fujio recently declared, 'If world history is a history of wars, you have to have trials for *each* war. And the same rules should apply at each trial'. But the IMTFE is condemned not just for itself, as it deserves, but as a symbol of wider injustices and weaknesses in the Occupation. In 1983 a conference in Tokyo was given over to an examination, and fairly comprehensive demolition, of the 'Tokyo Trial slant on history' – that is to say, the view of events between 1928 and 1945 held by the prosecution. This is now felt to be an unduly masochistic approach for Japanese citizens to adopt in the 1980s. In the words of Nakasone, 'It is considered progressive to criticise pre-war Japan for its faults and defects, but I firmly oppose such a notion. A nation is still a nation whether it wins or loses a war'.

The film *Tokyo Trial*, released in Japan in 1983 and New York in 1985, was made by Masaki Kobayashi, an avowed pacifist, and he took the opportunity, understandably, to condemn all wartime atrocities, not merely those of the Japanese. It could be objected, however, that his treatment of Japanese war crimes – which were after all a major point at issue in the trial which is his central subject – is sketchy and evasive in comparison with his lingering coverage of the Tokyo fire raid, the death pits at Bergen-Belsen and the use of napalm in Vietnam. A brief and scratchy clip from a Chinese propaganda film on the Rape of Nanking is intercut with unmistakably authentic and considerably more extended footage on Hiroshima.

The tenor of Kobayashi's film reflects sentiments widely held among the Japanese. Hiroshima has become the principal plea, to themselves and to outsiders, in extenuation of Japanese war guilt. It is particularly effective as applied to the collective sensibilities of America. When in 1950 a Japanese delegation was received on the floor of Congress, they took with them as a gift a cross of olive wood from a tree near the epicentre of the blast at Hiroshima – Christian symbolism to arouse Christian consciences.

From the perspective of the nuclear holocaust, Japan becomes victim not villain, attacked not attacker; it is no coincidence that the Japanese have built in Hiroshima a monument to the dead of Auschwitz, in an attempt to link themselves with the Jews as the war's principal sufferers. Anti-militarists, who are themselves often passionate critics of the atomic bombings, nevertheless fear that by obliterating all memory of what preceded Hiroshima and Nagasaki – cancelling the debt of guilt, as it were – the Japanese are paving the way for the mistakes and misdeeds of the 1930s to be repeated.

The indicators seem to be there – authoritarianism, revisionism, parroted appeals to patriotism, anti-Americanism, self-justification. America's bulwark against communism, the conservative old guard, has ruled uninterruptedly for close on forty years. The central bureaucracy remains in firm control. In public and private life, at work, at home and in school, the traditional patterns of loyalty, hierarchy, conformity, discipline are perpetuated. And those who forecast a return to the dark valley of the 1930s detect signs that Japanese ethnocentricity, heightened first by adversity and then by success, is taking on once more a tinge of xenophobia and fanaticism.

Unquestionably the Japanese are as proud now as they have ever been of Japan's two-thousand year continuity as a nation, her supposed racial purity and her consequent uniqueness. At the official level, the 1985 edition of 'The Japan of Today' alludes delicately but persistently to these motifs. 'The history and geography of Japan . . . have created an unusually homogeneous people. Over the centuries they developed institutions, customs and characteristics that have given them a strong sense of national identity and common purpose. The strength and stability derived from these features of the national life helped Japan undergo two major transformations in the last one hundred years, first in the late nineteenth century when it threw off a stagnant feudal system . . . and again in the twentieth century when it turned away from the tragic experience of World War II to create a new society. . . . While these two periods brought almost revolutionary change in both the political and social structure, this was accomplished without discarding traditional roots or impairing social continuity.' The homogeneity of her society was the excuse Japan offered for accepting no more than a handful of Vietnamese boat people, and it does much to explain the generally indifferent treatment of the Korean community, 600,000 strong, which constitutes Japan's only significant ethnic minority.

It is only a short step from strong sympathy with one's fellow countrymen to strong antipathy towards everyone else, and the signs of xenophobia are plain in Japan at every level, from the most trivial to the potentially dangerous. Foreign sportsmen – baseball professionals and amateur *sumo* wrestlers, imported for the sake of novelty and colour – are expected to be worth their fees but not to excel unduly at the national games. In a poll held by the Prime Minister's Office in 1980, sixty-four per cent of Japanese wanted nothing whatsoever to do with foreigners. Japanese girls who have lived abroad for any length of time have substantially reduced their chances of making suitable marriages; and Prime Minister Nakasone revealed that he has had, on occasion, to order vice-ministers to overcome their aversion to foreign travel for the good of the nation. All foreign residents are required to be fingerprinted; and no foreign nationals – even Koreans actually born in Japan – may be employed as public servants. In 1981 an official from the Ministry of Education, explaining the ban on foreign teachers, mused: 'I wonder if a foreigner is capable of eliciting in children reverence for the Emperor and the flag, the feelings aroused by viewing cherry blossoms'.

It is reverence for the Emperor which makes the watchdogs of ultra-nationalism and renascent militarism perhaps most uneasy. Not without reason, as the tone and tenor of a recent article, published in a reputable magazine, suggests. 'The Emperor', the article claims, 'is better evidence than any argument. Despite the Allied Powers' vindictiveness at the Tokyo War Crimes trials, our head of state was not tried. . . . The Emperor retained his throne because Japan, unlike Nazi Germany, was *absolved of crimes against humanity* [our italics]. . . . Though the national polity, as personified by the Emperor, underwent great changes through defeat and the Allied occupation it was not eradicated. All the great leaders of the World War II era – Stalin, Roosevelt, Churchill, Mussolini, Mao Tse-tung, Chiang Kai-Shek – are gone. Only one, our Emperor, is alive and in good health, the perfect symbol of national prosperity. In fact, have any of the so-called victorious nations in World War II been more successful in the last forty years than defeated Japan?'

In the Emperor's survival is seen not only further proof of his innocence, and Japan's innocence of war crimes, but evidence of

Japan's superiority over other nations – and for many Japanese the Emperor will forever continue as the focus of national conscious-ness. He owes his present popular status at least partly to the public relations campaign which the Imperial Household has waged unabated since the 'humanising' process first began in 1946. Though on a smaller scale than before the war, the House-hold itself has survived intact. Most of its spider's web of bureaus and offices have been preserved in practice, though on paper they have been amalgamated and re-named: the mundane-sounding Maintenance Division, for example, incorporates the former Office of Imperial Cuisine, Office of Imperial Works and Office of Imperial Stables. This means, according to one authority, that the palace 'has a wide range of cultural, traditional, moral, religious and even political elements that can be used as resources to rearrange the symbolic content of the Imperial institution in accordance with the changing conditions outside the palace gates'.

The Household's mission has been to adapt the Imperial institu-tion – itself passive – to its environment, making sure that it is in tune with the spirit of the times. In an era when Japan has never been more concerned with material success, for the Emperor to blend with his surroundings he has had to be presented, de-mystified, as the model of the urban *bourgeois,* and his family as the epitome of middle-class virtues, combining contemporary aware-ness with staunch support for traditional Japanese values. 'Each member has certain laudable and endearing qualities. The emperor is a sincere, hard-working man, a scientist and a doting grand-father. The empress is a warmhearted grandmother, skilled in calligraphy and the Japanese arts; the crown prince is a sports enthusiast as well as a devoted father and husband; Princess Michiko seems to embody all that is good and beautiful in the modern Japanese woman.'

In the eyes of its critics, however, it is in the very adaptability of the institution that the danger lies. The present environment is middle-of-the-road, middle-class, middle-brow and, in the world context, politically moderate. But if the climate were to become markedly more reactionary and the government more absolutist, the Imperial institution could again become a powerful force in its own right or, as in the past, a seal of authority to be set on the actions of others.

Awareness of this danger is perhaps behind the determination with which a wedge has been driven between the Emperor and the SDF. At one time he used to grant private audiences to high-ranking defence officials and SDF commanders, but this practice was stopped in 1973 after the Director-General of the Japan Defense Agency imprudently passed on some of the Imperial comments on Japan's armed forces. These were innocuous enough – Hirohito suggested that without copying the evil aspects of the old army, the SDF might benefit from adopting some of its better features – but the very idea that the Emperor might be taking an interest in military matters caused a public furore, and the Director-General had to resign.

The latent power of the Imperial institution is considerably strengthened by the Emperor's continuing connections with Japanese religious life. Hirohito's personal status still derives in part from the Shinto faith: the so-called 'renunciation of divinity' in fact did nothing to change the relationship between the Emperor, the nation's *kami*, and the people. He may not himself be worshipped as *kami*-incarnate, a living god, but he may – indeed must – intercede for his people with the principal Shinto deity, Amaterasu, who remains the particular *kami* of the Imperial family. Nothing short of the total obliteration of the Imperial institution and successful debunking of the dynasty's ancestry could have affected this relationship.

Popular interest in Shinto is still regarded to some extent as a barometer of nationalism – a symptom of nostalgia for the old 'national polity'. (It was Yoshida who in 1959 suggested that Shinto should be revived as a means of strengthening 'love of country'.) Since the end of the Occupation there have been frequent calls for the reinstatement of Shinto as the official national religion, and the state funding of Shinto shrines. In particular need of help is the Ise Shrine, dedicated to Amaterasu and Shinto's most holy place of worship; every twenty years the shrine building must be reconstructed at a different spot within the sacred precincts, and the recurring expense is quite beyond the shrine's own resources.

There has also been constant pressure for the re-nationalisation of the Yasukuni Shrine, principally from the eight million members of the War Bereaved Families Association. (One of the Association's early leaders was Oshinori Kaya, Tojo's Minister of Finance, sentenced by the IMTFE for conspiracy to wage aggressive war, but released after serving only four years in prison.) Since 1969 the LDP has repeatedly introduced into the Diet a bill to place Yasukuni under state management. As yet it has met with little success, but the visit of the Nakasone cabinet to Yasukuni in 1985 gave great encouragement to the traditionalists as a step towards official recognition of the shrine.

But perhaps the most conspicuous breach in the barrier erected between state and religion by the 1946 Shinto Directive has been the revival of National Foundation Day, the celebration on February 11 of the enthronement of the mythological Emperor Jimmu. This revival, finally achieved in 1966, was the result of years of agitation, and liberals were alarmed by the jubilation with which the restoration was received among ultra-nationalists. The Greater Japan Production Party crowed: 'The victory meant that the history and traditions of Japan which were wiped out by the Occupation Forces had been rightfully restored. It also meant that at least one phase of Japan's spiritual side had been liberated for the first time in twenty-two years.' It is significant, though hardly surprising, that the first Prime Minister to participate officially in the celebration was Yasuhiro Nakasone.

Gravitation towards a strengthened Shinto is just one aspect of a general quest for the resuscitation of traditional values. Many older Japanese are worried, even frightened by what they see as degeneracy in the young and a decline in general moral standards – a lack of discipline, a refusal to conform, rampant consumerism and individual ambition – which they attribute directly to the alien code of values imposed by the Americans in the 1940s.

The instinctive response is to look to the past for inspiration – and it is no accident that Yukio Mishima's edition of the *bushido* text *Hagakure* rapidly became a best-seller. In his own writings Mishima savagely attacked the vapidity and spinelessness of Japanese post-war society. 'We do not have an appropriate ideology or philosophy of life that enables us to live with a sense of spiritual satisfaction. . . . Mothers warn of the dangers of giving war toys to children. At school, teachers claim giving numbers to children and making them line up in single file is tantamount to militarist indoctrination, so children loiter about aimlessly like Diet representatives.' He demanded a new 'aesthetic patriotism', and in 1973 the echoes of his call sounded in the rallying cry of a new force on the political scene. The *Seirankai*, or Summer Storm Society, took as their watchword 'the politics of the heart', moral commitment and professional purity combined with a 'positive' approach to defence issues, constitutional revision, educational 'rectification' and a crusade against communism.

The association with Mishima did not go unnoticed; and while the 'Storm Troopers', as their critics liked to call them, were not fringe fanatics but registered members of the LDP, opponents of reaction were further disturbed by their formal initiation ceremony, or *keppan*, at which each nicked his little finger with a razor blade and signed the roster in blood – a ritual irresistibly reminiscent of the blood pacts of 1930s ultra-nationalists and 1980s *yakuza* or gangsters.

As for reactionary tendencies in the business world, in April 1984 the President of the Japan Teachers' Union accused the government of trying to revive the anti-democratic pre-war system of education 'in response to requests from industrial circles'. A good example of what he may have had in mind is to be found in the writings of oil tycoon Sazo Idemitsu, who saw his first task after welcoming a new recruit into the company as being to strip him of all trace of 'the new-fangled education alien to the Japanese spirit'.

Idemitsu (who read a message of condolence at Mishima's funeral) was a self-made millionaire, his wealth founded in a pre-war 'expansion programme' in Manchuria, Korea, Northern China and Formosa. When Japan's overseas possessions were confiscated, he naturally lost heavily, but in 1949 he was permitted by SCAP to begin distributing petroleum products, and with the beginning of the Korean War was presented with the opportunity to build up a tanker fleet and a huge oil empire.

In his *Be A True Japanese!*, published in 1971, Idemitsu violently attacked Occupation policies, and called for the abolition of a Constitution 'intended to sever the bond of mutual trust between the Imperial Family and the people'. The education laws were, he said, designed to 'pull down the dignity of the teacher' so that the Japanese spirit would disintegrate; the labour laws were intended to destroy the traditional foundations of 'mutual trust and assurance' between men and masters, as the 'shortest cut to forestall resurgence of Japan's industry'. (He never permitted unionisation in his company, whose employees formed instead 'one big family'.) A return to the old values was, he felt, both necessary and inevitable. 'A Japanese has traditional Japanese blood pulsating in his veins which cannot be replaced by anything alien. It is a pure blood inherited from his ancestors, made thicker and thicker by several thousand years of peaceful co-existence. It is the blood of mutual trust which binds the people to the Imperial Family . . . and therefore Japan is entirely different from nations ruled by force. . . . A nation based on infinite trust in the *Tenno* who transcends all concepts of might and right may be said unparalleled in the world. . . . Spring is coming and nothing can hold back the sprouting of young leaves.' Of all the slogans constantly reiterated by the militarists in the 1930s – racial purity, national uniqueness, loyalty to the Emperor as the father of his people – Idemitsu missed very few.

He would no doubt have approved of the present phenomenon of the *oendan* – all-male university clubs whose members, not unlike glorified cheerleaders, originally kept order at sporting events but these days are more often used to break up leftist meetings on campus. Militaristic in organisation and training – the members of each chapter are ordered by rank and seniority – the *oendan* affect uniforms and short hair, and like to compare themselves with *kamikaze* and *samurai*. With a motto like *Shitsujitsugoken* – 'Honour, duty, strength and loyalty' – it is not surprising that they are in great demand with employers both in legitimate business and in the underworld.

The notion of sterner discipline among youth is one that tends to appeal to many present-day parents in Japan. Early in 1985 a burglary was reported at a junior high school in Osaka; the policeman sent to investigate attracted the critical attention of pupils watching from the balconies around the central courtyard and when he dropped the tape measure with which he was measuring a broken window, somebody cat-called. Infuriated, he lined up the whole class, and demanded to know who had jeered; when no one owned up, he hit all eighteen boys, one of whom later needed medical attention. The school complained to the police station, and the officer was suspended from duty and threatened with prosecution – but the threat was lifted when the vast bulk of the correspondence which poured into both school and station proved to be in his favour. In July 1983 it was revealed that the superintendent of a private 'naval academy' had been beating, starving and freezing the pupils in his care – emotionally maladjusted and 'difficult' children whose parents had sent them to him in the hope that he might instil some sense of discipline in them with techniques of 'perfection through pain' learned during his days in the Imperial Navy.

The old soldiers of Empire are widely revered. In March 1974 Lieutenant Hiroo Onoda emerged from the jungles of Lubang (a small island about ten miles north of Mindoro in the Philippines) where for thirty years he had refused to acknowledge that the war was lost – and was hailed in Japan as a hero, a model of the traditional virtues of tenacity and loyalty to the Emperor. He now works at a mountain holiday camp, teaching children the virtues – courage, solidarity and obedience – which are necessary for one to 'live with nature'. 'We sent children through a lonely lane by themselves at night. Camp personnel masquerading as ghosts and evil monsters were waiting along the route to scare them. Few children could make the trek alone. But when they were allowed to go in a group of two or three, they all completed the course, although they were just as frightened. . . . The children really learned to appreciate friendship, and also that a group is mightier than an individual.'

The martial arts, once resolutely weeded out of the curricula of schools and universities, are enjoying a full-blooded revival, unchanged in purpose, content and method. Equally, the attempt to wean the theatre public away from 'feudal' drama has been singularly unsuccessful: the repertoires of *kabuki*, *noh* and *bunraku* (puppet) theatre continue to feature the classic loyalty and revenge dramas and battle pieces, and even cabaret acts fuse sex and the *bushido*. In the cinema, *chambara* – the *samurai* version of the western 'horse opera' – is unfailingly popular; and, nearer the knuckle as far as militarophobes are concerned, war films have had a hugely enthusiastic reception in recent years. Among the major summer successes in 1983 and 1984 were *The Great Japanese Empire* and *Zero*, a hymn to the Zero fighter.

1984 also saw the re-release of two wartime cartoons. The first, a 'short' commissioned in 1942 entitled *Momotaro the Sea Eagle*, was a thinly disguised version of Pearl Harbor in which the child Momotaro and his animal crew attack Ogre Island and destroy the enemy fleet assembled there; one of the sailors on the first battleship to be sunk has the voice of Bluto – lifted from a *Popeye* cartoon found in Paramount's Tokyo office after the outbreak of war. The second was a full-length sequel made in 1945 entitled *Momotaro and his Good Soldiers from the Sea*, this time a reworking of the Imperial Navy's airborne assaults on Manado, north of the Celebes, in January 1942. Momotaro and his crew (all domestic animals) come to free the peoples of Asia (jungle animals) from Western domination and attack the enemy's capital: Momotaro by now bears a strong resemblance to General Yamashita, the conqueror of Singapore. Among the western troops surrendering in panic are again Bluto and Popeye – who drops his spinach. The film ends in rural Japan where children, emulating their older brothers in parachute practice, jump out of the branches of a tree to land within a chalk outline of the United States.

The higher the militarist temperature seems to rise, the more favourable the climate becomes for the right-wing extremists who have always been part of Japanese political life. Despite all SCAP's efforts to stamp it out, Japanese ultra-nationalism resurfaced in the 1950s and survives into the present decade, looking and sounding much as it always did. Even during the Occupation itself, right-wing groups began to recoup some of their strength as the purge was lifted and pressure relaxed on prominent ultra-nationalist politicians, *zaibatsu* leaders and others who had traditionally protected and funded extremism. It has even been suggested that America was partly to blame for the resurgence, since certain rightist societies were recruited by G-2 to assist in information-gathering for the Red Purge.

Immediately after the formal conclusion of the Peace Treaty and the ending of American military control over Japanese civilian life, a rash of rightist 'incidents' erupted. On the first day of independence, a group of pilots met in Nagasaki to burn the white flag which had flown over their headquarters on the day of the surrender. Within a month the Bataan Death March had been dismissed in the press as American propaganda, and the flood of 'I Was

There' memoirs by generals and admirals was in full spate. In October 1952 a collection of documents was published from Sugamo Prison to win support for the release of convicted war criminals; and the number of visits to the Yasukuni Shrine soared from ten to ten thousand a day.

Societies which had been influential in the 1920s and 1930s before being suppressed by SCAP bobbed up again in the 1950s either under the same names – the National Essence Mass Party, the Flowers of Glory Association, and so on – or under new ones: the National Martyrs Youth Corps, for example, bore strong resemblances to the Association for Heavenly Action, and the Myriad Weapons Society to the Loyalists' Sincerity Group. Many of these societies survived precisely because they were small, isolated and hard to trace; others were too powerful to have been effectively obliterated. The *Butoku Kai*, for instance, was restored four months before the passing of the Self-Defense Forces Law in 1954, to promote a healthy martial spirit among the people of Japan. It had Yoshida's blessing, and assets of over a billion yen to be reclaimed from the Foreign Ministry.

There were, besides, a number of new, virulently anti-Communist groups which had proliferated after the Surrender, and continued throughout the 1950s to trumpet the beliefs which SCAP had tried so hard to discourage – restoration of the Emperor system, a pan-Asian fellowship under Japanese domination, the promotion of a true 'Japanese' Constitution, massive rearmament and the revival of traditional values. In the 1960s and 1970s these ideals were elaborated to encompass plans for a 'Showa Restoration', which would make the Emperor once again the locus of sovereignty; calls for the return of the Northern Territories by Russia; demands for an end to the so-called 'Yalta-Potsdam structure' – the condition of world affairs as determined by these two conferences, at which the United States and the Soviet Union were established as superpowers effectively dividing the globe between them.

Ultra-nationalists have made their presence violently felt from time to time as successors to the assassins of the 1930s. In 1960 during a television debate a seventeen-year-old fanatic stabbed to death Inejiro Asanuma, the chairman of the Japan Socialist Party. In 1961 another teenager broke into the home of Hoji Shimanaka, president of the company which publishes the monthly magazine *Chuo Koron*, killed the housekeeper and wounded Shimanaka's wife; he later explained that he had been offended by a novel serialised in a recent issue of the magazine which described the execution, in a dream, of the Imperial Family by a revolutionary mob. In 1968 an attack was made with a wooden sword on Soviet

Deputy Premier Nikolai Baibokov while he was visiting Japan. In 1971 a 22-calibre derringer and 175 rounds of ammunition were sent to Prime Minister Sato with the recommendation that he use them on himself. In 1972 an attempt was made on the life of a pro-Peking Diet member with sulphuric acid. In 1973 the Japan Communist Party Presidium Chairman was slashed with a fish-gutting knife. And in 1978 Prime Minister Ohira was attacked on the doorstep of his official residence.

Within the SDF too there have been signs of 1930s-style plots and conspiracies. In 1963, for instance, without the knowledge of the Japan Defense Agency, a group of SDF staff officers drew up the 'Three Arrows' plan – a study of the resources which might be needed and action which might be taken by Japan in the event of war between America and China, precipitated in Korea. (The three 'arrows' were an air force operating out of Guam, intercontinental ballistic missiles, and Polaris submarines.) Two years later the plan was leaked, to public uproar and Socialist accusations of an attempted rightist *coup d'état*. The military, it seemed, were not content to submit to civilian control; and even more alarming, the 'Three Arrows' scenario incorporated contingency plans for the suppression of internal insurrection which included censorship of the media and the imposition of controls over the Diet and the economy. And in case the resonant echoes of 1930s militarism were not loud enough already, it had appended to it the Tojo regime's *Basic Principles for the Empire's National Policies.*

But the most extreme form of ultra-rightism was personified in Yukio Mishima. Throughout his career as novelist, critic, playwright and film maker, he expressed profound contempt for what he saw as the flabbiness and decadence of the new 'democratic' Japan – 'the feminisation of the male'. In particular, his mind full of the principles of the *bushido*, he despised what Japan's once-proud fighting forces had become – 'a gigantic arsenal without a soul. . . . The SDF has continued to bear the cross of national dishonour since the defeat of the country'.

Mishima sought through the creation of a small private militia – the *Tate no kai*, or Shield Society, to revive the spirit of the *samurai*, first in the SDF and then in the country as a whole. On November 25, 1970, with four young members of the *Tate no Kai*, he overpowered the commander of the Eastern SDF in his office at Eastern Regional Headquarters in Tokyo, and demanded to be allowed to address the troops. From a balcony overlooking the parade ground, dressed in the quasi-military uniform he had designed himself for the Shields and wearing the headband of the warrior, inscribed with a slogan from *Hagakure*, he railed for ten minutes at a hastily-assembled crowd of a thousand off-duty soldiers, urging them to rise with him and demand the abolition of Article 9. Then he went back inside and into the commander's office, knelt on the carpet, and disembowelled himself with his short sword. His chief lieutenant made an ineffectual attempt to behead him with the long sword in accordance with *samurai* precepts, and himself committed *hara-kiri*. Another Shield successfully beheaded them both, and the survivors, placing the severed heads – headbands in place – neatly on the floor before the bodies, saluted and gave themselves up.

This act had, for Mishima at least, manifold significance. It was a personal response to his reading of the *Hagakure*, an expression of the belief that the attainment of a 'beautiful' death is the only satisfactory completion of a life which one has attempted to live 'beautifully'. To the man of action, whom Mishima so longed to be taken for, 'life frequently appears as a circle to be completed by the addition of one last point. . . . I should think that a death which in an instant completes one's world by the addition of a single point would afford a more intense feeling of fulfilment by far'. It was also perhaps an attempt to use shock and guilt as weapons – emphasising with his death the failure of the SDF to meet his expectations – to force the nation into an awareness of its own spiritual degeneracy. At root, though, it was a political act, an attempt to precipitate constitutional reform, specifically reform of Article 9.

But his death had few of the consequences for which he had hoped. Far from rising up, the SDF sniggered and catcalled as he made his appeal to their honour; Nakasone rejected his gesture as 'madness'; and more than any other single phenomenon, it has served to put those who fear resurgent militarism on their guard.

27

Demilitarised Japan

To the pessimist it might seem that two dangerous currents are converging in Japanese life, sweeping the country inexorably towards the rapids of 1930s-style militarisation. The one, the Mishima spirit, is a reactionary trend in public opinion, both informed and uninformed. The other, the Nakasone factor, is a forceful leadership channelling these energies to serve a defined political end – the reconstruction of Japan as a strong, possibly independent military power.

But in order to decide whether the Japanese people and the rest of the world are really facing a resurgent menace, one must put these portents in the right perspective. And this is not the perspective of the past – the China and Pacific Wars, and the barbarities of almost half a century ago – but the perspective of the present. Do the indicators of militarisation still seem significant in the context both of Japan's political development, and her international position? There is much in the condition of Japan in the 1980s, internal and external, to suggest that not only is she incapable of rising up to threaten the outside world, she no longer has a genuine will to do so.

Seeing Japan in sharp focus is not always easy. The western observer carries over into his assessment of the Japanese not only his inescapable cultural conditioning, but a battery of prejudices which more often than not have their roots in wartime propaganda and are reinforced by fear and envy of Japan's phenomenal economic success since then. Very little is taught about Japan in schools in Britain or the United States, and ignorance makes it hard to resist the line taken by the media – which on this subject is generally the line of least resistance.

It is easiest, and most titillating, to trot out the well-worn stereotypes – the stylised violence of the *samurai*, the courtly mystery of the *geisha*, the ant-soldiers of the Imperial Army, and so on *ad nauseam*. Conflict is more saleable than conciliation,

aggression than neutrality, past war than present peace, and renascent militarism makes a good story. At regular intervals articles,
books and films emerge whose one theme is the treachery, fanaticism and barbarity concealed behind the false, inscrutable smiles of
the bringers of stereo headsets, computer games and economy
motoring. Novelists cast their villains as bloated *zaibatsu* leaders,
de-purged war criminals, renegade *kamikaze* pilots, power-crazed
MITI bureau chiefs, forming a conspiracy to challenge the superpowers. Prophets of doom portray the commercial strategy of
Japan as a hundred-year war of aggression, equally as menacing as
her armed expansion in Asia in the 1930s. Stereotype feeds
stereotype, and any defence of Japan is regarded as an apologia
and treated with deep suspicion.

The West is not entirely to blame for the failure in communications. The Japanese are without doubt passionately interested in
themselves, in their own uniqueness, and devote a good deal of
time to self-analysis; this has led to what is known as the *Nihonjinron* boom, a spate of books – forty in one year alone – on 'what it
means to be Japanese'. But they are far less concerned to explain
themselves to others – insular to the point where, some observers
fear, under pressure they might turn ever more tightly in on themselves and become a nation with whom it is impossible for outsiders to deal. 'The stronger the criticism and censure from
outside, the more unanimous and firm becomes the reply of self-
assurance from inside. The present psyche of the Japanese is
almost on the verge of being pathological.'

If one wants accurate information about Japan, one must dig for
it. So what exactly is the evidence that militarisation is not a serious
threat in Japan, nor likely to become one?

*   *   *

The fundamental argument is, quite simply, that Japan is a
genuine democracy – the antithesis of a militarised state, almost by
definition. All societies are in a permanent state of flux – political,
economic, sociological, even geographic – but the rate of change
varies widely from nation to nation, era to era. For almost 250 years
in Japan, from the start of the seventeenth century, the *shoguns*
tried to keep alteration to a minimum, isolating the country almost
completely from the outside world in their efforts to preserve the
feudal structure which worked so notably to their own advantage.
But even they could not hold fast for ever. Almost imperceptibly
Japanese society changed, and with the violent incursion of the
western powers in the middle of the nineteenth century, the pulse

of progress quickened. The last of the *shoguns* was ousted, the Emperor restored and a Constitution promulgated, and a unified Japan embarked on a feverish programme of industrialisation. This in turn introduced a new dynamic into society; by the 1920s feudalism was in full retreat and a form of constitutional democracy, at least in embryo, seemed to be emerging.

From this position, the 'dark valley' of militarisation in the 1930s was a disastrous step backwards, a reimposition of feudal values and organisation. When the Americans arrived in 1945, they tended to regard militarisation as the whole story, ignoring or discounting all that had gone before. The SCAP reformers did not initiate democracy in Japan, as sometimes they appeared to believe. Nevertheless, in two crucial respects they greatly stimulated its development.

The Occupation dramatically accelerated the rate of change in Japan, initiating what has been in some ways the most significant period of progress in Japanese history. The trauma of defeat and occupation; the austerity of the immediate post-war years; the impact of SCAP reforms, resuscitating ideas which had temporarily been submerged – all these were spurs to what became known as Japan's 'economic miracle'. In three decades Japan has been transformed into a quintessentially middle-class urbanised nation, with a wide spread of wealth and education and a population which has virtually doubled since the war.

Secondly, and more important, America supplied the framework within which this accelerated change was to take place. Progress in the late nineteenth century occurred within the context of authoritarianism. Guiding Japan's evolution in the latter part of the twentieth century, as both catalyst and blueprint, has been the SCAP Constitution.

Despite the fact that the Japanese people had little to do with its design, the Constitution has survived for forty years almost entirely unaltered. The original meaning of some Articles may have been stretched by the courts – a Japanese legal phenomenon known as *kempo hensen*, 'constitutional transformation' – but there have been no formal amendments. This is not to say that attempts have not been made. But no doubt anticipating a counter-attack, MacArthur and his men employed the skills of trench warfare to safeguard their creation. Their defences against constitutional revision were two-fold: first, the requirement of a two-thirds majority in the Diet before any change could be made – the artillery and mortar barrage, as it were, aimed at breaking up an offensive at long range before it left the trenches; and second, the insistence on a national referendum – the sea of barbed wire and machine-guns enfilade which only the most determined assault would penetrate.

Over the years, a constitutional carapace imposed on the Japanese state from outside has gradually been absorbed, to shape Japanese society from within – shell become skeleton. In the words of Saburo Ienaga, an 'act of transubstantiation' has taken place, whereby the Constitution 'has become the flesh and blood of the Japanese polity', crystallising and consolidating it as a democracy. Political power is no longer the sole prerogative of a single warrior caste, but a weapon in the hands of the people, if they choose to wield it – and even the perennial predominance of the LDP is no real evidence to the contrary.

Without question many of the expedients adopted by the ruling party to keep itself in power are disreputable – jerrymandering, manipulating the media, juggling with electoral boundaries, and so on. And the stalwart backing the LDP receives from big business distorts the political environment. But the fact remains that the party achieved and retains power through the ballot box, not by coercion or force of arms. The fundamental reason for the regime's longevity is the success of its policies for restoring Japan's economy – policies to which none of the opposition parties can offer any attractive alternative.

The LDP has, besides, displayed considerable sensitivity to the wishes of the electorate: when the party's popularity declined steeply in the 1970s, its leaders rapidly reviewed and revised their policies to suit the changing climate. This may signify nothing more than self-interested political agility; but the end result is the same, a government which acts in response to the popular will – as good a working definition of democracy as any. As one commentator has observed, 'It would be an insult to the intelligence and political consciousness of the Japanese people to assume that sheer manipulation and dominance were the primary factors in the continuance of conservative rule.' What is ironic is that America's choice of leadership for Japan – a choice made purely on the basis of America's own global strategic objectives, with little or no consideration for the people of Japan – should have been so heartily endorsed by these same people for so long.

But while the Constitution has entered the life of Japan, so too has Japanese life entered the Constitution. Japan may be a democracy, but she is not a western, specifically an Anglo-American, democracy. She has taken America's gift and refashioned it to meet her own requirements. (There is a parallel here with the approach of many Asians, including thousands of Japanese, to Christianity. It is the ambition of movements like *Mukyokai* – 'Churchless Christianity' – to penetrate to what is universal in Christianity, rejecting dogma and institutions derived from western culture.) Democracy in Japan is centred not on the individual but the group, rooted not in individual but collective self-interest.

The operative group, however, is not the nation as a whole. Homogeneous as the Japanese state may feel itself to be racially, it is far from monolithic. The people of Japan neither identify themselves with their government, nor feel obliged to follow slavishly wherever it leads, and their society is as pluralistic as any other. Schisms, a healthy and natural feature of any democracy, are to be found in all aspects of life.

In the Diet, all shades of political opinion are represented, from extreme left to extreme right. The LDP itself is no integrated unitary power bloc, but an uneasy coalition of rival factions jockeying for advantage. In the economic sector, the giant conglomerates do not have the monopoly on political influence; at the grass roots level, mid- and small-scale enterprises all the way down to the family shop are regarded as almost more important to the LDP in terms of support at the polls, and their special interests must be catered for. Farmers, too, possess disproportionate power as the residents of de-populated electoral districts, and the agricultural lobby has so far been able to ensure that Japanese protectionism is maintained.

Right across the spectrum of religious, ethnic, environmental and regional affairs, more fissures appear. This is no totalitarian structure, and it allows full scope for dissent. Japan is still largely a gerontocracy; great respect is paid to age, and Nakasone was considered a strikingly youthful Prime Minister when he took office at 63. But in a country 40% of whose population is under forty, youth and radicalism have a clearly audible voice.

The reverence for traditional values which so alarms militarophobes is by no means universal. In some notable respects, Japanese youth are rejecting, or have rejected, their parents' philosophy. The surveys for which the Japanese have a passion have indicated, for example, that while the majority of those born before 1937 express respect and affection for the Emperor, the majority of younger people are either indifferent to the institution or positively in favour of abolishing it. The average young/middle-aged Japanese is beginning to break away from the ethic of self-sacrifice which his father felt to be obligatory, if the war was to be won and its ravages repaired; today's citizen is far more interested in staking his claim to a share of Japan's escalating standard of living. Most telling of all, perhaps, the old pattern of family life is disappearing. In a high-cost, high-density urban environment, there is less and less room for the extended family: the institution which was the hothouse for traditional values is being replaced by the western-style nuclear family.

It is in the context of a fragmented society that the significance of right-wing extremism should be assessed. Ultra-nationalism is not the tip of a broad-based iceberg of popular feeling, but simply one voice among many. And though strident, it will never be especially influential as long as the movement continues to lack the two main prerequisites – solidarity and money.

The representatives of the extreme right have always operated as a multitude of small groups, each owing loyalty to its individual *oyabun*. The 750 rightists who tried to break up the annual convention of the Japan Teachers' Union in 1973, for example, came from eighty-two separate groups. (There is a saying, 'Take two Japanese and you have a society.') And though the same *oyabun/kobun* groups crop up in a number of different societies, they have never attempted to pool their resources and form a concerted movement with a single coherent ideology and programme of political action. This is one of the reasons why they lack a mass following – others being, on the one hand, the decline as a class of the rural peasantry which used to provide so many of their supporters and, on the other, their failure to comprehend and promote the material aspirations of the industrial worker.

Even more seriously, perhaps, they have no reliable source of funds. Since the 1920s right-wing groups have been mostly parasitic, influencing events at second hand as the 'out-riders' of politicians or military men – and it is harder now for them to find hosts. In the 1960s rightists developed intimate associations with the underworld, as they had done in the pre-war era, and even if they did not participate in extortion and racketeering, they frequently lived off the proceeds. But in the 1980s many of the younger neo-rightists have foregone even this source of strength. Politically a good deal more radical than their predecessors, they share with the extreme left a contempt for the materialism and corruption of the old right wing.

In the complex of interests represented in this pluralistic society, there is one highly significant gap – a gap which suggests that far from being conspicuously militarised, Japan is actually *less* suspect in this regard than many of her critics. For the one group which could claim to be genuinely under-represented in Japan is the military.

The Japanese defence establishment, if one can call it that, is relatively small and under strict civilian control. Not only are military men prohibited from interfering in civilian policymaking, they are not even permitted to govern their own affairs. The SDF's Commander-in-Chief is the Prime Minister, and front-line commanders need his prior authorisation to act even in the event of a surprise attack. Defence policy – on the size of the armed forces, their weaponry, training and deployment – is formulated by the

Prime Minister and Cabinet, taking advice from a variety of specialist sources of which the Japan Defense Agency is only one and by no means the most powerful. Lacking the status of a full ministry, the JDA finds it hard to compete with such giants as the Ministry of Finance or the Foreign Ministry. And it is in any case itself civilian-controlled: the uniformed officers are heavily outweighed by the civilian bureaucrats, and the Director-General himself must be a civilian, in accordance with a constitutional provision (Article 66) which states that all Ministers of State shall be *'bunmin'* – 'literary persons' or civilians.

Nor is the power of the military greatly enhanced – as it is in many western countries – by connections with industry and big business. It is true that in so far as the *zaikai* or business community backs the LDP and the LDP has always backed the SDF, one can speak of general business support for rearmament. In addition, within the *zaikai* there are specific pressure groups for the Japanese armaments industry – most notably the Defense Production Committee which advises the *Keidanren*/Federation of Economic Organisations on defence and rearmament. (This has traditionally been dominated by Mitsubishi Heavy Industries.)

But until now the business community has seemed content to press for a modest though consistent increase in Japan's armed forces, and for a higher proportion of their weaponry to be produced at home. Holding business back from any more urgent demands is the fact that as yet there is relatively little money at stake.

If Japan were to approach arms production as she has approached the production of cars, her merchandise would doubtless be cheaper, more plentiful and more reliable than that of her competitors, profits would be huge, and the manufacturers would have an incentive to press for rapid expansion of the industry. But at present production is severely limited by restrictions on arms exports. These stem not from the Constitution, but from three 'principles' enunciated in 1967 by Prime Minister Sato – no sales to Communist countries; no sales to countries banned by United Nations resolution; no sales to countries at war, or liable to be at war. (Japan has repeatedly refused requests for arms from both Iran and Iraq.) In 1976 Prime Minister Takeo Miki extended the ban to block virtually all potential markets, partly perhaps in response to strong domestic criticism of Japan's role in supplying such commodities as napalm for use in Vietnam.

There is a good deal of evasion of the restrictions – straightforward smuggling (rifles for the Thai police labelled 'hunting equipment', Japanese-made American Armalite rifles turning up in Belfast), and the use of proxies or joint ventures. And the supply of arms to the United States is a notorious 'grey area'. Procurement orders are not subject to MITI approval in the ordinary way, and the outflow appears to be increasing, violating the spirit if not the letter of Sato's three 'principles'. (The Americans may not be at war, but there is no guarantee that the arms they order will not be passed on to countries which are.) An American subsidiary of Hitachi was recently discovered to be making a type of magnet which is at the core of a laserbeam generator being developed at Los Alamos for the Strategic Defense Initiative programme. And a formal Japanese/American 'technology transfer' programme was confirmed in November 1983.

Nevertheless, the ban on arms exports is generally effective, and as long as it remains in force, it is probably premature to talk of a significant 'military-industrial complex' in Japan. Japanese science and technology are still primarily developed as servants of industry rather than the defence establishment; and there is little sign as yet of the alliance and mutual backscratching of soldier, industrialist, research and development technocrat, and bureaucrat which many consider to be the single greatest threat to civilianism, and detect at its most potent in the United States.

*   *   *

Buried in the 1945 OSS survey of factors which might prevent America from achieving her objectives in Japan was the question, 'Does the creation of a political and social democracy limit the ability of the United States to utilize other means at its disposal?' If the 'other means' included the capacity to direct Japanese policy against the wishes of the Japanese people, the answer has to be 'yes'. In making Japan a democracy, the United States made the will of the Japanese people paramount – and the will of the Japanese people, generally speaking, is firmly against military escalation.

The peace movement in Japan, like Japanese society itself, has many facets. It encompasses political, religious and philosophical attitudes, all merging and blending with other currents in Japanese life. Unarmed neutrality is a principal plank in the political platform of at least one opposition party. Buddhist organisations like the ten-million-member Soka Gakkai (which has strong political representation in the Diet, in the form of the Komeito or 'Clean Government' party) are pacifist on religious grounds. From the sociological perspective, a posture of conciliation rather than confrontation is what comes most naturally to a group society – provided that the society is not under threat.

Overlaying all these elements and binding the peace movement together is a powerful emotional resistance to the threat of war, and to anything which might bring that threat closer. The resistance does not spring simply from the memory of millions of Japanese killed in action overseas or by air raids at home, the devastation of almost all Japan's cities, the years of humiliation and poverty which followed defeat: other nations suffered similarly without reacting in the same way. Japanese pacifism has behind it the unique stimulus of the atomic holocausts at Hiroshima and Nagasaki. An experience which no other nation has shared has produced an emotional revulsion against war in general, and nuclear war in particular, which no other nation can quite equal. With well over 350,000 people still entitled to special medical care for the after-effects of atomic bombing, Japan's 'nuclear allergy' leaves the public generally deaf to arguments of national pride and strategic necessity.

In the late 1970s there appeared the omnibus edition of a remarkable 'comic' strip entitled *Barefoot Gen* – a cartoon version of the bombing of Hiroshima and its aftermath by Keiji Nakazawa. He was seven when the bomb fell on Hiroshima where he lived with his family, and the story of *Gen*, centred round a child *hibakusha* or atom bomb survivor, is semi-autobiographical. Gen's father and brother are crushed and burned to death in their pulverised house and his mother dies a protracted death by radiation sickness, after which Gen is left to fend for himself in the contaminated wilderness. The story, and the way in which it is told, is peculiarly horrible: the cartoon frames are filled with burned and melting flesh, corpses decomposing and riddled with maggots, severed limbs, eyes pierced by glass splinters, omnipresent diseases, filth and stench. Its impact is the greater in that *Barefoot Gen* is not a political tract. Nakazawa is equally fierce in his condemnation of evils on the Japanese side which precipitated the war: the fact of the bomb, not the nation which dropped it, is the object of repugnance.

What is extraordinary and pertinent is that *Gen* was originally serialised from 1965 onwards in Japan's largest weekly children's comic. It is perhaps not surprising that in 1985 the poll conducted annually by *Asahi* on or near the anniversary of Hiroshima revealed that more people find themselves unable to forget the atomic bombings than in 1975. From this perspective one might say that *Thin Man* and the *Enola Gay* did more in a single day to demilitarise Japan than SCAP achieved in seven years of laborious pacification and democratisation.

In practical terms, the 'allergy' is expressed in the 'three non-nuclear principles' devised, like the ban on arms exports, by Eisaku Sato in 1967, and broadly upheld by succeeding LDP administrations ever since. Sato declared that in future Japan would not possess nuclear weapons, would not manufacture them, and would not permit their introduction into the country.

The government's attitude to these pledges, however, has been rather more flexible than that of the general public. It seems to many that if Japan wishes to shelter under America's nuclear umbrella, she cannot reasonably deny the Americans possession in Japan of the weapons on which the umbrella's weather-worthiness depends. (She already tolerates the use of American installations in Japan to control nuclear submarines in the surrounding waters, and to collect information essential to American nuclear strategy elsewhere in the region.) The solution has been to turn a blind eye while the Americans have repeatedly and more or less openly flouted the 'no introduction' provision. No less a source than the U.S. Navy Department's Dictionary of American Naval Fighting Ships reveals that vessels carrying nuclear warheads have been calling at Yokosuka regularly since 1959.

The breach of the rules, and the Japanese government's collusion in it, were first pointed out in America in 1974, and reiterated very publicly indeed in 1981 by Edwin Reischauer, former U.S. Ambassador to Tokyo. Although Japan might not permit the storage of nuclear weapons within American bases, he argued, she unquestionably sanctions port-calls by nuclear-armed warships and the transit of nuclear weapons through her territorial waters and air space. (Reischauer went on to allege that this arrangement is the outcome of a secret verbal agreement made in the 1950s. This the Japanese authorities angrily denied, but it is claimed that on February 26, 1958, in the midst of American/Japanese negotiations over the first renewal of the Security Treaty, the Commander of the U.S. Navy in the Pacific suggested to the American Joint Chiefs of Staff that permission to bring nuclear weapons into Japan be added as a secret 'unpublished annex' to the revised treaty.)

Reischauer's disclosures alerted public opinion, but failed to bring the government out into the open: here, as on so many other subjects, it seems wisest to the Japanese politicians to evade the issue. In the late 1950s Prime Minister Kishi extracted the promise that America would not attempt to make 'major changes' in the deployment or armament of U.S. forces in Japan – and the entry of nuclear weapons would patently be a 'major change' – without 'prior consultation' with the Japanese government. The current Japanese line is that if prior consultation has not taken place, neither has the introduction of nuclear weapons. It is American policy neither to confirm nor deny that a vessel is carrying nuclear weapons – and Japanese policy never to press the question. But what the government has never done is explicitly repudiate this or any other of the three principles – which, after all, do not even have the force of law.

Opposition to rearmament based on war memories and the emotional fallout of the atomic bombings would scarcely have survived through decades of change were it not for the one great, even unique strength that the Japanese peace movement possesses. It has a focus – and one which *does* have the force of law. Few other pacifists can point to their country's constitution as the sanction for their beliefs. And Article 9 presents a sterner challenge to the government than the non-nuclear principles, because it raises a problem that is more serious and harder to ignore than the occasional passage of American nuclear weapons through Japanese territory – that is to say, the incompatibility of the existence of the SDF with the basic law of Japan. The underlying meaning of Article 9 has never been seriously in doubt since MacArthur drafted his original version in which Japan renounced war 'as an instrumentality for settling its disputes and even for preserving its own security'. The intention of Article 9 as written by MacArthur, defended by Yoshida in the Diet, and accepted by the Japanese people was that Japan should never maintain a standing army. This was acknowledged at the time even by the U.S. War Department's Planning and Operations Division, whose most earnest desire it was that Japan *should* rearm. 'Legalistically it might be argued that the Constitution does not prohibit defensive armed forces. However, its preamble and the Occupation directives to date [April 1948] make it clear that the intention of the Constitution is to renounce war without qualification, to prohibit armed forces, and to rest the security of Japan in faith in the peaceloving peoples of the world.'

The 'legalistic argument' mentioned here is obviously the Ashida amendment – which in fact legal experts too tend to dismiss as a dishonest quibble. Even Yukio Mishima, who might have been expected to take advantage of any loophole allowing Japan to rearm, scorned to stoop that low. It was, he said, 'patently clear that under the theory of law, the Self-Defense Forces are unconstitutional, and defense, the nation's basic problem, continues to be evaded by *opportunistic legal interpretation*.'*

In theory, of course, the conflict between Article 9 and the existence of the SDF could readily be resolved. One way would

---

* This was, from the start, the opinion of the Japanese people, according even to Yoshida, who described the general reaction in 1954 as being quite simply that the passing of the SDF Law 'involved something illegal and unconstitutional, which was given a specious pretext for existence by laws enacted by a reactionary Government'.

be to revise the Constitution to make the SDF legal – in other words, to get rid of Article 9. This has been a plank in the LDP platform since the party's foundation in 1955. In that year a law was passed setting up a Commission on the Constitution to report on its origins and interpretation: if it was found to be an alien imposition, working contrary to the true interests of the Japanese people, it was suggested, it should be revised. And Article 9 was the prime candidate for 'reconsideration', though there were factions who, with visions of another Imperial restoration in mind, cherished dark designs against the principle of popular sovereignty and the provisions championing individual rights at the expense of traditional family bonds. (It is interesting, though not necessarily significant, that the chairman of the Commission was Kenzo Takayanagi, one of the leading defence attorneys at the IMTFE, and its members also included Ichiro Kiyose, who had made such notable efforts on Tojo's behalf.)

The Socialists, fearing that the alteration of even one Article might open the way to a wholesale scrapping of the Constitution, including the much-valued 'Bill of Rights', boycotted the Commission, leaving the floor to the conservatives. But the Commission's deliberations lasted seven years; and even though the majority concluded that the Constitution *had* been imposed by SCAP and was in no way authentically Japanese, by now the LDP had lost the majority in the Diet it needed for constitutional change. The revision movement lingered on under the leadership of Nobusuke Kishi, who had after all been imprisoned as a war criminal by the same 'aliens' who had imposed the Constitution: in 1981, though no longer in active politics, he headed the LDP Diet Members League for Formulation of an Independent Constitution, canvassing grass roots opinion in favour of a referendum. But the problem remains the same: Article 9 is taken as a test case for the durability of the Constitution as a whole, and too much else is at stake.

The alternative is to preserve the integrity of the Constitution by getting rid of the SDF – and this too has been tried. Since 1946 the Supreme Court has possessed the power to review legislation to ensure that it is consistent with the Constitution. The opponents of the SDF are convinced that the Self-Defense Forces Law and the Japanese Defense Agency Law are *not* consistent, and that if the Supreme Court could be persuaded to exercise its power of judicial review, it would have no alternative but to declare the existence of the armed forces unlawful. Repeated attempts have been made to provoke it into doing so.

There was some success in 1959 when the Tokyo District Court ruled the Security Treaty unconstitutional, and in 1973 the Sapporo District Court got as far as ruling that the SDF Law was unconstitutional. But in both cases higher courts subsequently overruled the decisions, on the grounds that the issues involved did not fall within the scope of judicial review. They were, it was claimed, essentially political issues, and it is for the legislative and executive and not the judiciary to determine political policy. The judiciary, it was argued, has power to review only those laws which are *obviously* unconstitutional – and the government at least claims that there are two sides to the argument over the SDF. (To many this argument seems to impose restrictions on the independence of the judiciary that were not intended by the drafters of the new Constitution. Article 9 clearly grants the court's authority to review legislation, and to deny this authority is to limit the judiciary's capacity to protect the people's constitutional rights against an authoritarian regime.)

The real issue is the government's extreme anxiety, apparently shared by the Supreme Court, to avoid any public pronouncement on the constitutionality of the armed forces. To declare them constitutional would undoubtedly provoke demonstrations, probably violent, by radical elements in the peace movement; to declare them *un*constitutional would set in train the machinery for revision of the Constitution, including a popular referendum, which could equally lead to civil disorder. Better by far, from the government's point of view, to leave the question hanging and the SDF's status uncertain.

Many western countries – perhaps the United States in particular – would find this situation unacceptable, and would want every ambiguity made plain, every conflict brought into the open and resolved one way or the other. But this is another instance where one detects a Japanese ghost in the Western democratic machine, complicating its workings. In Japan where harmony has the highest priority, divisions are to be minimised not emphasised, and attempts at evasion and deceit are accepted as inseparable from politics. Long is the West likely 'to be amazed at the Japanese tolerance for contradictory and even ludicrous explanation and meaning given by authorities to daily social patterns'.

There is, besides, the fact that what the Japanese people themselves want is contradictory. A majority wants to keep Article 9: emotionally the cost of relinquishing it would be excessive, since it seems to hold out hopes for peace, however fragile, which no nation would lightly abandon. But a majority – fluctuating along with the current perception of the Soviet threat – also wants to keep the SDF: again, the emotional price of dispensing with the country's sole defences, whatever their weaknesses, would be high. By taking full advantage of this inconsistency, the government is able to maintain the *status quo*.

The dilemma has so far been resolved by a working compromise.

Between 1976 and January 1987 a sop was offered to the public conscience in the form of a ceiling of one per cent of Gross National Product imposed on the defence budget. This, like the non-nuclear principles and the arms export ban, was an extra-constitutional measure, its purpose to reconcile the Japanese people to rearmament. Given Japan's huge GNP, even this tiny proportion represented heavy expenditure on arms – well over 16 billion dollars in 1986, some three times as much as the defence budget of South Korea, the next highest spender in the Far East. But psychologically the one per cent limit was soothing.

The one per cent ceiling became something of a political fetish, and Prime Ministers were forced to some dubious expedients to avoid breaching it. At the best of times, the defence budget was, and will presumably continue to be calculated by slightly questionable means. (It includes, for example, compensation paid for the physical and environmental damage caused by American bases in Japan, but excludes overseas development aid with manifest defence implications, and even the pensions of retired regular army officers and men. The Nakasone administration added to the distortion by deferring payment for weapons already ordered; adopting a different method of calculating GNP (a larger GNP obviously means a larger defence budget); and, in 1985, postponing the retirement age for members of the SDF, delaying the evil moment for paying lump-sum separation allowances to over six thousand retiring soldiers. All to no avail, for to meet the Mid-Term Defense Program (Financial Year 1986–1990) issued in September 1985, expenditure of 1.04% GNP was officially admitted to be required.

The failure of the artifice has forced the government formally to abandon the one per cent ceiling. The new compromise offered, for which the government 'earnestly seeks the understanding and co-operation of the Japanese people', is to adopt 'a new yardstick for the ceiling', replacing percentage with specified amount. For the remainder of the Mid-Term Defense Program the annual defence budget is to be 'held within the framework' of approximately 18.4 trillion yen, as proof that Japan remains committed to the 'exclusively defensive posture' which her leaders have been proclaiming since the Ashida amendment in 1946. This solution should be the more palatable since, as the government points out, this sum should be roughly equivalent to – one per cent GNP.

*   *   *

This is the context in which one should assess the strength and significance of the SDF. The average Japanese civilian fears nothing more than military involvement; the government holds defence spending well below what the patriot considers the level befitting a sovereign state; the very existence of a standing army is questioned at law. In these circumstances it is hardly surprising that Japan's modern armed forces resemble hardly at all the Imperial Japanese Army in its heyday.

The most obvious difference lies in the fighting spirit of the two armies. Old soldiers complain of the 'employee' mentality of the new force; the defence of the nation has become a service rendered for money, a nine-to-five job involving no more intense ideological commitment (and carrying considerably less prestige) than computer programming or electrical engineering. Many recruits join, in fact, to acquire precisely such skills as engineering, vehicle maintenance and man-management, with an eye to their return to civilian life. The regular term of service is short – two years for the Ground SDF, three for the Air and Maritime SDF – and less than fifty per cent of recruits join up for a second term. Many of the most promising are lured away even before the expiry of their first term by offers from private industry; the casualty rate was so high in the early 1970s that the JDA was forced to issue an informal warning to the *zaikai*, with veiled threats to withdraw defence contracts from firms found guilty of repeated poaching.

Japan's armed forces are not as isolated from the civilian community as they are in the West, but often live in ordinary residential areas, and are encouraged to mix socially rather than gravitating towards service clubs and associations. Under the Constitution, Japan, unlike virtually every other developed nation, is allowed no separate military legal authority; soldiers committing crimes are tried in the ordinary civil courts. This the hardliners consider detrimental to discipline – which is in any case harder to maintain among a force composed entirely of volunteers. In the new democratic Japan, anything that smacks of mindless regimentation is anathema, and the casual brutality of officers and NCOs to men is no longer commonplace – though this was a lesson it perhaps took longer to learn. (In February 1957 two members of the SDF died after what the press chose to describe as the 'Hiroshima Death March'. This was a regular training exercise, in the form of an inter-regimental contest, whose centrepiece was a 24-hour forced march, the stragglers helped along by their officers in traditional style with bamboo canes.)

The code of behaviour imposed on the contemporary serviceman is tame, practically ornamental in comparison with the demands made in the Imperial army, where 'fighting spirit' – a suicidal commitment to battle – was seen as the answer to superior force and arms. Today no more is required than the minimum subscribed to by armies all over the world. The watchwords the

SDF are offered are in essence those to be found inscribed on the granite benches overlooking the Hudson River at West Point – 'Honour', 'Obedience', 'Duty', 'Patriotism'.

In the shadow of Article 9, *esprit de corps* cannot thrive. The members of the SDF are denied any expression of pride in themselves, discouraged from distinguishing themselves in any way which might draw attention to their dubious legal status. During the war, soldier and civilian were one in the sense that the civilian was required to live up to standards of loyalty and self-sacrifice set by the soldier. Today they are one because the army is civilianised – in the words of one American warrior, 'stuffed full of all that democracy crap'.

Not unnaturally the change – many would say the decline – in the Japanese military ethos has affected morale within the SDF, and would appear too to have discouraged recruitment. As a profession, soldiering has enjoyed consistently low prestige since the war. A poll conducted in 1958 revealed that high school seniors ranked the soldier nineteenth on a scale of twenty-three in terms of social status (above farmer, carpenter and clerk) and twenty-second in terms of social necessity, with only the political boss considered less useful; and attitudes have not altered dramatically since then. Only recently have SDF officers felt at ease wearing their uniforms in the streets of Tokyo. Many teachers actively discourage their pupils from volunteering for the forces – some forbid the SDF to put up recruiting posters in their schools – and a certain number of universities have refused to accept SDF members on their extension courses.

In consequence, the SDF have consistently fallen short not simply of the 350,000-man level optimistically set by John Foster Dulles, but even of their authorised force levels of 180,000 for GSDF and 46,000 each for MSDF and ASDF. They are not quite reduced to accepting anyone and everyone who applies: automatically ineligible are ex-convicts, those judged mentally incompetent, and members of the Japanese Communist Party. But they have had to make the physical requirements for entry less stringent than they would like. In the mid-1970s there was, for instance, no absolute ban on soldiers who were colour-blind; and a considerable proportion of SDF members are older than is ideal. The JDA has said it feels the highest useful age for a soldier to be 45; but the average rifle squad of twenty men has four or five in their fifties, and in 1985 the retirement age was raised to 53.

Part of the problem, of course, is the pay. On their present budget, the SDF can hardly compete with industry in the wages they offer; and the national employment rate is high enough at present for the average Japanese to be free to choose. The govern-

ment does not actually want a huge standing army: camps of uniformed men are by far the most conspicuous evidence of a military
presence, prompting people to reflect upon the status of Article 9,
and 'personnel costs' are already the most expensive single item in
the defence budget. But without substantial regular forces the JDA
is left with the problem of how to meet an emergency.

At present the SDF are suspiciously top-heavy, with a disproportionately high ratio of officers and NCOs to men. It has
often been claimed that this is part of a deliberate strategy – that it is
the existence of a cadre of trained leaders which is crucial, and that
the lower ranks could be expanded rapidly in a crisis. But no one
has yet offered a satisfactory suggestion as to exactly how this
expansion is to be achieved. No emergency mobilisation procedure
is known to exist. All three services possess reserves, but they
receive less than a week's training in a year, and are in any case not
large enough to be in themselves an answer to the problem. To
propose conscription, even on a limited basis, would still be
electoral suicide for any government: it is, besides, against Article
18 of the Constitution which states, 'No person shall be held in
bondage of any kind. Involuntary servitude, except as punishment
for crime, is prohibited.' For all these reasons the SDF must try at
least to maintain recruitment levels, regardless of the cost.

The one per cent ceiling has also restricted the firepower of the
Japanese armed forces. True, the SDF already possess some highly
sophisticated weapons and have plans to acquire more. But,
equally undeniable, for the last ten years they have consistently
fallen short of these plans. The five-yearly 'mid-term defense programs', setting out what is needed if the guidelines projected in the
1976 National Defense Program Outline are to be achieved, have
no binding force, and are becoming little more than ideal shopping
lists, sops to the Pentagon. In effect, the final say in defence policy
has passed to the Finance Ministry.

As things stand, the SDF lack strength in depth. Much of their
existing equipment is out of date; in 1980 almost three-quarters of
the GSDF's tanks, for example, were twenty years old. New purchases are often incomplete: in 1983 the SDF bought their first two
E-2C early warning aircraft without spare parts, for lack of funds,
and the P-3C Orion anti-submarine aircraft was introduced without ground stations capable of analysing the type of signal it emits.
(The SDF are dependent to a remarkable degree on the ordinary
civilian telecommunications system (NTT) for their station-based
communications, having no network of their own.)

The JDA has often been accused of spending a disproportionate
amount of the money that is available on flashy frontline equipment inadequately maintained by logistical support, giving the

SDF style but no staying power. In June 1984 the U.S. Defense Department reported to Congress, that the stockpiles of ammunition called for under Japan's existing programmes would last less than thirty days. (The Mid Term Defense Program 1986–1990 has taken some steps to remedy this imbalance, allocating only twenty-five per cent of future budgets to 'frontal equipment' and far more than before to 'sustainability'.) There is also the problem of finding opportunities to test modern equipment and train with it; these are limited by a shortage of sites in over-crowded Japan, the necessity to conserve fuel, and the opposition of environmentalists. And finally there is the stipulation that Japan shall not possess weapons which have an offensive capability – no inter-continental ballistic missiles, for example, no aircraft carriers, no powerful long-range bombers. Very often the SDF are prevented from buying the best available defence tool simply because it can also be used in attack.

The end result is an armed force whose effectiveness is in doubt and whose precise function is unclear. The SDF are unquestionably powerful enough to deter, and probably to repress, internal disorder; but most previous administrations have felt that it would be political suicide to use them in earnest against Japan's own citizens. And it is beyond hope that they could defend Japan successfully against significant external attack.

The incessant violations of Japanese air space by Russian combat aircraft – approximately 900 a year, almost three a day, since 1981 – suggest that the Soviet Union for one considers Japanese air defences a joke. (The Soviet pilots frequently wave nonchalantly at their Japanese opposition as they are seen off.) Nor are war games any more reassuring. In 1975 one Japanese military analyst estimated that without American aid the Ground SDF might hold off a Soviet invasion for a week; the Maritime SDF might endure for a few days; and the Air SDF would last ten minutes. In 1985 a computer analysis based on the current actual strength of the SDF credited Japan with three days' overall resistance.

*   *   *

Given the central importance of the U.S./Japan relationship, it is easy to assume – as America often seems to do – that only these two nations are involved in the debate over Japanese rearmament. Japan needs and values the United States above any other single nation. Over the last four decades, America has been guide, sponsor, protector and cultural influence, and if the rearmament debate were simply a matter of face-to-face confrontation between America and the Japanese peace movement, Article 9 would indeed have been a remarkable creation to have survived.

But the truth is more complex. The peace provision is buttressed by forces beyond Japan's shores which have served both to counter American pressure and to limit the degree of rearmament to which even the most outspoken of Japan's hawks aspire. The international environment which before the war propelled Japan irresistibly towards arms and empire now equally inexorably holds her in check.

Broadly speaking, opposition to America's ambitions for Japan has come since the war from three sources – from the non-Communist states of the East Asian region, from the People's Republic of China, and from the Soviet Union. There have been marked variations in the motives, methods and effectiveness of their opposition, but cumulatively they have provided a strong countercurrent to the rearmament dynamic.

Amongst Japan's non-Communist neighbours resistance to her rearmament is more or less instinctive, a natural legacy of the years of colonisation, exploitation and indiscriminate brutality which almost all suffered during the Pacific War. And past resentments are reinforced by the nagging suspicion that Japan, once again the region's predominant economic power, is currently attempting to recreate the Greater East Asia Co-Prosperity Sphere, sucking her poorer neighbours dry to satisfy her own insatiable needs, and offering nothing in return. Japan's impact on the Asian economy, they claim, is that of the warship which, docking in a small port, swamps the sampans around it. Hostility in the region is barely concealed, and every so often it erupts into public demonstrations and official protests against Japan's 'economic imperialism', her restrictive trade practices and the arrogant behaviour of her businessmen abroad.

The ubiquity of anti-Japanese feeling works against escalated rearmament in various ways. General consciousness of Japanese war guilt – which from time to time the Japanese themselves have perfunctorily acknowledged – gives countries like the Philippines a degree of leverage which otherwise they would not have. More significant, in the prevailing climate the likeliest response to a rapid acceleration in Japan's rearmament would be a general arms build-up in the region. Any chain reaction of military escalation would destabilise the region to a hazardous degree. The alarmists who predict Japanese territorial expansion fail to acknowledge that she is no longer surrounded by a handful of disorganised, disunited, underdeveloped colonies, but by emergent nation-states strengthened by alliances among themselves and with the superpowers (Thailand and South Korea with America, Vietnam with Russia, North Korea with Russia and China, and so on).

A third restraint more powerful than either guilt or fear is economic necessity. Japan's 'economic miracle' has been heavily export-led. To sustain her export trade she relies on other nations as much as she has ever done for her raw materials and much of her fuel, and for markets for her goods. In a situation of such vulnerability she can afford few if any enemies.

The Japanese, it seems, have concluded that they are best advised to leave power politics to the new *samurai* nations, America and the Soviet Union, and accept their own role as the paradigm of a merchant nation. Shunning *sopu nashonarisumu*, or emotional soap-opera nationalism, they have chosen to adopt an 'omni-directional' foreign policy calculated to offend no one and enable Japan to trade comfortably with everyone. They abhor confrontation, favour equivocation and conciliation, and admit responsibility to no ideology but their own self-interest – *mai homu gaiko*, 'my-home-ism'. (The Japanese response, for example, to anti-Japanese riots and threatened trade boycotts in Bangkok and Jakarta in the early 1970s was a public apology and a generous package of concessions.)

The collapse of the Japanese Empire did very little to change Japan's perception of the role of her South East Asian neighbours, and her efforts to bind the regional economy together again began – with every encouragement from America – in the late 1940s. During the 1950s Japan stimulated trade by paying voluntary reparations of over 1.5 billion dollars to Burma, the Philippines, Indonesia and South Vietnam, and pledged a further 500 million dollars' worth of economic assistance to South Korea. Since then she has given direct aid to all these countries, plus Malaysia and Thailand, as well as establishing joint ventures and other types of investment.

The notion of 'Pacific Basin Co-operation' has been energetically canvassed – and Japan's efforts have not gone unrewarded. The Asian Pacific region (Australia included) provides raw materials, fuel, cheap labour, outlets for finished products, and access to third-party markets. It now accounts for thirty per cent of Japan's total trade, and is a market which is likely to become increasingly important in the future in the face of European and American protectionism.

Japan would be most unlikely to prejudice this happy state of affairs by increasing her military strength at a rate and to a level which her neighbours might consider excessive. Sensitivity to South East Asian opinion does much to explain, for example, her anxiety to avoid any move which might be construed as sending troops overseas. Many have questioned the propriety of Japanese participation in joint RIMPAC (or Rim of the Pacific) exercises. These are claimed to be purely for training purposes; but in recent years they have expanded to involve countries such as Britain and Australia, and now more closely resemble NATO exercises, which have both a defensive and an offensive function. The question of the 1000-mile radius for defence of the sea lanes is equally ticklish, with every nation in South East Asia on the alert for Japanese violation of its territorial waters.

In contrast with the unremitting suspicion of the non-Communist countries, China's attitude to Japan's military posture has fluctuated along with the rest of her foreign policy, volatile and unpredictable, in the years since the communist revolution of 1949. The era of Mao Tse-tung was characterised, as far as Japan was concerned, by vicious invective and by anti-Japanese mass demonstrations in Peking. The party leadership seized on even the joint communiqué issued from Shanghai at the end of President Nixon's historic visit in 1972 as an excuse to damn Japan in the eyes of the world. The People's Republic of China, it announced, 'firmly opposes the revival and outward expansion of Japanese militarism and firmly supports the Japanese people's desire to build an independent, democratic, peaceful and neutral Japan'.

The next decade, however, was an era of rapprochement. Going beyond the U.S., Japan formally recognised the People's Republic in 1972. By 1978 America was normalising relations with China, and the way was clear for a Treaty of Peace and Friendship between Japan and the PRC. To Japan's businessmen, China offered a market of one billion people, and virtually inexhaustible natural resources. Channels of private trade had been open, discreetly, since 1952; but in the ten years following formal recognition, bilateral trade multiplied almost ten-fold, making Japan the PRC's single largest trading partner.

Entente with America meant estrangement from Russia for the People's Republic: the 1978 Treaty of Peace and Friendship with Japan included a mutual pledge to resist 'hegemonism' – China's code word for the Soviet threat. By the beginning of the 1980s the possibility of a U.S./China/Japan military bloc seemed to be drawing closer. Surveys showed that Japanese public opinion increasingly favoured a strategic alliance of this kind; and for their part the Chinese announced that they were prepared to tolerate an increase in Japanese defence spending to two per cent GNP.

More recently, however, in the later years of Deng Xiao-ping's rule, the euphoria has evaporated on both sides. China has always faced considerable difficulties in her modernisation programme, and the so-called 'adjustment' policy of 1981 led to the cancellation or postponement of a good many export contracts; the China trade has generally been less immediately profitable than Japan had hoped. And for a variety of reasons Deng now favours a more even-handed policy towards the Soviet Union on the one side and America and her allies on the other. The build-up of Soviet troops on the PRC's northern borders continues; and, more positively, the Soviet Union has a great deal to offer at this stage of China's economic development. (It is one country, for instance, with which China can trade extensively by barter, freeing valuable foreign currency for dealings with the West.)

Deng's shifting perspective has resulted in a frostier, less sanguine Chinese attitude to the prospect of Japanese remilitarisation. It was protests from Peking, for example, which compelled Nakasone to cancel his proposed visit to Yasukuni in 1986. China's voice will continue to be loud and influential in the rearmament debate. She is, after all, a nuclear power, with the world's largest standing army. Almost more important, she is now an integral and permanent feature of Japan's economic perspective. Despite past disappointments, no one questions the PRC's long-term potential for absorbing growth in the Japanese economy, and she remains a useful hedge against protectionism elsewhere. Above all, Japan is wary of taking any action which might force China back into the arms of the Soviet Union.

The Soviet Union is, of course, the most interesting and potentially most significant factor in the rearmament equation. Ever since the completion of the Trans-Siberian Railway in the nineteenth century under the Tsars, the story of Russo-Japanese relations has been one of almost unrelieved hostility. Bitter competition for Korea and tracts of Manchuria and Mongolia found its first formal expression in the Russo-Japanese War of 1904/5, continued through a series of border clashes in the 1930s, and ended with the Pacific War and the Soviets arrayed along the 38th Parallel.

Once America had asserted control over Japan, however, Russia's goals altered. The objective was now, at the very least, Japanese neutrality, preferably unarmed, with a kind of 'Finlandisation' as the ideal. Since 1945, as Japan has remained firmly attached to America, the Soviet Union has both protested at every indication of Japanese rearmament and, latterly, made its own military presence in the region strongly felt.

On the face of it, the Soviet threat is what Japanese rearmament is all about – the hawks' principal and often-repeated justification. Certainly America takes this line, and from time to time the Japanese seem to be fully in accord, indulging in sabre-rattling of their own. But in reality a strong countercurrent runs beneath the surface, carrying with it the distinct possibility that the Soviet Union, far from being the main spur to rearmament, may become its most effective curb. As Nakasone pointed out thirty-five years ago in his 'representation' to MacArthur, Japan does not and cannot view the Soviets through America's eyes. Ideologically, strategically, economically, their perspectives are different.

Communism has had a curious history in Japan, appealing to widely disparate groups. It gathered impetus most noticeably during the Occupation years, when poverty and unemployment were rife, and activists long suppressed by the military régime were all at once given total (if shortlived) freedom of operation. There are those who believe that communism, with its orientation towards collectivity, is better suited to Japanese ways of thought than Western democracy will ever be; certainly in the early years of the Occupation it seemed a more marketable product.

Many Communist doctrines had also previously held resonances for the younger and more fanatical of the militarists themselves – the 'young officers' whose socialistic leanings so alarmed conservatives like Konoye and Yoshida. Early in 1945 Konoye went so far as to urge Hirohito to end the war on the grounds that the Imperial Japanese Army might otherwise become the focus for a socialist *coup d'état*. (Whatever evidence Konoye may have had, it died with him. But several incidents in the history of the military's relations with Russia in the 1920s and 1930s do indeed seem enigmatic – certain dealings over railway concessions, for instance, and the abrupt halting of the border war at Nomonhan.)

Whatever the significance of these past encounters with communism, the inescapable fact remains that even today the Japanese simply do not share America's ideological opposition to it. (They had no reservations, for example, in acknowledging and embracing the People's Republic of China, abandoning Taiwan. Their 1972 communiqué stated baldly, 'Taiwan is an inalienable part of the territory of the People's Republic of China', while America's reluctance to go this far has been an important factor in the deterioration of U.S./PRC relations.) Japan's anti-communism is not so much self-generated as derived from association with America; and it is not inconceivable, though still unlikely, that at some time in the future Japan might drift into the Soviet or Chinese orbit.

From the strategic point of view, too, Japan's perceptions of the Soviet Union vary fundamentally from America's – the principal difference being the framework in which the Russian threat is set. For the United States, the frame is the world and the objective a world balance of power. But the Japanese lack any comparable global perspective in strategic terms, and are interested in Russia only as Russia directly affects themselves. For Japan the framework is the East Asian region – and in this limited context, to avoid provoking the Soviet Union by rearming seems by far the most sensible course.

The Soviet Union exerts heavy military pressure on Japan, at closer range than America herself has ever experienced. The rapid Soviet arms build-up in Asia, accompanied by the relative decline of American military strength and China's apparent side-step, has given the Soviet Union a good deal of leverage on Japan. Japan shares with other nations the apprehension of Soviet power in the Middle East, and the threat to trade routes in South East Asia from the Soviet navy now firmly established in American-built facilities in Cam Ranh Bay.

But Japan faces a more immediate menace: it has been known that since the end of the 1970s the Soviet Union has had the capacity to invade Japan. Her effective arsenal includes missile sites in Siberia, and Backfire bombers stationed on the coast opposite the island of Sakhalin; and Vladivostok, the Russian Pacific Fleet's principal base, is only six hundred miles away. Psychologically most significant, the Soviet Union has remanned and fortified her bases in the so-called 'Northern Territories'.

The 'Territories' are four of the most southerly of the Kurile Islands which stretch from the eastern tip of Japan's northernmost island Hokkaido to the Kamchatka peninsula of Siberia. Historically the southernmost Kuriles are Japanese territory, but in 1951 Japan renounced her claim to them under the Peace Treaty with America, unaware that Roosevelt had agreed secretly at Yalta to hand them over to Stalin.* The islands are of key strategic importance to the Soviets, as they command the northern air and sea routes between Japan and the United States and guard one of the Soviet navy's major points of access to the Pacific. Bases were established there almost immediately; during the 1960s and early 1970s they remained largely inoperative, but since 1979 they have been armed with long-range artillery and ground-attack helicopter gunships. And Japan's sense of being in the front line is confirmed by the fact that the nearest base is a mere four-and-a-half miles away from Hokkaido, clearly visible on a fine day.

No longer is it so easy to believe that being an island nation will keep Japan safe from invasion – especially in the face of the kind of threats issued by the Soviet Union in the period when a strategic alliance between America, China and Japan seemed possible. And at the same time strategists fully realise that, short of nuclear weapons, Japan is virtually indefensible from within her own boundaries.

Japan's population and industrial megalopolis are largely concentrated on the eastern seaboard of Honshu island, exceptionally

* Japan subsequently renewed her claim to Iturup, Kunashir, Shikotan and the Habomai Islands, which many people believe do not belong to the Kuriles at all.

vulnerable to air strikes. Her long coastline and lack of strategic depth – at few places in the home islands is one more than 75 miles from the sea – make for easy invasion. The inadequacies of a conventionally-armed SDF as anything more than a 'high-tech' guerrilla force have already been discussed – and Japan is highly unlikely to acquire, or be allowed to acquire, nuclear weapons, whatever the prophets of doom may say. Domestic resistance to such a move is important – but American opposition is critical, and the United States has no desire to encourage nuclear proliferation even among its allies.

In other words, in the last analysis Japan is totally dependent on American defences, conventional or nuclear depending on the type and scope of the menace. It is hard, in any event, to imagine a conflict in which America would not be involved: few believe that the Soviet Union would invade Japan for any reason short of a super-power confrontation. In which case Japan is as safe – or unsafe – with small Self-Defense Forces as she would be with large ones. At present, providing that she maintains the minimum armed strength necessary to satisfy American requirements, she is as well defended as she ever can be. To arm further would be expensive, politically undesirable, diplomatically hazardous, provocative – and ultimately pointless.

Military power is not the only hold the Soviet Union has over Japan. It is simply the stick – and in the past few years the Soviets have simultaneously been making great play with the carrot of economic inducements. Here again the Japanese view is rather different from that of America. The United States prefers its allies to treat economic and strategic issues as necessarily related, and has tried to make this link in its relations with Japan. If Japan wants American military protection, it is claimed, she should open her markets to American products; conversely, if she wants the United States to accept her exports, she should increase the level of her military cooperation. Japan, not surprisingly, would prefer to treat trade and defence strategy as unconnected. This is the line she pursues with the United States, and consequently she feels justified in doing business with North as well as South Korea, Communist as well as Nationalist China.

The Soviet Union is a trading partner of enormous potential significance for Japan. As a supplier of fuel alone it could be crucial: Siberian coal, oil and natural gas could dramatically reduce Japanese dependence on the unreliable energy sources of the Middle East. Soviet satellites like Vietnam and North Korea have already proved to be valuable markets for Japanese goods as well as sources of foodstuffs and raw material. In the Mekong Delta Japanese interests are involved in oil exploration and shrimp cultivation, and Japan is now Vietnam's major supplier of trucks and bicycles.

Following the Soviet invasion of Afghanistan in 1979, the escalation of military activity in the Northern Territories, and the shooting down of Korean airliner KAL 007 with twenty-eight Japanese on board, Japan's trade relationship with the Soviet Union cooled. But in recent years the Russians have devoted considerable energy to fanning it back into life with what they have called their 'peace offensive'. Both sides have been working at the diplomatic level for rapprochement. In March 1985 Nakasone met Soviet leader Mikhail Gorbachev in Moscow at the funeral of previous Premier Anatoli Chernenko; this was the first Russo-Japanese meeting at head of government level for twelve years. The following October Nakasone wrote to Gorbachev asking for the resumption of negotiations on a peace treaty (the dispute over the Northern Territories being the ostensible reason why peace has been so long delayed)*. In the spring of 1987 Premier Gorbachev is to visit Tokyo.

At the strictly practical level, Japan has become ever more deeply involved in the Siberian pipeline project, despite President Reagan's bitterly-resented attempts to interfere. And the Soviets have made some startling concessions, apparently deferring to the Japanese credo 'The customer is king'. Miles of the red tape which has previously entangled foreign investment in the Soviet Union has been cut in order to encourage Japanese entrepreneurs. The Japanese are, for example, already engaged in forest clearance and timber exporting, food processing and machine-tool manufacture, and are busily setting up fast-food chains in Moscow. The potential for joint ventures is practically unlimited, with Japan supplying the technology, machinery and management, Russia the labour, raw materials and markets.

Outwardly Japan manifests continuing suspicion of Soviet ploys. The 'Defense of Japan' White Paper for 1986 identified the Soviet Union as Public Enemy Number One and described the 'peace offensive' as an attempt 'to separate the United States from its allies'. Inwardly, however, the Japanese keenly appreciate the persuasive force of both the stick and the carrot, and all the time the Soviet Union develops its capacity to combat America's wishes for Japanese rearmament.

---

* In 1956 Japan and the USSR signed a 'peace declaration' formally ending the hostilities declared in 1945, but no treaty was concluded.

EPILOGUE

Epilogue

Was Japan ever truly demilitarised? Is she now remilitarised? How significant was, and is, American involvement in Japan's affairs? When we set out to write this book, our aim was to counter the prevailing 'Yellow Peril' paranoia without falling into the opposite trap of post-Vietnam anti-Americanism. The situation has become too serious for anyone to indulge in rhetoric or extremism: a working compromise with Japan is essential.

The balance of the evidence clearly suggests that, far from remilitarising, Japan is fairly effectively demilitarised – partly in consequence of Occupation reforms, partly in response to external pressures, and partly through the will of the majority of the Japanese people themselves. For forty years the United States has been pressing Japan to upgrade her military strength; but though America may have helped to initiate rearmament in the 1940s and 1950s, her efforts to force the pace since then have largely failed. Where defence is concerned, there is a proven credibility gap between what the Japanese government says it is going to do and what it actually does. Even the advent of Nakasone has yet to produce a substantial surge in rearmament. The assurances of cooperation from Tokyo have grown louder and more confident, the complaints from Washington correspondingly less clamorous, but the underlying reality is still a profound concern for a tightly controlled budget and a prevailing creed of caution.

Demonstrably, America's policy towards Japan is sterile. The question is whether it ever was, or ever will be, the wisest approach to adopt. Japan's cooperation with the Western alliance is urgently needed – no one would take issue with America on this score. But are men under arms the most useful contribution she can make?

The arguments in favour of abandoning pressure to rearm and searching for an alternative policy are varied and cogent. The defence issue is a major cause of destructive misunderstanding between Japan and the United States. Nor is compelling Japan to spend more on defence a viable means of slowing down her economic offensive, the other principal source of friction. Many Americans believe that Japan's relative economic success is largely due to the 'free ride'. This may have been true during the critical period of capital accumulation after the war, but today Japan could sustain a defence budget of up to six per cent of GNP without losing more than one or two percentage points on her annual growth rate. The problem lies in America's failure to compete, not Japan's success. Besides, a Japan heavily rearmed would probably also be a Japan ready and willing to *export* arms, challenging American entrepreneurs in yet another field.

In so many respects the course America appears to be advocating for Japan is highly dangerous. Military escalation could well destabilise the Asian region, and it is open provocation to Japan's Communist neighbours. In the view of some observers, a renewed Japanese threat, real or perceived, would be enough to drive China out of alignment with the U.S. and back into the arms of the Soviet Union.

Others go further, and see in current U.S. policy the potential for alienating the Japanese themselves beyond recall. American hardliners have suggested that the best answer to Japanese obstinacy is the *shokku* or 'shock tactic' – the threat, for instance, to withdraw American troops and protection from Japan altogether. This, they imply, would make Japan toe the line. It seems far more probable, however, that such aggressive posturing would precipitate Japan away from the western alliance and into the non-aligned movement amongst countries whose anti-Americanism is running high – or, further still, into the Chinese, even the Soviet orbit. Alternatively, and no more desirably, Japan might finally be encouraged to fulfil the alarmists' worst forebodings and set herself up as an independent nuclear-armed power.

This last resort would surely spell disaster for the Japanese people – and in more senses than one. In encouraging rearmament, America could well be exposing Japan again to all the attendant evils of remilitarisation, from which her society remains peculiarly at risk. A long-established western democracy might be able to accommodate a greatly increased military establishment quite easily – America has had to do precisely this since the Second World War. But arguably a young, unorthodox oriental democracy still in the process of developing would not. In the search for a government which could be relied upon to resist communism, America forfeited or stifled those elements in Japan which in the West have proved to be strong bulwarks of democracy. In entrenching the conservative old guard in authority after the war they effectively endorsed centralisation, the pre-war bureaucracy, the domination of big business, and many of the traditional Japanese values which in the 1930s had provided a fertile seed-bed for militarism. The group ethic survived the impact of 'democratisation' triumphantly, and even today it is hard to predict how a people with a strong natural predisposition to discipline and dependence would react to a strengthened hierarchy and a greater degree of regimentation from above.

One last question remains. Is pushing the Japanese into an arms build-up morally defensible? The charge is not that America has abandoned Article 9; the policymakers cannot be accused of betraying something to which they never wholeheartedly subscribed. The point is that Article 9 exists, whether America regrets it or not, and that the Japanese people, generally speaking, have espoused it with enthusiasm. The Constitution as a whole, once America's 'gift' to Japan, has been absorbed into the fabric of Japanese society. The Americans no longer have any proprietary rights over it; and in inciting the Japanese to violate one of its Articles – for few people bother any longer to argue the constitutionality of Japanese armed forces – America is interfering in the internal affairs of another sovereign state.

President Reagan was once challenged as to why Washington, in its struggle to combat communism, is prepared to support régimes that are corrupt, brutal and dictatorial. He replied, 'What is the alternative?' In Japan an answer may be presenting itself – if the United States is prepared to contemplate an *entente* rather different from its international relationships in the past.

It is true that until the late 1970s all that Japan could realistically contribute to America's global strategy was access to bases and a modest quota of men under arms. But this is no longer the case. Japan is a leading industrialised nation, her potential expanding in virtually every sphere *except* the military. Now is the time for America to recognise what she has to offer and reassess future relations.

Japan is entering a new era in more than just the formal sense that the reign of Hirohito is coming to an end. Economically, she is moving into the post-industrial age – leaving to the newly-industrialising countries of the region (Taiwan, Singapore, South Korea) the basic industries on which her wealth has been built, and looking to a technological future. The 'science city' she has built at Tsukuba is intended to be in the vanguard of the world's research and development, and Japan is staking a great deal on its success, investing heavily in the primary resource of the twenty-first century – knowledge*.

---

* If Tsukuba prospers, it will no longer be possible to argue, as many Japanese do, that the Soviet Union will not invade because Japan has no natural resources of any value.

In other ways, too, the basis of the Japanese economy is changing, pointing to a less vulnerable and politically more potent future. Japan's financial services operation is already a significant source of invisible exports, and her overseas investment is expected to rise from $120 billion in 1985 to $556 billion in 1995, giving her valuable leverage over other countries.

This atmosphere of change seems to have been accompanied by a new readiness to accept international responsibility. For Japan, the relative decline of U.S. strength heralds a revision of the world order. In the new configuration, the burden which for years the United States has appropriated to itself alone will have to be shared by other nations, and Japan can now visualise herself as being among them. In 1980 a high-level study group commissioned by Prime Minister Ohira reported, 'We are living in an age when "Pax Americana" is nearing an end. . . . The days are gone when Japan could count on a system maintained single-handedly by the United States, be it in terms of military security, politics and diplomacy, or the economy. Japan must now contribute to the maintenance and management of the system as an influential member of the free world. There has been a shift from a world of "Pax Americana" to a world of "peace maintained by shared responsibilities"'.

In the late 1980s America is presented with the opportunity to steer Japan towards a new alliance, as once she steered her towards democracy. There would still be ample scope for directing the course of her international relations. Japan has recognised the need for a new force in world affairs without necessarily knowing how to transform herself into such a force. The move away from 'omnidirectionalism' would be momentous, and America's guidance is needed still.

But the new relationship would demand a striking change in America's own attitude. Her role would become that of *partner* rather than unquestioned leader, and she would be committed to collaboration rather than unilateral decision-making. Above all, she would have to accept that Japan's contribution to the partnership need not and should not take the form of men under arms unless Japan herself so determined. Together American *samurai* and Japanese merchant account for almost half the world's GNP, and a genuine partnership would have awesome power if the *samurai* could fully appreciate what the merchant has to offer.

The continued safety of the free world depends not simply on the strength to confront and deter military threats from the Soviet Union or elsewhere, but also on the ability to deny the spread of Soviet influence. The present international currency and free trade system must remain viable; democracies must be defended against economic and political instability, and the Third World rescued from its disastrous downward spiral. In this context Japan's principal contribution might well be to promote political stability through economic aid. In one region the threat to be averted may be chaos and a strategic vacuum, as in Turkey; in another, it will be communism, as in Central America, or in the South Pacific, where the Soviet Union is busy trying to build a presence through fishing and trade deals.

Being encumbered by no perceptible ideological commitment, Japan is often better placed than the United States to intervene in this way. America's hands are tied to some extent over aid to Turkey by a powerful Greek lobby in Congress. And Japan, with a foot in the camp of the non-aligned movement, could play a crucial role in wooing for the West various Third World countries which increasingly show signs of anti-Americanism.

Her *persona* as merchant does not, however, mean that Japan could not offer America 'military' support of any kind, simply that this would take the form not of men under arms but rather the components of high-technology weapons systems, and a willingness to share the fruits of future research and development with military applicability. And the use of bases in Japan's home islands would continue to be of vital strategic importance to the United States.

To some extent Japan is already playing the role we have sketched. She has permitted an increase in U.S. military facilities. She is a major contributor to the International Monetary Fund and the World Bank. Her 'overseas development assistance' has often been deployed before where it will best serve American interests – in the Philippines, to bolster the Marcos regime in the run-up to an 'election'; in Thailand after the North Vietnamese takeover of Kampuchea; in Pakistan after the Soviet invasion of Afghanistan. And America is already reliant on Japanese weapons components and drifting towards greater dependence. She has recently expressed interest in items such as semi-conductor lasers, heat-resistant ceramics, fibre optics, 'artificial intelligence' computers, night-time imaging systems and image-seeking missile guidance systems, many of which have obvious application to the SDI programme. (Indeed, Japanese involvement in SDI could be vital to its success.)

But the blow to national prestige which America would suffer in raising Japan to partnership is not the only price she would have to pay. There would be an emotional barrier to be overcome. America would have to accept the consequences of the Occupation, acknowledge Japan's status as a special case, and agree to bear virtually complete responsibility for her defence, leaving Japan to work out her own destiny for the SDF. This would mean reversing

[311]

the trend, setting aside the sentiments expressed in the Guam Doctrine – and this despite the fact that the bitter experiences of the Korean and Vietnamese wars have only strengthened the belief of many, perhaps most, Americans that Asia should be defended by Asians: in a good cause or not, too many American lives have been sacrificed already.

Against this huge concession – and it should be recognised by both sides as such – would be set Japan's strategically-oriented economic aid, political support, and her technological contribution to western defence. A price tag can readily be pinned to each partner's contribution, and a method of computation might be devised by which to balance the one against the other. If at the end of the day Japan was found still to be enjoying a free, or at least a cheap ride, then she should find a way of making up the difference. The Japanese economy is more than strong enough to support a rise of 300%, 500%, even 700% in the amount devoted to defence spending: the barrier to an increase of this kind has always been political and psychological rather than financial.

If, on the other hand, Japan was discovered to be more than paying her way, then America should recompense her: this is the meaning of partnership – and America may come to consider it money well spent. Sooner or later she must realise that she has little choice. She cannot carry on indefinitely without help – and her allies in the West are fully committed. Only Japan can make a significant new contribution, but this must be of a special kind. For the first time in two millennia the Japanese sword is sheathed, and America must come to terms with that fact.

Sources

Prologue

p. xiii **executions description** FO 371 76250, SCAP Public Information Office Release, Dec. 23, 1948; and an eye-witness account by the US Official Observer – William Sebald with Russell Brines, *With MacArthur in Japan: A Personal History of the Occupation* (Norton, 1965), pp. 172–6. **Himmler of the East** *The Times*, Dec. 23, 1948. **scaffold** hanging was also official mode of execution in pre-war J, substituted for strangulation in 1873 – Paul Heng-Chao Ch'en, *The Formation of the Early Meiji Legal Order; the Japanese Code of 1871 and its Chinese Foundation* (OUP, 1981), p. 40.

p. xv **eighth largest arms budget** Theodore McNelly, 'The Renunciation of War in the Japanese Constitution', in *Armed Forces and Society*, 13/1 Fall 1986, p. 85.

p. xvi **Japanese suffered** for first-hand reports of conditions by Allied civilians imprisoned at outbreak, see PROC/TS26/820. **tools of military masters** raises the wider question of the grounds on which whole populations can be blamed – see P. A. French, 'Morally Blaming Whole Populations' in eds. V. Held, S. Morgenbesser, T. Nagel, *Philosophy, Morality & International Affairs* (OUP, 1974), p. 266ff. **responsible government** USIPSP, reprinted in *PRJ* Vol. II. **American in substance** the British complained of not even being consulted in initial stages – FO 371 46449 F6699, J. C. Sterndale Bennett note,

Sept. 11, 1949; and cf. FO 371 46448 F7037, L. H. Foulds note, Sept. 18, 1945 describing US failure to submit text of MacA's authority to 'the Allied Powers for whom General MacArthur is supposed to be acting' as 'highly objectionable'.

p. xvii **new organisation** for a detailed description of GHQ SCAP, see D. Clayton James, *The Years of MacArthur: Triumph & Disaster 1945–64* (Houghton Mifflin, 1985), pp. 41–58.

p. xviii **Privy Council discussed** Ray A. Moore, review of *Senryo shiroku* (ed. J. Eto, Kodansha, 1981–2), in *JJS*, 10/1 Winter 1983.

p. xix **flawed from the outset** for the problems and status of social scientists in the Occ., see generally J. W. Bennett & Iwao Ishino, *Paternalism in the Japanese Economy: Anthropological Studies of Oyabun-Kobun Patterns* (Minnesota UP, 1963), Chaps. 1 & 2. **cut off from the outside world** Robert E. Ward, 'The American Occupation of Japan: Political Retrospect', in ed. Grant Goodman, *The American Occupation of Japan: A Retrospective View* (Kansas UP, 1968). **political surgery** Goodman, op. cit. p. vi. **despite a century of industrialisation** David E. Apter, *The Politics of Modernisation* (Chicago UP, 1967), p. 134. 'The modernising autocracy successfully integrated new roles and traditional ones'. **without the technique** e.g. Robert King Hall, *Shushin: the Ethics of a Defeated Nation* (Columbia, 1949), p. 6, on 'the unanswered question whether or not anyone, through any process of education, can fundamentally change the thinking of another people'; and Robert E. Ward & Frank J. Shulman, *The Allied Occupation of Japan, 1945–52: An Annotated Bibliography of Western-Language Materials* (Chicago, 1974), p. 1907. 'Its operational style was more pragmatic than theoretical in this respect.'

p. xx **accepted mode of organising society** Barrington Moore disputed that the product of the contact between the US and J was necessarily predictable. Dennis Smith, *Barrington Moore: Violence, Morality & Political Change* (Macmillan, 1983), p. 50. **science in its infancy** one must distinguish between the pre-World War II ideological question of whether planners should be permitted to plan the destinies of others, and the actual practice of the science itself, which became widespread only in the 1950s – W. G. Bennis, K. D. Benne, R. Chin, K. E. Corey, *The Planning of Change* (Holt, Rinehart & Winston, 1976), p. 10. **lowly and uninfluential** Bennett/Ishino, op. cit. p. 17. **ignorant of sociology** Bennett/Ishino, pp. 3, 28. **one major field study** John Embree's *Suye Mura*, 1939. See Bennett/Ishino, p. 3. **no-one knew how long** 'Perhaps the most important handicap of the Occupation was its impermanence. . . . It led, on the American side, to an excessive zeal and haste, ramming reforms down Japanese throats in a race against time without regard for Japanese opinion' – Martin Bronfenbrenner, 'The American Occupation of Japan: Economic Retrospect' in Goodman, op. cit. And cf. William P. Woodard, *The Allied Occupation of Japan 1945–52 & Japanese Religions* (E. J. Brill, 1972), p. 10. **the responsible officers** Woodard, op. cit. p. 17. **simple act of faith** Thomas Bisson, *Zaibatsu Dissolution in Japan* (Berkeley, 1954), pp. 39–40. 'A set of assumptions underlay the policy. . . . The most basic of these, perhaps, was that what had worked in the US would work in Japan,

that what was suitable for one was suitable for the other. . . .'

p. xxi **State Department turned** Michael Schaller, *The American Occupation of Japan* (OUP, 1985), p. 84.

p. xxiv **General Charles Willoughby** see Chapter 23 below. **'an honest mistake'** see p. 237 below.

p. xxv **Tojo's Execution file** NAS RG 338 Records of U.S. Army Commands 1942 – Records of the U.S. Eighth Army: Sugamo Prison Records 1945–52, Box 142 – 'Tojo, Hideki'. MacA had said that photographers at the executions 'would violate all sense of decency'. **the whole spectrum** Joseph Sykes, letter to the authors, Sept. 4, 1985. **would-be Marco Polos** Sykes, op. cit. **Civil Service drunks** Sykes, op. cit. **MacArthur's minions** NAW PPS Records, Box 19, Kennan/George Butterworth, Mar. 9, 1948. Cited in Schaller, op. cit. p. 125.

p. xxvi **Kades . . . Hussey** on Kades, see his own COH interview and Justin Williams, Sr., *Japan's Political Revolution Under MacArthur: A Participant's Account* (Georgia UP, 1979), pp. 33–51. On Hussey, see his own collected papers at the University of Michigan, Ann Arbor, and Williams, op. cit., especially pp. 52–4, 106–16. **universal morality** 'Meeting of Steering Committee with Committee on the Emperor, Feb. 6, 1946', and '2nd Meeting of Steering Committee with Committee on Civil Rights, Feb. 9, 1946', in papers of Charles Kades – J. Constitution. Formation During Diet Debate and Preliminary Proposals' Vol. VIII – within the papers of Justin Williams (JWP). **remembered him saying** George F. Kennan, *Memoirs*, Vol. 1 (Little, Brown, 1967), p. 390. **a college degree** Schaller, p. 28.

p. xxvii **baseball to Japan** Bronfenbrenner, op. cit. p. 12. **a stuffed pig** James, op. cit. p. 43. **Whitney devised 'I shall return!'** Williams, op. cit. p. 84. **Catherine II** NAW PPS Records, Box 19. Kennan/Butterworth, Mar. 9, 1948. **some of them acted** Clark Lee, *Douglas*

Sources

MacArthur. Quoted in Clay Blair, *MacArthur* (Doubleday, 1977), p. 84.

p. xxviii **bunch of bastards** Staff of *Mainichi Daily News, Fifty Years of Light and Dark: the Hirohito Era* (1975). **quite peculiar types** *The Yoshida Memoirs* (Heinemann, 1961), p. 53. **unsigned messages** Roger Buckley, article in ed. T. W. Burkman, *The Occupation of Japan: the International Context* (MacArthur Memorial, 1982), p. 82 n. 4. **sent him sandwiches** Yoshida, op. cit. p. 55.

p. xxix **personal appeal to MacArthur** JWP, 166.01. **part of psychological demilitarisation** see generally Kazuo Tsurumi, *Social Change & the Individual: Japan Before & After Defeat in World War II* (Princeton UP, 1970), pp. 138–179.

p. xxx **'strict instructions'** Robert Donihi, a prosecution attorney at Tokyo, believed these were given to Keenan as he boarded the plane for Tokyo. A Presidential car pulled up on the tarmac and a special messenger from Truman handed over a double-sealed envelope. Interview with authors, Sept. 1985. **most authoritative biographer** D. Clayton James, op. cit. p. vii. **biographies of him** Courtney Whitney, *MacArthur: His Rendezvous with History* (Knopf, 1956). Charles A. Willoughby and John Chamberlain, *MacArthur, 1941–51* (McGraw Hill, 1955). **Mr. Prima Donna** Truman, memo June 17, 1945. Robert Ferrell, *Off the Record: the Private Papers of Harry S. Truman* (1980), p. 47. **wearing his glasses** James, p. 360. **claiming credit** according to General Matthew Ridgway – quoted in Blair, op. cit. p. 3.

p. xxxi **State Department greatly irritated** Richard Barnet, *Allies: America, Europe and Japan since the war* (Simon & Schuster, 1983). **Dean Acheson snapped** quoted by Blair, p. 290. **about his funeral** James, p. 688. **surrounded by his enemies** Vice-Admiral John L. McCrae to John C. Perry, quoted in Perry's *Beneath the Eagle's Wings: Americans in Occupied Japan* (Dodd Mead, 1980), p. 69. **his fiercest critics claim** e.g. Schaller, pp. 46–7, 85–6. **least direct contact** James, p. 366. **the General's**

words E. H. Norman, quoted in Charles Taylor, *Six Journeys: A Canadian Pattern* (Anansi, 1977), p. 129.

p. xxxii **MacArthur really believes** FO 262 2056, Gascoigne/Dening, Dec. 1, 1947. **waves of enthusiasm** Gordon Daniels, 'The American Occupation of Japan' in ed. Roy A. Prete & A. Hamish Ion, *Armies of Occupation* (Wilfred Laurier UP, 1984), p. 167. **fondness for Western movies** Willoughby & Chamberlain, op. cit. p. 289. **radioactive cobalt waste** James, pp. 578–9. **could I have** speech to National Institute of Social Sciences, New York, Nov. 8, 1951. MacA Memorial Bureau of Archives, RG 10.

p. xxxiii **45 of 79** S. E. Finer, *The Man on Horseback: the Role of the Military in Politics* (Pall Mall, 1962), p. 1. **$400 billion & 22,000,000 men & women** eds. Asbjørn Eide & Marek Thee, *Problems of Contemporary Militarism* (Croom Helm, 1980), p. 17. **symptoms of militarisation** see Marek Thee, 'Militarism and Militarisation in Contemporary International Relations' in Eide/Thee, pp. 15ff. **power sharing** see Lucian W. Pye, 'Armies in the Process of Political Modernisation' in ed. J. J. Johnson, *The Role of the Military in Underdeveloped Countries* (Princeton UP, 1962), p. 69. **Eisenhower . . . military-industrial complex** quoted in Eide/Thee, p. 9. See also Volker R. Berghahn, *Militarism – the History of an International Debate 1861–1979* (Berg Publishers, 1981) for different meanings of the term 'militarism'. **Weimar Republic militarist** Berghahn, op. cit. p. 37. 'There can be militarism in the absence of a strong army, as in Weimar Germany. It was the all-pervasive "spirit of the uniform" which was the key to the problem.'

p. xxxiv **civilianism** Alfred Vagts, *A History of Militarism: Romance and Realities of a Profession* (London, 1938), p. 15. Cited in Berghahn, p. 9. **in this book militarisation/militarism** this distinction is for our own purposes. cf. Marek Thee, 'Militarism and Milit-

[315]

arisation', op. cit. p. 15 for a different distinction.

Chapter 1 – Militarised Japan: the nature of the problem

p. 3 **Japanism** 'perhaps the crucial question for post-war research into the history of J in the 1930s . . . namely what label can most appropriately be given to this period'. Olavi K. Falt, *Fascism, Militarism or Japanism? The Interpretation of the Crisis Years of 1930–41 in the J English-language Press* (Studia Historica Septentrionalia 8, 1985), p. 9. **militarised Japan was founded** for militarists as heirs to repressive state, see e.g. R. H. Mitchell, *Thought Control in Pre-War Japan* (Cornell UP, 1976), R. H. Mitchell, *Censorship in Imperial Japan* (Princeton UP, 1983), Ben Sun Kim, *Forced Political Reorientation in Japan* (Ph.D. Oklahoma, 1984, UMI 85–04326). **ranking equally** David A. Titus, 'The Making of the "Symbol Emperor System" in Post-War Japan', in *Modern Asian Studies*, 14/4 1980, p. 532. 'The theory of imperial prerogative justified a flourishing of autonomous and semi-autonomous institutions, whose leaders "advised and assisted" (*hohitsu*) the emperor in the exercise of his prerogatives.' **'government by assassination'** the title of Hugh Byas's book (Knopf, 1942). **legitimise their rule** the Imperial Institution's role as the ultimate source of legitimacy lies at the root of its longevity. R. J. Smith, *Japanese Society: Tradition, Self & the Social Order* (CUP, 1983), p. 12.

p. 4 **total war** see Jai-Hyup Kim, *The Garrison State in Pre-War Japan & Post-War Korea. A Comparative Analysis of Military Politics* (University Press of America, 1978), p. 45, for the rise of a total war ideology in Japan. But note e.g. Robert J. C. Butow, *Japan's Decision to Surrender* (Stanford UP, 1954), pp. 10–11: J did not attempt a rapid expansion of production as a whole, merely a more complete transfer of available resources. **'total defence state'** term in current use by *Osaka Mainichi* in 1930s –

see Falt, op. cit. **other vested interests** T. J. Pempel, *Policy & Politics in Japan – Creative Conservatism* (Temple UP, 1982), p. 27. **Way of Subject** ed. J. Victor Koschmann, *Authority & the Individual in Japan: Citizen Protest in Historical Perspective* (Tokyo UP, 1978), p. 48; and cf. Smith, op. cit. pp. 129–30 – there can be no distinction between private and public 'where the state itself is conceived to be a moral entity'.

p. 5 **Kyochokai** W. D. Kinzley, *The Quest for Industrial Harmony in Modern Japan: the Kyochokai 1919–46* (Ph.D. Washington U, 1984. UMI DA 8501064), cited in *Dissertation Abstracts International*, Vol. 45 No. 11, May 1985 3430. **no black listening** FO 371 54286 F910 USSBS Kawai interview.

p. 6 **indoctrination in schools** see generally Un Sun Song, *A Sociological Analysis of the Value System of Pre-War Japan as revealed in the Japanese Government Elementary School Textbooks 1933–41* (Ph.D. University of Maryland, 1958). e.g. p. 10 – in the six grades of elementary school 50% of teaching was value-oriented; and p. 40 – 'textbooks made the Japanese people', according to Tomitaro Karasawa. **Indoctrination in schools** extended throughout the Empire – see E. Patricia Tsurumi, *Japanese Colonial Education in Taiwan 1895–1945* (Harvard UP, 1977). **oath of loyalty** quoted in Gordon Daniels, 'The Evacuation of Schoolchildren in Wartime Japan', *PBAJS* 1977 Part 1. **centred on the Emperor** David A. Titus, 'Watsuji Tetsuro and the Intellectual Basis of Emperorism in Pre-War Japan: Some Initial Speculations', in *PBAJS* 1979 Part 1. **perversion of Shinto** see generally D. C. Holtom, *Modern Japan & Shinto Nationalism – a Study of Present-Day Trends in Japanese Religions* (Paragon, 1963).

p. 7 **Emperor is the State** for Yatsuka Hozumi's thought, see Richard Minear, *Japanese Tradition and Western Law* (Harvard UP, 1970). **rugged individualism** Steven Lukes, *Individualism (Blackwell, 1973), p. 26.* **basic**

unit is group see generally Yoshihara Scott Matsumoto, *Collectivity Orientations in Contemporary Japan* (Ph.D. The American University, 1957. UMI 21967). **interactionist/individualist** Smith, *Japanese Society*, p. 74.

Chapter 2 – The Peculiar Chosen People: planning the Occupation
p. 10 **Herman Melville** *White Jacket*, Chapter 36 – quoted in Arthur Schlesinger, Jr., 'America: Experiment or Destiny', *American Historical Review* No. 82 Feb.–June 1977, p. 521. Opposed to the destiny view is the idea of the American way as 'an experiment. The outcome is by no means certain' – op. cit. **Abraham Lincoln** speech at Springfield, Illinois, June 26, 1857. *Works*, II, p. 406. **Declaration of Independence** R. H. Kohn, *Eagle & Sword – The Federalists & the Creation of the Military Establishment in America 1783–1802* (Free Press, 1975), sees the American Revolution as 'a revolt against militarism'. And cf. Paul Heffron, *The Anti-Militarist Tradition of the Founding Fathers and its continuation in the writings of Carl Schurz, Charles A. Beard and Walter Millis* (Ph.D. Minnesota U, 1977). **Kissinger observed** 'The Specter of Protection', *Washington Post*, Oct. 8, 1985. **reshaping. . . Asia** Goodman, p. vi.

p. 11 **'savage apes . . . bestial Japs'** George W. Ware, Jr., *The Tokyo War Crimes Trial 1946–8: Case for the Defence* (M.A., University of Maryland, 1979), pp. 7, 16. **13% of Americans** Ware, op. cit. p. 18. **the Army and Navy** on Army planning for the Occupation, see generally Eric H. F. Svensson, *The Military Occupation of Japan: The First Years. Planning, Policy Formulation and Reforms* (Ph.D. Denver, 1966).

p. 12 **State Department . . . long-range planning** on planning for the Occ. within the State Department, see Michael J. Boyle, *The Planning of the Occupation of Japan and the American Reform Tradition* (Ph.D. Wyoming U, 1979).

OSS framed Svensson, op. cit. p. 22.
p. 13 **John K. Emmerson** for 'China Crowd' thinking, see his *The Japanese Thread: A Life in the U.S. Foreign Service* (Holt Rinehart, 1978). **swarthy, pudgy man** Emmerson, op. cit. p. 96. **alma mater** Boyle, op. cit. Chap. 2.

p. 14 **unquestionably liberals** Boyle, Chap. 2, likens them to the New Dealers of the 1930s, with reference to Thomas A. Krueger & William Glidden, 'The New Deal Intellectual Elite: A Collective Portrait', in ed. F. C. Jaher, *The Rich, the Well Born, and the Powerful: Elites and Upper Classes in History* (Illinois U, 1973). **Ballantine explained** COH: Joseph Ballantine. **Grew at least** Schaller, pp. 9–13. **'poor dear Japan'** Blakeslee Marlene J. Mayo, 'Planning Japan's Economic Future', paper for Columbia University seminar on Modern East Asia, Dec. 8, 1978, p. 22. **diplomacy a matter** Waldo Heinrichs, *American Ambassador* (Little, Brown, 1966), p. 341. **cousin of J. Pierpont Morgan** e.g. Howard Schonberger, 'T. A. Bisson and the Limits of Reform in Occupied Japan', *BCAS* 12/4 Oct.–Dec. 1980.

p. 15 **not even MacArthur** see e.g. Richard Tregaskis, 'Peace Caught Us Napping', *Saturday Evening Post*, Sept. 29, 1945. **maybe hundreds of thousands** MacA, characteristically, put the figure at a minimum of a million. MacA/Eisenhower, Jan. 25, 1946. *Foreign Relations of the United States* (FRUS) 1946, VIII, pp. 395–7. And see Chapter 14 below.

p. 16 **Emperor should be preserved** FO 371 46447 F4605 July 24, 1945. **33% of Americans** Christopher Thorne, *Allies of a Kind: the United States, Britain and the War Against Japan 1941–5* (Hamish Hamilton, 1978), p. 657. **Hara-kiri . . . Yoko Hama** Ware, p. 22. **tacit pledge** see Williams, op. cit. pp. 16, 99–100, for the view that this phrase was in effect a covert assurance that the Emperor system would be preserved, since to the Japan Crowd it was unthinkable that the people would want it abolished. And see Chapter 14 below. **Dooman responsible** Emmerson, p. 236.

p. 17 **little bastards** quoted by Theodore Achilles in Daniel Yergin, *Shattered Peace: the Origins of the Cold War and the National Security State* (Boston, 1977), p. 132. **decline in Japan Crowd** COH: Joseph Ballantine. 'The soft peace people . . . were completely superceded by the hard peace people . . . The idea of the Morgenthau peace, turning Germany and Japan into goat pastures, was uppermost in the minds of these people'. **New Deal economists** Diary, Chapter XII, pp. 266–8. Ballantine Papers, Hoover Institute. **Grew's nominees** Emmerson, p. 252. **divine revelation** cf. Williams, op. cit. p. 100. 'It cannot be overemphasised that SCAP acted on the basis of directives received from Washington'. **I still recall** Whitney, op. cit. p. 213.

p. 18 **BIPSD** reprinted in *PRJ*, Vol. II. **shown to various members** Emmerson, p. 200. **to embrace theses** Dooman/Kenneth Colegrove, July 30, 1955, quoted in COH: Eugene Dooman.

p. 19 **experiences in Yenan** especially pp. 179–213, 394–5. **Yenan a glamorous word** Emmerson, p. 216.

p. 20 **obviate any feeling** NAW RG 218 LEAHY 51 Marshall/MacA WARX 64221, Sept. 14, 1945. **Allied military involvement** see, e.g., Roger Buckley, *Occupation Diplomacy: Britain, the United States and Japan 1945–52* (CUP, 1982), Chapter 6. **the acquiescence of the Chinese** FO 371 46449 F6699. Note on file, J. C. Sterndale Bennett, Sept. 11, 1949. **initial suspicions** Buckley, op. cit. pp. 163–71.

p. 21 **bastion of European civilisation** Geoffrey Bolton, 'Australia and the Occupation of Japan', in *The British Commonwealth & the Occupation of Japan*, p. 15, proceedings of a symposium held in 1983 at the International Centre for Economic and Related Disciplines. **dismissed them both** FO 262 2054 Gascoigne/FO, Oct. 25, 1946.

Chapter 3 – First Encounters

p. 23 **Bowers recalled** COH: Faubion Bowers, pp. 14–15.

p. 24 **wave of suicides** *The Times*, Aug. 27, 1945. **fleeing with their planes** HP 10 B 23. **delaying the landings** see Arisue's account, 'Memoirs of Atsugi', quoted in Svensson, op, cit. pp. 137–8. **OSS memo** quoted by Lester Brooks, *Behind Japan's Surrender: the Secret Struggle that ended an Empire* (McGraw Hill, 1967), p. 367. **Tojo Doesn't Live Here** in *Free World*, Dec. 1945, p. 33. Quoted in Perry, op. cit. p. 4.

p. 25 **preferred a meerschaum** James, p. 358. **one bomb for every 15** Perry, p. 104. **2,259,879 . . . 600,000** Harry Emerson Wildes, *Typhoon In Tokyo* (Macmillan, 1954), p. 2. **200 a month** *Fifty Years of Light and Dark*, op. cit.

p. 26 **ersatz clothes . . . chocolate** Kazuo Kawai, *Japan's American Interlude* (Chicago UP, 1960), p. 135. **nutritional mulberry leaves** *Nippon Times*, Aug. 10, 1945. **36,000 . . . 32,624** Svensson, p. 147. **food drops** Svensson, p. 146. **knife attacks, telephone wires, dynamite** WO 268 768 Quarterly Historical Reports HQ British and Indian Division. (BRINDIV) **bullet holes** NAS RG 331 Box 5097 File 319.1 Mar. 27, 1946, Occupational Trends Japan and Korea. **American murdered** SNMAJK Dec. 1945. **Japanese sentenced** SNMAJK May 1946. **when a comparison** WO 268 768 BRINDIV, Fortnightly Intelligence Review No. 11, week ending Oct. 21, 1946. **303 . . . 953** SNMAJK Nov. 1946.

p. 27 **rash of traffic accidents** Mark Gayn, *Japan Diary* (William Sloane Associates, 1948), p. 40 **rape and licentiousness** e.g. the J govt. warned that unconditional surrender would mean 'prostitution and castration' for the J people. Allan M. Winkler, *The Politics of Propaganda: the Office of War Information* (Yale UP, 1978), p. 142. **ennobling influence** MacA, statement on the first anniversary of the Surrender, Sept. 2, 1946, in *PRJ* Vol. II, p. 756 **early respect modified** NAS

RG 331 Box 5097 File 319.1, op. cit. **SCAP's official bulletin** i.e. SNMAJK. **GI sentenced** SNMAJK Jan. 1946. **new draftees tolerant** Ian Nish, 'Britiain & the Occupation of Japan – some personal recollections', *PBAJS* 1979 Part 1. **MacA's inimitable phraseology** Wildes, op. cit. p. 326.

p. 28 **black-market whisky** SNMAJK Jan. 1946. **indiscriminate rape** NAW RG 59, Box 3812, State Dept. 740.00119 Control(Japan)/9-1545. H. Merrell Benninghoff, Headquarters XIV Corps US Army Korea/Sec. of State, Sept. 15, 1945. **half-apologetic attitude** *NYT*, Sept. 11, 1945. **Japanese war criminal wrote** FO 371 84036 FJ 1662/2 Japanese War Criminals Correspondence Oct.–Dec. 1949. **interview with Akira Ando** Gayn, op. cit. pp. 247–50.

p. 29 **women preferred** Wildes, p. 35. **Americans are drunkards** NAS RG 331 Box 5097 File 319.1 op. cit.

Chapter 4 – Spiking the Guns
p. 33 **tip off Etajima** *NYT*, Dec. 9, 1945. **delicate task** 'Note of the Japanese Government of August 14 [1945] to the Governments of the United States, Great Britain, China and the Soviet Union Expressing its Desire with Reference to the Execution of Certain Provisions of the Potsdam Declaration', in *Documents concerning the Allied Occupation and Control of Japan. Volume I. Basic Documents* (Tokyo, 1949), p. 19. **government's hope** 'Note of the Japanese Government', op. cit. p. 19. **Allies had expressed** FO 371 F 6567 FEC 'Statement of Policy on Disarmament, Demobilization and Disposition of Enemy Arms, Ammunition and Implements of War'. Earl of Halifax, Washington/Sec. of State for Foreign Affairs, Apr. 25, 1946.

p. 34 **with bands playing** FO 371 F 6567 op. cit. **scouts captured reconnoitring** Gayn, p. 153.

p. 35 **at Okinawa 7,400** Basil Liddell Hart, *History of the Second World War* (Pan, 1973), p. 716. **Japanese**

warrant officer WO 268 768 BRINDIV Fortnightly Intelligence Review No. 10, week ending Oct. 7, 1946. Part V. **British had also kept** FO 262 2056 Gascoigne/Dening, Mar. 12, 1947: MacA very critical of British. And cf. FO 371 F 9976 and 1125; and Louis Allen, 'Not so Piacular – A Footnote to Ienaga on Malaya', *PBAJS* 1980 Part 1. **indoctrination schools** Willoughby & Chamberlain, p. 301. **grim and unsmiling** FO 371 84036 FJ 1662/2 Oct.–Dec. 1949. **sloughed off** Rodger Swearingen, *The Soviet Union & Japan* (Hoover Institution, 1978), pp. 51–2.

p. 36 **as late as 1970** James, p. 91. **disarming Japan** in general, see draft of FEC 017, 'Statement of Policy on Disarmament', op. cit., FO 371 F 6567, and *MacA Reports*. **B-29 bombers . . . volunteer corps** NYT, Jan. 4, 1945, Apr. 18, 1945, June 22, 1945, July 12, 1945. **crossbows . . . explosive arrows** *NYT*, Aug. 30, 1946. **dummy weapons** Gayn, p. 70. **fencing sticks** Bowers, 'How Japan Won the War', *NYT Magazine*, Aug. 30, 1970.

p. 37 **their apparent disregard** *MacA Reports*, p. 140. **propellant charges detonated** Henry I. Shaw, 'The US Marines in the Occupation of Japan' (Marine Corps Historical Reference Series No. 24, Historical Branch, G-3, HQ US Marine Corps, 1961). **quantity of TNT** *NYT*, Sept. 22, 1945. **'Destruction Incorporated'** *MacA Reports*. **more dramatic end** NAW RG 218 LEAHY 45. Memo H. H. Arnold, Commanding General, Army Air Forces/ Sec. JCS, Dec. 13, 1945. **180 tons** GHQ Far Eastern Command, 'A Brief History of the G-2 Section, GHQ, SWPA and Affiliated Units', July 8, 1948, p. 102 **Mobile Command Post** NAW RG 218 JCS 388.3 1946–7 Japan, Section 1. C-in-C Allied Land Forces S.E. Asia/HQ Supreme Allied Command SEA, Oct. 9, 1945. **in US Army custody** NAW RG 319 (Army Staff) P & O Div. 1946–8 091 Japan. CinCFE/DoA WDGPO Radio, Oct. 9, 1947.

p. 38 **he ascribed . . . combat vehicles** ibid. **Allied investigators commented** NAW IPS Investigative Div. Case No. 43 – Burning of Confidential Documents. Memo re Tokyo PoW Information Bureau, Oct. 6, 1945. **order must be burnt** NAW IPS Investigative Div. Case No. 43 – Burning of Confidential Documents. Top Secret War Ministry order No. 363, Aug. 17, 1945 in IPS memo Feb. 13, 1946. **trucks and tunnels** *NYT*, Sept. 9, 1945. **tanks as tractors . . . surprise raids** Gayn, pp. 84–8, 155.

p. 39 **benefit from research** the West was alive to fact of J superiority in certain areas – FO 371 46464/80589, Erle Dickover address, Feb. 14, 1945. **enjoy intelligence . . . contrary to US interests** NAW RG 218 JSC 1946–7 091.31 Japan Sec. 3. 380.11 Japan CCS 35.05 'Intelligence for Control of Japan'. Joint Intelligence Committee 322/2, Feb. 25, 1946. **if any information** NAW RG 218 LEAHY 42. WAR 94446, JSC/MacA, Mar. 20, 1946. **amnesty from prosecution** John W. Powell, 'Japan's Germ Warfare: the US Cover-Up of a War Crime', *BCAS* 12/4, Oct.–Dec. 1980. **American medical experts** Powell, op. cit. p. 9.

p. 40 **Japanese had worked** Daniel Okimoto, *Ideas, Intellectuals and Institutions: National Security and the Question of Nuclear Armament in Japan* (Ph.D., Michigan, 1978), pp. 10–11. And cf. John Dower, 'Science, Society and the Japanese Atomic Bomb Project during World War II', *BCAS* 10/2 Apr.–June 1978: he argues that there was no concerted attempt to conceal the programme. **all atomic scientists . . . compounds** NAW RG 218 LEAHY 43 Japan 1946. MacArthur Communications. JCS WARX 79907 Oct. 30, 1945. **cyclotrons destroyed . . . agriculture** James, p. 88. **requirements in heavy industry** Edwin W. Pauley, *Report on Japanese Reparations to the President of the U.S., Nov. 1945 to April 1946* (Washington, 1948). **British had faith** Chihiro Hosoya, 'George Sansom – diplomat and historian', in

eds. I. Nish & C. Dunn, *European Studies on Japan* (Tenterden, 1979).

p. 41 **Burma lodged** Bowers, 'How Japan Won the War', *NYT Magazine*, Aug. 30, 1970. **FEC puzzled** FO 371 63706 F 109.

p. 42 **average retail prices** James, p. 155.

Chapter 5 – Rooting Out Evil: the purge

p. 43 **210,288 of Japan's leading citizens** Hans H. Baerwald, *The Purge of Japanese Leaders under the Occupation* (California, 1959), p. 80. This book is the source for most of the statistics and much of the factual information in this chapter.

p. 44 **32 members** *Nippon Times*, Aug. 30, 1945. **38 new . . . strongarm men** Gayn, pp. 14–15. **New Elite . . . skinning rabbits** interview with wife of Yasutoshi Maki, leader of New Elite Masses Party, Jan. 1947. HP 81 A 10. **NYT pointed out** Jan. 22, 1947.

p. 45 **Butoku Kai** *PRJ* Vol. I, pp. 67–9. **such evocative titles** HP 78 A 4, Appendix to Ag 091.

p. 46 **Japanese suggested** Baerwald, op. cit. p. 43. **Whitney dismissed the proposal** Whitney, conference with Kijuro Shidehara, Jan. 25, 1946. *PRJ* Vol. I, p. 18. **blasting from the command** Jan. 4, 1946. *PRJ* Vol. I, p. 14.

p. 47 **Yoshida argued** Yoshida/MacA, Dec. 21, 1946. JWP File 128.

p. 48 **anarchy, chaos and communism** Yoshida/MacA, Oct. 22, 1946, Oct. 31, 1946. JWP File 128.

p. 49 **statues . . . scrapped** NAS RG 331 3287-8 05931 File 9 'On Military Monuments'. **citizens of Nara** NAS RG 331 5404. CIE News Digest No. 3, Press Release from Nara MG team, undated – early 1947. **if you were purged** COH: Ai Kume, p. 23.

p. 50 **purge abused** e.g. Baerwald, p. 52. **Democratic Party** one of the four, Wataru Narahashi, wrote to GS pointing out that the purge was applied shortly before an election, and the appeal procedure delayed, leaving the purgees no time to campaign. Whitney/Yoshida, Apr. 21, 1947. JWP File 128. **view of the OSS** OSS/State Dept. Intelligence & Research Reports: Part II – Postwar Japan, Korea and SouthEast Asia. OIR Report No. 4518, 'The Purge Problem and the Japanese Peace Treaty', Sept. 25, 1947.

p. 51 **only 2%** Baerwald, p. 82. **US Army unwittingly** Gayn, pp. 68–9. **36 new members** HP 78 A 18. Adjutant-General B. M. Fitch/Imperial Japanese Government, Mar. 27, 1946. **Tottori Prefecture** WO 268 768 BRINDIV Fortnightly Intelligence Review, week ending Dec. 7, 1946.

Chapter 6 – Military and Magnates
p. 52 **ten families . . . 75%** Howard B. Schonberger, 'Zaibatsu Dissolution and the American Restoration of Japan', *BCAS* 5/2, Sept. 1973, p. 16. **assault on capitalism** Schonberger, op. cit. p. 18.

p. 53 **zaibatsu . . . equipment . . . intelligence gathering** T. A. Bisson, *Zaibatsu Dissolution in Japan* (Berkeley, 1954), p. 22. **almost feudal relationship** Schonberger, p. 18.

p. 54 **foundations for a Japanese middle class** Corwin D. Edwards, *Report of the Mission on Japanese Combines* (Washington, 1946).

p. 55 **impossible burden** on the vagaries of the dissolution programme, see generally Bisson, op. cit., and Eleanor M. Hadley, *Antitrust in Japan* (Princeton, 1970).

p. 56 **in dominating men** quoted in W. G. Beasley, *The Meiji Restoration* (Stanford UP, 1973), p. 111. **a great mistake** *The Yoshida Memoirs* (Houghton Mifflin, 1962), pp. 150–1. **it is believed** Bisson, p. 90. And cf. FO 371 76252 80381 – Comyns Carr. **blackmarketeers laundering** NAS RG 331 Box 5243 Oyabun-Kobun Conferences, July 24, 1947. J. F. Sullivan, memo of meeting with ESS.

p. 57 **way labour organised** see e.g. John Mullen and Chiyono Sata, *Labor Developments in Japan during*

the late 1940s and early 1950s: the papers of Richard L. G. Deverall in the Catholic University of America Archives, in JWP.

p. 58 **707 . . . 6.665,483** James, p. 176. **No democracy can be built** William MacMahon Ball, *Japan – Enemy or Ally?* (John Day, 1949), p. 112.

p. 59 **only 2000 owned 100 acres** Kawai, op. cit. p. 171. **Martin wrote** Edwin Martin, *The Allied Occupation of Japan* (Stanford UP, 1948), p. 87.

Chapter 7 – Changing Minds: the re-education of Japan
p. 61 **in the last week** WO 268 768 BRINDIV Fortnightly Intelligence Review No. 15.

p. 62 **Japanese schooling refashioned** NAS RG 331 Box 5405, files 'Parent-Teacher Associations' & 'General Materials – Directives & Activities on Japanese Education'. **drill sergeants** John W. Dower, *Empire and Aftermath: Yoshida Shigeru and the Japanese Experience, 1878–1954* (Harvard UP, 1979), p. 353. **Ministry of Education sacked** James, p. 297. **assistant principal** NAS 331.5097 Decimal File (Secret) 1945–52 .0008 Education. Summary of Information. CIS/OD/GA Branch. 'Ultranationalists in Local School', Jan. 7, 1948. **influenced by Dewey** Victor N. Kobayashi, *John Dewey in Japanese Educational Thought* (thesis, University of Michigan School of Education, 1964). **teacher reorientation . . . Teachers' Manual** HNMAOJ Vol. 11, Social, Part A: Education, p. 70ff.

p. 63 **one member of CIE** COH: Josephine Colletti McKean.

p. 64 **a typical wartime textbook** Masami Yamazumi, 'Textbook Revision – the Swing to the Right', *JQ* 28/4 Oct.–Dec. 1981. **reflective not customary morality** Ming-Huey Kao, *An Analysis of Moral Education in Japanese Public Schools* (Ph.D. South Illinois U, 1964). **schools radio . . . intense emotions** NAS RG 331 Box 5404, Educational Radio Programs. **spontaneity . . . hand grenades** NAS RG 331 Box 5467. **CIE**

Education Research Files. 'Bureau of Indoctrination'. Hatsu Tai No. 80: Vice-Minister of Education/Prefectural Governors, Directors of Higher Normal Schools and Normal Schools, Nov. 6, 1945. Hatsu Tai No. 100: Chief of Bureau of Physical Education, Ministry of Education/Principals etc., Dec, 26, 1945. Hatsu Do No. 20, Aug. 24, 1945.

p. 65 **in order to control content** on the control of textbooks, see generally Benjamin C. Duke, 'The Textbook Controversy', *JQ* 19/3 July–Sept. 1972. **first 'clean' textbook** Duke, op. cit. p. 345. **adult re-education** for range of activities, see NAS RG 331 Box 5242, file 'Bulletins CIE,' and Box 5243, file 'Media Plans'. **product was democracy** John W. Gaddis, *Public Information in Japan under American Occupation* (Geneva, 1950), p. 74.

p. 66 **a SCAP consultant** HP 76 B 19. **highest proportion of radio sets** Kawai, p. 221. **features included** NAS RG 331 Box 5404. Educational Radio Programs. **for adults . . . duty** Gaddis, op. cit. p. 80. And cf. HNMAOJ Vol. 11, Social, Part G: Radio Broadcasting.

p. 67 **domestic newsreels . . . resistance** Akira Iwasaki, 'The Occupied Screen', *JQ* 25/3 July–Sept. 1978. **reading rooms** NAS RG 331 Box 5404. Standard Operating Procedure for CIE Reading Rooms. **saxophone and Hawaiian guitar** HNMAOJ Vol. 11, Social, Part C: the Theater and Motion Pictures. **traditional memorized-speech** NAS RG 331 Box 5404. CIE News Digest No. 3. **Parent-Teacher Associations** COH: McKean, op. cit.

p. 68 **CIE was under instructions** SCAP General Orders No. 183, Sept. 22, 1945. **Press & Publications Division report** William J. Coughlin, *Conquered Press: the MacArthur Era in Japanese Journalism* (Pacific, 1952), pp. 21–2, 44. **'Now It Can Be Told'** Gayn, pp. 6–7.

p. 69 **censorship** see generally Coughlin, op. cit., and Jim

Hopewell, 'Press Censorship: A Case Study', in *Argus* (University of Maryland) 6/6, May 1971, pp. 19–20, 58–64. **since 1943** Jay Rubin, 'From Wholesomeness to Decadence: the Censorship of Literature under the Allied Occupation', *JJS* 11/1 Winter 1985. Rubin claims Occ censorship was partly modelled on the wartime US Office of Censorship. **minimum of restrictions** SCAPIN 16: Memorandum to Japanese Government Concerning Freedom of Speech, Sept. 10, 1945. *PRJ* Vol. II, p. 460. **adhere strictly to the truth** SCAP Code for Japanese Press, Sept. 24, 1945. **references to GI offences suppressed** *Asahi Hyoron* file, Oct. 1, 1948, in GWPC. The censors were taxed by a J review of Norman Mailer's *The Naked and the Dead*, which focussed on the behaviour of his GIs. 'They were suffered from the obsession [in which their wives committed irregularities] . . . Stimulated by the obsession and the physical requirement suppressed, dirty and foul words on the sex and the water-closet were exchanged among them, which formed the basis for their daily conversation'. **'blue-eyed nationals' . . . footprints** Richard L. G. Deverall, *The Great Seduction: Red China's Drive to bring Free Japan behind the Iron Curtain* (Tokyo, 1953). **forbidden to disparage . . . imperialism of the US** Hopewell, op. cit. p. 63. **a poem . . . Kikuhata** censorship report on issue of Jan. 23, 1948 in *Kikuhata* file, GWPC.

p. 70 **Lippmann's column** Coughlin, p. 47. **MacA's personal intervention** Coughlin, p. 51. **perhaps over-protective** Coughlin, pp. 54–5. **minutes of the ACJ** COH: Roger Nash Baldwin. **poem in Kikuhata** censorship report on issue of Sept. 15, 1946 in *Kikuhata* file, GWPC. **War and Peace** Hopewell, p. 63. **the Kama Sutra** Hopewell, p. 62.

p. 71 **banknotes . . . stamps** HNMAOJ Vol. 6, Social, Part A: Freedom of Religion. **flash list** COH: Baldwin, op. cit. **I shall get revenge . . . be expected** AFPAC Civil

Censorship Detachment, 'Perusal of Letters, Public Opinion and Literature, Oct.–Dec. 1945'. JWP File 234. **index of films** HNMAOJ Vol. 11, Social, Part C: the Theater and Motion Pictures. **Kurosawa** Rubin, op. cit. **film makers encouraged** HNMAOJ Vol. 11, Social, Part C. **Children of the Atom Bomb** Deverall, op. cit.

p. 72 **Mikado** COH: Bowers. And cf. p. 82 and source below. **Hellman . . . All My Sons** HNMAOJ Vol. 11, Social, Part C. **principal offender . . . repertoire** HNMAOJ Vol. 11, Social, Part C, p. 34. **Germans conquered England** COH: Bowers, p. 41. **revolutionary changes . . . art form** HNMAOJ Vol. 11, Social, Part C, p. 36 **tools of dictator** Marlene J. Mayo, 'Psychological Disarmament: American Wartime Planning for the Education and Re-education of Defeated Japan, 1943–5', in ed. T. Burkman, *The Occupation of Japan: Education and Social Reform* (MacArthur Memorial, Norfolk, 1982), p. 77. **Baldwin criticised** COH: Baldwin. **advice from OSS** OSS/State Dept. Intelligence and Research Reports, Part II: Postwar Japan, Korea and S.E. Asia. OIR Report No. 4246, 'The Development of Media of Information in Japan since the Surrender', Oct. 1, 1947. **the public is not** NAS RG 331 Box 5404. CIE News Digest No. 3.

Chapter 8 – Making Shinto Safe
p. 73 **UN Church** Stuart D. B. Picken, *Shinto: Japan's Spiritual Roots* (Kodansha, 1980), p. 53. **futurologist fulminated** Dan Gilbert pamphlet, New York Public Library. **SCAP officials** on Shintoism generally, and SCAP policies towards it, see William P. Woodard, op. cit. **Lieutenant Ishiroku** Hillis Lory, *Japan's Military Masters* (Viking, 1943), p. 37. **coordinated bowing** CAD 29th Weekly Report to FEC, week ending July 29, 1946.

p. 74 **nor were school teachers** NAS RG 331 Box 5466. Education

Research Files. Hatsu Kyo No. 101. Chief of Bureau of Textbooks, Ministry of Education/Metropolitan, Hokkaido and Prefectural Governors, July 9, 1948. **compilers . . . forbidden** NAS RG 331 Box 5404. Educational Radio Programs. F. B. Judson, note on meeting, Nov. 28, 1947. **one authority** Daniel Holtom, *Modern Japan and Shinto Nationalism* (Chicago UP, 1977), p. 176. **effort to keep** Woodard, p. 108.

p. 75 **cluster of beliefs** Woodard, p. 10. **cult required** A. Hamish Ion, 'The Formation of the Nippon Kirisutokyodan, 1941 – A Case Study of Church-State Relations', *PBAJS* 1980 Part 1, p. 98. 'As the Emperor-God, conveniently, was also Commander-in-Chief of the Army, Shinto served as a spiritual bond between the military and the civilian population'.

p. 76 **Japanese Cabinet . . . incentive to peace** NAS RG 331 Box 3287. Cabinet meeting, Dec. 5, 1947. **war-dead shrines** NAS RG 331 Boxes 3288–9. And cf. Woodard, pp. 157–63. **passing on** NAS RG 331 Box 3288. Memo W. K. Bunce, Chief of RCR Division/Donald Nugent, Chief CIE, June 19, 1951.

p. 77 **exaggerated respect** NAS RG 331 Box 3288. File 9 – On Military Monuments. **he deeply embarrassed** on MacA and Christianity in J, see generally Lawrence S. Wittner, 'MacArthur and the Missionaries: God and Man in Occupied Japan', *Pacific Historical Review* 15/1 Feb. 1971. **championing Christianity** Woodard, p. 16. And cf. Toshio Nishi, *Unconditional Democracy – Education and Politics in Occupied Japan 1945–52* (Hoover Institute, 1982): Nishi claims this was because it was a faith imbued with 'a spiritual repugnance of war'. **did not go to church . . . Mount** Woodard, p. 241. **on one occasion** Woodard, p. 241. **Reminiscences** Douglas MacArthur, *Reminiscences* (McGraw Hill, 1964), p. 322. **Protestant equivalent of the Pope** John Gunther, *The Riddle of MacArthur* (Harper, 1950), p. 75.

p. 78 **best defence against communism** he referred to Christianity as 'an invincible spiritual barrier against the infiltration of ideologies which seek by suppression the way to power and advancement'. MacA, Press Release on selection of Tetsu Katayama as Prime Minister, May 24, 1947. *PRJ* Vol. II, p. 770. **electoral appeal** James, p. 291. **Christmas trees** Woodard, p. 137. **missionaries** NAS RG 331 Box 5242, file 'Bulletins CIE' Vol. 1 No. 9, Oct. 18, 1947. Policy of the Occ 'to facilitate the entry of Christian missionaries into Japan'. **special privileges** Wittner, op. cit. **Protestant evangelist campaign** James, p. 290. **wartime broadcasts . . . soldier** Gayn, p. 101. **MacA the source** though Ray Moore emphasises (in his review of Roger Buckley, *Occupation Diplomacy* in *JJS* 10/1 Winter 1983, p. 243) the Japanese government's role in encouraging the Emperor and Empress 'to show a personal interest in Christianity to indicate their receptivity to Western culture and American democracy'. **Billy Graham** *NYT*, July 4, 1964. **Williams wrote** Williams/Guy Swope, June 10, 1948. JWP 106.04. **the Vatican** FO 371 F 19602 British Legation to Holy See/Japan & Pacific Dept, FO, July 6, 1948. **Christianity made little progress** Wittner, op. cit.

p. 79 **GIs stole supplies** Wittner, op. cit. **largest golf course** Woodard, pp. 195–6.

Chapter 9 – Ah-So San: the humanising of the Emperor

p. 80 **spiritual leader by lineage** possessing what Max Weber called 'hereditary charisma' – not personal, but by virtue of being incumbent of Imperial throne. Song, pp. 55, 255. **high priest . . . lifetime** Picken, op. cit. pp. 37, 40.

p. 81 **no-one seems certain . . . the sound** on the origin of the Imperial Rescript, and Reginald Blyth's role, see Woodard, pp. 250–68; Wilhelmus H. M. Creemers, *Shrine Shinto after*

World War II (E. J. Brill, 1968); and COH: Harold Henderson. **all of them** Ray Moore, review of Jun Eto, *Senryo shiroku*(Kodansha, 1981–2) in *JJS* 10/1 Winter 1983, p. 250. **what he did deny** Woodard, p. 267. **the Shinto Publication Committee** Picken, p. 40.

p. 82 **government in the new Japan . . . unity of the people** Constitution of Japan, preamble and Chapter 1, *PRJ* Vol. II, p. 671. **publicly censured** *NYT*, Dec. 7, 1948. **performance of The Mikado** Prince Takematsu, the Emperor's brother, and two other members of the Imperial family attended the performance. 'The party smiled throughout but did not applaud.' Takematsu, leaving a few minutes before the end, said he had found it 'very interesting'. *NYT*, Jan. 30, 1948. **NYT editorial** Feb. 3, 1948. **liable to tax** HP 90 B 2 – on Imperial Institution. **Hirohito's glasses** David A. Titus, 'The Making of the "Symbol Emperor System" in Postwar Japan', *Modern Asian Studies* 14/4 1980, p. 565 n. 77. **the Palace at Akasaka** JWP 109.08.

p. 83 **14 former members** HP Section 19 B. **MacArthur is the navel** HP Section 79 B. **long-term public relations** Toru Takemoto, *Failure of Liberalism in Japan: Shidehara Kijuro's Encounter with Anti-Liberals* (UP of America, 1978), p. 163. Shidehara, appointed PR man for the Emperor, answered questions on his behalf from the *NYT* and AP. **endearing facts** *NYT*, Jan. 8, 1947. **his sea shells** *Nippon Times*, Jan. 1, 1947. **princesses** *NYT*, Aug. 14, 1946. **square dancing** Kawai, p. 87. **Emperor's tours** not without precedent in the knowledge of the Japanese people. The elementary school *shushin* textbooks told of Emperor Meiji's tours of the northern provinces in 1878. Song, p. 84.

p. 84 **ruler of 80 million** *NYT*, Feb. 20, 1946. **facial tic** Gayn, pp. 138–40. **one young woman** *NYT*, Feb. 20, 1946. **First Down-to-the-Earth Sovereign** *Nippon Times*, Jan. 1, 1947.

Chapter 10 – Prescription for Peace: rewriting the Constitution

p. 85 **Potsdam Ordinance** Williams, p. 187. **potsudamu** Bowers, 'How Japan Won the War', *NYT Magazine*, Aug. 30, 1970.

p. 86 **SCAP flew members** NAS RG 331 Box 5097. Memo Lou G. Van Wagoner/Special Assistant for Occupied Areas, Nov. 21, 1950.

p. 87 **MacA claimed** *PRJ* Vol. II, p. 660. **Walzer** Michael Walzer, *Just and Unjust Wars* (Allen Lane, 1978), p. 113. **Hague Convention** John D. Montgomery, *Forced To Be Free: the Artificial Revolution in Germany and Japan* (Chicago UP, 1957), p. 4. **Hussey expressed concern** in an address to the Foreign Service Institute, Apr. 5, 1947. **Blakeslee felt** Dale Hellegers, 'Constitution and Law Reform in Post-war Japan', in ed. L. H. Redford, *The Occupation and its Legacy to the Post-war World* (MacArthur Memorial, 1976).

p. 88 **Atlantic Charter** as the Japanese Foreign Ministry pointed out in its initial response to the American Initial Post-Surrender Policy. Moore, op. cit. p. 249. **Japanese hotly denied** see for example Takemoto, op. cit. pp. 169–73. **Stalin's suggestion** as paraphrased by Harry Hopkins, Truman's Special Secretary, in May 1945. Cited in Takemoto, p. 169. **advised by the CIA** for whom he was then working. HP 93 D 10.

p. 89 **he promptly wrote** Hussey/ Kades, Nov. 12, 1958. HP 93 B 5. **amendments, not all insignificant** they included the substitution of two Diet chambers for one; the deletion of a provision for the nationalization of land ownership; the deletion of the Diet's right to review Supreme Court decisions. Williams, pp. 116–17. **Shimizu Cho** Ben Sun Kim, *Forced Political Reorientation in Japan: A Study of the Impact of Defeat on Japanese National Consciousness* (Ph.D. Oklahoma, 1984), Chap. 8. **Foreign Ministry** Moore, p. 253. **unofficial groups** James, p. 122. **Emperor expressed interest** when Government Section approached the CLO to learn Konoye's proposals, they were told that his work had been done exclusively for the Emperor. (Memo of meeting Rowell/Mr. Sone, CLO, Dec. 10, 1945. HP 21 B.) And cf. N. Ito, *New Japan: Six Years of Democratisation* (Japan Peace Study Group, 1952) for the claim that the Emperor had initiated constitutional reform in September 1945.

p. 90 **SWNCC 228** reprinted in ed. Theodore McNelly, *Sources in Modern East Asian History and Politics* (New York, 1967). **before Japan was defeated** McNelly, 'Constitution and Law Reform in Postwar Japan', in ed. Redford, *The Occupation and its Legacy*, op. cit. Constitutional revision is listed as a possibility in an OSS planning document of May 16, 1945 – R & A 3034, 'Working Outline for Analysis of Policy Issues Regarding Japan'. And Kades claimed that he arrived in J at the very start of the Occ with draft directives on constitutional reform. (COH: Charles Kades). **Atcheson conferred with Konoye** James. p. 120. **Whitney prepared** *PRJ* Vol. II, p. 622. **advised by Atcheson** McNelly, 'Constitution and Law Reform', op. cit.

p. 91 **none an expert** William Sebald (later Political Adviser in Tokyo), who had been appointed to the POLAD office in response to SCAP's specific request for an expert in Japanese law, was not consulted. Hussey/Reischauer, Sept. 20, 1963. HP 93 A 65. **Lincoln's Constitutional History** Hellegers, op. cit. **Abbé Sièyes** Hellegers, op. cit. **compendium of constitutions** Hellegers, op. cit. **'Record of Events'** 'Record of Events on 13 February 1946 when proposed New Constitution for Japan was submitted to the Foreign Minister, Mr. Yoshida, on behalf of the Supreme Commander'. In the papers of Charles Kades, within JWP. Also in HP, Group 26.

p. 92 **psychological shaft** Whitney, *MacArthur*, p. 251. But cf. Takemoto, p. 193: it was one which the Japanese did not understand at the time. **only hope of survival** memo, Col. H. E. Robison. HP Group 23.

p. 93 **it is extremely unlikely** Hussey/Kades, Nov. 12, 1958. HP 93 B 5. Hussey's discomfort is understandable; but even if the existence of the Memorandum was a secret, the events of the meeting were by now well-publicised. Gayn, in *Japan Diary* (pub. 1948), had published an account which corresponds in outline and some of the more striking details with the Memorandum, while containing several inaccuracies. Where he got his information is not known: he refers to a memorandum written by Hussey and 'read to the staff at a general meeting'. If this is true, Gayn's source could have been one of a number of GS officials. **Katayama observed** Hellegers, op. cit.

Chapter 11 – Savage Apes

p. 97 **officer's diary entry** FO 371 51048 U 6867, Webb's report to UNWCC, Sept. 10, 1945. **atrocities** for descriptive account of Japanese atrocities, see e.g. E. F. L. Russell, *The Knights of the Bushido* (Dutton, 1958).

p. 98 **narcotics** see e.g. *The Opium Trade 1910–41* Vol. 6, 1927–41 (Scholarly Resources Inc., 1974). In 1939 joint representations were made by the US and British Ambassadors to the Japanese Government to stop the semi-official traffic in narcotics. **fear of reprisals** FO 371 51051 U9420. State Dept. Press Release 653, Sept. 4, 1945. **record sales of war bonds** Ware, op. cit. p. 9.

p. 99 **88%** Ware, p. 18. **Tojo and his gang** Ware, p. 11. **'minor'** our division of war criminal proceedings within Japan into major and minor trials reflects the jurisdiction of the courts at which these trials were held. In Japan only the IMTFE had jurisdiction to try alleged breaches of the *ius ad bellum*. (Outside Japan, Australian military tribunals also claimed this jurisdiction). In this book the defendants at the IMTFE are called 'major' war criminals; all the others are 'minor'. For

a comprehensive account of the Allied proceedings and courts' jurisdiction in S.E. Asia, see Philip R. Piccigallo, *The Japanese On Trial: Allied War Crime Operations in the East 1945–51* (Texas UP, 1971). **Russian propaganda timing** e.g. *Materials on the Trial of Former Servicemen of the Japanese Army Charged with Manufacturing and Employing Bacteriological Weapons* (Foreign Languages Publishing House, Moscow, 1950). **Chungking UNWCC** Piccigallo, op. cit. p. 5. **5700 . . . 4405 . . . 984** Piccigallo, pp. 264–65. **Portuguese Timor** FO 371 57432 U6650.

p. 100 **British Admiralty complaint** FO 371 57429 U8041, Nov. 18, 1946. **call a halt** FO 371 76252 F6005, JCS/SCAP, Apr. 1, 1949, relaying FEC recommendations to member governments. **British decision not to prosecute** FO 371 76254 F16343. **Churchill quote** FO 371 92699 FJ1664/1 – Lord Hankey's letter to *The Times*, Aug. 6, 1951; and see meeting with Lord Henderson.

p. 101 **1000 suspects . . . Kyushu University** FO 371 7654 SCAP Information Bulletin No. 19, Oct. 19, 1949. **inconceivable war crimes trials not held** see Maxine Jacobson Heller, *The Treatment of Defeated War Leaders* (Ph.D. Columbia, 1965. UMI 65–13, 954) in DIA, op. cit. p. 4786. 'The failure of the Allies to punish World War I leaders was frequently alluded to by Allied officials during World War II. Plans were consequently made fairly early during the war for the punishment of Axis leaders'. **monument to the futility of militarism** Saburo Ienaga, *Japan's Last War* (Blackwell, 1979) emphasises the value of public knowledge as a major weapon against war, with an enlightened public preventing irrational war, regardless of economic or strategic pressures influencing the élite.

p. 102 **Nuremberg tribunal** for a discussion of origins and problems, see Bradley F. Smith, *Reaching Judgment at Nuremberg* (Deutsch, 1977) and, with relation to the IMTFE,

Richard Minear, *Victor's Justice: the Tokyo War Crimes Trial* (Princeton UP, 1971). See also Buckley, *Occupation Diplomacy*, op. cit. pp. 106–22. **outlaw aggressive war** cf. Bradley F. Smith, *The American Road to Nuremberg: the Documentary Record 1944–45* (Hoover Institution Press, 1982), p. x. 'Intent is in many ways the crucial issue raised by these materials'. **putting on trial and punishing them** Bradley Smith, *The American Road*, op. cit. p. 30. Stimson/Roosevelt, Sept. 9, 1944, 'Punishment of these men in a dignified manner consistent with the advance of civilisation will have all the greater effect upon posterity'. **Stimson** on Aug. 8, 1932 Stimson had denounced the Japanese as 'lawbreakers' for their aggression in Manchuria – Armin Rappaport, *Henry L. Stimson and Japan 1931–33* (Chicago UP, 1963). Yet on Nov. 28, 1944 he opposed Col. W. C. Chanler's suggestion of trial for 'aggressive war' as being too innovative. Smith, *American Road*, p. 51; and cf. Henry L. Stimson and McGeorge Bundy, *On Active Service in Peace and War* (Harper, 1948), p. 587 n. 3. **conventional legal wisdom** see Hendrik Jan Van Eikema Hommes, *Major Trends in the History of Legal Philosophy* (North-Holland Publishing Co., 1979). **what had been established** the prevailing view was that of Dicey – 'A law is any rule which will be enforced by the courts'. See *Political Science Quarterly*, Vol. 69 (1954), where F. S. Burin describes A. L. Goodhart's assertion to the contrary as 'anachronistic'. **Stimsonianism** Arthur Schlesinger's definition, quoted by Richard Minear, cited by Kano Tsutomi, *JI* Vol. 11/3 Winter 1977, p. 263.

p. 103 **doubts in Japanese minds** FO 371 57429 U 7297. Gascoigne/FO, Sept. 24, 1946. 'Numerous Japanese publications have advanced strong arguments against the legality of international trials'. **United Nations** at the UN, agreement on a definition of aggression was not reached until 1974. Benjamin B. Ferencz, *An International Criminal Court – A*

Step Toward World Peace (Oceana Publications, 1980), Vol. 1, p. xii. **problem facing State Dept.** British inclined to let 'the Americans take charge'. LCO2 2983, Dean/War Office, Nov. 14, 1945 and Jan. 5, 1946. **policy too soft** NAW RG 59 Box 3812, State Dept. Papers 740.00119 Control (Japan)/9–1245, Sept. 12, 1945. **67% . . . extreme harshness** Ware, p. 27. **Acheson quote** NAW RG 59 Box 3812, State Dept. Papers 740.00119 Control (Japan)/9–645, Acheson/Ballantine, Sept. 6, 1945.

p. 104 **promise of usefulness in demilitarisation** FO 371 57424 U2160. Sansom/FO, stating the purpose of the IMTFE to be 'to stimulate in Japan a public sense of responsibility for national policy'. **include South Africa** FO 262 2047. FO/UKLIM, Jan. 4, 1946.

Chapter 12 – A Creature of International Law
p. 105 **nothing un-American** FO 371 63820. Reed/Shawcross, Nov. 11, 1947. **Machine Gun Kelly** authors' interview with Robert Donihi, Oct. 1985. **to bed before dinner** FO 371 69831. Shawcross/Jowitt, Jan. 23, 1948. **an embarrassment from Washington** FO 371 69834 FI7784, Gascoigne/FO, Dec. 1, 1948. MacA's own opinion; and, according to Gascoigne, the root problem in controlling Keenan was that he was a personal friend of Truman.

p. 106 **cohesive machine . . . not burdened** NAW RG 331 Box 593, Item 5. Darsey/Keenan, Apr. 26, 1946. **recuperative visits** R. Dingman, reviewing *Documents on New Zealand External Relations, Vol. II – The Surrender & Occupation of Japan* (1982) in *JAS* 43/4 Aug. 1984, is critical of MacA for allowing Keenan back after his first visit to Saratoga Springs to dry out. **genius in his way** Donihi, op. cit. **office boy** FO 371 57427. Reed/Attorney General, Apr. 16, 1946. **shared the Stimsonian view** see his post-Tokyo book, Joseph Berry Keenan and Brendan Francis Brown,

Crimes Against International Law (Public Affairs Press, Washington, 1950). p. 161. 'Unless there is honest faith in a higher law, restraining the unjust acts of those who are entrusted with the shaping and execution of national policies, and unless the world community puts that faith into effect by the continued implementation of this law, through international treaties and undertakings, and thereafter enforces international criminal law by judicial process, savagery and barbarism will assume grotesque and apocalyptic forms of frightfulness.' **civilisation today . . . again and again** NAW RG 331 Box 611, Item 3. Keenan memo, Jan. 24, 1946. Text formed basis for opening address.

p. 107 **IPS viewed its task** first draft of Charter in NAW RG 331 Box 596, item 11. And cf. FO 371 57422 U5. FO/British Embassy, Washington, Jan. 15, 1946, noting 'State Dept. propose limiting jurisdiction of the court to crimes against the peace', and urging extension. **did not suit Keenan** NAW RG 331 IMTFE Chief Prosecutor, Box 6 Items 7–8, Folder 40. Notes for Meeting with Sec. of War, Jan. 5, 1946. **public opinion dissatisfied** FO 371 57422 U745, Jan. 14, 1946.

p. 108 **traced back to 15th century** Natalie Jean Ferringer, *Crimes Against Humanity: a Legal Problem in War and Peace* (Ph.D. Virginia U, 1980. UMI 8022670). **judges in their own cause** 'The core of justice I take to be the exclusion of arbitrariness. Hence the great importance of the growth of legality, or the rule of law, which is slowly seen to carry with it the implication that no one can be a judge of their own cause.' Morris Ginsberg, *On Justice in Society* (Cornell UP, 1965), p. 10. **Toyoda case** transcript LCO2/2982; correspondence FO 371 76253.

p. 109 **Keenan's justification** FO 371 57432. Speech to FEC Committee No. 5 – War Criminals, June 25, 1946. **Nathan and Morgan** Ware, p. 34.

p. 110 **Eichelberger story** Robert J. C. Butow, *Tojo and the Coming of War* (Princeton UP, 1961), p. 455. **clear evidence of destruction** see generally NAW RG 331 IPS Investigative Division Case No. 43, 'Burning of Confidential Documents', inc. Six Air Force Order, Larsh memo, Takujiro Inoue letter July 1, 1947.

p. 111 **Time magazine** Feb. 3, 1947, p. 25, cited by Ware, p. 128. **no nonsense about rights** Tojo was well aware of the purpose of Fihelly's questions. Butow, op. cit. p. 480 (Fihelly/Tojo, Feb. 26, 1946). **interrogated by Fihelly** Butow, p. 477.

p. 112 **once Fihelly's interrogatories lodged** Robert Donihi interview, Oct. 1985. **the major war criminal** FO 371 54286 F556, Dec. 18, 1945. MacDermot/FO. **could not face humiliation** FO 371 54286 F2759. British Naval Liaison Officer, memo, Dec. 17, 1945. **Chiang Kai-shek** FO 371 51050 U8966. British Embassy, Chungking/FO **an end to fighting in China** Butow, *Japan's Decision to Surrender* (Stanford UP 1954) p. 19.

p. 113 **Konoye may have misconstrued** COH: Harold Henderson. And cf. Robert Donihi recalled that during the IPS investigation (conducted by Darsey) Konoye's closest friend, Jimmy Kawasaki, said that Konoye had misinterpreted American intentions. **Konoye's personal secretary** NAW RG 331 'Sources of Information: Confidential', Case No. 260 – Ushiba. **sybaritic and unwholesome** *Life*, June 26, 1947. Butow, *Tojo*, op. cit. p. 493. Robert Donihi remembers Tanaka offering to arrange 'temporary wives' for the IPS lawyers in Tokyo. **unless Tojo PM . . . it would be difficult** Tanaka's testimony, T15, 873; denied by Tojo, T36, 309.

p. 114 **prior to trial** NAW RG 331 Box 626, Item 8. Morgan/Keenan, Apr. 26, 1946. **Tanaka medical reports** see NAW RG 331, IPS-11, Case No. 234 – Tanaka, Ryukichi. **be gentlemanly** NAW RG 331 IPS-11, Case No. 234. Sasakawa/Edwards.

Chapter 13 – Crimes and Criminals

p. 115 **large staff . . . 277/232** SCAP Press Release on disbanding IPS – FO 371 80155. **Williams entrusted** NAW RG 331 Box 593, Item 7. **Keenan/IPS** staff, Apr. 22, 1946. **IPS remained flexible** NAW RG 331 Box 31, Item 10. Note of meeting, May 4, 1946, finalising 'method of coordination of the work of preparation and trial'.

p. 116 **12,000 documents** Ward and Shulman, op. cit. p. 344. **digested source material** NAW RG 331 Box 624, Items 2–4. **teams of attorneys . . . long-term watching briefs** FO 371 57428, see e.g. Keenan/IPS staff, May 8, 1946.

p. 117 **rebuttal outcry** see Ware, pp. 120–21. **one linguist two days** NAW RG 331 'IPS Chief Prosecutor', Box 31. Memo May 7, 1946. **Comyns Carr** Arthur Strettell Comyns Carr, b. 1882; called to Bar 1908; Liberal MP East Islington 1923–24; QC 1924; Bencher Gray's Inn 1938; knighted 1949.

p. 118 **frightful job** FO 371 57427 U5116. Carr/Attorney General, Mar. 19, 1946. **Carr drafted indictment** FO 371 57427 U5116. Reed/Attorney General, Apr. 16, 1946. **first 1500** NAW RG 331 Box 623, Item 9.

p. 119 **assuring Hitler** NAW RG 331 Box 610. Carr/Keenan, Feb. 15, 1946.

p. 120 **Tojo/Togo confusion** Count 25. See T15827 and T16120–1. Togo deleted, but substitution of Tojo not permitted. **full of errors** NAW RG 331 Box 599, Item 5. CLO/SCAP, May 8, 1946. **deviousness** NAW RG 331 Box 610. Carr/Keenan, Apr. 12, 1946.

p. 121 **repetitious, long-winded** NAW RG 331 Box 610. Lopez/Keenan, Apr. 13, 1946. **Brabner Smith's view** NAW RG 331 Box 610. Smith/Keenan, Apr. 14, 1946. **British intelligence conclusions** FO 371 57428 U6329. UKLIM Inter-Service Intelligence Committee Special Report No. 1, May 17, 1946. **proposal to Stimson** Smith, *American Road*, p. 10 – by Col.

Murray C. Bernays. And cf. Richard N. Current, *Secretary Stimson: A Study in Statecraft* (Archon, 1970), p. 218. 'In the early 1900s he had found "conspiracy" a useful charge in prosecuting American business men. It would do as well, he thought, in the prosecution of Nazi war criminals.'

p. 122 **representative of a larger group** Stimson and Bundy, *On Active Service*, op. cit. p. 586, quoting Diary, Nov. 21, 1944. **Stimson a lawyer** Rappaport, op. cit. p. 202. 'Much of Stimson's attitude toward international affairs derived from his legal training. . . . He approached treaties and their violations as a prosecuting attorney approached an individual who transgressed municipal law.' **Japanese situation infinitely more complicated** FO 371 57427 U5116. Carr/Attorney General, Mar. 11, 1946. **far-fetched theory of history** Minear, op. cit. pp. 125–59. e.g. 'The Tokyo Tribunal failed miserably in its attempts to write the history of the pre-war years'. And cf. *JE* Vol. 11 Special Issue 1984 for revisionist views of the trial. **Carl J. Friedrich** ed. Douglas G. Haring, *Japan's Prospect* (Harvard UP, 1946), p. (vii).

p. 123 **national policy adopted** A. Comyns Carr, article in *Far Eastern Survey*, May 18, 1949. **Tojo joined conspiracy** the Tribunal judged Tojo to have become a principal conspirator as of March 1937. Butow, *Tojo*, p. 511. **Tanaka Memorial** see generally W. F. Morton, *Tanaka Giichi and Japan's China Policy* (Dawson, 1980). **James Cagney** ed. Marlene J. Mayo, *The Emergence of Imperial Japan: Self Defense or Calculated Aggression?* (D. C. Heath, 1970), p. xi. **stopped looking for Tanaka Memorial** COH: Joseph Ballantine.

p. 124 **little concrete evidence** NAW RG 331 Box 593. Darsey memo, Dec. 9, 1945. **selection not mechanical** Solis Horwitz, 'The Tokyo Trial' in *International Conciliation* No. 465, Nov. 1950, pp. 494–98. **peg out incidents** FO 371 57427 U5163 & U5236. Keenan: 'The Indictment includes the survivors of those who . . . appear to have major responsibility for most of the phases.'

p. 125 **two additional accused** Shigemitsu and Umezu. FO 371 57426 U4295, UKLIM/FO. **five separate sources** NAW RG 331 IPS-11. 'Apprehension of War Criminals', File 99e. Memo Mar. 18, 1946.

p. 126 **enterprising Newsweek reporter** Ware, p. 85. **Shidehara . . . blunders** OSS/State Dept. Intelligence Research Reports. Part II Postwar Japan, Korea and S.E. Asia. Situation Report R & A No. 3479.55, Aug. 27, 1948. **national unity essential** *ibid.* **indictment aroused interest** *ibid.* **sense of relief** the Japanese public were aware that the Imperial Family was 'not inviolate' – especially after the arrest of Prince Nashimoto. FO 371 51051.BFP/FO, Dec. 9, 1945.

Chapter 14 – The Shadow of the Emperor
p. 127 **political nature** *JE* Special Issue 1984, p. 65. And cf. FO 371 69834 F16716 – attempting to find justification for not trying the Emperor, in anticipation of Parliamentary question. **Keenan and Tojo's testimony** Minear, pp. 113–14, Note 83. And cf. *JE* Special Issue 1984, p. 66. 'Keenan . . . went to extraordinary lengths to force Tojo to testify to the emperor's exemption from responsibility.'

p. 128 **Brannon's cri de coeur** Pritchard, Vol. 22, 'Petition for Review on Behalf of Kido, Koichi'. **why Emperor not indicted** see e.g. Moore, review of Buckley, *Occupation Diplomacy* in *JJS* 10/1, op. cit. p. 240. 'My own research suggests that the final decision was made in MacArthur's headquarters.' **America anticipated the day** Alva C. Carpenter, Chief of SCAP's Legal Section, announced at a press conference, 'No person in Japan is immune from being named as a war criminal'. *Mainichi*, Oct. 25, 1945. **JCS on Nov. 29, 1945** NAW RG 218 Japan 1946, WARX 85811. **Soviet formal Notes** FO 371

92698 FJ 1662/1. Franks/FO, Jan. 29, 1951. **'Destroy him'** NAW RG 218 'Japanese War Criminals', CA 57235.

p. 129 **Emperor not indicated** FO 371 57428 U6078, June 24, 1946. **capital political blunder** FO 371 57422 U750. FO/British Embassy, Washington, Dec. 26, 1945. And cf. FO 371 57423 F1194 'major political blunder', and FO 371 51051 U8787, Dominions Office/Australian Government, Aug. 17, 1945 – 'capital political error'. **Russians made no mention** FO 371 27426 U4332, note dated Apr. 23, 1946; and U4758, UKLIM/FO May 1, 1946.

p. 130 **breach of faith** Bonner F. Fellers' memo of Oct. 2, 1945, in Woodard, op. cit. pp. 360–61. See also *JJS* Vol. 10/1, Moore op. cit. p. 251: citing the Japanese 'official view that Japan, in accepting the Potsdam Proclamation, had entered into an international agreement with provisions that both sides were obliged to honour'. **Potsdam meant preservation of Emperor** see Fellers' memo, op. cit. And cf. Stimson and Bundy, op. cit. p. 267, describing the wording of the Potsdam Declaration regarding the Emperor as 'masterful'. **OWI refrained from castigating Emperor** Allan M. Winkler *The Politics of Propaganda: the Office of War Information* (Yale UP), p. 142. **Chichibu rightist** (transl. and intro.) Mikiso Hane, *Emperor Hirohito and His Chief Aide de Camp. The Honjo Diary 1933–36* (Tokyo UP, 1982), p. 50. **suit our interests** FO 371 54286 F3512. Foulds' note, Feb. 27, 1946.

p. 131 **until Mar. 1946** NAW RG 331 Box 623, Item 8. Keenan/Legal Staff, Mar. 28, 1946. **proved Emperor's guilt conclusively** FO 371 69831. Carr/Shawcross, Jan. 2, 1948. **Carr's belief** there is a suggestion in a note on file FO 371 69833 F16333 of a conversation on Nov. 17, 1948 that Carr may have changed his mind; he thought that 'a fair-minded tribunal would probably have acquitted the Emperor if he had been brought to trial'. **guilty of conspiracy even though** NAW RG

331 Box 599, Item 6. Memo Brown, Pollack and Taranto/Keenan, May 23, 1946.

p. 132 **Hirohito did have power** see generally Mikiso Hane, op. cit. And cf. Ben Ami Shillony review, *JJS* 10/12 Summer 1984, pp. 524ff.; and FO 371 76250 80080, E. H. Norman's assessment of Saionji Harada memoirs, p. 17. **concept of family** Song, op. cit. p. 135, citing Kizaemon Ariga. **sense of other-worldliness** Douglas G. Harin, 'Religion, Magic and Morale' in ed. D. G. Haring, *Japan's Prospect* (Harvard UP, 1946), p. 246. Cited Song, p. 72. **order their conduct** Song, p. 148. **seems a restraining force** Mikiso Hane, p. 62.

p. 133 **throat cut** FO 262 2056. Gascoigne/Dening, Jan. 22, 1947. **Emperor's decision to end war** see generally Butow, *Japan's Decision*, op. cit. **responsible to Imperial ancestors** GHQ FEC Military Intelligence Section, Historical Division. Statements of Japanese Officials on World War II. **a stronger force for peace** cf. FO 371 69914, Gascoigne's *Japan: Annual Report for 1947*, p. 4. 'While Hirohito himself wishes, I think, sincerely to assume the role of a democratic monarch, Imperial Household officials are antagonistic to the democratisation of the palace and the consequent diminution of their own prestige.'

p. 134 **Emperor's letter to Sansom** FO 371 54286 F3512, Jan. 29, 1946.

Chapter 15 – The Case for the Prosecution
p. 135 **Hollywood premiere** *Time*, May 20, 1946, p. 24. Quoted in Minear, p. 3, Butow, *Tojo* p. 484. **hot court** FO 371 57429 U6601 Humphreys/ Scott Fox, July 16, 1946. 'The judges are fighting among themselves, and have now struck work altogether at the heat in court, and the whole Trial is dragging along at a slower tempo than even I, always the pessimistic prophet, thought possible. In the Legation we play tennis at 85 degrees and just drip placidly.'

p. 136 **miserable-looking lot** first draft of William J. Sebald, *With MacArthur In Japan* (in the East Asia Collection, McKeldin Library, University of Maryland), Chapter 8, Aug. 28, 1963. **Indien, Kommen Sie** Attorney Hayashi, reported in *Nippon Times*, May 7, 1956. **saved by penicillin** Pritchard, Vol. 22. 'Proceedings in Chambers', Aug. 23, 1946. **Sebald not in sympathy** Sebald, *With MacArthur*, op. cit.

p. 137 **zaibatsu spearheaded . . . Keenan announced** FO 371 57429. Gascoigne/FO, Nov. 5, 1946.

p. 138 **no discrimination against French** FO 371 57429. Gascoigne/FO, Nov. 5, 1946. **routine tactical exercises** see Tojo's Affidavit T36193. 'The Supreme Command drew up strategic operational plans against potential enemies in peace time the same as the army branch so designated in every nation did.'

p. 139 **judgement on Tojo** T49,845–8.

p. 140 **precedent** cf. Telford Taylor, *Nuremberg and Vietnam: An American Tragedy* (New York, 1970), p. 207. 'Somehow we failed ourselves to learn the lessons we undertook to teach at Nuremberg, and that failure is today's American tragedy.' **Bertrand Russell** ed. John Duffett, *Against the Crime of Silence: Proceedings of the International War Crimes Tribunal, Stockholm and Copenhagen*. **droning testimony** NAW RG 331 Box 593, Item 7. Keenan/ IPS staff, Apr. 22, 1946. **frustrated by Webb** Webb's background as principal investigator of Japanese atrocities against Australian soldiers may have led MacA to expect him to be more overtly a counterbalance to SCAP liberalism outside the courtroom. See Grant Goodman, 'MacArthurian Japan: Remembered and Revised', *International Studies*, 1983/1. p. 3. Webb 'seemed to epitomise popular Australian racial and political animosity toward Japan at that time'. **Morrow row** OCP 'Trial of Tojo – China Aggressive Phase'. **second-rate show** Ware, p. 84.

p. 141 **Hirota . . . prosecution allegations unanswered** but he did initially object to the Indictment on various grounds – for example, that the acts alleged were 'acts of the Japanese government acting in its sovereign capacity as a government'. Pritchard, Vol. 22, 'Proceedings in Chambers', June 12, 1946. **Hirota . . . jumped on** Saburo Shiroyama (transl. John Bester), *War Criminal: the Life and Death of Hirota Koki* (Kodansha, 1977), p. 149. **Richard Storry** *Times Lit. Supp.*, May 12, 1978, p. 520. **worried to death** FO 371 57429 U8295. Dec. 26, 1946.

p. 142 **American shysters** LCO2 2992. Gascoigne/FO, May 15, 1947. **fair not speedy** FO 371 57429 U8063. Gascoigne/FO, Nov. 23, 1946. **grave misgivings** T915–935, June 18–19, 1946. And cf. Keenan's application for *all* witnesses to give direct evidence in affidavit form – T2549.

p. 143 **pig in Far China** NAW RG 331 Box 599, Item 6. 'Conference on Matters in Relation to Expedition of the Trial', June 24, 1947, p. 15. **best evidence rule introduced halfway through trial** Minear, p. 122. **acted not acted upon** FO 371 76250 F1146. E. H. Norman summary, p. 18. **Iron Curtain speech inadmissible** Ware, p. 106.

p. 144 **communism not relevant** Ware, p. 104. **Tojo affidavit** T36,485. **prevention of communism** this argument found favour with Mr. Justice Pal, but his motives have been the subject of debate – see e.g. Saburo Ienaga, *Japan's Last War*, op. cit., and *JI* Vol. 11/3 Winter 1977, pp. 264–78, debate between Ienaga and Minear. **acme of barbarism** Martin Bronfenbrenner, *Fusako and the Army: An Episode of Occupation* (Hokuseido Press, 1952), p. 26. 'However much they might read of Japanese atrocities and war crimes . . . to their minds, America's exports of atrocities would always exceed her imports.'

Chapter 15 – The Case for the Defence
p. 145 **defence attorneys' view of job facing them** T214–15 Major Ben Bruce Blakeney: 'Those of us American

defense counsel who wear the uniform of the armed forces of our country, I think also have the right to speak for America. We speak for American, for Anglo-Saxon, for Anglo-American, for democratic views of justice, of fair play. We speak for the proposition that observing legal forms, while ignoring the essence of legal principles, is the supreme atrocity against the law. It is to the commission of this atrocity that the invitation is extended by the Indictment.' May 14, 1946. **all these disadvantages** for general tenor of defense counsel's attitude, see OCP. **funds, lodgings, food** Ware, p. 91. **attorneys contributing 1000 yen** Ware, p. 70. **Webb persuaded SCAP to arrange** Ware, p. 86.

p. 146 **another ten million yen** *Nippon Times*, May 7, 1956. **Valentine Deale** *NYT*, Dec. 19, 1948. **flowers gracefully** *ibid.* **too polite and courteous** OCP 'Trial of Tojo'. **waste of time** T905 and T907. **Japanese in charge** e.g. OCP Telecom, Owen Cunningham: draft press release, Feb. 14, 1947. In preparing the defence opening statement 'American counsel have only served as advisers and have participated to a very little extent in the selection of the substance'.

p. 147 **not an advocate of Japanese cause . . . sole purpose conviction** OCP, Cunningham address to American Bar Association, Seattle, Sept. 7, 1948. **erroneous presumption** OCP, Cunningham address to ABA, op. cit. **frown on American counsel** FO 371 57423 U1666. Report of Carr's meeting with US War Dept. **fair, legal nor impartial** T198. **Webb's atrocities inquiry** see FO 371 51048 U7124.

p. 148 **conducted armed aggression** NAW RG 331 Box 593, Item 5. May 28, 1946, Golunsky/Keenan. **hounded out by Keenan** interview, Robert Donihi. **Myron C. Cramer** FO 371 57429 U7247. Sansom/FO, Sept. 16, 1946. **defence contended . . . trouble with Russians** OCP, 'Trial of Tojo'. **political harangue** Ware, p. 93.

alternate judges LCO2 2983. British Embassy, Washington/FO, Dec. 31, 1945– 'no alternates in view of the problems of accommodation, transportation, and the difficulties of local arrangements'; and cf. NAW RG 218 LEAHY 53 Box 9. CinCAFPAC/War Dept., Dec. 22, 1945. **I would be deceiving you** Ware, p. 98.

p. 149 **by Cunningham's calculations** OCP 'Trial of Tojo'. **gravest blot** FO 371 63820. Gascoigne/FO, Nov. 10, 1947. **counsel extremely enterprising** see OCP 'Telecom: Owen Cunningham'. **Marshall's Affidavit** FO 371 F16755. Gascoigne/FO, Apr. 27, 1948. And cf. OCP Telecom, Sept. 25, 1947 and ff.

p. 150 **committee of judges' report** LCO2 2992. McDougall/ Members of IMTFE, Mar. 27, 1947. **mess . . . fulsome apologia** LCO2 2992. Patrick/Lord President of the Court of Session, Mar. 29, 1947.

p. 151 **easily be a complete breakdown** LCO2 2992. Northcroft/New Zealand Chief Justice, Mar. 28, 1947.

p. 152 **shipping losses . . . Apostolic Delegate** FO 371 63820 F14788. Gascoigne/FO, Oct. 14, 1947. **driven by economic blockade . . . first fuse** FO 371 63820 F13150. Gascoigne/FO, Sept. 11, 1947. **British revelations** FO 371 F13150. Gascoigne/FO, Sept. 11, 1947.

p. 153 **Muto and Koiso** FO 371 69831. Gascoigne/FO, Dec. 16, 1947. **Doihara, Araki and Hashimoto** FO 371 63820. Gascoigne/FO, Oct. 14, 1947. **abusive cross-examination** OCP 'Trial of Tojo – Preface'. **cloven hoof** FO 371 63820. Carr/Shawcross, Oct. 6, 1947.

p. 154 **even more disastrously** FO 371 63820. Carr/Shawcross, Oct. 21, 1947.

Chapter 17 – Tojo's Defence of Japan
p. 155 **Hagakure** see *Mishima on Hagakure – The Samurai Ethic and Modern Japan* (Penguin, 1977), p. 58.

transl. Kathryn Sparling. **Seikai Shunju . . . Horitsu Shimpo** FO 371 57429 SCAP CIE Media Analysis Division, Sept. 11, 1946.

p. 156 **ridiculed ignominious failure** Butow, *Tojo*, p. 468. **Remember Pearl Harbor . . . gum** Ware, p. 102. **undignified mutual recriminations** OSS/State Dept, op. cit. Aug. 27, 1948. **shot its bolt** FO 371 69914. Japan: *Annual Report for 1947*, p. 1. **sworn testimony three days** OCP 'Trial of Tojo'.

p. 157 **Tojo's Affidavit** T36,171– 36,488, plus exhibits. **Aritomo Yamagata** Roger F. Hackett, *Yamagata Aritomo in the Rise of Modern Japan 1838–1922* (Harvard UP, 1971), p. 172 – pointing out a personal connection between Yamagata and Tojo's father. **sincerity of extreme significance** the root seems to lie in Zen Buddhism – Caldarola, p. 85. 'The life which Zen points to is the life of integrity . . . its alternative is the partial and fragmented life, the life of alienation, of posturing and insincerity.' And cf. Song, p. 222.

p. 158 **US frustrating Konoye peace initiative** T36,270. **USSR broke Neutrality Pact** T36,484. **denial of preparations for war** T36,242– 36,248. And cf. T36,285 – 'Japan's preparations for possible hostilities against America and Britain were made as emergency measures.' **military encirclement** T36,273. **Hawaiian islands defence** T36,274. **clearly discernible** T36,275. **if we swallow American demands** T36,302.

p. 159 **Japan made unbearable concessions** T36,291. **waging an economic war . . . fruits of victory** T36,292. **take up arms** T36,281. **exhaustion of liquid fuel** T36,322. **most conducive time** T36,281–2. **'have' nations** T36,194–5. **not too hopeful of winning** T36,282–3. **America's spiritual poverty** R. Courtney-Browne, *Tojo: The Last Banzai* (Angus & Robertson, 1967), p. 26. And cf. Butow, *Tojo*, pp. 16–17.

p. 160 **expression of His Majesty** T36,327–8.

p. 161 **Tojo accepts responsibility** T36,488. **Tojo's Affidavit** FO 371 69831. Gascoigne/FO, Jan. 25, 1948. **crude and strident** FO 371 F16755. Gascoigne/FO, Apr. 27, 1948, calling it 'an outrageous document . . . written by a former editor of the *Jiji Shimpo*'.

p. 162 **Carr's version of Keenan story** FO 371 69831. Carr/Shawcross, Jan. 2, 1948. **Cunningham has recorded** OCP 'Trial of Tojo'. **transcript of Tojo/Keenan/Fihelly debacle** T36,533–5. **accused Tojo** T36,535.

p. 163 **scored heavily in every exchange** FO 371 69831. Gascoigne/FO, Jan. 25, 1948. **President is highest authority** T36,783. **Vichy government** FO 371 69831. Gascoigne/FO, Jan. 25, 1948, encl. 4. **MacArthur foresaw possibility . . . probably profound** FO 371 69831. Gascoigne/FO, Jan. 25, 1948.

Chapter 18 – Judges and Judgements
p. 164 **Yasuaki Onuma** *JE* Vol. 11, Special Issue 1984, pp. 63–4.

p. 165 **when I got out here** LCO2 2992. Memo by Lord Patrick, enclosed with letter Lord Normand/Lord Jowitt, Feb. 5, 1947 (Patrick Memorandum). And cf. LCO2 2992. Erima Northcroft/New Zealand Chief Justice, Mar. 18, 1947. **Lord Patrick appointment file** LCO2 2986. **obvious political motive** for Gascoigne's opinion, see FO 371 69834 F17460. Gascoigne/Dening, Nov. 25, 1948. The SEA Dept. of the FO noted on Dec. 13, 1948, 'Krishna Menon . . . expressed disquiet at the attitude adopted by Mr. Justice Pal'. See also Ian Nish, 'India and the Occupation of Japan', *International Studies*, 1983/1.

p. 166 **Patrick's view, the waverers** Patrick Memorandum, op. cit. **an extraordinary document** Patrick Memorandum, op. cit. **Webb resentful at rejection** cf. *FEER*, Aug. 29, 1983. Iwao Hoshi, commenting on

Ian Buruma's article on the IMTFE in the previous issue, says that at Webb's request he wrote about the scholastic doctrine of just war, war crimes and their punishment, as Webb considered the court's mandate 'a not quite convincing legitimization of the proceedings and was concerned about whether the trial could be based on natural law'.

p. 167 **Bench in disarray** Patrick Memorandum. **this is dreadful** FO 371 F13724. Gascoigne/FO. Feb. 14, 1948. **fellow judges as jury** LCO2 2992. Mar. 18, 1947, Northcroft letter.

p. 168 **Canberra Conference** Patrick's opinion, expressed to Gascoigne. LCO2 2992. Gascoigne/FO, Oct. 9, 1947. **Australia had lost interest** LCO2 2992. Gascoigne/FO, Oct. 9, 1947. **insignificance of New Zealand** FO 371 63820 F15007. Gascoigne/FO, Nov. 11, 1947. **dumbfounded . . . sudden death** FO 371 63820 F15007. Gascoigne/FO, Nov. 11, 1947. **Cramer not suitable . . . nevertheless** FO 371 63820 F15007. Gascoigne/FO, Nov. 11, 1947. **deplorable . . . shelving responsibility** FO 371 63820 F15007. Gascoigne/FO, Nov. 11, 1947. **edited by judges . . . butchered** OCP 'Trial of Tojo'.

p. 169 **trial statistics** Minear, p. 5, and Ward and Shulman, p. 341. **9,500,000** FO 371 F14750. Gascoigne/FO, Mar. 5, 1948.

p. 170 **Pal's memorial service** Richard Minear, 'In Defense of Radha Binod Pal' [sic], *JI* Vol. 11/3 Winter 1977, p. 264.

p. 171 **SCAP prudently forbade publication** Ward & Shulman abstract, p. 345; and *Nippon Times*, May 7, 1956. But cf. FO 371 69834 F17460, Gascoigne/Dening, Nov. 25, 1948. Pal 'came to Japan with the fixed intention of "torpedoing" any judgements condemning the defendants. Before Justice Pal arrived . . . his ten colleagues on the Court had signed a document to the effect that any dissenting judgement which might be delivered would not be published. Pal, however, insisted on the publication of his totally dissenting judgement'. SCAP also forbade publication in Japan of A. F. Reel's *The Case of General Yamashita* – see *Washington Post*, Oct. 24, 1949. **sentences lenient** *NYT*, Nov. 21, 1948 reported Kido's son 'found dancing in the corridor' at the life sentence given his father – having presumably feared hanging. **not want clemency** in his Petition for Review to MacA following conviction, Tojo wished it 'to be strictly understood that no request is made of the Supreme Commander for clemency or for reduction of sentence meted out by the Tribunal'.

p. 172 **public eulogy** FO 371 69834 F17784. Gascoigne/Sec. of State for Foreign Affairs, Dec. 1, 1948. Keenan praised for having 'contributed immeasurably to the cause of humanity and the further development of international law'. **further major case** Toyoda; the acquittal they won reflected badly on the convictions at the IMTFE. **MacArthur consulted the Allies** FO 371 69833 F16062. Gascoigne's report, Nov. 28, 1948. **approval of a majority** reservations were expressed by Dutch and Indian representatives. FO 371 69833. Gascoigne/FO, Nov. 28, 1948.

p. 173 **seven defendants** there was an eighth application by Shigemitsu, not filed in time to be heard with the first seven. FO 371 76254 F3841. **one judge broke ranks** *Nippon Times*, Dec. 10, 1948. **most unfortunate** FO 371 69834. UKLIM/FO, Dec. 13, 1948. **'ill-judged' press reports . . . not above question** FO 371 69834 F18518. Gascoigne/FO, Dec. 13, 1948. **complete misunderstanding . . . neglect it** FO 371 F17083. Gascoigne/FO, Dec. 2, 1948.

p. 174 **rescue a few remains** defence attorney Hayashi in *Nippon Times*, May 7, 1956. **Douglas opinion** FO 371 76252 F10639.

Chapter 19 – Alien Soil
p. 175 **political failure** FO 371 69832. Note on file, Oct. 23, 1948. **only to a limited degree** OSS/ State Dept. Intelligence Research Reports. Part II: Postwar Japan, Korea and S.E. Asia. Situation Report R & A No. 3479.59, Dec. 3, 1948. **genuine resentment** FO 371 69833. Gascoigne/FO, Nov. 17, 1948. **unsuccessful** OSS/State Dept. Intelligence Research Reports. Part II: Postwar Japan, Korea and S.E. Asia. Situation Report R & A No. 3479.55, Aug. 27, 1948. **standards of justice . . . in the new Constitution** Chap. 3, Article 39. 'No person shall be held criminally liable for an act which was lawful at the time it was committed.'

p. 176 **not the servant of society** Talcott Parsons, *The System of Modern Societies* (Prentice Hall, 1971), p. 136. 'Even recently, Japan's legal institutions seem weaker than those of pre-Revolutionary Russia.' **modern law a veneer in Japan** René David & J. E. C. Brierley, *Major Legal Systems in the World Today* (Stevens, 1968), pp. 20, 450–60. And cf. Minear, *Japanese Tradition*, op. cit. p. 192. 'Resistance to a western concept of law in pre-war Japan had deep social and psychological roots.' **no transcendent laws** Koschmann, p. 8. Neither Buddhism nor Christianity succeeded in establishing transcendent morality, both being defeated by a 'core value system based on a "rather naive communal religion – functional, affirmative, this-worldly"'. **group's own value system** William M. Wallace, *Cultural Values and Economic Development: A Case Study of Japan* (Ph.D. Washington, 1963. UMI 64,6443). See also Matsumoto, op. cit. p. 204. 'The concept of group duty rather than individual right, religious principle, or Good or Evil determines ethical behaviour.' And JWP 107.06, Williams/Colegrove, Mar. 18, 1948. 'Precedent means everything to the Japanese, ethics (in the Christian sense) absolutely nothing.' **demands of filial piety** George de Vos, 'The Relation of Guilt Toward Parents To Achievement and Arranged Marriage Among the Japanese', in *Psychiatry* Vol. 23, Aug. 1960 No. 3. See also the discussion of Kanzo Uchimura's guilt feelings in Robert Lee, 'Service to Christ and Country: Uchimura's Search for Meaning' in ed. Ray A. Moore, *Michigan Papers in Japanese Studies*, No. 5, 1981. De Vos's point is that in Japanese psychology guilt is related primarily to ego rather than super-ego functions. NB The concept of filial piety is much wider than the narrow western understanding of the term, and (in the 1930s) encompassed 'ancestor worship, the worship of Shinto deities, reverence of the Emperor and service to the nation, and setting the parents' minds at ease'. Song, p. 140. **explain their barbarity** see generally ed. Michael Howard, *Restraints on War: Studies in the Limitation of Armed Conflict* (OUP, 1979).

p. 177 **Yuji Aida** Y. Aida, *Prisoner of the British – A Japanese Soldier's Experiences in Burma* (transl. Hide Ishiguro & Louis Allen, Cresset Press, 1966), p. 45. **two American anthropologists** Geoffrey Gorer, 'Themes in Japanese Culture' in *Transactions of the New York Academy of Sciences*, Series II 5(5), 1943; and Weston La Barre, 'Some Observations on Character Structure in the Orient: the Japanese', in *Psychiatry*, 8, 1945. **control their sphincters** Gorer, op. cit. in William A. Haviland, *Cultural Anthropology* (Holt Rinehart & Winston, 1983), p. 153. **smashes his toys** FO 371 46464 80589. 'Diagnosis of Japanese Psychology', Part II, Apr. 27, 1945. **Maruyama's suggestion** Masao Maruyama, 'Theory and Psychology of Ultranationalism' (1946), in ed. Ivan Morris, *Thought and Behaviour in Modern Japanese Politics* (OUP, 1963), p. 19. **erosion of individual responsibility** Scalapino, op. cit. p. 130 makes the further point that 'respect for individual personality' was also stunted.

p. 178 **Imperial institution** *In re Masuda* 1945 (I War Crimes Reports 71). Japanese defence counsel argued (unsuccessfully but perhaps accurately) that given the relation between Emperor and soldier, 'it was not possible to apply "the liberal and individualistic ideas which rule usual societies unmodified to this totalistic and absolutistic society"', in L. C. Green, *Superior Orders in National and International Law* (A. W. Sijthoff International Publishing Co., 1976). **Japan unable to do wrong** Maruyama, op. cit. p. 9. And cf. Hillis Lory, *Japan's Military Masters* (Viking, 1943), p. 34. Japan is 'an enemy without ethics. . . . Whatever promotes the rule of a sacred Emperor is right'. **Report on Mentality** FO 371 76251 F5338. Assistant Commissioner Prisons, Singapore/FO, Mar. 30, 1949. And cf. Tsurumi, pp. 147–53. **Vietnam atrocities** see e.g. eds. R. A. Falk, G. Kolko, R. J. Lifton, *Crimes of War: a legal, political-documentary and psychological inquiry into the responsibility of leaders, citizens and soldiers for criminal acts in war* (Vintage Books, 1971), esp. pp. 462–48, Peter G. Bourne, 'From Boot Camp to My Lai'. **GIs and Japanese directly comparable** testimony of Jean Chesneaux – 'concerning contemporary American war crimes, a reference to Tokyo seems much more germane and relevant than the reference to Nuremberg', in Duffett, op. cit. p. 53. And cf. Seymour Melman, *In the Name of America: the Conduct of the War in Vietnam by the Armed Forces of the United States as shown by published reports* (Clergy & Laymen Conference about Vietnam, 1968).

p. 179 **brutalising effect** R. John Pritchard, 'The Nature and Significance of British Post-war Trials of Japanese War Criminals 1945–8', *PBAJS* Vol. 2, 1977 Part 1, p. 191. Pritchard suggests that brutal training 'affected the judgement' of those responsible for systematic maltreatment of prisoners-of-war. And cf. Tsurumi, pp. 115–19 on violence as a deliberate technique of army socialisation. **racial hatreds** See Herbert P. Bix, *JI* 8/2 Spring 1983, p. 236. **military subcultures everywhere** Geoffrey Best, 'Restraints on War by Land Before 1945', in Howard, op. cit. pp. 24–26. **Japanese society antipathetic** 'The gulf between hostile attitudes and institutional structure inherited from the Tokugawa era and Western democracy was too great to bridge.' Ardath W. Burks reviewing Robert Scalapino, *Democracy and the Party Movement in Prewar Japan: the Failure of the First Attempt* (California, 1953), in *Political Science Quarterly* 69 (1954), pp. 285–7.

p. 180 **needed the cultural milieu of the west** E. Wight Bakke, *Revolutionary Democracy: Challenge and Testing in Japan* (Archon, 1968). He likens America's effort to a tree cut off above the roots and then transplanted. And cf. Sannosuke Matsumoto, 'The Roots of Political Disillusionment – "Public" and "Private" in Japan', in Koschmann, op. cit. p. 31. 'A system of government must be a manifest crystallisation of the way of life of the nation in which it operates.' **did not see individual self-interest** Japanese society emphasises 'collective goal attainment'. Talcott Parsons, *The System of Modern Societies* (Prentice Hall, 1971), p. 134 **not psychologically equipped** e.g. Koschmann, pp. 1–30. **fundamental revolution needed** 'Only with a change in the ethics and value judgements of the Japanese can there be hope for . . . a lasting democratic political order.' Robert King Hall, *Shushin: the Ethics of a Defeated Nation* (Columbia UP, 1949), p. vii. **meaning and coherence to the term democracy** see also NAS RG 331 Box 5243 for media plans; activities of the League of Political Education, founded on May 18, 1947; Japan Civil Liberties Union, etc. **Information Officers** see generally NAS RG 331 Boxes 5215–30. 'CIE Information Division Administrative Branch.' **November schedule** NAS RG 331 Box 5223 'Information Program (General) 52a'. **war guilt** 158th US Army Dept. Weekly Report on Japan, Dec. 24, 1948, mentions one documentary and two feature films informing Japanese people of leaders' war guilt.

p. 181 **tighter into the group** Bennett/ Ishino, p. 213. 'Paternalistic organisations, in either their bene-

volent or cynically exploitative phases, arise to meet needs for security not provided by other means.' **soldiers better able to cope** Matsumoto, p. 219, citing Edward Shils' summary of Samuel A. Stouffer et al., 'The American Soldier: Combat and its Aftermath', in *Studies in Social Psychology in World War II*, Vol. II, 1949, pp. 130–49. 'American soldiers under battle situations subordinated individualistic interests and adopted primacy in group values much as the Japanese have been forced [to do] under less dramatic but nonetheless stressful economic conditions.' **most Japanese in oyabun/kobun relationships** Chie Nakane, *Japanese Society* (Penguin, 1970). Koschmann, p. 11, sees 'traditional habits' rooted in 'linguistic and thought patterns'.

p. 182 **first became aware of oyabun/ kobun system** NAS RG 331 Box 5243; and cf. JWP; FO 262 2056. See also Bennett/Ishino, op. cit., and Harry Emerson Wildes, 'Postwar Politics in Japan, II', in *American Political Science Review*, pp. 1149–62. **Hokkaido labour bosses** JWP File 53 – Harry Emerson Wildes' report submitted Sept. 30, 1946. **system endemic in Japanese life** JWP 105.3. Williams/H. S. Quigley, Nov. 11, 1947. 'Every aspect of Japanese life is influenced if not controlled by the oyabun and their stooges.'

p. 183 **information campaign** see Williams, op. cit. Chapter 3. **pointing out the threat** e.g. *Nippon Times*, Dec. 3, 1947.' The scum of the underworld is living again the customs of an era when his progenitors wore two swords' – i.e. the *samurai* of feudal Japan. **Howard Handleman** FO 262 2056 F76099, for Gascoigne's comments. **bootblacks . . . official favours** *Nippon Times*, Nov. 23, 1947. **Sunday conference** described by J. F. Sullivan, memo Nov. 10, 1947, NAS RG 331 Box 5243, 'Oyabun/Kobun Conferences'. **awful fools** Hauge & Sullivan, memo Dec. 5, 1947. NAS RG 331 Box 5243 'Oyabun/Kobun Conferences'. **public mention taboo** see

Sullivan memos of Jan. 5, Jan. 14, and Jan. 28, 1948. NAS RG 331 Box 5243 'Oyabun/Kobun Conferences'.

Chapter 20 – From Enemy to Ally
p. 187 **humanitarian grounds** MacA's 'Report of Japan's Food Situation for Herbert Hoover, Chairman of the Famine Emergency Committee,' May 6, 1946, *PRJ* Vol. II, p. 749. And cf. his speech 'In Support of Appropriations for Occupation Purposes', Feb. 20, 1947, *PRJ* Vol. II, p. 764. 'As a consequence of the illtreatment including starvation of Allied prisoners in J hands, we have tried and executed many J officers upon proof of responsibility. Yet can we justify such punitive action if we ourselves in reversed circumstances, but with hostilities at an end, fail to provide the food to sustain life among those J people over whom we now stand guard within the narrow confines of their home islands?'

p. 188 **OSS secret memorandum** OSS Research & Analysis Branch, R & A 3034. 'Working Outline for Analysis of Policy Issues Regarding Japan', May 16, 1945. Library of Congress, Washington.

p. 189 **within a fortnight of Yalta** Joseph Grew, *Turbulent Era: A Diplomatic Record of Forty Years, 1904–45* (Houghton Mifflin, 1952), p. 1443. **Grew urged** Grew/Henry Stimson, May 12, 1945. DoA Records, RG 165, ABC 336, 'Russia in the Far East'. Cited by Schaller, p. 9. **Russia's intention to 'turn' Germany** Bruce Kuklick, *American Policy and the Division of Germany: the Clash with Russia over Reparations* (Cornell UP, 1972), p. 230. **the first shot** P. M. S. Blackett, *Fear, War and the Bomb: Military and Political Consequences of Atomic Energy* (1949). **one American observer** NAW RG 59 State Dept. Papers, Box 3812. 740.00119 Control (Japan). H. Merrell Benninghoff, HQ XIV Corps US Army/Sec. of State, Sept. 15, 1945. **aware of US/Soviet tensions** rumour was prevalent in the autumn of 1946 that Tojo would 'escape death and be used in the event of war between Russia and America'. Interrogation Mitsuhiko Komato, WO 268 768, BRINDIV, op. cit. **Rear-Admiral Sadatoshi** Ikuhiko Hata, 'The Postwar Period in Retrospect', *JE* Vol. XI, Special Issue 1984, pp. 13–14. **study of atomic warfare** Akira Iriye, *Power and Culture: the Japanese-American War, 1941–45* (Harvard UP, 1981), p. 266. **Truman stormed** Harry S. Truman, *Memoirs* (Doubleday, 1955), pp. 600–6. **Stalin claimed** Kenneth W. Condit, *The History of the Joint Chiefs of Staff: the Joint Chiefs of Staff and National Policy, Volume II, 1947–9* (JCS, 1978), Chapter 1.

p. 190 **declaration of World War II** Supreme Court Justice William O. Douglas, quoted in Emmerson, op. cit. p. 283. **Alanbrooke recorded** Arthur Bryant, *Triumph in the West 1943–46* (Collins, 1959), entry for Nov. 18, 1945, pp. 395–6. **men of Moscow** FO 262 2054. Despatch No. 177, Gascoigne/ FO, Aug. 7, 1946. **strategic importance of Japan** CIA Report 'Strategic Importance of Japan', May 21, 1948. Records of the CIA, ORE 43–48.

p. 191 **in economic terms** on US economic diplomacy in the post-war years, see generally Michael Schaller, *The American Occupation of Japan: the Origins of the Cold War in Asia* (OUP, 1985), and 'Securing the Great Crescent: Occupied Japan and the Origins of Containment in Southeast Asia', *Journal of American History* Sept. 1982. Also Robert Pollard, *Economic Security and the Origins of the Cold War: the Strategic Ends of US Foreign Economic Policy, 1945–50* (Ph.D., University of North Carolina, 1983); and William S. Borden, *The Pacific Alliance; the US and Japanese Trade Recovery* (Wisconsin UP, 1984). **security interest of the US** NAW RG 218 1721/43. Records of JCS. Report to JCS on 'Program for Assistance to the General Area of China', Jan. 16, 1950. **economic penetration** Macmahon Ball, op. cit., p. 187. **in March 1948** R. H. Hillenkoetter, Director CIA/Truman, Mar. 31, 1948. CIA Records.

p. 192 **reorganisation of foreign policy making** Schaller, pp. 83–5.

p. 193 **Kennan had first** Schaller, pp. 86–8. **altruism serving strategic ends** Michael J. Baun, 'The Marshall Plan: a Study of Morality and Foreign Policy', in ed. Kenneth Thompson, *American Moral Leadership in the Third World* (UP of America, 1985), pp. 43–60. **economic crank-up** NAW FEC Records Box 222. Edwin Martin/General Hilldring, Feb. 26, 1947. **full-scale reassessment** i.e. SWNCC 360. **two great workshops** Dean Acheson, 'The Requirements of Reconstruction', *Department of State Bulletin 16*, May 18, 1947, pp. 991–4. **both affected** Schaller, p. 86. **Kenneth Royall** US Senate, Congressional Record, 80th Congress, 2nd Session (1948) XCIV pt. 1, 1363–4.

p. 194 **NSC 13/2** *FRUS* 1948, VI, pp. 858–62. **seldom can** Macmahon Ball, p. 102.

p. 195 **virtually compelled** see e.g. Schaller, p. 116; James, p. 173 **Review Board selected by Draper** Kawai, p. 147. **I am certain** *Nippon Times*, Mar. 28, 1948. Cited by Robert Textor, *Failure in Japan* (John Day, 1951), p. 58. **Anti-Monopoly Law** Eleanor Hadley, 'Japan: Competition or Private Collectivism?', *Far Eastern Survey* 18, Dec. 14, 1949. And the process continues – see D. W. Anthony, 'The Economic and Political Background to Recent Proposed Changes in Japan's Anti-Monopoly Legislation', *PBAJS* 1976 Part 1. **coalescing around banks** Bronfenbrenner, op. cit. p. 21. **priority production aid** Dower, *Empire and Aftermath*, op. cit. pp. 342–3. **auspices of Miti** Dower, p. 343.

p. 196 **I will not permit** *PRJ* Vol. II. p. 762. **National Public Service Law** on the passing of the NPSL, see Williams, pp. 217–221. **sterner moves** Dower, pp. 339–40. **repressive policy** interview Shigeru Wada, Apr. 16, 1985. **government perceived**

... reactionary e.g. CIA Records, R & A, OIR Report No. 4678, Aug. 15, 1948. 'The Democratic Liberal Party: A Resurgence of Conservative Forces in Japan'. In 1951 a member of GS wrote presciently, 'Japan will remain in all probability under extreme conservative leadership [which] will, moreover, foster and encourage various conservative trends in Japanese life, many of which will endeavor to revive pre-war institutions and concepts'. Since the conservatives were the focus of power, America would have to work through them and would become identified with them. 'The polarization of Japanese politics combined with the present conservative trends in Japan and United States efforts to establish a practical means of providing for Japan's security have gone far to alienate from the United States the Japanese liberals and intelligentsia who in many ways may be regarded as the most democratic elements in the country. The United States is thus finding itself in the difficult position of undermining its own previous efforts to make Japan a democratic country.' JWP 104.18, unsigned memo, Dec. 3, 1951.

p. 197 **no provision in Peace Treaty** OSS/State Dept. Intelligence & Research Reports. Part II: Postwar Japan, Korea and S.E. Asia. OIR Report No. 4518, 'The Purge Problem and the Japanese Peace Treaty', Sept. 25, 1947. And cf. FO 371 92699 FJ 1664/1, memo to Lord Henderson, July 25, 1951. **his cabinet contained** Bowers, 'How Japan Won the War', *NYT Magazine*, Aug. 30, 1970. **pressure for the release** a parole system had been established as early as March 1950. Yoshida/MacA, Mar. 28, 1950. JWP File 128. And cf. FO 262 2085 – interview with Governor of Sugamo and information on legislation enabling release or parole of the remaining prisoners. **proceeds of army raw materials** Kent E. Calder, 'Kenryo vs. Shomin: Contrasting Dynamics of Conservative Leadership in Postwar Japan', in ed. MacDougall, *Political*

Leadership in Contemporary Japan (Michigan Papers in Japanese Studies No. 1, 1982). **shift in criteria** Baerwald, pp. 2–3, 10, 41, 99–100. **without recourse to formal procedures** Baerwald, p. 79 n. 7.

p. 198 **central committee of the JCP** MacA/Yoshida, June 6, 1950. JWP File 128. **anti-Communist hysteria** Schaller, p. 134. **anti-Communist pamphlets** NAS RG 331 Box 5217. File – Labor Materials. **Special Investigation Bureau . . . IPR** Dower, p. 365.

Chapter 21 – Continuity in Change
p. 200 **underlying continuity** for a rejection of the 'reverse course' theory on quite different grounds, see Williams, op. cit., Chapter 11. **logical outcome** for the so-called 'reverse course' as a coming to prominence of ideas long in the background, see e.g. Marlene J. Mayo, 'American Wartime Planning for Occupied Japan: the Role of the Experts', in ed. Robert Wolfe, *Americans as Proconsuls: United States Military Government in Germany and Japan* (Southern Illinois UP, 1984). **Stimson summarised** Stimson/Royall, Nov. 21, 1947. Stimson papers, Yale University – cited by Schonberger, 'Zaibatsu Dissolution', op. cit. p. 26.

p. 201 **by retaining intact** Herbert P. Bix, 'Japan: the Roots of Militarism', in ed. Selden, *Remaking Asia: Essays on the American Uses of Power* (Pantheon, 1974), pp. 320–1. **mass demonstrations . . . sitdown protest** Gayn, pp. 226–32. **public warning** Warning Against Mob Disorder or Violence, May 20, 1946, *PRJ* Vol. II, p. 750. **major press dispute** Gayn, pp. 21–3, 253–4, 263–5, 328–35. And cf. Coughlin, pp. 85–102.

p. 202 **October offensive . . . Imboden visited** Gayn, pp. 328–31. **according to Gascoigne** FO 262 2054. Gascoigne/FO, Oct. 25, 1946. **never intended to create** Bronfenbrenner, p. 22.

p. 203 **Emmerson wrote** Emmerson, p. 262. **CIA reported** Research & Analysis, OIR Report No. 4678, Aug. 15, 1948. 'The Democratic Liberal Party: a Resurgence of Conservative Forces in Japan.'

p. 204 **violence on railways** Chalmers Johnson, *Conspiracy at Matsukawa* (California, 1972). **seriously considered it** on July 4, 1949 he said J might have to ask whether the JCP 'should longer be accorded the validity, sanction, and protection of the law'. James, p. 239. And cf. CIA Records, Intelligence Memo No. 209, 'Vulnerabilities of Communist Movements in the Far East', Sept. 20, 1949, pp. 10–11. 'Should the [Japanese] government feel free in the future to outlaw Communism (and the recent dissolution of the leftist Korean organizations may point in this direction) . . .' **Yoshida stated firmly** Yoshida/MacA, Aug. 9, 1949. JWP File 128.

p. 205 **Fearey** NAW RG 59 Notter Papers Box 64. T-Documents 337–373. **Wall Street combines** FO 262 2061 Gascoigne/Dening, June 10, 1948. **left-wing orthodoxy** e.g. Gabriel Kolko, *The Roots of American Foreign Policy* (Beacon Press, 1969); and ed. David Horowitz, *Corporations and the Cold War* (Modern Reader/Bertrand Russell Peace Foundation, 1969).

p. 206 **immediate post-war period** see e.g. G. William Domhoff, 'Who Made American Foreign Policy 1945–63?', in Horowitz, op. cit. **what I have been trying** telephone conversation Forrestal/Reese H. Taylor, Mar. 25, 1947. Forrestal Papers, Princeton University, Box 73. Quoted by Kolko, op. cit. **Forrestal able to 'tap'** Schaller, p. 85. **invited Eberstadt** Domhoff, op. cit. p. 41. **President of Westinghouse** Draper/MacA, Jan. 7, 1948. HP 72 A 13. **B. F. Goodrich Co.** George Vaught/Edward Welsh, June 29, 1948. HP 72 A 17.

p. 207 **Kern sympathised with Japan** Schaller, p. 93. **one critic** Harold Lavine, Nov. 19, 1982. Cited in Schaller, p. 93. **vitriolic Newsweek leaders** e.g. *Newsweek* Jan. 27, 1947,

'Behind the Japanese Purge: American Military Rivalries'. And cf. *Newsweek* Dec. 1, 1947, Dec. 29, 1947. **Imboden of CIE** NAS RG 331 5097. Imboden/ Nugent, May 4, 1949. **it is the belief** NAS RG 331 5097. Nugent/Chief of Staff, May 27, 1949. **American Council for Japan** on the American *zaibatsu*, the ACJ, *Newsweek* and the Kauffmann Report, see generally Howard Schonberger, 'Zaibatsu Dissolution and the American Restoration of Japan', *BCAS* 5/2, Sept. 1973, pp. 21–6, and 'The Japan Lobby in American Diplomacy', *Pacific Historical Review* 46/3 Aug. 1977, pp. 327–59. **Ballantine's advice** Schonberger, 'Zaibatsu Dissolution', p. 30 n. 65.

p. 208 **in his report** the Kauffmann Report is to be found in the Robert L. Eichelberger Papers, Duke University Library, and also in HP 72 A 2. **Army much in sympathy** MacA claimed, for example, that Royall must have made his speech of Jan. 1948 to keep 'his own boys' – i.e. US big business – quiet. FO 371 F 69885. **Pentagon responsible for budget** FO 371 F 4367/662. **fount and magnet** Kolko, p. 30.

p. 209 **role played by Draper** Schaller, pp. 111, 114–21. **Kern pictured Draper** FO 371 69887. H. A. Graves/D. F. McDermot, May 1, 1948. **antipathy mutual** MacA/ Draper, Jan. 9, 1948. HP 72 A 15.

p. 210 **Kennan wrote** Kennan, *Memoirs* Vol. I, pp. 371–2. **Theodore H. White reported** in *Fire in the Ashes* (1953), p. 375. Quoted in David Horowitz, *The Free world Colossus* (Hill & Wang, 1965), p. 107.

p. 211 **military more prominent** cf. Foreign Office comments – e.g. FO 371 4646/662. Minute by F. S. Tomlinson, Mar. 30, 1948. 'The main impetus for the New Deal certainly seems to come from the War Department'. **Williams' description** Williams, p. 18. **Kades bitterly disappointed** Williams, pp. 50–51. **not so potent** FO 262 2061. Gascoigne/Dening, June 10, 1948. **good for at least five years** FO 371 F 1368/662. Gascoigne/Dening,

Jan. 9, 1948. **Parkinson's disease** James, p. 360. **biggest single threat** Schaller, p. 121.

p. 212 **unscheduled press conference** interview with press correspondents, Mar. 19, 1947, *PRJ* Vol. II, p. 765. And cf. FO 262 2056, Apr. 16, 1947. Gascoigne/Dening: MacA said the State Department 'were taken somewhat by surprise when he made his public statement'. **broad influence exercised** Condit, op. cit. p. 487. **planned to repeat** FO 262 2056. Gascoigne/Dening, Apr. 14, 1947.

Chapter 22 – An Honest Mistake: the origins of Article 9

In this chapter we owe a particular debt to the work of the leading authority on Article 9, Professor Theodore McNelly, and are grateful for permission to draw liberally on his articles: 'The Renunciation of War in the Japanese Constitution', *Political Science Quarterly* 77/3 Sept., 1962; 'The Origin and Meaning of the Disarmament Clause of the Japanese Constitution', *Proceedings of the 4th Kyushu International Cultural Conference*, 1977; 'General Douglas MacArthur and the Constitutional Disarmament of Japan', *Transactions of the Asiatic Society of Japan*, Third Series, Vol. 17. Oct. 1982; 'The Renunciation of War in the Japanese Constitution: its Significance for Peace and Security in Asia', *Armed Forces and Society*, Vol. 13 No. 1, Fall 1986.

p. 213 **SWNCC 150** Reinhard Drifte, 'Further Reflections on the genesis of Article 9 of the Japanese Constitution', *PBAJS* 6/2, 1981.

p. 214 **Working Outline** OSS R & A Branch, R & A Report 3034, May 16, 1945. **apparently took for granted** e.g. in Oct. 1945 Sec. of State Byrnes sent instructions to Atcheson in POLAD which clearly envisaged the future existence of Japanese armed forces. John Welfield, 'Japanese Rearmament 1945–55' in ed. Hosoya, *Japan and Postwar Diplomacy in the Asian-Pacific*

Region (Occasional Papers No. 1, International University of Japan, 1984), p. 197. **last-ditch attempt** meeting with the Japanese Cabinet, Feb. 22, 1946. **Kades did once** McNelly, 'General Douglas MacA', pp. 9–12. **Hirohito said in Sept. 1945** interview in *NYT*, Sept. 25, 1945.

p. 215 **those who knew Shidehara** e.g. his private secretary, Karamatsu Kishi. See McNelly, 'General Douglas MacA', p. 5. **his son has insisted** McNelly, 'General Douglas MacA', p. 4. **Shidehara is on record** in a diary kept by Hitoshi Ashida, brought in evidence during the proceedings of the Commission on the Constitution, Apr. 5, 1957. See McNelly, 'General Douglas MacA', p. 23. **it has been suggested** Frank Rizzo, for example, claimed that in Feb. 1946 GS was specifically told that Article 9 was MacA's idea; only after the outbreak of the Korean War was it attributed to Shidehara. JWP 110.11. And cf. COH: Ballantine. **Shidehara might have suggested** Tatsuo Sato, *Neparu no Ito Hirobumi* (Keiseisha, 1972), pp. 26–28. Cited by McNelly, 'General Douglas MacA', p. 28. **in hope of persuading MacA** see Drifte, op. cit. **official account** *PRJ* Vol. I, pp. 82–118. **it was Kades** McNelly, 'General Douglas MacA', p. 8.

p. 216 **the notes handed to Whitney** see McNelly, 'The Origin and Meaning', pp. 256–60, for several different versions of the MacA notes. **document mysteriously disappeared** McNelly, 'General Douglas MacA', p. 16. **Baldwin remembered** COH: Baldwin, p. 496. **outlawry of war** e.g. address to the American Legion in Los Angeles, Jan. 26, 1955. James, p. 666. **Article 9's birth** Hussey – well placed to judge, and author of the official account of the drafting of the Constitution (*PRJ*, Vol. I) – privately ascribed authorship to MacA. e.g. Hussey/Ray Sakakibara, June 25, 1958, expressing the opinion that Article 9 would be more vulnerable to revision if it were 'brought out' that

MacA had initiated it. HP 93 E 2. **'a sound idea'** MacA's comment on Imperial Rescript of Jan. 1, 1946. *PRJ* Vol. II, p. 471. **according to Frank Rizzo** answers to a questionnaire framed by Dale Hellegers. JWP 110.11.

p. 217 **McNelly explains** 'General Douglas MacA', p. 30. **plan for a control commission** sent by Byrnes to Ernest Bevin on Mar. 1, 1946 and discussed by FEC thereafter. F 7117/405/23. NB Rizzo maintained that neither he nor others in GS were aware of the existence of this plan. JWP 110.11. **Kades deleted** C. L. Kades and Yoshihisa Komori, '"Kosenken Hoki" wa Muyo Datta', in *Gendai* Vol. 15/8, Aug. 1981, p. 40. Cited by McNelly, 'General Douglas MacA', p. 17. **Ashida was taking advantage** on the distinction between 'war' and 'arms', see McNelly, 'General Douglas MacA', pp. 1–4.

p. 218 **tradition of the Founding Fathers** Paul Heffron, *The Anti-Militarist Tradition of the Founding Fathers and its Continuation in the writings of Carl Schurz, Charles A. Beard and Walter Millis* (Ph.D. Minnesota U, 1977). **Government Section accepted** McNelly, 'General Douglas MacA', p. 31; and 'The Origin and Meaning', pp. F5 8–9, 12–13. *NYT* **leader** Aug. 29, 1946. **pacifist from an enemy country** COH: Baldwin, p. 441. **even Yoshida** in House of Representatives, June 28, 1946. Dower, p. 379.

p. 219 **McNelly points out** 'The Origin and Meaning', p. F5 13.

Chapter 23 – The Dragon's Teeth: Willoughby's embryo army

p. 220 **instructions from Washington** HP 91 A 2, p. 15. **bitter feuds** amongst the papers of Whitney there was one cabinet-full which Whitney did not want made available to the public until after his death; it was believed to contain evidence of the 'guerrilla activities' within SCAP. Kades/Williams, Apr. 24, 1972. JWP 109.32.

p. 221 **a sort of FBI** James, p. 86. And cf. Willoughby and Chamberlain, op. cit. **I'm no reformer** Gayn, op. cit. **nor was Willoughby happy** Willoughby and Chamberlain, p. 297.

p. 222 **written approvingly of Mussolini** Robert Textor, *Failure in Japan* (John Day, 1951), p. 191. **more crap from SCAP** HP 76 B 4. **preserve military penal codes** Hussey/Whitney, Sept. 25, 1946. HP 10 B 33. **intimate combat association** *MacA Reports*.

p. 223 **investigated Bisson** Howard Schonberger, 'T. A. Bisson and the Limits of Reform in Occupied Japan', *BCAS* 12/4 Oct.–Dec. 1980. **Washington apprehensive** *MacA Reports*, p. 255. **Loyalty Desk** Truman instituted a 'loyalty program' – unprecedented in American history – in 1947, 'designed to root communists and their sympathisers out of government'. Alonso Hamby, *Beyond the New Deal: Harry S. Truman and American Liberalism* (Columbia UP, 1973), pp. 170–1, citing Alan D. Harper, *The Politics of Loyalty 1946–52* (Westport, 1969). **leftists and fellow-travellers** Willoughby and Chamberlain, p. 304. **coordinated with the FBI** Willoughby and Chamberlain, p. 304. **papers of Justin Williams** File 104.10. Memo for record, June 30, 1947. **American military police** draft memo Hussey/Whitney, Dec. 20, 1946. HP Section 81 B. **one of the legal officers** HP 84 B 3.

p. 224 **the Deputy Chief . . . doctrines we profess** Hussey/Whitney, Sept. 9, 1947. HP 84 B 8. **Bisson** Schonberger, op. cit. **fell foul of McCarthy** Dower, p. 545 n. 46. **a disgruntled person** Emmerson, p. 325. **it was the Army** HP 91 A 2 p. 13. **Willoughby disobeyed orders** FO 371 83013 Fergusson/Gascoigne, Feb. 11, 1950 – quoted by Schaller, p. 251.

p. 225 **190 Japanese generals** *MacA Reports*. **mission received by Willoughby** Wildes, p. 72. **contact with Arisue . . . 1970s** Welfield, op. cit. p. 202. **two other ventures** Welfield, p. 206.

p. 226 **a chequered career** when MacA was fired in 1951, Willoughby destroyed most sets, which had reached page proof stage, but MacA appears to have preserved at least one set, with related material. He forbade publication, apparently fearing that Army historians would drastically amend the MacA/Willoughby version of events; but after his death they were published unaltered – but with an Army caveat. James, p. 669. **Hattori built** Welfield, p. 208. **military pensions stopped** memo CLO/SCAP, Feb. 2, 1946, and memo Chief Finance Division/Chief ESS, Aug. 1, 1946. HP 14 B 1–16.

p. 227 **friend of Hussey** 'Mossy'/Hussey, no date. HP 92 A 8. **communal farms** HP Sections 14 B, 19 A 2 p. 13; and Gayn. p. 155. **Hussey even alleged** HP 91 A 2 p. 13. **the Russian Mission** memo from G-2, Nov. 14, 1946. HP Section 13.

Chapter 24 – Unsheathing the Sword
p. 228 **State Dept. against the DoA** Schaller, pp. 98–106, 164–77, 247. **Kennan would have preferred** Schaller, p. 171.

p. 229 **troops were demobilised** Condit, Chapter 1. **mandatory that we employ** NAW RG 319 P & O Div. Decimal File 1946–8 091. Japan TS. Section 1a Part 1. P & O Military Survey 73265, Apr. 19, 1948. **playing with fire** Condit, Chapter 1. **growing interest in rearmament** *Newsweek*, Aug. 4, 1947. Cited by Welfield, p. 215. **focus of this interest** on significance of Ashida's role in Japanese rearmament, see Welfield, p. 201.

p. 230 **on Aug. 29 . . . Willoughby** Haruhiko Fukui, 'Japanese Rearmament and US–Japanese Security Relations', in ed. Kosobud, *Northeast Asia and the United States: Defense Partnerships and Trade Rivalries* (Chicago Council on Foreign Relations, 1983), p. 58. And cf. Welfield, p. 205. **presented by Eichelberger** Fukui, p. 62. **crucial 'US Policy'** Schaller, p. 104.

Forrestal ordered Schaller, p. 124.

p. 231 **policy now being re-examined** NAW RG 319 P & O Div. Decimal File 1946–48. 091 Japan, Cases 1–88. Memo HAB, War Dept., General Staff/General Schuyler, Feb. 14, 1948. **Draper revealed** NAW RG 319 (Army Staff) P & O Div. Decimal File 1946–48.091 Japan TS. Box 19 Section 1. Memorandum of interview between MacA, Draper and Kennan, Mar. 21 1948. **Eichelberger discussing with Willoughby** Fukui, p. 60. **Eichelberger mused** *Osaka Mainichi*, Feb. 12, 1949. Quoted in Textor, op. cit. p. 217. **P & O Div. Military Survey** NAW RG 319. P & O Div. Decimal File 1946–48 091 Japan TS Section 1a Part 1. Military Survey 63265, Apr. 19, 1948. Plus attached 'Memorandum for Record' by Lt. Col. W. Milner, Jan. 10, 1949. **possible organisation of armed forces** P & O Military Survey 73265 also suggested 'exploring the question' of having the Japanese Constitution amended to permit rearmament. **ACJ hosted a luncheon** Welfield, p. 216. **US Air Force weather plane** Condit, Chapter 15.

p. 232 **NSC 68** James, p. 405. **Alanbrooke reported** Bryant, op. cit. pp. 394–5, 398, entries for Nov. 17 and 21, 1945. **MacA believed . . . fifth-rate military power** memorandum of interview MacA/Draper/Kennan, Mar. 21, 1948, op. cit.

p. 233 **explosive international reaction** MacA/DoA, June 12, 1948. JWP File 131. **small arms** Mac/DoA, July 28, 1949. JWP 131.43. **according to Eichelberger** *NYT*, Sept. 13, 1948. **MacA conjured up** *NYT*, Mar. 1, 1949. **pave the way for American bases** *NYT*, Jan. 1, 1950. 'It is in this connection that General MacArthur's statement comes, as something like an official interpretation that Japan has not renounced whatever means of defense can be found short of maintenance of an army, navy and air force.' **in June 1950** and cf. interview he gave to *NYT* on May 30, 1950, putting the case for Japan's unarmed neutrality.

Yoshida's reasoning Dower, pp. 387–8. And cf. Fukui, p. 66. **sometimes blamed** e.g. Clay Blair, *MacArthur* (Doubleday, 1977), pp. 266–8. **analogy with Switzerland** Blair, op. cit. p. 38.

p. 234 **State Dept. abandoned hopes** Schaller, p. 247. **even before the Korean War** Schaller, pp. 277–8. **thwarted attempt by Willoughby** Welfield, pp. 225–6.

p. 235 **created by Potsdam Ordinance** JWP File 49.11. **Williams informed** memo for the record, July 13, 1950. JWP 49.11 **P & O Div. had written** Military Survey 73265, Apr. 19, 1948, op. cit. **American puppet force** Welfield, p. 228. **Hussey suggests** HP 91 A 2 p. 14. **government wrote individually** Welfield, p. 259 n. 79. **special vehicles** John Dower, 'The Eye of the Beholder', *BCAS* 2/1 Oct. 1969. **pressure from Dulles** Dower, *Empire and Aftermath*, pp. 386, 430–1, 449.

p. 236 **without war potential** Dower, op. cit., p. 382. **full effectiveness** Dower, pp. 439–40. **private understanding** Welfield, p. 232. And cf. Reinhard Drifte, *The Security Factor in Japan's Foreign Policy, 1945–52* (Frances Pinter, 1983). Drifte suggests that Yoshida agreed both to concede American bases in Japan after the restoration of sovereignty, and to limited rearmament in principle, while Dulles agreed to exclude mention of rearmament from the Peace and Security Treaties. **Yoshida told the nation** Dower, p. 437. **Tokutaro Kimura** Dower, pp. 396–7. In Oct. 1948 Yoshida had appealed to MacA (Yoshida/MacA, Oct. 17, 1948, JWP File 128) for permission to depurge Kimura and make him Attorney General. MacA refused on the grounds that Kimura had been a director of the IRAA during the war, and the national director of the *Butoku Kai*.

p. 237 **Liberal party lost** Welfield, p. 239. **Lippmann called** Schaller, p. 197. **it was made clear** Dower, p. 431. **American interference beyond disguising** despite precautions: e.g. emphasis on 'urgent necessity of avoiding premature disclosure of any action taken to loan heavy armament to the NPR': the loan programme was to be called 'Special Far East Command Reserve Program'. Memo for Sec. of Defense, Feb. 9, 1951. NAS RG 218 CCS 383.21. Section 24. **Yomiuri Shimbun wrote** Sept. 3, 1953. Quoted by Ben Sun Kim, op. cit. **an honest mistake** Richard Nixon, 'To the Japanese People', printed in *Contemporary Japan* XXII 7–9, 1953.

p. 238   **rebirth of MSDF** see generally James E. Auer, *The Postwar Rearmament of Japanese Maritime Forces, 1945–71* (Praeger, 1973).

p. 239   **forced to wear American uniforms** Commission on the Constitution Reference Document No. 46, July 1960. Cited in Auer, op. cit. p. 47. **supported by . . . military hierarchy** HP 75 A. **horrified the reformers** HP 75 A 7, 75 A 11. **based on American model** Auer, p. 56.

p. 240   **sailors sent to Korea** Auer, pp. 63–7. In Dec. 1950, when Russia charged America with using Japanese troops in Korea and preparing to rebuild Japan's armed forces, the State Dept. accused the USSR of telling 'a naked lie'. *NYT*, Dec. 15, 1950. **Burke described** Auer, pp. vii–viii. **Burke's idea** Auer, p. 73. **Joy added** Welfield, p. 230.

p. 241   **Nomura wept** Auer, p. 94. **Japanese aviators to assist Chiang** Schaller, p. 185. **in Dec. 1945 Edwin Pauley** Pauley/MacA and Truman, Dec. 6, 1945. *FRUS* 1945: Far East Vol. VI. **one patriot remarked** Burford Brandis, 'The States and Japan', *Georgia Review* No. 3, 1949, p. 8. **MacA proposed reactivation** Dower, p. 383.

p. 242   **authorised unconditionally** by SCAP memo of Mar. 8, 1952. Fukui, p. 61. **Japanese nuclear scientists pressed** Gaddis, op. cit., points out that by 1949 a Japanese atomic physicist had won the Nobel Prize. **SCAP by no means reluctant**

some elements within SCAP had in any case objected on principle to the restrictions on freedom of research. They attempted to insert a guarantee of total academic freedom into the new Constitution, but were overruled on the grounds that 'the Allies intend to severely restrict some kinds of research and entirely forbid others'. 'Meeting of the Steering Committee with Committee on Civil Rights, Feb. 2, 1946', in Kades papers within JWP. **scientists were permitted** see e.g. SCAP Reports on Control and Surveillance of Atomic Energy Research and Development in Japan, 1946–9 in NAW RG 218 JSC 1946–7. CCS 383.21 Japan. Sections 12–15. By Sept. 1947 the ESS had a 'Special Projects Unit' vetting proposed research projects in the field of atomic energy. SCAP Report Mar.– Aug. 1947, Sept. 29, 1947. **obscure this from the Allies** Japanese scientists were given permission to publish their research on the blasts at Hiroshima and Nagasaki, with the proviso 'No special publicity should be given the decision established above, since ill-informed people would conclude Japanese were being allowed to engage in general research in field of atomic energy in contradiction to FEC policy on such matters'. JIC 406/1, Sept. 27, 1948, in NAW RG 218 JCS 1946–7 CCS 383.21 Japan Sections 12–15. **materials confiscated** e.g. CSGPO/SCAP, WAR 86474, July 23, 1948; CAD/SCAP, WAR 81765, Dec. 24, 1948; and Report for Jan.–Apr. 1949, July 16, 1949. All in NAW RG 218 JCS 1946–7 CCS 383.21 Japan. Sections 12–15. The FEC directive merely ordered SCAP to *impound* such materials. **Army Dept. memo** the memo is mentioned in a 'Note by the Secs. to the JCS on Control and Surveillance of Atomic Energy Research and Development in Japan', JCS 1380/70 (NAW RG 218 JCS 1947–7 CCS 383.21). It is not on the file, however – having possibly been removed? The 'Note' mentions 'field investigations' by SCAP designed to evaluate the plant, personnel and research potential of the better laboratories, and establish the identity and location of key personnel.

Chapter 25 – Pressure to Rearm
p. 245 **destroyers . . . tactical aircraft** Robert W. Barnett, *Beyond War: Japan's Concept of Comprehensive National Security* (Pergamon-Brassey, 1984), p. 18. **the SDF – strength** Mid-Term Defense Program 1986–90. **Mid-Term Defense Program** published by the Japan Defense Agency. *Defense Bulletin* Vol. IX No. 1, September 1985. **Chinook helicopters** *World Armaments and Disarmament: Stockholm International Peace Research Institute Yearbook* (SIPRI) 1985 (Taylor and Francis, 1985).

p. 246 **HAWK-Patriot** Mid-Term Defense Program 1986–90, p. 2. **world's major recipient** SIPRI Yearbook 1985. **buy from Europe** J. W. M. Chapman, 'The transfer of German underwater weapons technology to Japan, 1919–76', in ed. Nish & Dunn, *European Studies on Japan* (Paul Norbury, 1979). **howitzers from Britain** SIPRI Yearbook 1985.

p. 247 **highest export figures** SIPRI Yearbook 1985, pp. 372–3. **military electronics** Helena Tuomi and Raimo Vayrynen, *Transnational Corporations, Armaments and Development* (St. Martin's Press, 1982), p. 81. **rocketry** e.g. CIA Papers, Special Report SC No. 00606/64a 'Rocket Research in Japan', Feb. 14, 1964. **better than Exocet** Saburo Okita, quoted in Barnett, op. cit. p. 68. **preeminent . . . ceramics** Chalmers Johnson, 'East Asia: Another Year of Living Dangerously', *Foreign Affairs – America and the World 1983*, p. 721. **small-size nuclear weapons mooted** John K. Emmerson and Leonard Humphreys, *Will Japan Rearm?* (AEI/Hoover, 1973), p. 34. And cf. Gaston J. Sigur, 'Power, Politics and Defense', in ed. James H. Buck, *The Modern Japanese Military System* (SAGE, 1975). **nuclear industry has flourished** and Zbigniew Brzezinski suggests (in *The Fragile Blossom*, Harper and Row, 1972) that 'there are grounds for suspecting' that money spent on R & D and atomic energy is 'not unrelated to defence'. It is interesting that it was Nakasone who in 1954 proposed in the Diet that nuclear energy be exploited, launching Japan's post-war programme of atomic energy development. (See Daniel Okimoto, *Ideas, Intellectuals and Institutions: National Security and the Question of Nuclear Armament in Japan* – Ph.D. thesis, University of Michigan, 1978, p. 22.) **fourth biggest producer** *The Times*, July 26, 1986. **28% of energy needs** *FEER*, July 5, 1984. **industry depended** Nagai Susumu, 'Going Ahead with Atomic Power – A Dangerous Choice', *JQ* 25/1 Jan.–Mar. 1978, p. 13. **export atomic technology** in agreeing to participate in America's SDI programme, Japan is in effect agreeing to export nuclear weapons technology. **agreement with PRC** *FEER*, July 5, 1984. And cf. *Japanese Press Summary*, Aug. 1, 1985.

p. 248 **Tokai-mura** Susumu, op. cit. p. 17. **fast-breeder reactors** Susumu, p. 17. And cf. *Japanese Press Summary*, Oct. 14, 1985. US Dept. of Energy approached MITI with proposal for cooperation in fast-breeder reactor development. **threat to arms control** Takashi Mukaibo, quoted in Barnett, p. 74. **monitors activity in straits** Maeda Hisao, 'A Perilous Plan for Japan's Security', *JQ* 13/3 Oct.–Dec. 1984. **ten years** *FEER*, Sept. 22, 1983, quoting 1983 study by Research Institute for Peace and Security, ed. Kosaka Masataka and Kenneth Hunt. **Pentagon spokesman asserted** *Yomiuri*, June 16, 1985. **joint US/SDF exercises** *FEER*, Sept. 22, 1983. **studies of feasibility** *FEER*, Dec. 20, 1984, p. 27. **integrate command structures** Shuichi Kato, 'Conformity and Americanization: Postwar Japanese Society at 40', in *Asahi Journal*, Aug. 16–23, 1985.

p. 249 **as Manchukuo to Tokyo** Saburo Ienaga, *Japan's Last War* (Blackwell, 1979), p. 244. **Central Command HQ** *FEER*, Oct. 4,

1984, Dec. 20, 1984. **America spends on R & D . . . Middle East** Johnson, op. cit. p. 724. **Ikutaro Shimizu suggests** quoted in Hisao Iwashima, 'Recent Defense Debates in Japan', in ed. Shiratori Rei, *Japan in the 1980s* (Kodansha, 1982), p. 102.

p. 250 **collective defence** *FEER*, Dec. 20, 1984, pp. 26–7. And cf. Michael T. Klare, 'Restructuring the Empire: the Nixon Doctrine after Vietnam', *BCAS* 5/2 Sept. 1973, pp. 58–9. **Dulles' Pacific Pact** e.g. Shaw Fawn Kao, 'US Strategic Policy Toward Occupied Japan', in ed. Kenneth Thompson, *US Leadership in Asia and the Middle East* (University of America, 1985), p. 117. **Guam Doctrine** Alastair Buchan, *The End of the Post-War Era: A New Balance of World Power* (Dutton, 1974). **Nixon/Sato communiqué** excerpts in Emmerson and Humphreys, pp. 128–131. **reduction of American installations** Okimoto, op. cit. p. 103. **Brown was alleged** Iwashima, op. cit. p. 106.

p. 251 **Reagan's sustained effort** Gaston J. Sigur, 'The US–Japanese Relationship and US Policy in Asia and the Pacific', in eds. Sigur and Young C. Kim, *Japanese and US Policy in Asia* (Praeger, 1982), p. 9. **régime in the north** South Korea's President Chun Doo Hwan described it as 'the most tightly closed, tightly regimented and ideologically militant Asian communist régime in the world today'. Address to Washington Press Club, Washington DC, Feb. 3, 1981; and see generally eds. Gerald Curtis and Sung-joo Hun, *The United States–South Korea Alliance: Evolving Patterns in Security Relations* (Lexington Books, 1983). **in last ten years** JDA White Paper, 1986.

p. 252 **militarist private school** Albert Axelbank, *Black Star Over Japan – Rising Forces of Militarism* (Allen & Unwin, 1972), p. 213. **under his influence, Nixon** Wildes, p. 119. **Nakasone's first opportunity . . . Build-Up Plan** Emmerson and Humphreys, pp. 20–41.

p. 253 **Security Treaty . . . take second place** Emmerson and Humphreys, p. 25. **echo of Tojo's affidavit** *Observer*, Sept. 28, 1986.

p. 254 **excised peace dove** Brzezinski, op. cit. **carried out on the cheap** Johnson, p. 725. **critics claim** e.g. Shuichi Kato, 'Conformity and Americanization', op. cit. **misplaced confidence** 'Prime Minister Nakasone's English', *Bungei Shunju* – quoted in *Articles from the Japanese Press*, June 1985. **technology transfer and SDI** *FEER*, Aug. 1, 1985; *Times*, Sept. 10, 1986. **in January 1983** Johnson, p. 725. **a nation must shed** Fukatsu Masumi, 'A State Visit to Yasukuni Shrine', *JQ* 33/1 Jan.–Mar. 1986.

p. 255 **average intelligence of American** *Observer*, Sept. 28, 1986. **connection with Mishima** Henry Scott Stokes, 'Mishima, A Movie and Nakasone', *JQ* 31/1 Jan.–Mar. 1984. **needs the Emperor** Tashio Usui and Takeshi Endo, 'Politicizing the Emperor', *Asahi Journal*, Jan. 3–10, 1986. **campaigned for support of Ise** Wilhelmus H. M. Creemers, *Shrine Shinto After World War II* (E. J. Brill, 1968), pp. 184–8. **without such monuments** Masumi, op. cit. And cf. Keeichiro Kobori, 'A Letter on Gratitude to the War Dead', *JE* Vol. 11, Special Issue 1984; Kobori argues that in failing to honour the war dead the government is severing the Japanese people's links with their ancestors.

p. 256 **precedents** Masumi, op. cit. **Japan had followed** *Japanese Press Summary*, Aug. 15, 1985. **representation to MacA** JWP 166.1.

Chapter 26 – Remilitarised Japan
p. 259 **candidate for Governorship** Nakane, op. cit. p. 45. **Tanaka bribe** L. W. Fisher, *The Lockheed Affair: a Phenomenon of Japanese Politics* (Ph.D. Colorado U, 1980, UMI 8021572). And cf. Kent E. Calder, '*Kenryo* vs. *Shomin*: Contrasting Dynamics of Conservative Leadership in Postwar Japan', in ed. MacDougall, *Political Leadership in Contemporary Japan* (University of Michigan, 1982). **essentially tooth-**

less Nakane, op. cit. p. 123, 'The writing of first-hand reports is not regarded in Japan as a fitting occupation for an established man.' And see Dick Wilson, *The Sun at Noon: An Anatomy of Modern Japan* (Hamish Hamilton, 1986), pp. 120–21.

p. 260 **considerable influence on government policy** M. Y. Yoshino, *Japan's Managerial System – Tradition and Innovation* (MIT Press, 1968), p. 92. **trade unions** T. J. Pempel, *Policy and Politics in Japan: Creative Conservatism* (Temple, 1983), p. 31. 'Organised labor has never provided a support base for government in Japan', as in western democracies; rather, it has 'played a preponderantly opposing role'. Organised labour is numerically stronger than in the US (weaker than in Britain), but fragmentation severely weakens its political influence. **more than simply financial** Kitazawa Nasakuni, 'Militarism in the Management Society', in ed. J. Victor Koschmann, *Authority and the Individual in Japan: Citizen Protest in Historical Perspective* (Tokyo UP, 1978), pp. 200–206. 'Postwar militarism seems to have developed under the guise of social management, or the technological control of society.' **real power of civil service** Chalmers Johnson, 'Japan – Who Governs? An Essay on Official Bureaucracy', in *JJS* 2/1 Autumn 1975. **right to make policy** though within 'a broad ideological framework'. Pempel, *Policy*, p. 23.

p. 261 **bureaucracy unscathed** Pempel, *Policy*, pp. 15–16. **the civil service** would the bureaucracy obey a socialist administration? Pempel, p. 23. **adapting democracy** Dower, p. 415. **genuine reverse course** Justin Williams has pointed out that the term 'reverse course' was originated by left-wing Japanese scholars in the 1950s, and only later misapplied to describe Washington's alleged change of heart in 1947/8. In 'Constitution and Law Reform in Postwar Japan', in ed. Redford, *The Occupation and its Legacy to the Postwar World* (MacA Memorial, 1976); and letter to the authors, Dec. 6, 1986. **recentralisation** Dower, pp. 346–8, 357–61. **school boards** Dower, pp. 351–2. **control over teachers** Dower, p. 356.

p. 262 **education a security concern** . . . **Amano Outline** Dower, pp. 354–5. **To Matsunaga moved** *Japan Times*, July 20, 1957. **inspirational pap** Edward Norbeck, 'The American Occupation of Japan: Social Retrospect', in Goodman, op. cit. p. 28. **Image of the Ideal Man** Yoshiaki Iisaka, 'The State and Religion in Postwar History', *JJS* 7/3–4, Summer–Autumn 1972. **Kimi ga yo** *Tenei*, Oct. 1947. NAS RG 331 Box 3287–8. **once more designated** Masami Yamazumi, 'Textbook Revision – the Swing to the Right', *JQ* 28/4 Oct.–Dec. 1981. **twice a day** *Asahi Shimbun*, Apr. 2, 1986.

p. 263 **Masayuku Fujio declared** *FEER*, Aug. 14, 1986. Nakasone was compelled to dismiss Fujio after 49 days, when his remarks on Japan's annexation of Korea sparked a diplomatic row. But the first statement of his successor as Education Minister was a call for greater 'patriotism' and singing of the *Kimi ga yo. Observer*, Sept. 28, 1986. **standardisation of textbooks** Benjamin C. Duke, 'The Textbook Controversy', *JQ* 19/3 Jul.–Sept. 1972. **Ienaga case** Saburo Ienaga, *Japan's Last War* (Blackwell, 1979). And cf. Duke, op. cit.

p. 264 **one scholar** Allen Francis Ketcham, *World War II Events as represented in Secondary School Textbooks of former Allied and Axis Nations* (Ph.D. Arizona, 1982). **Marcos remarked** Kenneth B. Pyle, 'Japan Besieged: the Textbook Controversy', *JJS* 9/2 Summer 1983. **textbook scandal** see e.g. Pyle, op. cit.

p. 265 **article by Asahi Shimbun** 'Teachers, Children and School', *JI* 9/1 Spring 1974. **Ministry of Education issued guidelines** David Egler reviewing Hyoe Murakami, *Japan: the Years of Trial 1919–52*, in *Journal of Asian Studies* 42/3 May 1983. **omit war-related questions** Ian Buruma, 'Ethics in textbooks a matter of dispute', *FEER*,

Sources

Aug. 15, 1985, p. 45. **Japanese intel-
lectuals . . . internal migration** Ben-
Ami Shillony, 'Japanese Intellectuals
During the Pacific War', in *PBAJS* 1977
Part 1.

p. 266 **brief flurry** Ienaga, op.
cit. **change in attitude** Ienaga,
pp. 247–56. But cf. Louis Allen, 'Not So
Piacular – A Footnote to Ienaga on
Malaya', *PBAJS* 1980 Part 1, pointing
out that Ienaga himself, in emphasising *Allied* harshness, might be accused
of justifying Japan. **Ikeda and Robertson agreed** Ienaga, p. 255. **Okano
was declaring** Ienaga, p. 250. **an undigested lump** Ian Buruma, 'Liberator
or aggressor, a matter of identity',
FEER, Aug. 15, 1985, p. 43. **reexam-
ine the Occupation** Eiji Takemae, 'My
Impressions on taking part in the Symposium' – i.e. International Centre for
Economic and Related Disciplines Symposium, *The British Commonwealth and
the Occupation of Japan* (International
Studies 1983/1), p. 89. And cf. Hayao
Shimizu, 'The War and Japan: Revisionist Views', *JE* Vol. 11, Special Issue
1984, p. 3. **critic Jun Eto** see *Senryo
shiroku*, ed. Eto (Kodansha, 1981–2)
and Ray A. Moore's review in *JJS* 10/1
Winter 1983, pp. 251–2.

p. 267 **Takanori Irie** 'The Lingering
Impact of Misguided Occupa-
tion Policies', *JE* Vol. 11, Special Issue
1984, p. 23. **recent TV documentary**
Roger Buckley, *Japan Today* (CUP,
1985), p. 16. **Fujio declared** *FEER*,
Aug. 14, 1986. **1983 conference in
Tokyo** Takemae, op. cit. **unduly
masochistic** see e.g. Masaaki Tanaka,
The Fiction of the Nanjing Massacre.
words of Nakasone Fukatsu Masumi,
'A State Visit to Yasukuni Shrine', *JQ*
33/1 Jan.–Mar. 1986. **Tokyo Trial**
FEER, Aug. 18, 1983.

p. 268 **extenuation of war guilt**
Pritchard, Vol. III p.(i) acknow-
ledges the 'observable tendency of the
Japanese public to turn a blind eye to
[atrocities] and to concentrate instead
upon the broader political and strategic
dilemmas', and suggests it is because
the *Asahi Shimbunsha Index* ignores the

atrocities evidence. **monument to
dead of Auschwitz** *FEER*, Aug. 23,
1984. And cf. Ian Buruma, 'The politics
of peace', *FEER*, Aug. 15, 1985; and
'Isaiah Ben-Dasan', *The Japanese and the
Jews* (1970) **first adversity and then
success** Kim, op. cit. Chapter 2.

p. 269 **indifferent treatment of
Koreans** *Japan's Minorities:
Burakumin, Koreans, Ainu, Okinawans*
(Minority Rights Group, 1983).
foreign sportsmen *FEER*, Nov. 1, 1984.
64% of Japanese 'Where aliens are
hardly human', *Guardian*, Dec. 5, 1985.
girls who have lived abroad *Guardian*,
Dec. 5, 1985. **Nakasone revealed**
Guardian, Dec. 5, 1985. **foreign resi-
dents fingerprinted** *Mainichi*, Aug. 25,
1985. **I wonder if** 'Japan Vetoes
Foreign Teachers', *Asahi Shimbun*,
Apr. 8, 1985. **the Emperor is better**
Shoichi Watanabe, 'Hirohito: World
War II's Last Survivor', *Voice*, Jan. 1985.

p. 270 **one authority** Titus, op. cit.
p. 568. **each member** Titus,
p. 557. **practice stopped in 1973** Osamu
Inagaki, 'The Jieitai: Military Values in
A Pacifist Society', *JI* 10/1 Summer
1975, p. 13.

p. 271 **barometer of nationalism**
Creemers, op. cit. 'Summary &
Conclusions'. **calls for reinstatement
of Shinto** Creemers, pp. 184–8. And cf.
FEER, Aug. 15, 1985; and Iisaka, op. cit.
renationalisation of Yasukuni Iisaka,
op. cit. **National Foundation Day**
Karl H. Dixon, *The Extreme Right Wing in
Contemporary Japan* (Ph.D. Florida,
1975), pp. 42–3.

p. 272 **first Prime Minister** Toshio
Usui and Takeshi Endo, 'Poli-
ticizing the Emperor', *Asahi Journal*,
Jan. 3–10, 1986. **we do not have . . .
representatives** Mishima, 'An Ideology
for an Age of Languid Peace', *Journal of
Social and Political Ideas in Japan* 2/2,
Aug. 1964; and *Tate no kai*, pamphlet
distributed Nov. 3, 1969. **Seirankai**
J. Victor Koschmann, 'Hawks on the
Defensive: the *Seirankai*', *JI* 8/4 Winter
1974. And cf. Dixon, op. cit. Chap. 4.
NB The *Seirankai*'s foreign affairs

specialist in the 1970s was Masayuki Fujio. **President of JTU** *JQ* 31/3 Jul.-Sept. 1984, *Chronology* Apr. 13, 1984.

p. 273 **Sazo Idemitsu** Idemitsu, *Be A True Japanese*, privately printed in 1971 for the sixtieth anniversary of Idemitsu Kosan Co. Ltd. **oendan** Charles Fleming, 'The Bully Boys in Black', *Tokyo Journal*, Aug. 1985.

p. 274 **burglary at junior high** 'Policeman Thrashes Teenage Taunters', *Sankei Shimbun*, Feb. 15, 1985. **private naval academy** *FEER*, July 14, 1983. **Hiroo Onoda** 'Onoda Teaches Children To Love Nature', *Voice*, Nov. 1984. **martial arts revived** Hiroyuki Hamada, *Postwar Martial Arts Program in Japanese Higher Education: Case of Nippon College of Physical Education* (Ed. D. thesis, College of William and Mary in Virginia, 1984). **repertoires of kabuki** Leonard A. Humphreys, 'The Japanese Military Tradition', in ed. Buck, op. cit.

p. 275 **war films** *FEER*, Aug. 16, 1984. **the militarist temperature** Rosamund Goldie, 'Mishima and the Military: a sociological study of Mishima's novels and the military in Japan', in eds. Nish and Dunn, op. cit. **ultranationalism resurfaced** see generally Ivan Morris, *Nationalism and the Right Wing in Japan: a study of postwar trends* (OUP, 1960); and Dixon, op. cit. **rash of rightist incidents** Richard L. G. Deverall, *The Great Seduction* (Tokyo, 1953).

p. 276 **societies bobbed up** Morris, op. cit. Appendix IV. **Butoku Kai restored** FO 371 1192/23 BBC Monitoring Report, Mar. 20, 1954. And cf. Morris, pp. 242-3. **new anticommunist groups** Masayuki Takagi, 'Right Wing Draws Public Attention', *JQ* 27/4 Oct.-Dec. 1980. **presence violently felt** Takagi, op. cit. p. 480.

p. 277 **Three Arrows plan** Ienaga, op. cit. And cf. Axelbank, pp. 18, 51, 59, 176. **feminisation of the male** *Mishima on Hagakure: the Samurai Ethic and Modern Japan* (Penguin, 1979), p. 25. **arsenal without a soul** Mishima, 'An Appeal', *Sande Mainichi*, Dec. 13, 1970. **November 25, 1970 . . . gave themselves up** Dixon, pp. 257-9.

p. 278 **personal response to Hagakure** Mishima had written *Hagakure Nyuman/Introduction to Hagakure*, a personal interpretation of *samurai* ethics, in 1967. **life frequently appears** *Mishima on Hagakure*, p. 18. **awareness of spiritual degeneracy** cf. Kodama Mansion incident, Fukushima Akira, *JI* 11/1, 1976, p. 70. **madness** Akira, op. cit., p. 71.

Chapter 27 – Demilitarised Japan

p. 279 **perspective of the present** Akira Iriye, *Power and Culture: the Japanese–American War, 1941–5* (Harvard UP, 1981), p. 266. 'The onset of the atomic age made it certain that the world would not go back to the pre-war status quo.'

p. 280 **at regular intervals** 'Paranoia invents the rebirth of the Yellow Peril', *FEER*, Aug. 1, 1985. **Nihonjinron boom** Hiroshi Minami, 'The Introspection Boom: Whither the National Character?', and Tsutomu Kano, 'Why the Search for Identity?', *JI* 8/2 Spring 1973. **the stronger the criticism** Shumpei Kumon, 'Some Principles Governing the Thought and Behaviour of Japanists (Contextualists)', *JJS* 8/1 Winter 1982, p. 6. **Japan is a genuine democracy** Theodore McNelly, *Politics and Government in Japan* (UP of America, 3rd ed. 1984), p. 255. And cf. Pempel, op. cit. p. 4. **societies . . . flux** see eds. W. G. Bennis, K. D. Benne, R. Chin, K. E. Corey, *The Planning of Change* (Holt, Rinehart and Winston, 1976), p. 2.

p. 281 **a form of constitutional democracy** see Robert A. Scalapino, *Democracy and the Party Movement in Pre-war Japan: the Failure of the First Attempt* (California, 1953). **context of authoritarianism** E. Herbert Norman, *Japan's Emergence as a Modern State: Political and Economic Problems of the Meiji Period* (Institute of Pacific

Relations, 1940), p. 207. **meaning stretched** see Tomosuke Kasuya, 'Constitutional Transformation and the Ninth Article of the Japanese Constitution' (trans. P. S. Taylor), in *Law in Japan* (Vol. 18, 1985), pp. 1ff.

p. 282 **gradually been absorbed** Tsurumi, op. cit. p. 4. The Constitution has brought with it 'a radical alteration in the value orientation of the society as a whole'. **shell become skeleton** 'Once institutions are established they tend to become dynamic and hence influence the values and the expectations of the population.' Pye, op. cit. p. 72. **act of transubstantiation** Ienaga, op. cit. p. 245. **expedients disreputable** Pempel, *Policy*, p. 307. **revised their policies** see Masahide Shibusawa, *Japan and the Asian Pacific Region* (Croom Helm for the Royal Institute of International Affairs, 1984), p. 21. 1960 Security Treaty opposition was 'an experiment in the dynamics of internal politics'. **it would be an insult** Pempel, *Policy*, p. 307. **not a western democracy** see generally Nobutaka Ike, *A Theory of Japanese Democracy* (Westview Press, 1978), p. 5. 'Conceivably one could take the position that only democracy based on individualism, the democracy found in the west, is genuine, but that would be rather egocentric.' **refashioned it** see J. Victor Koschmann, 'Soft Rule and Expressive Protest', in ed. Koschmann, *Authority and the Individual in Japan: Citizen Protest in Historical Perspective* (Tokyo UP, 1978), pp. 1–30. **approach of Japanese to Christianity** see ed. Gerald H. Anderson, *Asian Voices in Christian Theology* (Orbis, 1976), and ed. Douglas J. Elwood, *Asian Christian Theology – Emerging Themes* (Westminster Press Philadelphia, 1980), p. 61. 'We have to free Christianity, the universal values of Christianity, from western cultural particularism'. (And cf. Kiyoko Takeda Cho, 'Inquiry Into Indigenous Cultural Energies' in ed. Elwood, op. cit.) **mukyokai and acculturation** Carlo Caldarola, *Christianity – the Japanese Way* (E. J. Brill, 1979).

p. 283 **rooted in collective self-interest** R. Scalapino and Masumi Junnosuke, *Parties and Politics in Contemporary Japan* (Berkeley UP, 1964), p. 153 – 'an open society made up of closed components'. Cited in Kim, op. cit. And cf. Pempel, *Policy*, p. 3. Also see Nakane, p. 152 – 'Japanese "democracy" is a community sentiment'. **far from monolithic** Pempel, *Policy*, pp. 11, 16. **as pluralistic as any other** see ed. T. J. Pempel, *Policymaking in Contemporary Japan* (Cornell UP, 1977), p. 310, challenging the 'Japan Inc.' thesis, and Pempel, *Policy*, op. cit. p. 11. (But cf. Pempel, *Policy*, pp. 25–6, pointing out that though Japan is pluralist, it nevertheless has 'relatively broad bases of commonality in such things as speech, upbringing, and information, if not in specific values and objectives [which] minimizes or at least clarifies the areas of potential disagreement, confusion and misunderstanding that can often arise in more diversified societies'.) **LDP not unitary bloc** Pempel, *Policy*, p. 35 – 'a vague amorphous amalgam'; and Calder, op. cit. **more fissures appear** Pempel, *Policy*, p. 26 – 'The relatively undifferentiated homogeneity of the Japanese populace is complicated by many lines of organisational and social cleavage'.

p. 284 **lack solidarity** e.g. Morris, pp. 403–4; and Dixon, p. 314. **750 rightists** Dixon, p. 72. **lack mass following** Morris, pp. 404–5; and Dixon, p. 315. **no source of funds** Dixon, pp. 315–16. **civilian control** see e.g. Ian Gow, 'Civilian Control of the Military in Post-war Japan: *Bunmin Tosei* and *Bunkan Tosei*', *PBAJS* 6/2 1981. And cf. Theodore McNelly, 'Disarmament and Civilian Control in Japan: A Constitutional Dilemma', in *Occasional Papers/Reprints Series in Contemporary Asian Studies* No. 8, 1982.

p. 285 **outweighed by civilian bureaucrats** Ikuhiko Hata, *A Historical Record: Japanese Rearmament*. (*Bungei Shunju*, 1976), pp. 154–5. And cf. Bix, op. cit. p. 349 n. 7. **Defense Production Committee** David R.

Hopper, 'Defense Policy and the Business Community: the *Keidanren* Defense Production Committee', in Buck, op. cit. **little money at stake** in 1954 the *Keidanren* DPC voted to limit weapons manufacture to large companies, none of which would depend on arms for more than a fraction of its income. Fukui, op. cit. p. 78; and cf. Hopper, op. cit. **restrictions on arms exports** Reinhard Drifte, 'Japan and Regional Arms Control in the Asia–Pacific Region', *PBAJS* 1981 Part 1. **Miki extended the ban** see e.g. Reinhard Drifte, 'Appearance and Reality: Japan's Defence Policy of Defence', *PBAJS*, 1984 Vol. 9. **arms to the US . . . grey area** Drifte, 'Japan and Regional Arms Control', op. cit.

p. 286 **American subsidiary** *Asahi*, June 21, 1985. **servants of industry . . . potent in US** Herbert Bix, 'The Japanese Challenge: US–Japanese Relations at Mid-Decade', *BCAS* 17/4 Oct.–Dec. 1985, p. 30. **the OSS survey** OSS R & A 3034. 'Working Outline for Analysis of Policy Issues Regarding Japan', May 16, 1945. **one opposition party** i.e. Japanese Socialist Party. **conciliation not confrontation** Song, op. cit. p. 102, points out that even while the total defence state of the late 1930s was being built, Japanese elementary schoolchildren were taught, 'We Japanese are fundamentally peaceloving people, but in case of a national emergency, we have made it our duty to serve the country courageously, forgetting self and family'.

p. 287 **emotional resistance** Shibusawa, op. cit. p. 16. **unique stimulus** the first sector of Japanese society to focus on the atomic bombings was the governmental propaganda machine, in the uncertain days following the surrender. e.g. *Nippon Times*, Aug. 12, 1945, 'Cruel Havoc Wrought By New Bomb'; Aug. 26, 'Terrific Power of A-Bomb is Bared'; Aug. 18, '"Difficult To Believe What We Did"', says Flier of Attack on Hiroshima'. The Emperor's Surrender Rescript itself spoke of 'a new and most cruel bomb'. **350,000 people**

Fukui, p. 77. **Barefoot Gen** omnibus published by Project Gen, Tokyo, 1979. Originally serialised in *Shukan Shohen Jampu*. **Asahi poll** July 20, 1985. **the allergy** an additional reason is given by Richard F. Kosobud, *Northeast Asia and the US: Defensive Partnerships and Trade Rivalries* (Chicago Council on Foreign Relations, 1983), p. 4. 'A nuclear umbrella could be thought of as exposing Japanese territory to the risk of nuclear weapons use.' **devised by Sato** Okimoto, p. 24.

p. 288 **more flexible** currently flexible enough to allow participation in the SDI programme, which might be counted as manufacture of nuclear weapons. **it seems to many** e.g. Masamori Sase – to rely on the Security Treaty but deny its military implications is to behave like an 'international eccentric'. Quoted by Kenneth B. Pyle, 'The Future of Japanese Nationality: An Essay in Contemporary History', *JJS* 8/2 Summer 1982. **control nuclear submarines** Toyoda Toshiyuki, 'The Decreasing Credibility of Nuclear Deterrence', *JQ* 31/3 Oct.–Dec. 1984. **no less a source** *JQ* 31/3 Apr.–June 1984, *Chronology* Jan. 9, 1984. **pointed out in 1974** by Admiral Gene Larocque in testimony before Congress. Okimoto, p. 43 n. 18. **Reischauer** see editorial 'The Nuclear Policy of the Japanese Government', *JQ* 28/4 Oct.–Dec. 1981; and Yagisawa Mitsuo, 'Maintaining Japanese Security', *JQ* Summer 1983, p. 359. **agreement in the 1950s** there were also rumours of an agreement concluded in 1960 between the Japanese Foreign Minister and the American Ambassador, Douglas MacArthur II. Okimoto, p. 43 n. 30. **Feb. 26, 1958** Ikuhiko Hata, 'The Postwar Period in Retrospect', *JE* Vol. 11 Special Issue 1984, p. 20. And cf. Komori Yoshihisa, 'The Reischauer Statement: What the Press Omitted', *JE* Vol. 8/4. **Kishi extracted promise** Okimoto, p. 18. **patently a 'major change'** Okimoto, p. 19.

p. 289 **Article 9 is a focus** see Taketsugu Tsurutani, *Japanese Policy* and East Asian Security (Praeger, 1981), p. 110. 'The postwar Constitution is important to understanding Japan's external conduct in the past three decades only in the sense that it provided an extremely effective and plausible *pretext* for the pattern of conduct that had in itself nothing to do with its apparent pacifism. Major sources of postwar Japanese conduct reach much further back than either August 1945 or the promulgation of the peace Constitution.' **legalistically it might be argued** NAW RG 319 P & O Div. 091. Japan TS(Sec. 1–a). Military Survey 73265, Apr. 19, 1948. **legal experts tend to dismiss** McNelly, 'The Renunciation of War in the Japanese Constitution', *Armed Forces and Society* 13/1 1986, p. 83. **patently clear** Mishima, 'An Appeal', *Sande Mainichi*, Dec. 13, 1970. **according to Yoshida** *The Yoshida Memoirs*, op. cit. p. 189.

p. 290 **Commission on the Constitution** see e.g. McNelly, review of John M. Maki, *Japan's Commission on the Constitution: the Final Report* (Washington UP, 1981), in *Monument Nipponica* 36/3, 1981. **factions cherished dark designs** McNelly, review of Maki, op. cit. **Socialists . . . boycotted** McNelly, review of Maki, op. cit. **the revision movement lingered on** editorial, 'The Current Cry for Constitutional Revision', *JQ* 28/1 Jan.– Mar. 1981. And fascination with the topic persists – 'NHK television's docudrama on the constitution was seen by millions'. Moore, op. cit. **repeated attempts** see e.g. McNelly, 'The Constitutionality of Japan's Defense Establishment', in Buck, op. cit. And cf. Alfred C. Oppler, 'The Sunakawa Case', *Political Science Quarterly*, 76/2. See also Hisahiko Okazaki, *A Grand Strategy for Japanese Defense* (UP of America, 1986), which points out that the 'Hyakuri Air Base Suit' has been going on for over twenty years.

p. 291 **Japanese tolerance for contradictory** Robert J. Smith, op. cit. p. 59. And cf. Drifte, 'Appearance and Reality', *PBAJS* 1984/9. **majority**

wants to keep Douglas H. Mendel, 'Public Views of the Japanese Defense System', in Buck, op. cit. More recent polls have produced similar results. **a majority fluctuating** Fukui, p. 73.

p. 292 **political fetish** Kosaka Masataka, 'Japan's Defense Options: Pragmatism or Symbolism?', *Sankei Shimbun*, Jan. 15, 1985. **questionable means** Bix, 'The Roots of Militarism', op. cit. pp. 307–8. **postponing retirement age** *Mainichi Shimbun*, Dec. 17, 1984. **the new compromise** . . . **1% GNP** Japanese Cabinet Press Release, Jan. 24, 1987.

p. 293 **employee mentality** Osamu Inagaki, 'The *Jieitai*: Military Values in a Pacifist Society', *JI* 10/1, Summer 1975, pp. 8–11. **informal warning** Thomas M. Brendle, 'Recruitment and Training in the SDF', in Buck, op. cit. **code of behaviour** Humphreys, op. cit.

p. 294 **low prestige** Brendle, op. cit. **automatically ineligible** . . . **colour blind** Brendle, op. cit. **older than ideal** 'Japan's Old Soldiers Don't Fade Away', *Mainichi Shimbun*, Dec. 17, 1984.

p. 295 **it has been claimed** e.g. Brendle, op. cit. **against Article 18** though in 1970 Nakasone insisted that an explicit ban on conscription be dropped from the proposed Defense White Paper. **fallen short of plans** Ikeuchi Fumio, 'The 1986–90 Medium Term Defense Plan', in *JQ* 31/3 Oct.– Dec. 1984. **ideal shopping lists** *FEER*, Sept. 22, 1983. **final say** Fukui, pp. 78–9. **SDF lack strength in depth** Tsurutani, op. cit. p. 78. **GSDF's tanks** Fukui, p. 69. **E2C-Orion** Drifte, 'Appearance and Reality', op. cit. **dependent on NTT** Fukui, p. 70.

p. 296 **US Defense Dept. reported** Fumio, op. cit. **opportunities to test** Fukui, p. 69. **prevented from buying the best** Erik Fromm (quoted in Barnett, p. 42) claims that the Japanese 'considered AWACS in 1977 for the MiG-25 threat and selected the less capable E-2C. Oddly, this was done *because* AWACS had command

and control (i.e. "battle-management") capability, and because the E-2C had a *shorter* range: these negative judgments were based on Japan's "defense only" principles'. **effectiveness . . . unclear** Chalmers Johnson claims ('Another Year of Living Dangerously', op. cit. p. 726) that 'Japan has no established mechanism for crisis management, no mechanism for a wartime leadership structure, no mechanism for joint operations of Japan's three services . . . and no plans for the fulfilment of military objectives as distinct from the mere purchase of military hardware'. **violations of air space** 'Japan Reacts to Soviet Airspace Violation', *Tokyo Shimbun*, Nov. 30, 1984. **in 1975 one analyst** Osamu Kaihara, former secretary of the National Defense Council. James H. Buck, 'The Japanese Military in the 1980s', in Buck, op. cit.

p. 297 years of colonisation Japan occupied for more than three years every country now an ASEAN member. Charles E. Morrison, *Japan, the United States and a Changing S.E. Asia* (UP of America, 1985). **sucking neighbours dry** Shibusawa, p. 74. **general arms build-up** General Indar Jit Rikhye, interview with authors, Oct. 21, 1985. **more powerful . . . economic necessity** Evelyn Colbert, 'National Security Perspectives: Japan and Asia', in Buck, op. cit.

p. 298 can afford few enemies 'No major nation in the world is as constrained by fear of economic pressure as is Japan today. The US, despite its obvious economic trials and tribulations, is fundamentally strong and resilient in its economic capability.' Tsurutani, p. 26. **Japanese have concluded . . . mai homu gaiko** Pyle, op. cit. **omni-directional policy** cf. Takeo Miki's view that 'a basic tenet of Japanese policy was that no country was an "enemy"'. Barnett, p. 108. **my-homeism** a phrase more generally used in a domestic context – see Tada Michitaro, 'The Glory and Misery of My Home', in ed. Koschmann, op. cit.

pp. 207–217. **Japanese response** Morrison, op. cit. p. 36. And cf. Shibusawa, p. 75. **voluntary reparations** Shibusawa, p. 42. Initially these took the form primarily of credits that could be used to buy Japanese goods. Later Japan's foreign aid programme was established to replace the reparations agreements. Morrison, p. 35. **US \$500 million** Shibusawa, p. 41. **Pacific Basin Co-operation** See e.g. *PBAJS* 1981/1, Special Issue on the concept of the Pacific Community. **30% of total trade** M. White, 'Trade Interdependence in the Asian Pacific Region and some Japanese perspectives on a Pacific Community', *PBAJS* 1981/1.

p. 299 expanded . . . resemble NATO *Asahi*, Oct. 10, 1985. **1000-mile radius ticklish** see e.g. General Sayidiman Suryohadiprojo, Indonesian Ambassador to Japan in 1983, quoted by Barnett, p. 115. Morrison, p. 43. **vicious invective** e.g. 'Support the Just Struggle of the Japanese People Against the Japan/US Treaty of Military Alliance' (Foreign Language Press, Peking, 1960) which refers to the 'fascist violence' used by the government of Nobusuke Kishi, 'the US lackey in Japan', to force through the renewal of the Security Treaty and the visit of President Eisenhower, 'the god of plague'. **Shanghai communiqué** cited in Paul Seabury, *America's Stake in the Pacific* (Ethics and Public Policy Center, 1981), p. 69. **era of rapprochement** Shibusawa, pp. 63–68. **channels of private trade** McNelly, *Politics and Government in Japan*, op. cit, p. 232. **largest trading partner** Wolf Mendl, 'Japan's Relations with China – the Key to Asia's Future?', *PBAJS* 1981 Part 1. **hegemonism** McNelly, 'The Renunciation of War in the Japanese Constitution', *Armed Forces and Society*, op. cit. p. 10. **surveys showed** e.g. US International Communication Agency Research Report, 'Japanese Perceptions of Security Issues', July 31, 1980. Results of surveys carried out Apr.10–13, 1980 after Soviet invasion of Afghanistan. **Chinese announced 2%** Tatsumi Okabe, 'Japan's Relations with China in the 1980s', in eds. Gaston Sigur and Young C. Kim, *Japanese and US Policy in Asia* (Praeger, 1982), pp. 97–116. **'adjustment' policy** Shibusawa, p. 171.

p. 301 **communism's curious history** for a discussion of the appeal of Marxism after the war, see Okimoto, pp. 54–5. **Konoye Memorial** delivered Feb. 1945. Robert J. C. Butow, *Japan's Decision to Surrender* (Stanford UP, 1954), p. 45. **Nomonhan** FO 371 24699 F 3473. Tokyo Embassy Minute May 22, 1940, stressing superiority of Soviet German-made) equipment, in particular flame-throwing tanks. 'There would have been no alternative to retreat if the Soviet Army had chosen to continue to fight.' **lack global perspective** Yoshio Okawara, quoted in Barnett, p. 27.

p. 302 **capacity to invade** Thomas Robinson, 'US Policies Toward the Soviet Union and China in Asia', in eds. Sigur and Kim, op. cit. p. 143. **Backfire bombers** Johnson, op. cit., p. 724. **Northern Territories** McNelly, *Politics and Government*, pp. 237–8. **key strategic importance to Soviets** for this reason, Roosevelt's wisdom in granting them to Russia was queried in the Senate. Responding for the JCS, Omar Bradley conceded that they were 'under present circumstances . . . not completely satisfied concerning [the Kuriles'] security. However, in view of the current world situation, it is believed that the interests of the US are best served by leaving the permanent status of the area to be determined at a future date when international tensions have been eased'. NAW RG 218 BRADLEY 1949–53. Bradley/Watkins, Sept. 21, 1951. **virtually indefensible** on the 'undefendable Japan' theory, see Fukui, pp. 81–2. And cf. Tsurutani, p. 34. 'The whole nation is a mammoth exposed precision instrument interconnected by sensitive joints and delicate links. . . . An enemy could easily cause paralysis.' **Japan subsequently renewed** *NYT*, Dec. 23, 1949.

p. 303 **'high-tech' guerrilla force** McNelly, 'The Renunciation of War', *Armed Forces and Society*, op. cit. p. 8. **trade and defence strategy unconnected** J. W. M. Chapman, 'Japan and a Pacific Community', *PBAJS* 1981/1.

p. 304 **peace offensive** Shigeru Kido, 'A Thaw in Tokyo–Moscow Relations', *Sekai*, Jan. 1985. **Nakasone met Gorbachev** *FEER*, Mar. 28, 1985. **customer is king . . . joint ventures** *FEER*, Sept. 11, 1986. **outwardly Japan manifests suspicion** 'Menace from Moscow', *FEER*, Aug. 21, 1986.

Epilogue
p.307 **proven credibility gap** Edward A. Olsen, *US–Japan Strategic Reciprocity: A Neo-Internationalist View* (Hoover Institution Press, 1985), p. 114.

p. 308 **sustain a 6% budget** Radha Sinha, *Japan's Options for the 1980s* (Croom Helm, 1982), p. 7, citing H. Patrick & H. Rosovsky, *Asia's New Giant: How the Economy Works* (1976), p. 45. **Japan export arms** Stephen E. Ambrose, *Rise to Globalism: American Foreign Policy Since 1938* (Penguin, 1983), p. 413, emphasises the importance of the international arms trade to the US and European countries 'paying for their oil and other imports with arms sold to the Third World exporters of raw materials'. **destabilise the Asian region** Tsurutani, pp. 40–42, points out that the East Asian region is already acutely unstable. 'East Asian nations still lack a strong tradition of . . . mutual interaction not only because they are generally "new" as actors in the regional international arena but also because of their mutual divergence in culture and history. . . . Rigidity of attitude, abiding mutual distrust and fear of deception and betrayal remain powerful forces behind the behaviour of Asian states.' **into the arms of the USSR** in Mar. 1982 the Director of MITI's Trade Policy Bureau said, speaking hypothetically, 'if the US and Europe do not trade with Japan . . . we would probably join the communist bloc'. Shibusawa, p. 162. **exposing Japan to remilitarisation again** see e.g. the views of Michio Morishima in the Seki/Morishima debate, summarised in *JE* 11/1 1980, pp. 63–8. **a young, unorthodox oriental democracy** 'Militarism as it affects the external social structure can be either designed or unanticipated. Designed militarism flows from the strength and conscious effort of military officers to influence and modify certain social structures. Unanticipated militarism develops from a lack of effective traditions and practices for controlling the military establishment.' Morris Janowitz, 'Armed Forces and Society: A World Perspective', in ed. Jacques van Doorn, *Armed Forces and Society: Sociological Essays* (Mouton, 1968). p. 23.

p. 309 **science city** Gene Gregory, 'Science city: the future starts here', *FEER*, Mar. 28, 1985. **primary resource . . . knowledge** cf. Barnett, pp. 10–11, 'Knowledge is Power'.

p. 310 **overseas investment** Nomura Research Institute figures, cited *FEER*, Sept. 4, 1986. **revision of the world order** Tetsuya Kataoka, 'Reagan in Asia – An Assessment', in ed. Morton A. Kaplan, *Global Policy: Challenge of the 80s* (Washington Institute for Values in Public Policy Inc., 1984), p. 168. The decline of the US economy 'has had quite direct strategic consequences'. **high-level study group reported** Comprehensive National Security Study Group, *Report on Comprehensive National Security* (July 2, 1980), summarised and interpreted in Barnett, *Beyond War*, op. cit. **without knowing how** 'The question for the coming years will be whether and how Japan can reinforce its international position and status while remaining essentially an economic power' – Shibusawa, pp. 8–9. **depends not simply on the strength to confront** 'In the Japanese view, the US concept of security is often too narrowly con-

strued in military-strategic terms. Chae-Jin Lee and Hideo Sato, *US Policy Toward Japan and Korea* (Praeger, 1982). **present international system viable** see also Henry Kissinger, *Washington Post*, Oct. 8, 1985. **defended against instability** Nayan Chanda, *FEER*, Nov. 6, 1986, citing State Dept. Congressional testimony. 'Strong and vibrant free enterprise economies are our best defense against the blandishments of the Soviet Union and its surrogates'.

p. 311 **stability through economic aid** Barnett, p. 10. 'Administration of a stable, growth-oriented and reliably outward-looking interdependent economic system is the bedrock of Japan's own security and by far Japan's greatest contribution to the security of other countries in the East Asian region.' And cf. Ryohei Murata, quoted in Barnett, pp. 95–6, and Morrison, pp. 41–2. **South Pacific** *FEER*, Nov. 6, 1986. **powerful Greek lobby** Richard Perle, quoted by Barnett, p. 36. **signs of anti-Americanism** see generally eds. Alvin Z. Rubenstein and Donald E. Smith, *Anti-Americanism in the Third World and its Implications for US Foreign Policy* (Praeger, 1985). **increase in US facilities** *FEER*, Aug. 21, 1986. **overseas development assistance** Kubota Akira, 'Foreign Aid – Giving With One Hand?', *JQ* 32/2. **drifting toward dependence** Olsen, p. 121. **items such as** *FEER*, Aug. 1, 1985.

p. 312 **price tag** e.g. USA spends $40–45 billion per annum on Asian regional security. Japan spends less than $12 billion on defence, where an American-size percentage of GNP would mean expenditure of $87 billion on defence. Olsen, pp. 141–2. In 1985, the US had a $50·billion deficit in mercantile trade with Japan. **America must come to terms** this might be seen as upholding one of the values which Roosevelt urged should be promoted when the war was over – 'freedom from fear – which, translated into world terms, means a world-wide reduction of armaments to such a point and in such a fashion that no nation will be in a position to commit an act of physical aggression against any neighbour anywhere in the world'. Cited in Eide/Thee, op. cit. p. 9.

Index

Index

Index